1st Edition 2006

Bahrain
The Complete **Residents'** Guide

Passionately Publishing...

Bahrain Explorer 1st Edition   ISBN 13 - 978-976-8182-52-4   ISBN 10 - 976-8182-52-0

Front Cover Photograph – Pete Maloney

Printed and bound by Emirates Printing Press, Dubai, United Arab Emirates.

Explorer Publishing & Distribution
PO Box 34275, Zomorrodah Bldg, Za'abeel Rd, Dubai
United Arab Emirates
Phone   (+971 4) 335 3520
Fax   (+971 4) 335 3529
Email   Info@explorerpublishing.com
Web   www.explorerpublishing.com

Bahrain Explorer 2006
The Complete Residents' Guide

Also available in this series:
Abu Dhabi, Bahrain, Dubai, Geneva, Hong Kong, London, New York, Oman, Qatar, Singapore, Sydney

Forthcoming titles in this series (2007):
Amsterdam, Barcelona, Dublin, New Zealand, Paris, Shanghai

Contributing Authors
Brig Rooke, Edel Moroney, Maureen Spencer, Rory Adamson & Susie Spratt

Publisher
Alistair MacKenzie

Editorial
Managing Editor Claire England
Lead Editors David Quinn, Jane Roberts, Matt Farquharson, Sean Kearns, Tim Binks, Tom Jordan
Deputy Editors Helen Spearman, Jake Marsico, Katie Drynan, Rebecca Wicks, Richard Greig, Tracy Fitzgerald
Editorial Assistants Grace Carnay, Ingrid Cupido, Mimi Stankova

Design
Creative Director Pete Maloney
Art Director Ieyad Charaf
Senior Designers Alex Jeffries, Iain Young
Layout Manager Jayde Fernandes
Designers Hashim Moideen, Rafi Pullat, Sheteeq Marakkatepurath, Sunita Lakhiani
Cartography Manager Zainudheen Madathil
Cartographer Noushad Madathil
Design Admin Manager Shyrell Tamayo
Production Coordinator Maricar Ong

Photography
Photography Manager Pamela Grist
Photographer Victor Romero
Image Editor Henry Hilos

Sales and Marketing
Area Sales Manager Stephen Jones
Marketing Manager Kate Fox
Retail Sales Manager Ivan Rodrigues
Retail Sales Coordinator Kiran Melwani
Corporate Sales Executive Ben Merrett
Digital Content Manager Derrick Pereira
Distribution Supervisor Matthew Samuel
Distribution Executives Ahmed Mainodin, Firos Khan, Mannie Lugtu
Warehouse Assistant Mohammed Kunjaymo
Drivers Mohammed Sameer, Shabsir Madathil

Finance and Administration
Administration Manager Andrea Fust
Financial Manager Michael Samuel
Accounts Assistant Cherry Enriquez
Administrators Enrico Maullon, Lennie Maugaliuo
Driver Rafi Jamal

IT
IT Administrator Ajay Krishnan
Senior Software Engineer Bahrudeen Abdul
Software Engineer Roshni Ahuja

Contact Us
Reader Response
If you have any comments and suggestions, fill out our online reader response form and you could win prizes. Log on to **www.explorerpublishing.com**

General Enquiries
We'd love to hear your thoughts and answer any questions you have about this book or any other Explorer product. Contact us at **info@explorerpublishing.com**

Careers
If you fancy yourself as an Explorer, send your CV (stating the position you're interested in) to **jobs@explorerpublishing.com**

Designlab and Contract Publishing
For enquiries about Explorer's Contract Publishing arm and design services contact **designlab@explorerpublishing.com**

PR and Marketing
For PR and marketing enquries contact **marketing@explorerpublishing.com**
pr@explorerpublishing.com

Corporate Sales
For bulk sales and customisation options, for this book or any Explorer product, contact **sales@explorerpublishing.com**

Advertising and Sponsorship
For advertising and sponsorship, contact **media@explorerpublishing.com**

Explorer Publishing & Distribution
Office 51B, Zomorrodah Building, Za'abeel Road
PO Box 34275, Dubai, United Arab Emirates
Phone: +971 (0)4 335 3520, **Fax:** +971 (0)4 335 3529
info@explorerpublishing.com
www.explorerpublishing.com

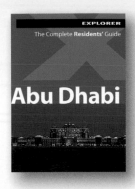
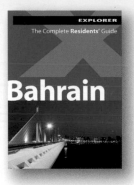
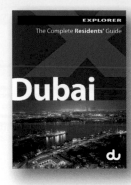

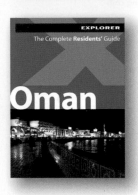
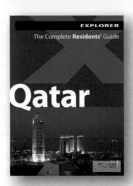

Novotel Al Dana Resort
The Hotel in a beach resort setting

Enjoy the art of value-added hospitality and the splendour of traditional Bahraini architecture by the sea. 172 spacious rooms and suites. A private beach. 3 gourmet restaurants. Modern health club, business centre and conference rooms. A unique experience of a lifetime in the heart of the city. Call us a hotel or a resort... at Novotel Al Dana, business and leisure is always a pleasure!

NOVOTEL
ACCOR
hotels

AL DANA RESORT

Tel.: +973 17 298008, Fax: +973 17 298338. Email: reservations@novotel-bahrain.com
www.novotel-bahrain.com - www.novotel.com - www.accor.com

ONCE UPON A TIME...

Learn what life was like before gleaming skyscrapers and traffic jams, when Dubai was no more than a sandy fishing village. These memories, shared by locals who have seen the city change immeasurably, offer a fascinating glimpse into life in simpler, and yet infinitely more difficult, times.

Supported by

بنك دبي الوطني
National Bank of Dubai

TELLING TALES
AN ORAL HISTORY OF DUBAI

Phone (971 4) 335 3520 • **Fax** (971 4) 335 3529
Info@Explorer-Publishing.com • www.Explorer-Publishing.com
Residents' Guides • Visitors' Guides • Photography Books • Activity Guidebooks • Maps

EXPLORER

Passionately Publishing...

A square book but not for squares

Explore Dubai's decadent range of restaurants, bars, cafes and clubs in this beautiful book with stunning images and informative reviews. More than just a guidebook, it's at home on a coffee table while you're out on the town.

Hashim MM
AKA: Speedy Gonzales
They don't come much faster than Hashim – he's so speedy with his mouse that scientists are struggling to create a computer that can keep up with him. His nimble fingers leave his keyboard smouldering (he gets through three a week), and his go-faster stripes make him almost invisible to the naked eye when he moves.

Jane Roberts
AKA: The Oracle
After working in an undisclosed role in the government, Jane brought her super sleuth skills to Explorer. Whatever the question, she knows what, where, who, how and when, but her encyclopaedic knowledge is only impressive until you realise she just makes things up randomly.

Helen Spearman
AKA: Little Miss Sunshine
With her bubbly laugh and permanent smile, Helen is a much-needed ray of sunshine in the office when we're all grumpy and facing harrowing deadlines. It's almost impossible to think that she ever loses her temper or shows a dark side... although put her behind the wheel of a car, and you've got instant road rage.

Jayde Fernandes
AKA: Pop Idol
Jayde's idol is Britney Spears, and he recently shaved his head to show solidarity with the troubled star. When he's not checking his dome for stubble, or practising the dance moves to 'Baby One More Time' in front of the bathroom mirror, he actually manages to get some designing done.

Henry Hilos
AKA: The Quiet Man
Henry can rarely be seen from behind his large obstructive screen but when you do catch a glimpse you'll be sure to get a smile. Lighthearted Henry keeps all those glossy pages filled with pretty pictures for something to look at when you can't be bothered to read.

Kate Fox
AKA: Contacts Collector
Kate swooped into the office like the UK equivalent of Wonderwoman, minus the tights of course (it's much too hot for that), but armed with a superhuman marketing brain. Even though she's just arrived, she is already a regular on the Dubai social scene - she is helping to blast Explorer into the stratosphere, one champagne-soaked networking party at a time.

Ieyad Charaf
AKA: Fashion Designer
When we hired Ieyad as a top designer, we didn't realise we'd be getting his designer tops too! By far the snappiest dresser in the office, you'd be hard-pressed to beat his impeccably ironed shirts.

Katie Drynan
AKA The Irish Deputy
Katie is a Jumeirah Jane in training, and has 35 sisters who take it in turns to work in the Explorer office while she enjoys testing all the beauty treatments available on the Beach Road. This Irish charmer met an oil tycoon in Paris, and they now spend the weekends digging very deep holes in their new garden.

Ingrid Cupido
AKA: The Karaoke Queen
Ingrid has a voice to match her starlet name. She'll put any Pop Idols to shame once behind the mike, and she's pretty nifty on a keyboard too. She keeps us all ticking over and was a very welcome relief for overworked staff. She certainly gets our vote if she decides to go pro; just remember you saw her here first.

Ivan Rodrigues
AKA: The Aviator
After making a mint in the airline market, Ivan came to Explorer where he works for pleasure, not money. That's his story, anyway. We know that he is actually a corporate spy from a rival company and that his multi-level spreadsheets are really elaborate codes designed to confuse us.

Kiran Melwani
AKA: Bow Selector
Like a modern-day Robin Hood (right down to the green tights and band of merry men), Kiran's mission in life is to distribute Explorer's wealth of knowledge to the fact-hungry readers of the world. Just make sure you never do anything to upset her – rumour has it she's a pretty mean shot with that bow and arrow.

Abdul Gafoor
AKA: Ace Circulator
After a successful stint on Ferrari's Formula One team Gafoor made a pitstop at our office and decided to stay. He has won our 'Most Cheerful Employee' award five years in a row – baffling, when you consider he spends so much time battling the traffic.

Andrea Fust
AKA: Mother Superior
By day Andrea is the most efficient manager in the world and by night she replaces the boardroom for her board and wows the pants off the dudes in Ski Dubai. Literally. Back in the office she definitely wears the trousers!

Ahmed Mainodin
AKA: Mystery Man
We can never recognise Ahmed because of his constantly changing facial hair. He waltzes in with big lambchop sideburns one day, a handlebar moustache the next, and a neatly trimmed goatee after that. So far we've had no objections to his hirsute chameleonisms, but we'll definitely draw the line at a monobrow.

Cherry Enriquez
AKA: Bean Counter
With the team's penchant for sweets and pastries, it's good to know we have Cherry on top of our accounting cake. The local confectioner is always paid on time, so we're guaranteed great gateaux for every special occasion.

Ajay Krishnan R
AKA: Web Wonder
Ajay's mum and dad knew he was going to be an IT genius when the found him reconfiguring his Commodore 64 at the tender age of 2. He went on to become the technology consultant on all three Matrix films, and counts Keanu as a close personal friend.

Claire England
AKA: Whip Cracker
No longer able to freeload off the fact that she once appeared in a Robbie Williams video, Claire now puts her creative skills to better use – looking up rude words in the dictionary! A child of English nobility, Claire is quite the lady – unless she's down at Jimmy Dix.

David Quinn
AKA: Sharp Shooter
After a short stint as a children's TV presenter was robbed from David because he developed an allergy to sticky back plastic, he made his way to sandier pastures. Now that he's thinking outside the box, nothing gets past the man with the sharpest pencil in town.

Alex Jeffries
AKA: Easy Rider
Alex is happiest when dressed in leather from head to toe with a humming machine between his thighs – just like any other motorbike enthusiast. Whenever he's not speeding along the Hatta Road at full throttle, he can be found at his beloved Mac, still dressed in leather.

Enrico Maullon
AKA: The Crooner
Frequently mistaken for his near-namesake Enrique Iglesias, Enrico decided to capitalise and is now a regular stand-in for the Latin heartthrob. If he's ever missing from the office, it usually means he's off performing for millions of adoring fans on another stadium tour of America.

Alistair MacKenzie
AKA: Media Mogul
If only Alistair could take the paperless office one step further and achieve the officeless office he would be the happiest publisher alive. Wireless access from a remote spot somewhere in the Hajar Mountains would suit this intrepid explorer – less traffic, lots of fresh air, and wearing sandals all day - the perfect work environment!

Firos Khan
AKA: Big Smiler
Previously a body double in kung fu movies, including several appearances in close up scenes for Steven Seagal's moustache. He also once tore down a restaurant with his bare hands after they served him a mild curry by mistake.

Welcome to the brand-new Bahrain Explorer – the guidebook your life has been waiting for. Bursting out of its cover with all the information residents need, this guide will add so much to life in Bahrain you won't know how you ever managed without it!

Our team of locally based writers includes some of the most knowledgeable and experienced resident experts on living in Bahrain, ensuring you get only the most vital and relevant advice and information for all areas of life. Whether you're new in town or have lived here for years, visiting friends and family or just here for business, this guide will show you more about this fascinating country than you ever thought possible.

For an overview of the country, **General Information** gives you an insight into Bahrain's history, geography and heritage, as well as everything you need to know when first arriving. The **Residents** chapter provides useful information on all aspects of life, including employment, visas, housing, schools, hospitals and a whole host of insider tips to help you ease into living in Bahrain. **Exploring** describes the heritage, culture and attractions that can be found in every corner of all of Bahrain's islands, and lists the essential things every visitor must see and do during their time here.

To make the most of your leisure time, **Activities** has comprehensive listings of all the choices to fill up your free time with sports, activities, hobbies, clubs, groups and societies. In the **Shopping** chapter we have great listings for what to buy and where to buy it, and a guide to the best of Bahrain's shops, stalls and malls. While **Going Out** features reviews of the best restaurants, cafes, bars and nightclubs in the country.

Enjoy getting more out of Bahrain!

The Explorer Team

Now it's over to you...

Just because you didn't get involved in the making of this book doesn't mean you can just sit on your laurels. We've done our best to uncover all the facts about

living in Bahrain, but we accept – and it hurts to say this – that we might have left things out. Which is where you come in. We want to know what we've done wrong, who we've missed and where we can improve. Have we left out your ice-sculpting club or dissed your favourite restaurant? Tell us! And don't forget that compliments are also gratefully received, so feel free to send in as many expressions of unadulterated praise as you want.

Visit our website to fill in our Reader Response form, and tell us exactly what you think of us.

www.explorerpublishing.com

Bods Behind the Book...

A lot goes into the production of our Complete Residents' Guides – sweat, tears, late nights, laughter, talents, tantrums, dedication, prayers, moral support and a colourful collection of vocabulary have all been offered selflessly by members of the Explorer family over the last few months. They all deserve a shake of the hand, a pat on the back, and copious air kisses for their contributions.

Our creative genius aside, there's a whole extended Explorer family to thank. A big shout goes out to the tireless efforts of our roving reporters and backstage hands. These are the people who work just as hard as us (sometimes harder), and yet still manage to hold down their day jobs. Thank you to everyone who had a hand in the creation of this masterpiece – here they are:

Our team of reporters who deserve medals for their contributions to food and drink research – Alia Salman, Anthony Knapton, Bobby de Havilland, Bryson Wood, Carol Ayas, Carole Litherland, Christina Fantcehi, Clare Cunningham, Emma Garrett, Geraldine Davey, Hilary Picton, Jeneene Mackie Jennifer Downey, Jennifer Doporto, Lydia Auld, Mark Kane, Michael Spratt, Michelle Powell, Monique Groh, Orla Rudman, Phoebe Middleton, Rory Adamson, Shannelle Adel, Susie Keeble, Teresa Sarnsworth, Toby Auld and Ziad Matar.

Thanks also go to the following for their help: Anand and Tony from Emirates Printing Press, Maher and Peter (Maps), Tariq Salaam, Mr. Juma Obaid Alleem (Director of Censorship – Dubai) and not forgetting Jasim, Cassale, Salem, Samy and Ten Ten.

Extra special thanks to long-suffering partners Alan, Alex, Arnel, David, Dominik, Felicitas, Fraser, Grace, Greg, Justin, Jodie, Marjan, Miki, Nijula, Peter, Raihanath, Raji, Robert, Sadanand, Sadhiya, Sajithkumar and Sunitha: well done for putting up with our bad moods, late nights and general deadline frenzy. And to the youngest Explorers – Amy, Caitie, Dan, Dylan, Fiza, Hannah, Kanyon, Lauren E, Lauren G, Louise-Alodia, Lourdes-Amely, Mohammed Shaaz, Peter-Vincent, Sean, Shahaha, Shahhina, and Shahinsha – your mummies and daddies will be home soon!

Come and have a go if you think you work hard enough...

If you fancy yourself as an Explorer and want a piece of the action send your details to Jobs@Explorer-Publishing.com and mark the email subject with one of the following: Food Reporter (if you want to write for your supper), Freelance Writer (if you think you have insider info to contribute), Editorial (if you want to join the ranks of our esteemed production team), Design (if you have professional creative skills), Research (if you think you could be an Explorer investigator).

Rafi VP
AKA: Party Trickster
After developing a rare allergy to sunlight in his teens, Rafi started to lose a few centimeters of height every year. He now stands just 30cm tall, and does his best work in our dingy basement wearing a pair of infrared goggles. His favourite party trick is to fold himself into a briefcase, and he was once sick in his hat.

Shyrell Tamayo
AKA: Fashion Princess
We've never seen Shyrell wearing the same thing twice – her clothes collection is so large that her husband has to keep all his things in a shoebox. She runs Designlab like clockwork, because being late for deadlines is SO last season.

Sunita Lakhiani
AKA: Designlass
Initially suspicious of having a female in their midst, the boys in Designlab now treat Sunita like one of their own. A big shame for her, because they treat each other pretty damn bad!

Roshni Ahuja
AKA: Bright Spark
Never failing to brighten up the office with her colourful get-up, Roshni definitely puts the 'it' in the IT department. She's a perennially pleasant, profound programmer with peerless panache, and she does her job with plenty of pep and piles of pizzazz.

Tim Binks
AKA: Class Clown
El Binksmeisterooney is such a sharp wit, he often has fellow Explorers gushing tea from their noses in convulsions of mirth. Years spent hiking across the Middle East have given him an encyclopedic knowledge of rock formations and elaborate hair.

Sean Kearns
AKA: The Tall Guy
Big Sean, as he's affectionately known, is so laid back he actually spends most of his time lying down (unless he's on a camping trip, when his ridiculously small tent forces him to sleep on his hands and knees). Despite the rest of us constantly tripping over his lanky frame, when the job requires someone who will work flat out, he always rises to the editorial occasion.

Tissy Varghese
AKA: PC Whisperer
With her soft voice and gentle touch, Tissy can whip even the wildest of PCs into submission. No matter how many times we spill coffee on our keyboards she never loses her temper – a real mystery, especially as she wakes at 3am every day to beat the Sharjah traffic.

Shabsir M
AKA: Sticky Wicket
Shabsir is a valuable player on the Indian national cricket team, so instead of working you'll usually find him autographing cricket balls for crazed fans around the world. We don't mind though – if ever a retailer is stumped because they run out of stock, he knocks them for six with his speedy delivery.

Tom Jordan
AKA: The True Professional
Explorer's resident thesp, Tom delivers lines almost as well as he cuts them. His early promise on the pantomime circuit was rewarded with an all-action role in hit UK drama Heartbeat. He's still living off the royalties – and the fact he shared a sandwich with Kenneth Branagh.

Shefeeq M
AKA: Rapper in Disguise
So new he's still got the wrapper on, Shefeeq was dragged into the Explorer office, forced to pose in front of a camera, and put to work in the design department. The poor chap only stopped by to ask for directions to Wadi Bih, but since we realised how efficient he is, we keep him chained to his desk.

Zainudheen Madathil
AKA: Map Master
Often confused with retired footballer Zinedine Zidane because of his dexterous displays and a bad head-butting habit, Zain tackles design with the mouse skills of a star striker. Maps are his goal and despite getting red-penned a few times, when he shoots, he scores.

Laura Zuffa
AKA: Travelling Salesgirl
Laura's passport is covered in more stamps than Kofi Annan's, and there isn't a city, country or continent that she won't travel to. With a smile that makes grown men weep, our girl on the frontlines always brings home the beef bacon.

Mohammed T
AKA: King of the Castle
T is Explorer's very own Bedouin warehouse dweller; under his caring charge all Explorer stock is kept in masterful order. Arrive uninvited and you'll find T, meditating on a pile of maps, amid an almost eerie sense of calm.

Mannie Lugtu
AKA: Distribution Demon
When the travelling circus rode into town, their master juggler Mannie decided to leave the Big Top and explore Dubai instead. He may have swapped his balls for our books but his juggling skills still come in handy.

Motaz Al Bunai
AKA: Car Salesman
Motaz starts every day with a tough decision, namely, which one of his fleet of exotic cars he's going to drive to work. If he ever takes a break from his delightful designing, he could always start his own second-hand car garage – Motaz's Motors.

Maricar Ong
AKA: Pocket Docket
A pint-sized dynamo of ruthless efficiency, Maricar gets the job done before anyone else notices it needed doing. If this most able assistant is absent for a moment, it sends a surge of blind panic through the Explorer ranks.

Noushad Madathil
AKA: Map Daddy
Where would Explorer be without the mercurial Madathil brothers? Lost in the Empty Quarter, that's where. Quieter than a mute dormouse, Noushad prefers to let his Photoshop layers, and brother Zain, do all the talking. A true Map Daddy.

Matt Farquharson
AKA: Hack Hunter
A career of tuppence-a-word hackery ended when Matt arrived in Dubai to cover a maggot wranglers' convention. He misguidedly thinks he's clever because he once wrote for some grown-up English papers.

Pamela Grist
AKA: Happy Snapper
If a picture can speak a thousand words then Pam's photos say a lot about her - through her lens she manages to find the beauty in everything – even this motley crew. And when the camera never lies, thankfully Photoshop can.

Mimi Stankova
AKA: Mind Controller
A master of mind control, Mimi's siren-like voice lulls people into doing whatever she asks. Her steely reserve and endless patience mean recalcitrant reporters and persistent PR people are putty in her hands, delivering whatever she wants, whenever she wants it.

Pete Maloney
AKA: Graphic Guru
Image conscious he may be, but when Pete has his designs on something you can bet he's gonna get it! He's the king of chat up lines, ladies – if he ever opens a conversation with 'D'you come here often?' then brace yourself for the Maloney magic.

Mohammed Sameer
AKA: Man in the Van
Known as MS, short for Microsoft, Sameer can pick apart a PC like a thief with a lock, which is why we keep him out of France and pounding Dubai's roads in the unmissable Explorer van – so we can always spot him coming.

Rafi Jamal
AKA: Soap Star
After a walk on part in The Bold and the Beautiful, Rafi swapped the Hollywood Hills for the Hajar Mountains. Although he left the glitz behind, he still mingles with high society, moonlighting as a male gigolo and impressing Dubai's ladies with his fancy footwork.

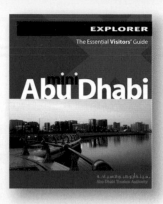

Residents' Guides

All you need to know about living, working and enjoying life in these exciting destinations

 Abu Dhabi
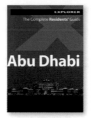 Amsterdam
 Bahrain

 Barcelona
 Dubai
 Dublin
 Geneva
 Hong Kong

 Kuwait
 London
 New York
 New Zealand
 Oman

 Paris
 Qatar
 Shanghai
 Singapore
 Sydney

∗ Covers not final. Titles available Winter 2007.

Activity Guides

Drive, trek, dive and swim... life will never be boring again

 off-road UAE
 off-road Oman
 trekking Oman
 underwater UAE

Mini Guides

The perfect pocket-sized
Visitors' Guides

* Covers not final. Titles available Winter 2007.

Mini Maps

Wherever you are,
never get lost again

* Covers not final. Titles available Winter 2007.

Photography Books

Beautiful cities caught through the lens

Contents   General Info

Residents

Contents   Exploring

An in-depth look at the areas worth exploring in Bahrain and all the attractions to be found there, including museums, heritage sites, parks, beaches and amusement centres, and what can be found in Bahrain's neighbouring countries.

Activities

With enough to keep everyone busy, from beach lovers and theatre players up to even the most ardent extreme sports enthusiasts, Bahrain has a variety of sports and activities to keep you busy. Comprehensive listings for all the sports, activities, clubs and relaxation available.

Contents   Shopping

From large and flash malls to traditional, atmospheric souks, there's a massive range of shopping opportunities in Bahrain. There are reviews on each mall and shopping area and the sections on where to find whatever you want to buy.

Going Out

Whether you love fine dining or street-side shawarma, this chapter opens up Bahrain's culinary delights with independent reviews of all the 'must-do' places. There's also a rundown of cinemas and theatre options.

MEDECINS SANS FRONTIERES

أطبــّــاء بــلا حــدود

Unconditional Medical Aid. where needed. when needed.

2002 WINNER OF THE UAE HEALTH FOUNDATION PRIZE

MSF has been counting on you, and millions have been counting on MSF. Your continuous support has helped relieve pain and suffering of thousands of people around the world.

YOUR DONATIONS are actually supplying medicine, aiding war casualties, administrating vaccinations, providing prenatal care, fighting epidemics, and improving water and sanitation practices and facilities.

YOUR DONATIONS help MSF be an aid against, and a witness to all that endanger humanity, where needed and when needed.

PLEASE DONATE. Help us help them.

YOUR DONATION WILL MAKE A DIFFERENCE

General
Information

EXPLORER

General Information

Highlights...

Tomorrow's Bahrain Today [p.6]

Bahrain is currently undergoing rapid expansion (no surprise there then – as the entire GCC has the same hunger for a makeover) and there are a number of exciting retail, business, commercial and property developments on the horizon. There are islands, residential complexes and financial developments all currently under construction or in the planning stage so if you're planning to see yesterday's Bahrain you better catch it today!

Bahrain Overview

Geography

Bahrain is an archipelago of 33 islands with a combined area of 707 square kilometres situated in the Arabian Gulf. It sits off the east coast of Saudi Arabia about halfway between Saudi Arabia and Qatar. Iran lies 200km to the north-east. Bahrain is roughly the same size as Singapore. The Arabian Gulf has an average depth of only 35 metres and most of it in the vicinity of Bahrain is much shallower than this.

The main island of Bahrain is 586.5 square kilometres. It is linked by causeways to Muharraq, which holds the international airport, and Sitra, where the country's main industrial area is based. There are numerous other small islands, but they are mainly uninhabited and are mostly nesting sites for migratory birds. Most development in Bahrain is concentrated on the northern third of the main island, which is undergoing extensive reclamation.

Bahrain is almost completely flat, the highest point being Jebel Ad Dukhan (which means Smoke Mountain), which stands a mere 134m above sea level in the central region. The majority of Bahrain's oil wells are in this area, which consists of limestone rock covered with saline sand.

Bahrain's name is derived from the Arabic words 'thnain Bahr' (two seas) and refers to the sweet water springs under the sea, which mix with the salt water. This is believed to be responsible for the beauty of Bahrain's natural pearls. Historically, Bahrain was known as an area of greenery in contrast to the region's deserts, as for centuries, the northern and western coastal belts were watered by a large number of natural springs. In the last 40 years, however, this has changed, and the island is a lot less lush than it used to be. As increasing demands have been made on the underground springs and on the land itself, many of the island's natural date palms and other plants have disappeared.

The country represents a fascinating blend of traditional Arab and western cultures. Unlike many of its regional neighbours, Bahrain has a large local population living alongside its expatriate population. Its development and modernity is reflected in the high-rise buildings of the ever-expanding commercial district, but a rapidly dwindling number of traditional houses can still be seen in Manama and Muharraq. The traditional way of life still remains, however, particularly among older Bahrainis.

History

Bahrain has a rich history that dates back several thousand years. International archaeologists have found that Bahrain has been inhabited for at least the last 7,000 years, and there is evidence of two distinct civilizations, Dilmun and Tylos, 2,000 years apart. Dilmun was a Bronze Age trading empire that lasted about 2,000 years. Its strategic position on the Mesopotamia/Indus Valley trade route meant that it became a watering place for ships carrying goods and it soon became a strategic trading post with well-developed social systems.

As a spring-watered garden land, Dilmun stood out in contrast to the deserts around. In the Babylonian Epic of Gilgamesh, Dilmun has been described as 'paradise', where there is a constant abundance of sweet water and the brave and the wise enjoy eternal life.

Some scholars have suggested that Bahrain may be the site of the biblical Garden of Eden. Dilmun was absorbed by the Assyrian and Babylonian empires, and in 323BC, the Persian Empire's domination of the region was ended by the arrival of Alexander the Great. Although there is no direct evidence that the Greeks conquered Bahrain specifically, the islands were renamed Tylos, a Greek name, and there is evidence that Greek influence was strong. New trade routes opened and Tylos remained a prosperous trading port within the Greek Empire for the next 600 years.

In the seventh century, Bahrain received a personal invitation from the Prophet Mohammed (Peace Be Upon Him) to convert to Islam, and many of the island's inhabitants did so.

In the early 16th century, Bahrain was invaded by the Portuguese, who were attracted by its trade relations, pearl exports and boat building industry. In 1602, an uprising ousted the Portuguese and the islands became part of the Persian Empire. However, in 1783 the Persians were expelled upon the arrival of the Al Khalifa family, Bahrain's current ruling family.

In 1861 Bahrain signed a treaty with Britain, who offered protection from the Ottomans in exchange for unlimited access to the Gulf. Oil was discovered in the 1930s. This was great timing: with the development of the Japanese cultured pearl industry, the world's natural pearl market was collapsing, so the oil money was a very welcome source of income. The British Empire took note, and the main British naval base in the region was moved to Bahrain in 1935, with the senior British official in the Middle East following in 1946. However, in the 1950s, increasing anti-British sentiment and the rise of Arab nationalism led to the announcement by Britain of its intention to leave the Gulf. Bahrain proclaimed its independence on August 14, 1971.

As the price of oil rocketed during the 1970s and 1980s, Bahrain developed in great strides. It also capitalised on its superior level of development and education to make it the region's centre for banking. Despite the Gulf-wide economic downturn of the late 1980s, Bahrain remained relatively prosperous. In 1986, the King Fahd Causeway was opened between Bahrain and Saudi Arabia, which boosted business and brought in tourists from Saudi Arabia, particularly of the weekend variety, who enjoy its relaxed social environment.

In the 1990s, Bahrain struggled with internal unrest. The relative decline in oil wealth, and employment pressures from an increasing population, the majority of whom are Shia Muslims, led to calls for democratic reforms and a more equal distribution of wealth. The refusal by the ruling Sunni elite to consider these calls led to widespread rioting in the mid 1990s and a severe government crackdown.

Bahrain's initial move towards democracy after this period took place in 1992 when the late Emir, Sheikh Isa bin Salman Al Khalifa, established the Shura (Consultative) Council. The members of the Shura Council were appointed by the Emir and included senior figures from business, civic and political positions who were deemed competent to give advice on policy and state matters. This was a welcome move, but it was another 10 years before a further major shift towards democracy took place.

However, recent years have seen the beginning of democratic reform in the kingdom. The king remains the supreme authority and the ruling family continues to hold all-important political and military posts, but the reform process has broadened the power base in Bahrain. In 2001, reforms intended to transform the country into a constitutional monarchy were proposed and supported overwhelmingly by Bahrainis.

The following year, elections were held for a 40 member parliament, the Council of Deputies, a dozen of whom are Shia. This was the first poll in nearly 30 years, since the National Assembly was dissolved in 1975. Since then, the country has enjoyed increasing freedom of expression and an improvement in human rights.

As part of the reform process, the 12 administrative areas, which had little autonomy, have been consolidated into five autonomous municipal areas. The new law has given the municipalities administrative and financial autonomy and clearly demarcated their responsibilities over public spaces, roads, beaches and the environment. Bahrain is home to the US Navy's Fifth Fleet, and has been a major non-NATO ally since 2001.

Economy

Bahrain Overview

Bahrain has a vibrant and growing economy based primarily on its petroleum production and refining industries, which account for 60% of export receipts and government revenue, and the financial sector, which is the largest employer and the largest contributor to GDP (over US$2 billion). In recent years the government has concentrated on diversifying the economy and the kingdom now has significant tourism, trading, construction, metal smelting and ship repairing sectors.

The industrial growth rate is 2% per annum. Total GDP is around US$10 billion with an annual growth rate of 5.6%. Per capita GDP is approximately US$ 14,000 (all 2003 figures). Bahrain's main export markets are other GCC countries and Arab states (37%), Asian countries (35%), the US (16%) and Europe (7%). Bahrain is a member of the GCC together with Kuwait, Oman, Qatar, Saudi Arabia and the UAE.

The six states are in the process of instituting a free trade area between all the members and signed a Customs Union in January 2003 unifying their tariff rates. They have also set 2010 as the target for a single currency within the GCC.

Bahrain has recently signed a Free Trade Agreement with the United States, which is expected to increase trade with the US significantly in the coming years. The Bahrain dinar is pegged to the US dollar, with a fixed exchange rate of US$1 = BD0.376.

Bahrain's main exports are aluminium, textiles, petroleum and petroleum products, and its main imports are crude oil, machinery and equipment, chemicals, foodstuffs and construction materials. Bahrain is the base for the headquarters of many international companies operating in the Gulf region. It has an excellent transport and communications infrastructure and the government is working to make the kingdom business friendly to both local industry and international investors.

Manama Overview

Manama is the capital city of Bahrain and is the centre for government, the diplomatic community, business, entertainment and shopping. Situated along the north-west coast of Bahrain Island, Manama is a 15 minute drive from the airport on Muharraq Island. Manama is connected to Muharraq by three multi-lane bridges.

Manama is a historic city but its development over the past 20 years has resulted in an ultra-modern metropolis with continuous construction changing its skyline. New hotels, shopping malls, office buildings, entertainment venues and residential complexes, which seem to spring up overnight like mushrooms, are an omnipresent feature of the city. Banking and financial services are the mainstay of the commercial life of the city and many multinational companies have located their regional headquarters in the city.

Given the small size of Bahrain, Manama is easily accessible to the whole population of the kingdom. Bahrain's unemployment rate is estimated at 15% of the working population. This mainly consists of school leavers and young adults reflecting the large portion of the population under 25 years old (57%). The government has undertaken a number of initiatives to address the unemployment problem, including a Bahrainisation program to encourage firms to replace expatriate workers with Bahrainis.

Expatriates, numbering over 260,000, represent 38% of the population, but the 194,000 expatriate workers represent 59% of the workforce. Bahrainisation has had limited success as much of the work carried out by expatriates is not attractive to Bahrainis. Employers also complain about the general absence of an acceptable Bahraini work ethic.

The government also commissioned MacKenzies to review the employment situation and issue a report with recommendations on how to improve the employment situation for Bahrain nationals. The report was issued in early 2005 and the government is now instituting programmes to implement the recommendations despite protests from members of the local Chamber of Commerce, who say that the proposed reforms (which include raising the minimum wage and work permit charges for expatriate labour to make it more expensive to hire expatriates than Bahrainis) would cripple their businesses.

Tourism Developments

Tourism is an important and growing sector of the Bahrain economy accounting for 10 – 12% of GDP. Approximately five million visitors arrived in Bahrain in 2004; 80% of these came across the Saudi causeway and the number includes visitors from Saudi Arabia who make multiple trips during the year. Tourism falls into two main categories: middle- to high-end tourists from Europe and Asia who want a holiday in the sun in relative luxury, and short-term tourists from the region, particularly from Saudi Arabia.

Non-Arab tourists are few and far between and are mainly families or small groups. Backpackers and low-end holiday makers are rare in Bahrain. The second group comprises families who enjoy the relaxed atmosphere in Bahrain and groups who visit Bahrain for weekends to sample the entertainment and friendly environment. Tourists are catered for by Bahrain's broad range of hotels ranging from relatively cheap guesthouses and apartments to world class hotels.

There are eight five-star hotels, 10 four-star, 20 three-star and over 40 one to two-star, where facilities are limited and pretty basic.

Tourism received a major boost with the opening of the Bahrain F1 Racetrack in 2004, the first ever in the region. Approximately 30,000 people attended the first Grand Prix with most of the foreign visitors coming from Europe. Needless to say, hotel prices skyrocketed, with most hotels only accepting bookings for a five-night F1 package at five or six times the normal rate.

Tourists are attracted to Bahrain for the weather, unique ambience (which is completely different from the average European package experience), diving and water sports, local culture and the relaxed friendly atmosphere. Bahrain also enjoys a comparatively liberal social climate (when compared to some other GCC countries), good shopping and minimal travel restrictions.

The growth of tourism in Bahrain is reflected in the number of multi-million dollar developments in the kingdom, with a large tourism component and the refurbishment and extension of many of the major hotels. It must be said, however, that Bahrain still hasn't quite got the tourist bit right. Most of the major tourist attractions are woefully lacking in basic amenities such as guides, toilets, souvenir shops and refreshment facilities. The government has plans to combat these problems with training schemes. Further information on tourism in Bahrain can be found at www.bahrain.com.

Key Bahrain Projects

Bahrain is currently experiencing a construction boom with business, shopping, tourism and residential developments underway throughout the kingdom. The major developments are:

Bahrain Financial Harbour (BFH)

BFH is a $1.3 billion integrated financial community development being built on 380,000 square metres of reclaimed land adjacent to Manama's existing commercial centre. The development will incorporate commercial, residential and leisure components (hotels, shops, restaurants, and a marina). Construction started in 2004 and is scheduled for completion in 2009. Phase one is already well advanced and the remainder of the 10 phases will be completed in stages over the next four years. Non-Bahrainis can buy properties on the development and will be entitled to indefinite residence permits for as long as they retain ownership.

Details: www.bfharbour.com

Durrat Al Bahrain

Durrat is a 20 square kilometre city resort development on 13 islands of reclaimed land to the south of Bahrain Island and 35 minutes drive from Manama. The development will incorporate 2,000 villas, 3,000 apartments, hotels, promenades, shops, restaurants, a marina, a golf course, sporting facilities, spas and entertainment venues. Development has been ongoing for several years and will continue until 2009/2010. Pre-sales for the first phases have already taken place.

Details: www.durratbahrain.com

Amwaj Islands

Amwaj is a 2.8 square kilometre residential and resort development on reclaimed land adjacent to Bahrain International Airport and a short drive from Manama across the new bridge and Muharraq Ring Road. The development will incorporate canal-side villas and apartments, hotels, shops, restaurants, marinas and a theme island. Development began in 2001 and the reclamation was completed in 2006. Pre-sales for the first five phases has already taken place, and the first residents will move into their premises in 2007. Non-Bahrainis can buy properties on the development and, as in the BFH, will be entitled to indefinite residence permits for as long as they retain ownership.

Details: www.ossisonline.com

Al Areen

Al Areen is a $750 million integrated residential and leisure development being built on 2,000,000 square metres of land at Al Areen Wildlife Park, 35 minutes drive from Bahrain International Airport. The development will incorporate luxurious themed hotels, therapeutic medical services, sports, residential, entertainment and leisure facilities. The Banyan Tree Desert Spa and Resort, which is already open, is aimed primarily at family and health-orientated tourism, while the rest of the development will be completed by 2008. 100% of the land parcels have already been sold.

Other major projects which are in the pipeline include the Northern City complex, a government-financed residential development in the north of the island and the Bahrain/Qatar Causeway.

Bahrain key projects

International Relations

Bahrain has excellent relations with its neighbours and the rest of the world. Since the settlement of the long-running battle with Qatar over ownership of the Hawar Islands, Bahrain has not been involved in any international disputes and while it generally supports pan-Arabic initiatives, it takes a neutral stance on global affairs. It is a member of the GCC along with Kuwait, Oman, Qatar, Saudi Arabia and the UAE. Internationally, the kingdom is a member of, among other organisations, the United Nations, the IMF, the WTO, Interpol and the G-77. It has recently signed a Free Trade Agreement with the United States; the only country in the region to do so. All regional countries and most major international ones have embassies or consulates in Bahrain. All of these are located in Manama, primarily in or near the Diplomatic Area in the city centre. Bahrain is regarded internationally as one of the most stable and best-governed countries in the region.

Government & Ruling Family

Bahrain is a constitutional hereditary monarchy with a bicameral parliament consisting of an elected House of Deputies (40 members) and a Shura Council (40 members) appointed by the king. There are no political parties in Bahrain, but political societies exist and members stand for election. The current breakdown of the House of Deputies is Sunni Islamists (9), Independents (21) and others (10).

لمملكة البحرين حققت حاضراً   وطوزت ما قد شيّدته الأوائل

Bahrain's ruling family

The Executive Branch of the government consists of the king, HRH King Hamad bin Isa Al Khalifa, the crown prince, HRH Prince Salman bin Hamad Al Khalifa and the prime minister, HH Shaikh Khalifa bin Salman Al Khalifa. The king succeeded his father, HH Shaikh Isa bin Salman Al Khalifa, as the ruler of Bahrain in 1999. HH Shaikh Khalifa bin Salman Al Khalifa was appointed prime minister in 1971 and has held the post since then. HRH Prince Salman bin Hamad Al Khalifa is the king's eldest son and first in line for the throne.

> ### GCC easy as ABC
>
> *If you want to drop in on your neighbours, then go prepared. Be it for a shopping spree in Dubai, a luxury holiday in Abu Dhabi, to find tranquility in the wilderness of Oman or to see the colourful heritage of Kuwait, don't leave Bahrain without an Explorer!*

The king has three other children – HRH Shaikh Salman, HRH Shaikh Abdullah and HRH Shaikha Najla. The Al Khalifa family has ruled Bahrain since 1783 when Ahmed bin Mohammed Al Khalifa came to Bahrain from Qatar. The heads of the family were known as sheikhs or emirs until October 2002 when the title of king was adopted by the head of state.

Bahrain has won worldwide recognition for its efforts to promote democracy and transparency in government. Bahrain is divided into five governorates – Capital, Muharraq, Northern, Central and Southern – which assume the duties of local government. There are also 12 municipalities, which are governed centrally. The central government is administered through a number of ministries including Islamic Affairs, Foreign Affairs, Interior, Transportation, Justice, Defence, Cabinet Affairs, Oil, Electricity and Water, Consultative and Representatives Council, Finance, Information, Works and Housing, Industry & Commerce, Municipalities Affairs & Agriculture, Education, Labour, Health and Social Affairs. In addition there are a number of national bodies that report to the Executive Branch through their chief executives and chairmen.

Facts & Figures

Population

The latest National Census taken for Bahrain (2001) showed a total population of 650,000 people. The latest official estimates for 2003 (see www.bahrain.gov.bh) give the population as

690,000. Of this total 428,000 (62%) are Bahrainis and 262,000 (38%) are non-Bahrainis. The total workforce is 330,000, of which 136,000 (41%) are Bahrainis and 194,000 (59%) are non-Bahrainis. The majority of the non-Bahraini population are male workers. The annual population growth rate is 2.1%. The average family has six or seven members. A large percentage of the local Bahraini population falls into the younger age groups. The life expectancy is around 73 years for women and 70 years for men (source: UN Human Development Report 1997).

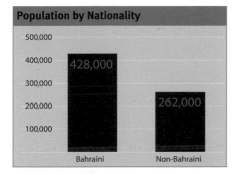

Population by Nationality

500,000	
400,000	428,000
300,000	
200,000	262,000
100,000	
	Bahraini Non-Bahraini

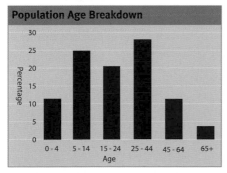

Population Age Breakdown

Percentage / Age: 0-4, 5-14, 15-24, 25-44, 45-64, 65+

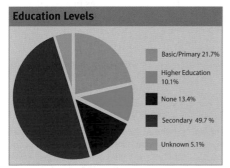

Education Levels

- Basic/Primary 21.7%
- Higher Education 10.1%
- None 13.4%
- Secondary 49.7%
- Unknown 5.1%

National Flag

The Bahrain national flag is red and white, the white portion on the hoist side having five points. Red is a traditional flag colour in the region and the five white points represent the five pillars of Islam. The flag flies on all government buildings and is widely displayed on National Day (16 December) and all public and religious holidays. The flag is also prominent during public appearances of members of the royal family. During the past two or three years, Bahrain has made several attempts to enter the *Guinness Book of Records*, the most bizarre of which was the making of the world's largest flag. The Bahrain flag, which was large enough to cover a football pitch, was ceremonially unfurled on the pitch of the National Stadium in the presence of a representative from the Guinness Book of Records. Letters to the GDN pointed out the incongruous nature of a flag which was too big to be flown, but the authorities did not seem to be deterred. The largest flag that is actually flown is on an enormous flagpole in the desert near Hamad Town and can be seen from many kilometres away.

National flag

Local Time

Bahrain is three hours ahead of UCT (Universal Coordinated Time), formerly known as GMT, so when it is 12:00 in Bahrain, it is 09:00 in London, and 18:00 in Tokyo. This, of course, changes when other countries adopt summer time.

Social & Business Hours

Traditionally in Bahrain, social hours are Mediterranean in style. In general, people get up early, have an afternoon siesta, and stay up and eat late in the evening. With increasing commercial demands, this is changing to a certain extent, particularly in the sectors serving international interests.

Government hours are 07:30 to 14:30 from Saturday to Wednesday. Thursday and Friday are the official government (and almost all schools) days off. However, in the private sector, the hours and weekends are more varied. Most of the trading and manufacturing companies work a Saturday to Thursday afternoon week, with split-shift days, which are generally 08:00 to 13:00 and 15:00 to 18:00.

Shop opening hours generally start and finish one hour later, but the newer shopping malls open from 10:00 to 22:00. Supermarkets are generally open from 08:00 to 22:00, but there are several 24 hour supermarkets, cold stores and pharmacies.

Local commercial banks work from 07:30 to 12:00 from Saturday to Wednesday and many branches are open from 15:30 to 17:30 during those afternoons. Most banks work from 07:30 to 12:00 on Thursdays. International banks follow similar working hours to local banks, but some have six-day coverage.

Working hours at embassies vary, but are generally from 08:00 till 14:00 from Saturday to Wednesday. Most have contact details on their answering machines for cases of emergency. In recent years there have been calls to move and regulate the weekend to Friday/Saturday, to work more in line with international timing, but it is likely that Bahrain will continue to have a split weekend.

Public Holidays

Most public holidays are dates that are of importance in the Islamic calendar. The Islamic calendar started from the year 622AD, the year of Prophet Mohammed's journey (Hijra) from Mecca to Medina. The Islamic year is called the Hijri year and denoted by AH. The Hijri year is based on lunar months and is 11 to 12 days shorter than the Gregorian calendar. Religious public holidays therefore fall upon different dates in the Gregorian calendar on a year-to-year basis (approximately 11 days earlier each year).

As the start of religious holidays are based on the sighting of the moon, quite often holidays that occur at the beginning of an Islamic month are only announced officially 12 hours before the start of the holiday. This often leads to great uncertainty on the part of schools and business establishments, and has occasionally resulted in one or other of the neighbouring countries deciding to start the holiday a day before the rest of the Gulf states, which leads to all sorts of confusion.

Every year one or two local scientists urge the authorities to set the holiday dates according to scientific principles, but this has not so far been accepted. Holidays such as New Year and National Day follow the Gregorian calendar.

Public Holidays – 2007	
New Years Day	1 Jan
Eid Al Adha	3 Jan
Islamic New Year	20 Jan
Ashoora - 2 days	29 Jan
Prophet's Birthday	31 Mar
Labour Day	1 May
Eid Al Fitr - 3 days	13 Oct
National Day	16 Dec
Accession Day	17 Dec
Eid Al Adha - 3 days	20 Dec

Electricity & Water

Other options → **Electricity & Water [p.66]**

Water and electricity are both supplied by the government through the Ministry of Electricity and Water. The electricity supply is 220 volts and 50 cycles. The socket type is the same as the three-point square plug British system. There are very few shortages for most of the year, with the exception of the hottest summer months, July and August, when the demand placed on the system by the increased use of air-conditioning units occasionally causes localised shortages for up to a few hours.

The mains tap water is desalinated and drinkable in the major residential areas, but is heavily chlorinated, so most people prefer to drink 'sweet water' purchased from local purification factories, or locally bottled mineral water at BD 1 for a five-litre bottle. This has lead incredulous newcomers to Bahrain to report home that 'oil is cheaper than water in the Gulf'.

There are different brands of water available and companies are listed in the *Yellow Pages*, but the main companies supplying five-litre bottles are Al Manhal, Tylos and Aquacool, who will make

Sights of the National Museum

regular deliveries to your home. Hotels and restaurants serve local and international brands of bottled water.

Photography

Normal tourist photography is acceptable, but tourists should avoid photographing government and military buildings. When photographing locals, you should ask for permission, particularly when wishing to take photos of women. There is a wide choice of film available and processing is usually fast and relatively inexpensive. APS, 35mm and slide film can all be processed, although the cost of processing and developing APS and slide film is still relatively high.

Environment

Climate

The summer in Bahrain can get extremely hot and humid. From June to September, temperatures average 35°C (97°F) during the day, sometimes reaching 48°C at the height of summer. From November to April the weather is much more pleasant, with warm days and cool nights. Temperatures at this time range from 15°C to 24°C. The coolest months of the year are generally December and January, when the island experiences northern winds, and at night the temperature sometimes drops to 10°C.

Flora & Fauna

Bahrain is naturally greener than many of its Gulf neighbours and is home to a variety of plants and animals. Most of the plants that are found in Bahrain are salt-tolerant and desert-resistant types, of which the palm tree is the most common. However in addition, Bahrain's scrubland supports a number of specially adapted species of plant, the most common of which is the bean caper (*Zygophillum qatarense*).

During the winter, if there has been a reasonable amount of rainfall the scrubland suddenly bursts into a colourful display of tiny flowers. Otherwise, this is the most impoverished area of Bahrain in terms of flora. Animals include snakes and other reptiles, hares, scorpions, hedgehogs and gazelles. The northern region is more lush and

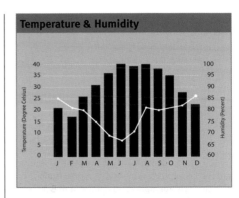

Temperature & Humidity

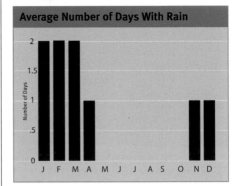

Average Number of Days With Rain

holds cultivated areas growing fruit and vegetables, as well as palm plantations. Most of the gardens and plantations in this area are on private land, so you would need an invitation to visit, but sometimes you're lucky and a hospitable owner will let you have a wander around.

The birds that breed in the green areas include the White-cheeked Bulbul, Graceful Warbler and Ring-necked Parakeet. On the road from Awali to Zellaq there are mesquite plantations near the racecourse at Sakhir which are host to hundreds of migrating passerines during the spring. Sakhir racecourse also has a lake where ducks can often be seen, as it is one of the few remaining freshwater areas on the island.

One main source of interest lies on the eastern shores of Bahrain. These hold mudflats, which were previously quite extensive, but have diminished in recent years. These were recently discovered to be of international importance as a wintering ground for migrating wading birds in the autumn. Over 40 species have been recorded, including the Broad-billed Sandpiper, Curlew Sandpiper and Bar-tailed Godwit. Further south near the Bahrain Yacht Club, flamingoes can be seen almost all year round.

Around Bahrain, the shallow saline waters support a rich marine life, including mackerel, shrimps, pearl oysters, dugong, green turtles and sea snakes. Another notable wildlife site is the site of the dwarf mangrove stands at the southern end of Tubli Bay. This tidal habitat is a nursery ground for many species of fish and crustaceans and was in fact the first recorded breeding site for the Black-winged Stilt in Bahrain. Herons can often be seen roosting here during the winter months. This is officially a protected area, but is still subject to illegal rubbish dumping and landfill, and Bahrain's conservationists regularly warn that unless the problem is countered, the area and species contained within it are threatened with destruction. 20km to the south-east of mainland Bahrain are the Hawar Islands.

Made up of a group of 16 islands, all flat and some with low cliffs, Hawar is topographically different to the main Bahrain Island and is home to some locally rare birds. The islands are the breeding ground of up to 200,000 Socotra Cormorants between October and February, and Western Reef Herons, Caspian Little Terns, Greater Flamingos, ground-nesting Ospreys and Sooty Falcons can also be seen. Visitors are welcome on the main Hawar Island, but visits to the outer islands require special permission. Ask the Hawar Islands booking office for further details.

Protection

Protection of the environment is a concept that exists in Bahrain, but often loses out to commercial concerns. There are relatively few areas marked as conservation sites, despite the presence of a few rare species of wildlife, but with a growing environmental awareness in Bahrain over the last few years this is likely to improve in the future. Certainly the amount of recycling that now exists is a result of initiatives taken in the last few years.

Similarly, the greater awareness and empowerment that has occurred as a result of the democratic reforms has placed environmental issues at a higher priority than previously, particularly in the case of concerns about pollution near industrial areas. This is especially true in Sitra, where local people have complained about noxious emissions from various factories and power plants.

Culture & Lifestyle

Culture

Bahrain's culture is rooted mainly in Gulf Arab historical traditions and Islamic culture. Islam is more than just a religion, it is a way of life, and impacts on everything in daily life, from what to eat or drink, to what to wear and to how social life should be conducted. That said, Bahrain is a welcoming and tolerant country, with a long history of responding to outside influences and its culture to a certain extent reflects this. Foreigners have the freedom to practise their religion, and alcohol is served in restaurants, hotels and bars, and is sold in off-licences to non-Muslims. Women, although conservative, are a visible part of the workforce and daily life, and unlike in Saudi Arabia, are allowed to drive and walk around unescorted.

In the Bahraini culture hospitality and courtesy are prized, and visitors are often charmed by the friendliness of the people. Over the last 35 years, however, Bahrain has undergone rapid economic development and this has changed daily life considerably. There has been a resultant impact on the culture, primarily in that people are more hurried and less relaxed than they were 20 years ago. Traditional pastimes have also given way to more modern and universally practised activities.

Most shopping now takes place in the malls and supermarkets, rather than in the souks, and while local coffee shops are still plentiful, international coffee house chains are increasingly popular with the young. However, traditional aspects of life continue to be apparent and Bahrainis have a strong pride in their roots and their ability to retain their essence while modernising, so this is unlikely to change.

Most Bahrainis continue to wear national dress, socialise often with their extended family and celebrate weddings in colourful occasions of feasting and music. Frequent mass weddings are organised by local religious and social organisations for the benefit of less wealthy couples.

To western eyes the inevitable photograph in the *Gulf Daily News* (GDN) of a group of happy grooms 'tying the knot' without a bride in sight seems strange, but separate celebrations for the brides are held at other venues where women only are admitted. Arabic culture in music, poetry and art is encouraged, and widely enjoyed. One of the wonderful aspects of Bahrain is that foreigners can continue to live within their own culture, and also enjoy what Bahrain offers, for a truly rich multicultural experience.

Language

Other options → Language Schools [p.148]
Learning Arabic [p.77]

Arabic is the official language, but English is generally used for commercial purposes. Most Bahrainis speak fairly good English, and many speak Farsi, Hindi and Urdu. Arabic is not particularly easy to pick up, mainly because English is widely spoken so you don't get much of an opportunity to practise, but most people are very appreciative if you make the effort to throw in a few Arabic words here and there. Road signs, shop names and restaurant menus are generally in both Arabic and English.

Religion

Islam is the official religion of Bahrain, and is practised by 85% of the population. The majority of the Bahraini population (about 75%) are followers of the Shia sect, but the ruling family follows the Sunni sect of Islam. Freedom of worship is permitted to other faiths including Christianity, Hinduism, Parseeism, Judaism and Buddisim. The basis of Islam is that there is only one God, and that Prophet Mohammed (Peace Be Upon Him) is His Messenger.

There are five main pillars of Islam, to which all followers must adhere: the testimony of faith, prayer, charity, fasting during the holy month of Ramadan and performing the Hajj pilgrimage at least once in a lifetime. Friday is Islam's holy day. The month of Ramadan is considered to be a holy month for Muslims, as it marks the period in which the Holy Quran was revealed to Prophet Mohammed.

The beginning of the month is marked by the sighting of the new moon, confirmed by a judiciary panel. During Ramadan, Muslims are expected to strive to a higher level of spirituality, and this is done in part by fasting during daylight hours. In the evening, the fast is broken by the Iftar meal. In Bahrain, working hours during Ramadan are shortened to six hours a day for Muslims. Some organisations extend this to non-Muslims too, who are also cautioned that it is illegal to eat, drink or smoke in public places during daylight hours, as a sign of respect to those who are fasting. The daily Ramadan timings are listed in the daily newspapers. In practice, Ramadan is a time where all official business slows down considerably. However, the upside is that there is a celebratory atmosphere throughout the country every evening for a month. In the villages, Bahrainis distribute dishes between houses most evenings for Iftar and Ghabgas (the late night meal and social gathering). It is somewhat ironic that food imports, particularly of meat, soar during the fasting month of Ramadan, but people party most of the night and lavish spreads are de rigueur. Mosques are full for evening prayers and you can feel the collective surge of community spirit and faith. Many hotels and cafes erect colourful tents for the whole month and Bahrainis and expatriates alike gather to socialise, eat and play a range of traditional games.

Ramadan ends with a three-day holiday and celebration, Eid Al Fitr, the Feast of the Breaking of the Fast. The other main celebration is Eid Al Adha, the Feast of the Sacrifice, which marks the end of the annual Hajj pilgrimage to Mecca.

While Christmas is not usually referred to by name in official media, it is openly celebrated in Bahrain and many of the clubs and hotels hold 'festive season' activities. These are often well attended by the large expatriate population, many of whom choose to spend it in an extended family and friends environment.

Diwali, the Hindu Festival of Light, is also celebrated by the large Hindu population. While many celebrate in their homes, the various Indian clubs and some hotels also hold parties to mark the occasion. Some Bahraini companies allow Christian and Hindu employees to take the day off for Christmas and Diwali, although this depends upon the whim of the boss.

Mosque grounds

Basic Arabic

General

(If you) **Please**	Lauw sammaht
God willing	Inshaa'a l-laah
No	La
Please (in offering/invitation)	Tfadhal
Praise be to God	Al hamdu l-illah
Thank you	Shukraan / Mashkoor
Thank you very much	Shukraan jazeelan
Yes	Naam / Aiwa

Greetings

Fine, thank you	Al hamdu l-illah bikhair
Good Evening	Masaa al khair
Good Evening (in reply)	Masaa an-noor
Good Morning	Sabaah al khair
Good Morning (in reply)	Sabaah an-noor
Goodbye	Maa as-salaama
Goodbye (in reply)	Allah yisullmak
Goodnight	Tisbah ala khair
Greeting (Peace be upon you)	As-salaam alaykum
Hello	Marhaba
Hello (in reply)	Marhabteyn
How are you?	Kayf haalak? (m) / Kayf haalik (f)
Welcome	Hala
Welcome (in reply)	Hala / Hayak'allah

Introduction

I am from...	Anaa min...
America	Amreekee (m) / Amreekeeyah (f)
Britain	Breetaanee (m) / Breetaaneeyah (f)
Europe	Orobeeyah (m) / Orobeeyah (f)
India	Hindee (m) / Hindeeyah (f)
Kuwait	Kuwayti / Kuwaitiyah
South Africa	Janoob afreekee (m) / janoob afreekeeyah (f)
My name is...	Ismi...
What is your name?	Shismik (m) / Shismich (f)
Where are you from?	Min wayn inta?

Questions

Also	kamaan
And	Wa
From	Min
How many / much?	Chem / Kem
How?	Kayf? / Eshloon?
In / at	Fee
There isn't	Ma fee / Ma koo
This/that	Haatha
To / for	Eila
What?	Shinu?
When?	Mata?
Where?	Weyn?
Which?	Aywho?
Who?	Miyn? Miynoo?
Why?	Lesh?

Taxi / Car Related

Airport	Mataar
Behind	Wara / khalf
Between	Beyn
Close to	Qareeb min
Corner	Zaawya
Desert	Al Barr
East	Sharq
First	Ewwil
Hotel	Finduk
In front of	Jiddaam
Left	Yisaar
Next to	Jamb
North	Shemaal
On top / Upstairs / Up	Fowg
Opposite	Mugaabil
Petrol Station	Mahattat banzeen
Restaurant	Mataam
Right	Yimeen
Road	Tareeg
Roundabout	Dawwaar
Sea / beach	Bahr / Shaatee
Second	Thaani
Signal(s)	Ishaara(at)
Slow down	Bateea / Eshway eshway
South	Janoob
Stop	Kif
Straight ahead	Seeda
Turning	Leff
West	Gharb

Accidents

Accident	Haadeth
Insurance	Ta'meen
Licence	Roksaht al qiyadah
Papers	Waraq al seyaara
Police	Poolíis / Makhfar Shurta
Policeman	Shurti
Policemen	Shurtiyyin
Sorry	Aasif (m) / Aasifa (f)

Numbers

Zero	Sifir
One	Waahid
Two	Ithnayn
Three	Thalaatha
Four	Araba'a
Five	Khamsa
Six	Sitta
Seven	saba'a
Eight	Thamaanya
Nine	Tiss'a
Ten	Ashra
Fifty	Khamseen
Hundred	Miyya
Thousand	Alf

National Dress

Most Bahrainis wear traditional dress, which consists of a long sleeved, floor length 'thobe' or 'dishdasha' for men. This is almost always white, although in winter months navy blue and brown are common. On their heads they wear a white crocheted skull cap covered by a white cloth called a 'ghutra' folded into a triangle, topped by a black double-ringed 'agaal', which was originally the rope with which camels were hobbled. The 'agaal' holds the 'ghutra' in place and can come in handy as a weapon.

On one occasion an irate gentleman was seen using his 'agaal' to lash the unfortunate pickup driver who had scraped his Mercedes on a roundabout. Sometimes, particularly in winter, a red and white checked 'ghutra' is worn, but the white one is more common in Bahrain.

For special occasions, sheikhs or important businessmen may also wear a thin black or gold robe, a 'bisht', over the thobe. Bahraini women are conservative, and while some do not wear the full black 'abaya', many of them wear the 'hijaab' (head scarf) and clothes that cover their bodies. Some women also wear black stockings and gloves, and thick veils. It can be quite disconcerting to notice that the driver of the car next to you at the traffic lights or hurtling towards you down a narrow street is completely covered.

There was considerable dissent, mainly on grounds of safety, when it was decided recently that women would be allowed to drive when dressed in this way, but the law stands. Visitors and expatriates are advised to show respect for the local culture when it comes to dress.

While sleeveless and tighter-fitting outfits for women are increasingly seen, particularly in clubs and restaurants, it is advisable to dress more modestly in the souks, malls and places where there are a lot of Bahrainis or Asian expatriates, if you don't want to have people staring at you.

Food & Drink

Other options → **Eating Out [p.191]**

As a cosmopolitan country with a large expatriate population, Bahrain offers almost every type of international cuisine. This ranges from the expensive to the very reasonable, so there really is something to suit every taste and budget. While many restaurants are located in hotels, some of the best restaurants are found in the suburbs.

Bahrain's licencing regulations allow restaurants to hold alcohol licences even if they are not part of a hotel, unlike in Dubai. For details on where to eat out, please refer to the Going Out section.

Supermarkets in Bahrain have been improving their choice of products yearly for the past 10 years. The main supermarket chains, which are Jawads, Al Jazira and Al Osra, all offer products and brands from all over the world in addition to local produce, and are styled on the supermarkets of the UK and US. However, there are plenty of smaller supermarkets and fruit/vegetable shops which often stay open late, or even round the clock, and offer excellent quality at lower prices, so it's worth looking around to establish your favourites.

Meat and fish can be found both in the supermarkets and the local markets or souks, and there are several small Asian food shops that sell fruit and vegetables from the Far East.

Local Cuisine

What people refer to as 'local' cuisine in Bahrain is actually a blend of various Middle Eastern cuisines, primarily Lebanese and Iranian as well as dishes from the Indian subcontinent. The larger hotels serve Arab food in their main restaurants, including wide-ranging buffets serving all the meze and salads particular to the region alongside biryanis and machboos (spiced rice dishes cooked with meat or fish).

In addition, you would really miss out if you didn't visit the various stalls selling shawarma (lamb or chicken sliced from a spit and served with tahina sauce and salad in pita bread and commonly known as flip-flop sandwiches) and Bahraini tikka (black-lemon spiced meat served with bread). Food from these stalls is very reasonable and represents a large percentage of the 'fast food' eaten in Bahrain.

There are numerous juice stalls throughout the country and these should not be missed: it is a delight to have freshly-squeezed juice so easily and cheaply available, particularly if you have been traipsing around the souk on a hot day.

Alcohol

Alcohol is served in licenced outlets. These include clubs, restaurants and bars, the latter being required to be associated with a hotel. Alcohol is also sold in licenced booze shops, such as BMMI and Gulf Cellar.

The law states that alcohol may only be sold to non-Muslims, but in practice this is not rigidly enforced and at weekends the car parks outside the alcohol

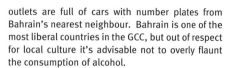

outlets are full of cars with number plates from Bahrain's nearest neighbour. Bahrain is one of the most liberal countries in the GCC, but out of respect for local culture it's advisable not to overly flaunt the consumption of alcohol.

Vociferous protests have been staged against the few establishments that serve alcohol and are situated in residential areas mainly populated by Bahraini families. It is also wise to remember that it is illegal to drive after drinking any alcohol whatsoever.

Shisha

Shisha, the water pipe sometimes called the hubbly-bubbly, is smoked throughout the Middle East and Bahrain is no exception. It is a popular pastime, often enjoyed in the local cafes while socialising with friends. Shisha comes either as plain tobacco (zehloun), or in a variety of flavours including green apple (iskanderani), double apple (tafahatain), strawberry (farowla) and grape (anab).

It's a completely different type of smoking from cigarettes or cigars, as the water smoothes the smoke, for a more soothing effect, and even people who don't smoke should try it at least once. In Ramadan when the festive tents are set up throughout Bahrain, shisha is very popular with Bahrainis and foreigners alike.

You don't often see Bahraini women smoking in public, but a row of ancient Bahraini grannies sitting on the floor smoking shisha pipes is a common sight at bridal parties being celebrated in private houses.

Pork

Pork is the most stringently taboo food for Muslims, so you don't find it featuring widely on menus. That said, it is served in many restaurants catering to westerners, but is clearly marked so that there is no confusion. The taboo extends to the storage, preparation and handling of pork, so restaurants that serve it, or supermarkets that sell it, must have completely separate refrigeration, handling and serving areas.

Entering Bahrain

Visas

Other options → **Entry Visa [p.42]**
Residence Visa [p.42]

Entry Visas

Citizens of the GCC countries (Saudi Arabia, the UAE, Kuwait, Qatar and Oman) do not require visas to enter Bahrain. Citizens of 35 countries, which include the USA, Australia, Canada, Japan, New Zealand, most EU countries, Norway and Switzerland can obtain a tourist visa on arrival for BD5 or US$13.25. This is for two weeks and can be extended for a further two for BD5, and BD40 for a second extension of up to one month. Citizens from all other countries require visas from the appropriate embassies prior to arrival in Bahrain. British passport holders receive a three month visa on arrival, which can be extended for a further three months for BD5. For full details, check the Ministry of Immigration's website: www.evisa.gov.bh, where you can check visa requirements for every nationality, and in many cases can apply for a visa online.

Visit visas only are issued at the Saudi Causeway entry to Bahrain. All other visas are issued either at the port, airport or the ministry in Manama.

E-tickets and Electronic Check-in

While the visa documentation is computerised in Bahrain the use of smart-cards or e-gate services is not currently applicable.

The Bahrain-Saudi Causeway

Meet & Greet

Meet and Greet services are available at Bahrain Airport through tour operators, hotels and airlines. These tend to be located outside the customs area in the main arrivals area. The Bahrain Airport Authorities have a Customer Service Counter in the arrivals area and will deliver documents to arriving passengers for a small fee; BD 3 or US$ 8. They can also arrange for Meet and Greet inside the prohibited areas in special cases.

The journey from the plane to the customs area for disembarking passengers is relatively short, approximately 10 minutes. There is no viewing platform in arrivals but as all arriving passengers use the same exit into the arrivals hall it is relatively easy to spot them. People who know the airport tend to designate their own meeting points (cafe or shop), and as the airport is small this does not generally present a problem.

There is a duty free shop in arrivals (after immigration and before customs). There are also banks, ATMs, car hire, hotel booking and customer service booths in the arrivals hall. Luggage trolleys are available for personal use and porters are also available at a minimum charge of 100 fils per bag.

A word of warning: if the baggage from your flight arrives on the carousel before you get to the baggage area to pick it up, a porter will probably have taken it off the carousel before it disappears back into the baggage loading area, so you need to check the ever-growing pile of suitcases beside the end of the carousel, in case yours is there. There's nothing more frustrating than waiting for your suitcase to arrive and then finding when the carousel stops that it has been sitting there for the past half an hour.

Customs

There are three customs locations when entering Bahrain: Bahrain International Airport, Bahrain Port and the Saudi Causeway. At the airport all bags are checked electronically and some are checked manually (picked at random, or if anything suspicious has been discovered during the electronic testing). Sometimes video tapes are taken away to be checked before you can bring them into Bahrain. In this case, you either have to wait until the check is finished, or return to the airport the next day to collect your cassette.

Customs at the port, and in particular the causeway, range from a perfunctory manual scan to a thorough investigation of the luggage and the vehicle, though normally the customs checks are not onerous. In general no customs duty is imposed on the personal effects of people entering Bahrain, though there is a BD 300 ceiling on the value of personal items.

Forbidden items include firearms, items produced in Israel, pornographic material, drugs, ivory and cultured pearls. Another word of warning: for some obscure reason, codeine is a banned substance in Bahrain, even though it is available off the shelf in other countries. If you are taking any medication containing codeine and you have to bring it with you to Bahrain, make sure you have a doctor's note.

The duty free allowances are generally: two litres of spirits, two litres of wine, and 2,000 cigarettes, but allowances differ depending on which country the visitor is coming from. Visitors are advised to check their allowances on www.bdutyfree.com/services/allowances before travelling. People in transit to Saudi Arabia via the causeway should note that no pork products, alcohol, pornographic material (which can include anything as seemingly innocuous as underwear adverts in women's magazines, or family beach photographs), or non-Muslim religious objects or literature are allowed into Saudi Arabia and the consequences for attempting to bring them in can be severe.

Leaving Bahrain

Bahrain airport is one of the easiest and most hassle-free airports in the region (if not the world) to arrive at or depart from. Different airlines indicate different check-in time requirements from one to two hours, but one hour is normally sufficient. Bags are security checked before entering the check-in area and again before entering the departure concourse.

Checks are electronic with additional random personal body checks. Different airlines have different reconfirmation rules and in general it is advisable to reconfirm all tickets two to three days before flying. Again, each airline has its own rules for children travelling unaccompanied and parents or guardians should get full details from their airline when booking the tickets. There is a BD 3 departure tax for all international destinations (usually included in the price of your ticket).

Bahrain's mosques

Travellers' Info

Health Requirements

Vaccinations for cholera, typhoid and yellow fever are recommended but are not required by law unless coming from an infected area. Bahrain is not in the malaria belt. Health services in Bahrain are generally good but travel insurance is advised, including emergency evacuation insurance for certain illnesses/accidents.

Health Care

Other options → **General Medical Care [p.70]**

Medical services in Bahrain are generally good but private medical insurance is advisable for short-term visitors. Residents are entitled to free medical services in government institutions but many expatriates take out private medical insurance to give them access to private medical services. Public health services are adequate for most occasions but the waiting time can be extensive and in-patient aftercare is sometimes impersonal and haphazard.

Visitors to Bahrain should be aware of the dangers of heat stroke, sun stroke and other sun/heat related ailments. Temperatures of 45°C with high humidity in the summer months can severely affect people unused to such conditions. The GDN gives the previous day's weather details and the forecast for the coming day. The Maximum Apparent Temperature is a similar concept to the wind chill factor found in European forecasts and is calculated from the actual temperature, the level of humidity and the wind speed.

In other words, it's what it actually feels like and can be well over 50°C during July, August and September. The rule of thumb is to drink lots of water and to wear a hat and a generous application of factor 50 when going out. Most hotels have doctors on hand or on call. The ambulance service is on a par with most developed world services.

Travel Insurance

General insurance should cover most activities in Bahrain. Visitors who intend to go diving or horse riding should ensure that their policies cover these risks. Visitors intending to use the F1 track for test driving will need to arrange insurance when booking the drive.

Embassies

Embassies		
American Embassy	1727 3300	13-E4
British Embassy	1757 4100	12-A3
Chinese Embassy	1772 3800	14-D3
Danish Embassy	1772 5119	14-C4
Dutch Embassy	1753 0704	11-E3
Egyptian Embassy	1772 0005	14-A3
French Embassy	1729 8600	12-C2
German Embassy	1753 0210	12-B2
Indian Embassy	1771 2785	14-B2
Iranian Embassy	1772 2400	14-A4
Italian Embassy	1725 2424	na
Japanese Embassy	1771 6565	14-A1
Jordanian Embassy	1729 1109	12-C2
Lebanese Embassy	1778 6994	4-A3
Norwegian Embassy	1781 3088	12-C2
Omani Embassy	1729 3663	12-C2
Pakistani Embassy	1724 4113	14-A2
Philippino Embassy	1725 0990	13-D3
Qatari Embassy	1772 2922	14-A4
Russian Embassy	1772 5222	13-D3
Saudi Arabian Embassy	1753 7722	12-B1
Swedish Embassy	1782 5004	12-C2
Swiss Embassy	1753 1166	11-E3
Syrian Embassy	1772 2484	14-A4
Thai Embassy	1782 2110	4-C3
UAE Embassy	1774 8333	14-D2

Female Visitors

Women don't have problems while visiting Bahrain, in the sense that there is not overt harassment and it's a fairly safe place. However, female visitors do receive unwanted stares on occasion and if you don't want to draw attention to yourself, it's best to avoid wearing tight or revealing clothing, and walking in downtown Manama or on Exhibition Avenue alone at night. In general, if you feel uncomfortable, ask a passerby for help, or go into the nearest hotel or cafe.

Travelling with Children

Children are a visible part of daily life in Bahrain and you often see families out with children until even quite late at night. This can be somewhat irritating if you are in the cinema watching a tense adult thriller and there's a crying baby whose parents are determined not to miss a minute of the film.

Shopping malls and hotels cater for families with play areas and sometimes extra entertainment, particularly at weekends or during holidays. The daily newspapers have 'What's On' sections and hotels tend to advertise if they are having a special activity. On Wednesdays, the GDN features several pages of upcoming events.

Most long-term visitors belong to social clubs in Bahrain and that's where they tend to spend family time, but there are a few public park areas, such as Andalous Gardens, the Manama Corniche and the Marina Club Corniche. Restaurants are often fairly welcoming to families and have children's menus.

Physically Challenged Visitors

In general, facilities for people with disabilities are limited. Most of the larger hotels have wheelchair facilities, but in other places there are rarely ramps designed with wheelchairs in mind. The malls and some supermarkets have designated special needs parking spaces, but these are quite often filled by other drivers who enjoy the larger space and don't want to walk far. Bahrain International Airport has facilities to assist disabled travelers and if you are booking a hotel room and need wheelchair facilities, it is advisable to check this point specifically with someone who understands what you mean.

Dress Code

Compared to some of its neighbours, Bahrain is fairly relaxed in its attitude to dress. However, the local population is conservative by nature and respect for their culture is appreciated. Revealing or tight-fitting clothing in the wrong environment will generate attention, so save these for the private beaches, nightclubs or restaurants. In malls, downtown and sightseeing, it is advisable to wear clothes below the knee and covering shoulders.

Women visiting the Grand Mosque are provided with abayas and hijaabs with which to cover themselves. In terms of climate, lightweight clothing is suitable for most of the year, but in the winter months (December to February) you may need slightly warmer clothes and possibly a jacket in the evening. Ironically in the summer months, you may have to go out armed with an extra layer as while outside it is boiling, the air conditioning makes malls and the like a little breezy!

Dos and Don'ts

The 'do' part is easy: do make an effort to see what Bahrain has to offer. It is a unique place in the Gulf, with a particular charm and culture. You will feel this more strongly the wider the range of people you try to interact with. Bahrain is particularly special in that it has a large and varied expatriate population, but also a local population that is very accessible and often welcoming. It's a mini cosmopolitan city-state, with a village background.

The 'don'ts' are also simple: don't break the law. Drugs are illegal, as is pornography and prostitution. Driving after having consumed alcohol, any at all, is illegal. The Islamic culture does not encourage public displays of affection between the sexes. Male visitors should never offer to shake the hand of a Bahraini woman, or touch her in any way. In general, the best guide is an appreciation of the cultural sensitivities and a dose of common sense.

Safety

The crime rate in Bahrain has historically been very low and it is often one of the first things that new residents comment on. However, it has risen in the last couple of years, particularly petty crime against low-income foreign workers and smash-and-grab offences against parked cars in the Exhibition Road area. Be discreet with large amounts of cash, your belongings and travel documents; keep anything valuable in the hotel safe. There are few tricksters about, but be sensible. Road safety is definitely a major issue in Bahrain.

With people from all over the world on the roads, there are a number of different and exotic styles of driving about. Your best bet is to drive according to international traffic regulations, but expect to encounter aggressive habits from fellow road users. Make sure your insurance is current and never drive without your licence on you.

Police

Police in Bahrain are divided into Public Security forces and Traffic Police. The Public Security officers wear pale green uniforms, while Traffic Police uniforms are white in the summer and light green and white in the winter. The majority of Public Security police are armed with handguns, but when on duty guarding strategic locations, such as embassies and ministries, they tend to be better armed.

Traffic police cars are white and black, with blue lights on the roof. Public Security vehicles are mostly SUVs and are generally dark blue, again with blue lights on the roof.

While the police are generally approachable, many of them speak no English, so may not be much help if you are lost. The emergency number for the police in Bahrain is 999. To report a traffic accident, the number is 199. However, for accidents where the cars can be moved, the drivers should go directly to one of the Traffic Directorate offices and obtain an accident report from there (see Driving p.26). In some instances, the local police station will direct you to the nearest post office (confusing!) where a motorcycle cop is on duty to register minor accidents.

Lost/Stolen Property

If you have lost any property in Bahrain, the most useful thing to do once you have spoken to the people employed in the place where you lost it (the shop or restaurant, for example) is to put a notice up on the nearest supermarket noticeboard and hope for the best! As far as passports and travel documents are concerned, you should contact your own embassy or the airline (if it's a ticket) directly, and they'll tell you what to do.

Bahrain Tourist Info Abroad

Bahrain's official tourism agencies are controlled by the Ministry of Cabinet Affairs and Information. The main offices in Bahrain are listed in the table.

Bahrain does not have any tourism offices overseas and directs any international tourism queries to its embassies in the various countries.

Bahrain Tourist Info

Ministry of Cabinet Affairs & Information	1778 1888
Ministry of Cabinet Affairs & Information Tourism Affairs	1720 1210
Bahrain Tourism Office	1721 1025

Places to Stay

Other options → **Weekend Breaks [p.115]**

Bahrain's target tourist market is in the middle to upper range and is well supplied with hotels and serviced apartments, but does not have any official youth hostels or campsites. There are over 80 hotels in the Manama area with over 7,000 rooms available.

All hotels and apartments are generally up to international standards for their rating though some of the three-star and below hotels might be regarded as below standard by visitors from the developed world. Serviced apartments range from top-class luxury apartments (many of which are attached to the upper level hotels and therefore have excellent facilities), to very basic apartments which are mostly let to weekend visitors and which vary significantly in cost.

Hotels

Five Star	Beach Access	Phone	Web	Map
Banyan Tree Desert Spa and Resort	–	1784 5000	www.banyantree.com/bahrain	9-D2
Crowne Plaza	–	1753 1122	www.crowneplaza.com	12-C1
Diplomat Radisson SAS P.215	–	1753 1666	www.radissonsas.com	12-C2
Gulf Hotel P.219	–	1771 3000	www.gulfhotelbahrain.com	14-C2
Regency InterContinental	–	1722 7777	www.intercontinental.com	11-E3
Ritz-Carlton, Bahrain Hotel & Spa	✓	1758 0000	www.ritzcarlton.com/resorts	3-E1
Sheraton Hotel	–	1753 3533	www.sheraton.com	12-A2
Mövenpick Hotel Bahrain P.213	✓	1746 0000	www.moevenpick-hotels.com	2-C4
Four Star				
Al Bander Hotel & Resort P.195	✓	1770 1201	www.albander.com	6-E4
Al Safir Hotel P.201	–	1782 7999	www.alsafirhotel.com	4-C2
Elite Hotel	–	1782 7600	www.baisan.com	14-E2
Golden Tulip Bahrain	–	1753 3000	www.goldentulipbahrain.com	12-B2
Novotel Al Dana Resort P.vii	✓	1729 8008	www.novotel-bahrain.com	12-D1

Hotel Apartments

	Phone	Web	Area	Price (BD)
Al Fanar Plaza	1774 1496	na	Umm Al Hassam	50 per night
Elite Luxury Apartments	1782 2999	www.eliteapartments.net	Seef	45 per night/750 per night
Gulf Executive Residence P.57	1772 6178	www.gulhotelbahrain.com	A'ali	tbc
Elite Suites	1755 8888	www.elitesuites.com.bh	Sanabis	100 per night

Hotels

Bahrain has a smaller number of hotels than most of its neighbours, but they cover the full range from unrated hotels with the most basic accommodation, to five-star, international-standard establishments. The lower-rated hotels vary in quality; generally the older ones are a bit run down, but they are cheap. The four and five-star hotels offer very good facilities and service, and are quite reasonably priced for what you get, particularly compared to the European market. The only 'beach' hotels are the Novotel, Al Bander and the Ritz Carlton, along with the Mövenpick, which has a beach on an inland lagoon near the airport, while the other five-star hotels are 'city hotels' more suitable for business travellers, although they all have swimming pools and gym facilities. While some hotels have websites, it is easier to make reservations on the phone. The classification system is largely in line with international standards and is monitored by the government. Hotel prices range from BD 20 per night for a double room in a one-star hotel, up to BD 1,700 per night for a chalet at the Ritz Carlton. However, beware of hotel prices during the F1 weekend at the beginning of April. As previously mentioned, hotel prices skyrocket then, with most hotels only accepting bookings for a five-night F1 package at five or six times the normal rate.

Hotel Apartments

A cheaper alternative to booking into a hotel, particularly if you are staying for more than a week, is to rent furnished apartments. These can be rented on a weekly, monthly or yearly basis and there are several places offering this service. In addition to cost, the other main advantage is that if you are staying in Bahrain for a while, you will feel more comfortable and settled than if you are a hotel guest, without the hassle of having to buy your own furniture and linen. The apartments come fully furnished including household appliances and linen, and have maid services, if you choose that option. Quite a few expatriates and their families start off life in Bahrain in these apartments while they look for a house or longer-term apartment to rent. Check the GDN classified ads pages for estate agents.

Hostels

There are two youth hostels in Bahrain, one close to Manama and one in Muharraq, near the airport. Both provide beds and washing facilities only and the costs are BD 7.500 for a single room with bath and BD 4.500 each for sharing a double room with bath. Members of clubs can get discounts. They are part of the Youth Hostelling Association (YHA), but don't use the online reservation services. Note that the Muharraq telephone number is also a fax number and it can be difficult to contact them by phone.

Hostels		
Al Jaffar Youth Hostel	Sanabis	1772 7170
Al Muharraq Youth Hostel	Muharraq	1772 9919

Campsites

Other options → **Camping [p.123]**

There are no official campsites in Bahrain, but there are areas widely known as being camping sites. These are in the desert near Sakhir, in the middle of Bahrain, but they do not provide any form of communal facilities; it's strictly 'back to nature'! The camping season is January and

Bahrain Main Hotels

Al Bandar Resort
Map Ref → 6-E4

Situated near the southern tip of Sitra, within a short drive of Manama city, this resort has a wide range of facilities including swimming pools, a health club, squash courts, a bowling centre and other sports and watersports activities around their private beach. Rooms are either cabana style or in chalets and there are activities for kids and a variety of food and dining options.

Al Safir Hotel
Map Ref → 4-C2

Al Safir Hotel is located close to the city centre with easy access to the airport and the sea. The hotel is a good place for families and business travellers, and facilities include a swimming pool and jacuzzi, laundry, dry cleaning, babysitting services and a complimentary shuttle bus. There is also a business centre with secretarial services, a 20 person boardroom and car rental assistance.

Bahrain Main Hotels

The Crowne Plaza
Map Ref → 12-C1

Located in the Diplomatic Area in the business centre of Manama, the Crowne Plaza has 246 rooms including 10 standard suites and two royal suites. Its facilities include an outdoor swimming pool, two gymnasiums, a beauty salon, shops and babysitting services, two restaurants, coffee shops, a nightclub and a business centre with four conference halls, meeting rooms and office services.

The Diplomat Radisson SAS Hotel
Map Ref → 12-C2

Centrally located in the heart of the Diplomatic Area, Manama's business centre, the Diplomat has 246 rooms including 20 suites. Sports and leisure facilities include an outdoor swimming pool, a gymnasium and a beauty salon and there is a good selection of popular restaurants and bars. The business centre offers 10 meeting and conference halls and VIP rooms.

The Gulf Hotel
Map Ref → 14-C2

Just a five-minute drive from the city centre, The Gulf Hotel has 352 rooms including eight suites. Its facilities include an outdoor swimming pool, a gymnasium, a beauty salon, shops and babysitting services. It has several restaurants and bars that offer some of the best eating out in Bahrain. A serviced apartment block is currently under construction in the hotel grounds.

Golden Tulip Bahrain
Map Ref → 12-B2

Located in the city centre, the Golden Tulip has 250 rooms including eight suites. Previously known as the Hilton Hotel, its facilities include a swimming pool, sports and health facilities, beauty salon, shops and babysitting services. It has several restaurants, lounge bars, coffee shops and a ballroom. It also has a fully serviced business and communications centre.

The Mövenpick
Map Ref → 2-C4

The Mövenpick is a new hotel located next to the airport, within 15 minutes of the city centre. It has 106 rooms including 10 suites and eight luxury suites. Facilities include restaurants, a bar, a coffee shop, shops, a ballroom, a pool, a gymnasium, a beauty salon and babysitting services. It also has a fully serviced business centre and six meeting/conference rooms.

Novotel Al Dana Resort
Map Ref → 12-D1

The Novotel is an attractive resort conveniently located for both business and leisure on the causeway between Manama-Muharraq, just minutes from the airport or Manama city. Equipped with 172 rooms, there are extensive fitness and recreation facilities including a gym and a private beach. There is also a host of dining and entertainment options.

The Ritz Carlton Hotel and Spa
Map Ref → 3-E1

Situated on the seafront in the exclusive area of Seef, just 10 minutes drive from the city centre, the Ritz Carlton has a large expanse of private beach and its own marina. With 264 rooms including 22 suites and villas on its 20 acre site, it also has nine quality eating out restaurants, the luxurious Ritz-Carlton Spa and comprehensive business facilities.

The Sheraton Bahrain Hotel
Map Ref → 12-A2

The Sheraton is near the Diplomatic Area and has 260 rooms. Its facilities include several restaurants and lounge bars, an outdoor swimming pool, a health club, two ballrooms, four meeting rooms and three boardrooms (up to 800 capacity). The futuristic twin towers of the Bahrain World Trade Centre adjacent to the hotel are steadily climbing skywards and are due for completion in 2006.

February, when the weather is cooler and it is pleasant to be outside overnight. The private tents range from the very basic to huge elaborate tents with their own toilets, electricity generators and satellite dishes.

In the case of the more luxurious campsites, the owners basically relocate their weekend social life from town to the desert for the month. It is a fun time, but it is worth finding your own quiet spot if you can, to better appreciate the solitude and escape that the desert provides. Al Jazayer Beach Chalets are popular with families and young single Bahrainis and cost only BD 3 to rent for 24 hours, but the area is not well maintained, the beach is dirty and the facilities fairly basic.

Getting Around

Other options → Maps [p.22]
Exploring [p.85]

By far the easiest way to get around Bahrain is by car, either your own or in a taxi. Bahrain has a recently renovated bus service, which will get you around the city extremely cheaply. The buses are relatively new and air-conditioned and are clearly marked on the front and side with their destinations. However, there is no easy access to bus timetables, which means catching one is a bit of a hit-and-miss affair.

Explore the GCC

If you're travelling within the region, go prepared with one of the Explorer Residents' Guides. Whether its shopping in Dubai or Abu Dhabi, exploring Oman's great outdoors, soaking up the history in Kuwait or living in luxury in Qatar, we've got the GCC covered.

A reasonably priced option is to jump into one of the 'shared taxis' or taxi pickup trucks that roam around the streets of Manama. These will get you where you want to go cheaply, but will pick and drop others off along the way; an interesting opportunity to meet local residents, but only if time isn't a big issue! Walking and cycling are limited, and there are no trains or trams.

Air

Other options → Meet & Greet [p.18]

Bahrain Airport is located at the extreme north of Bahrain, on the island of Muharraq. There is only one terminal, but while the airport is fairly small, it is modern and boasts a good Duty Free area. It is currently undergoing a process of expansion, in order to cater for the growth in passenger numbers. There are a number of regional airlines serving Bahrain – with regular flights to the other countries in the GCC.

The UAE is particularly well served, and there are a couple of low-cost carriers that offer good deals. Direct flights are available to a large number of destinations, although flights to the USA will require a connection to be made in Europe, and most Asian destinations tend to need a connection in Hong Kong or Singapore.

The headquarters of Gulf Air, which was originally owned by the six countries of the GCC, is in Bahrain. Four GCC states have pulled out of Gulf Air, mainly because they have set up their own national airlines, so it is now owned by the remaining two, Bahrain and Oman. Gulf Air offers a wide range of destinations, although fares can be high because of the relative lack of competition.

Airlines		
Aer Lingus	www.aerlingus.com	1722 2633
Air India	www.airindia.com	1722 3850
Air Mauritius	www.airmauritius.com	1727 3001
Alitalia	www.alitalia.com	1722 2637
American	www.aa.com	1753 1000
Balkan Bulgarian	www.balkan.com	1721 4231
British	www.ba.com	1758 7777
Cathay Pacific	www.cathaypacific.com	1722 6226
Cyprus	www.cyprusairways.com	1722 0849
Egypt Air	www.egyptair.com.eg	1720 9264
Emirates	www.emirates.com	1758 8700
Ethopian	www.flyethiopian.com	1722 3315
Gulf Air	www.gulfairco.com	1772 2200
Iran Air	www.iranair.com	1721 0414
Japan	www.jal.com	1722 3315
Jet	www.jetairways.com	1722 7114
Kenya	www.kenya-airways.com	1722 5040
KLM	www.klm.com	1722 9747
Kuwait	www.kuwait-airways.com	1722 3332
Lufthansa	www.lufthansa.com	1782 8762
Malaysia	www.malaysia airlines.com	1728 0440
Pakistan	www.piac.com.pk	1722 3808
Qantas	www.qantas.com	1721 1585
Qatar	www.qatarairways.com	1721 6181
Royal Brunei	www.bruneiair.com	1721 3434
Royal Jordanian	www.rja.com.jo	1722 9294
Saudi Arabian	www.saudiairlines.com	1721 1550
Singapore	www.singaporeair.com	1721 3054
Sri Lankan	www.srilankan.aero	1722 4819
Transworld	www.twa.com	1722 3315
Turkish	www.turkish airlines.com	1721 1896
Yemen	www.yemenia.com	1722 5322

Airport Bus

There is no dedicated airport bus service in Bahrain. All the major hotels provide their own bus service, many of which charge a modest fee (not more than BD 5 for the transfer). There is a regular bus service that runs between Bahrain Airport and Dammam Airport, but this is available only to passengers holding an airline ticket from Dammam.

Boat

Although Bahrain is a group of small islands, boats are a surprisingly unimportant part of most people's lifestyles. It is possible to rent a boat, or arrange trips on a tourist dhow, through Al Bander Club in Sitra or the Marina Club in Manama. The Ritz Carlton Hotel also offers boat rental services to its guests.

The one major opportunity for boat trips is taking a trip to Hawar – an island off the south-east coast of Bahrain, very close to the coast of Qatar. The boat trip to Hawar takes about an hour. There is a four-star hotel on the island, which offers reasonable accommodation and an acceptable restaurant. The island is well-known for its abundant bird life and the hotel also offers a variety of activities and some watersports.

Bus

Bahrain has a privately run bus service, which serves most of the country. The buses are all air-conditioned and the service is cheap. A ticket will cost only a few hundred fils, payable in cash (there are no prepaid passes available) and buses are reasonably frequent. However, timetables and route guides are not readily available, so finding

Manama Bus Depot

the right bus at the right time can be something of a hit-and-miss affair. Buses are primarily used by the expatriate workforce and are not geared up for the tourist industry.

Car

Other options → **Transportation [p.77]**

Bahrain's road system is fairly well developed, but recent years have seen a surge in the number of cars owned and this has led to increasing pressure on the country's roads. These are currently undergoing expansion, but as a result there are a few temporary bottlenecks in and around Manama, where new lanes are being added to highways, or flyovers are being built.

Most of the major roadworks are due to be completed by the end of the year. In any case, the country is so small that even a 'long' journey with a traffic jam doesn't usually exceed 30 minutes. It's just that Bahrain residents have got used to being able to get almost anywhere they want to in under 20 minutes! In the centre of Manama the roads are older and are limited to one or two lanes.

The highways are generally three or four lanes and well-maintained. Blue signs indicate the main areas within the country and brown signs show heritage and tourism sites, and other places of interest. Roads are also named on smaller blue signs and these are often either numbers or names of prominent people in the country's recent history. However, most people don't refer to the roads by their official names, and in fact, with a few exceptions, probably don't even know what they are officially called.

People refer to the roads primarily by landmarks they pass, which could be notable roundabouts, hotels, buildings or shops. So instead of being told, 'go down Khalifa Road', you could quite easily be told 'it's along Love Lane in Adliya, behind the Ferrari showroom'.

Driving Habits and Regulations

While the road infrastructure meets international standards, the general standard of driving is not. Although driving is perhaps of a higher standard than many of the neighbouring countries, there are nonetheless regular accidents. The main issue is discipline. Drivers are often somewhat self-centred, lacking lane and speed discipline. People also regularly use mobile phones when driving, which reduces their awareness. Although there have been calls to ban this, it hasn't happened yet.

One of the main reasons for the state of the driving standards is that the traffic police are not overtly seen to be enforcing existing laws strictly enough. So for example, although there are laws governing the use of seatbelts and restrictions on children travelling in the front seat of a vehicle, you often see unbelted children sitting on their parent's lap (even sometimes on the driver's lap!), but traffic policemen won't bother to stop the car and apprehend the driver.

Speeding is often cited as the reason for serious accidents on Bahrain's roads, but there are few speed cameras, even on highways where speeding is very common. When given, speeding fines are BD 50 and parking fines are BD 5. If you have unpaid fines, you have to settle them when you go for your annual car registration. Generally, traffic levels are fairly light, although at rush hour (07:00 – 08:00 and 13:30 – 14:30) traffic can build up, requiring drivers to add about 15% to journey times through busy areas.

None for the Road

There is a zero tolerance policy for drinking and driving in Bahrain. This means that there is no legal acceptable 'drinking limit'. It is strictly prohibited, and if you have had anything to drink at all you are just as guilty as if you've had a lot. The penalty for being caught is generally one night in jail and a BD 500 fine, so you are much better off taking a taxi or asking a friend who hasn't been drinking to drive you home. Most car insurance policies are void if the driver is drunk, which means that a drunken accident can be an expensive proposition.

Speed Limits

The speed limits are 100 km/h on motorways and 80 km/h on dual carriageways. The speed limit around certain pedestrian areas is 50 km/h. On-the-spot fines are becoming less frequent, but if you get one, you often have to go directly to the Traffic Directorate to pay it. Speed cameras are not particularly common, but are becoming more so. If you're driving a rental car and it's captured on film speeding, the fine will be passed on to you by the rental company.

Driving Licence

Visitors from European countries can drive on their existing driving licence simply by getting it endorsed by the Traffic Directorate. This endorsement can be done by the car rental company. Other nationalities require an international licence, which must also be endorsed by the Traffic Directorate. Once a driving licence has been endorsed, a driver may drive any passenger car with the owner's permission. Drivers must carry their driving licence and either originals or copies of the car ownership and insurance cards (these are credit card sized cards; a rental company will normally provide copies only) with them whenever they are driving.

Accidents

If you are involved in an accident, a police report is required before repairs can be made. If the cars are movable, all parties involved should take their cars to the nearest Traffic Directorate office, which will take statements, assess the damage on the cars and apportion blame. If the cars are too badly damaged to be moved, a Traffic Officer will come out to the site of the accident and make the report on the spot, but you may have to wait a long time for this to happen. The number you need to call is 1768 8888. Unfortunately, when you have an accident in this part of the world, particularly if it is a bad one, you become roadside entertainment and people will slow down to watch, or even park their cars to get a better look. The good thing is though, that most people are genuinely kind-hearted and will help if you ask them to.

Crash, Bang, Move

There is a common misconception in Bahrain that cars may not be moved in the event of an accident until the Traffic Police have inspected the accident. This used to be the rule, but is no longer the case, and in all events, any car that is involved in an accident should be moved out of the way of oncoming traffic as soon as possible.

Parking

In most areas of Bahrain, except the Diplomatic Area and the centre of Manama, parking is not difficult to find and you will not have to walk a long distance from your car.

In busy areas where parking is more of a problem, there are parking meters. These take between 50 and 100 fils per half-hour and most have a two-hour maximum slot. If you overstay and you get caught the fine is BD 5, so it is really not worth taking the risk. In the souk parking meters only apply from Saturday to Wednesday from 09:00 till 13:00 and 15:00 to 18:00, and on Thursday mornings only. In the Diplomatic Area they operate from Saturday to Wednesday from 08:00 till 13:00 and in Exhibition Avenue from Saturday to Thursday from 14:00 till 18:00. Outside those times parking is free.

General Info

Getting Around

Car Rental Agencies

Avis Rent-A-Car	1753 1144
Bahrain Car Hiring Co.	1753 4343
Budget Rent A Car	1753 4100
Elite Rent-A-Car	1731 1883
Europcar P.79	1769 2999
Express Rent-A-Car	1753 2525
Hanco Rent-A-Car	1731 0656
Hertz Rent A Car	1732 1358
National Car Rental	1731 1169
Thrifty Car Rental	1773 5991

Taxi

The main taxi service in Bahrain is government regulated, but the actual taxis are privately owned, and therefore range from old cars seemingly held together with string to smart new cars lovingly cared for by their owners. Regardless of the type of car, the fare on the meter is identical. Taxis are easily identified by orange panels on the front and rear wings. Taxis to and from the airport are subject to a BD 1 surcharge. On the meter, a ride from the airport to Manama should cost in the region of BD 3. A journey within Manama should not run to more than BD 2 on the meter.

It's the law

Don't be fooled by a taxi driver claiming not to have a meter; all taxis have them fitted by law. However, they will often try to get a higher fare by pretending not to have a meter, (check behind the tissue box by the gear lever), or that the meter is broken. If they refuse to use the meter, you can choose to get out and find another more honest taxi driver.

Taxis can be flagged down anywhere and, indeed, will often try to give you a lift even when you are not looking for one. Generally, taxi drivers have a good knowledge of Bahrain's roads and are unlikely to get lost. However, they may speak only basic English. There are two telephone limousine services in Bahrain, both of which offer a reliable reasonably priced, metered, air-conditioned telephone taxi service (Speedy Motors – 1768 2999 and Bahrain Limo – 1726 6266). However, at peak times, they can become overbooked, so it is worth planning ahead if you want to make use of their services, especially in the early morning or mid-afternoon.

Taxi Companies

Airport Taxis	1726 0208
Bahrain Limo	1726 6266
Speedy Motors	1768 2999

Train

There are no tram or train services in Bahrain.

Walking

Other options → **Hiking [p.127]**

It is safe and enjoyable to stroll around the old Manama Souk. The whole area is a maze of small roads and alleys, ideally suited to exploring on foot, although it can be unpleasantly hot and sticky during the summer months. There is also a corniche along the northern shore of Manama (the Regency Corniche) which is pleasant to walk on. You will often find people out walking along the corniche during the months from December to March, but in the summer, when temperatures can reach 40°C, often with quite severe humidity, walking is not always pleasant.

Money

Cash is still the preferred method of payment, although the use of credit and debit cards is becoming more widespread. Most shops and restaurants will accept cash or credit cards, although in the souk area, cash is by far the preferred form of payment (and often the only accepted method). The Saudi riyal is readily accepted everywhere, at a rate of just over 10 Saudi riyals to one dinar. As the dinar is pegged to the US dollar, dollars will often be accepted as a last resort. However, outside of hotels, this would generally be an exception, not the rule.

Local Currency

The monetary unit is the Bahraini dinar (BD), which is divided into 1,000 fils. Notes come in denominations of 500 fils, BD 1, BD 5, BD 10 and BD 20. Coin denominations are 5 fils, 10 fils, 25 fils, 50 fils and 100 fils, but in practice the 5 and 10 fils coins are hardly used any more. The dinar has been pegged to the US dollar for many years at a rate of US$ 1 to BD 0.377. Exchange rates for all major currencies are listed in the daily newspapers.

Banks

Bahrain considers itself to be the banking centre of the region, and is well represented with banks.

Exchange Rates

Foreign Currency (FC)	1 Unit FC = x BD	BD 1 = x FC
Australia	0.27	3.60
Bangladesh	0.01	175.81
Canada	0.32	3.08
Cyprus	0.78	1.28
Denmark	0.06	16.65
Euro	0.45	2.23
Hong Kong	0.05	20.57
India	0.01	119.47
Japan	0.003	311.05
Jordan	0.53	1.88
Kuwait	1.29	0.77
Malaysia	0.10	10.02
New Zealand	0.26	3.89
Oman	0.98	1.02
Pakistan	0.006	158.71
Philippines	0.007	139.49
Qatar	0.10	9.66
Saudi Arabia	0.10	9.95
Singapore	0.23	4.39
South Africa	0.06	16.68
Sri Lanka	0.003	270.98
Sweden	0.05	20.89
Switzerland	0.29	3.47
Thailand	0.009	108.55
UAE	0.10	9.74
UK	0.65	1.53
USA	0.38	2.65

Rates updated — January 2006

There are a number of international banks, in addition to many local and regional banks offering a full range of banking services. The head offices are all located in Central Manama, the Diplomatic Area, or in Seef, but most of the major banks have a number of branches and ATM machines available in outlying areas. In addition, most banks in Bahrain have the facility to access funds from other banks' ATM machines, but be aware that they will charge you 500 fils for the privilege. ATM machines are available in most malls and many major supermarket branches; information is available at the banks' branches. Opening hours for banks are varied, though most banks will have at least one branch that is open between 08:00 and 16:00 from Saturday to Thursday. Most banks offer money exchange services, though not all carry a large quantity of foreign currency unless you call in advance.

ATMs

ATMs are widely distributed in Bahrain in all high-street banks and shopping malls, the major hotels, major commercial areas, at the airport and other sites. Different banks have different conditions but most ATMs will accept major cash and credit cards, Cirrus, Benefit and Plus. Some ATMs dispense cash in both dinars and US dollars. Most ATMs operate using both Arabic and English.

Main Banks

Ahli United Bank	1758 5858
Arab Bank	1754 9000
Bahrain Credit	1778 6000
Bahrain Saudi Bank	1757 8999
Bank Melli Bahrain	1722 9910
Bank of Bahrain & Kuwait	1722 3388
BankMuscat	1721 8686
BNP Paribas	1753 1152
Citibank	1722 3344
Habib Bank Ltd.	1722 8522
Housing Bank for Trade & Finance	1722 5227
HSBC	1722 4555
National Bank of Bahrain	1722 8800
Shamil Bank of Bahrain	1758 5000
Standard Chartered Bank	1722 3636
United Bank Ltd.	1722 4030

Money Exchanges

There are many money exchanges in Bahrain, particularly concentrated in Central Manama around the souk area, and there are branches in most major towns, as well in some malls and other major shopping districts. Rates tend to be far more favourable than those given in the hotels. Money can also be exchanged in most banks, though they may not have large amounts of most foreign currencies. Opening hours vary, but in general they are open from 08:00 to 19:00, with a break from 13:00 to 15:00 for lunch, from Saturday to Thursday. Branches in malls tend not to close for lunch. There are also unofficial independent money changers in the souk. These tend to be elderly men sitting on tin chairs at intersections and it is advisable to avoid using their services.

Credit Cards

Credit cards are widely accepted in hotels, shops and restaurants. Common sense should be applied; a shop that focuses on selling small volume, low value goods is unlikely to accept credit cards. Equally, local budget restaurants are unlikely to have the facility. Some smaller local traders, particularly in the souk, will seek a premium when payment by credit card is requested, or at least will be happy to offer greater discounts for cash.

Exchange Centres

Al Fardan Khalil Ebrahim Exchange	1725 3627
Al-Zamil Exchange Est.	1721 2313
Ali Yousif Exchangers	1727 7720
Arab Exchange Co	1721 3313
Bahrain Financing Co	1722 8888
Bahrain India International Exchange Co	1721 0330
BEXMONEY	1727 5275
Dalil Exchange	1722 3464
Haji Yousif Al Awadi Exchange	1721 0800
World Exchange Centre	1721 1900
Zenj Exchange	1722 4352

Tipping

It is not mandatory to tip anywhere in Bahrain. However, it is established practice to tip around 10 – 15% of the bill in most restaurants and cafes. Many restaurants include service charges, but these usually go to the restaurant and not to the staff who served you.

Media & Communications

Newspapers/Magazines

The two main English newspapers in Bahrain are the *Gulf Daily News* (GDN) and the *Bahrain Tribune*, which are widely available in shops, hotels and stores and cost 200 fils.

There are several local Arabic newspapers available: *Akhbar Al Khaleej*, *Al Ayam* and *Al Wasat News*. The major international newspapers are available one or two days after publication and generally at several times the published price. Some of the British Sundays may be missing some of their supplements – the *Sunday Times Magazine* is not available, although the paper's other supplements are usually included.

English papers predominate but other languages are also catered for with limited circulation. These tend to be sold only in the major hotels and selected large shops and shopping malls. Censorship on foreign newspapers is minimal, though certain editions have occasionally been unavailable in the past when they have included articles critical of the local government or lifestyle.

There are a number of English magazines published in Bahrain which provide information on a range of subjects: *Bahrain This Month* (events, lifestyle and local news), *Bahrain Confidential* (business and lifestyle), *Arabian Motors* (vehicle purchase & lease), *Arabian Homes* (property), *Gulf Industry* (oil and industry), *GFI* (Finance), *Bahrain Woman* (female interests), *Arabian Night* (top-end profiles and products), *MEED* (business) and *Coeds* (youth magazine).

Further Reading

Other options → Websites [p.35]

Tourist brochures are available at the Tourist Information Office (1721 1025) and all major hotels. There are no other definitive guide books. *Bahrain This Month* has an events/entertainment section.

Post & Courier Services

Other options → Postal Services [p.68]

Bahrain's postal service is a department of the Ministry of Transportation. It is rather old fashioned, and although it rarely actually loses items of mail, it is not uncommon for items to suffer delays on occasion. A letter to the UK, USA or Australia can take between three days and a week to arrive. Most mail is delivered to post office boxes rather than to street addresses; all companies have a PO box and so do many individuals. Otherwise, people usually receive their mail through their employer's PO box.

It is possible to have mail addressed to a physical address, but this is less common and tends to slow mail delivery down. Letterboxes are not particularly widespread, and in general, the easiest way to get mail sent is to take it directly to the nearest post office. There are post office branches in most of the bigger towns. Many international courier companies have a presence

Courier Companies

Al A'Ali Cooling Cargo	1787 4187
Aramex International	1733 0434
Barid Mumtaz	1734 3366
DHL Express	1772 3636
FedEx	1733 4448
Indian Cargo Services	1729 2033
Memo Express	1723 2173
Overseas Courier Service	1721 3825
Sky Net Worldwide Express	1771 7939
TNT International Express	1732 2353
UPS (United Parcel Service)	1722 3123

eeZee prepaid packages that include:

- FREE Missed Call Alert
- FREE Voicemail
- FREE email account
- FREE call back features

And much more such as:

- SMS diverting
- Send and Receive SMS messages while roaming
- Info and Entertainment Services from the World of WoW
- Make and Receive calls while roaming*

*Available in selected countries.

For more information call 107, visit any Experience Shop or our website:

www.mtc-vodafone.com.bh

in Bahrain and there is a great deal of competition within this industry, so it pays to shop around for the best price.

Radio

There are many radio stations broadcasting in Bahrain in Arabic, English and also in several Asian dialects. The four main English-language stations are Bahrain 96.5 FM (playing a mix of music, mostly modern, with news, sports and features), Bahrain 101 FM (a mix of modern music and news), BBC World Service (offering substantial coverage of news and current events) and Voice of America (offering news, features and music). The first two stations have occasional competitions but the prizes are more nominal than substantial.

Television/Satellite TV

Other options → **Satellite TV & Radio [p.69]**
Television [p.69]

There are five local Bahrain channels (Channels 55, 44, 4, 38 and Bahrain Sports Channel) which broadcast mainly in Arabic with occasional films and programmes in English. There are over 40 satellite channels available, which can be purchased in various packages, costing from BD 5

to over BD 50 per month. Subscribers can pick and choose their package, mainly in English and also in several Asian dialects. Major sports events are televised live on big screens in pubs and clubs throughout Manama and the adjoining areas. The following spots are always a safe bet to be showing the big game: the British Club, the Rugby Club, Bahrain Yacht Club, Warblers Bar, the Country Club, the Sherlock Holmes (Gulf Hotel) and Fiddlers (Diplomat Hotel).

Telephones

Other options → **Telephone [p.67]**

The landline service is effectively a monopoly run by the state-owned Batelco. There are two mobile service providers: Batelco and Vodaphone. Bahrain is currently liberalising its communications services and other service providers are expected to enter the market over the coming years. Both services are now efficient in terms of local and international calls but getting new lines or changes in services can still be a time-consuming and frustrating experience. Phone boxes are available throughout Bahrain and take both coins and pre-paid cards that can be purchased in most cold stores. Calls using hotel lines can be expensive; up to twice the basic tariff.

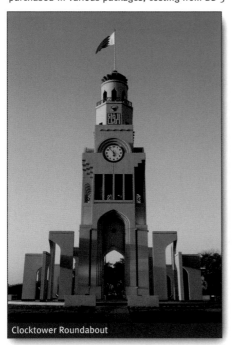
Clocktower Roundabout

Area Codes & Useful Numbers

Airport taxis	1726 0208
All land line numbers start with	17XX XXXX
Bahrain country code	973
Batelco Customer Services	1788 3030
Call before you dig	101
Coast Guard information	1770 0000
Directory enquiries	181
Directory enquiries - mobile	188
Drainage	1778 3711
Electricity	1724 1111
Fire, Ambulance & Police	999
Flight information	1733 9339
International call enquiries	191
Local call assistance	100
Mobile telephones	3XXX XXXX
Roaming assistance	(+973) 3961 1196
Roaming assistance national	196
Telephone and fax faults	121
Telex. leased circuits & private network ISDN	8000 1180
Traffic accidents	1768 8888
Wake up call	151
Water	1772 7500
Weatherline	1723 6236

Importing electronics from China?

We've got the connections.

No one knows China like we do.

Whatever you're importing, plug into DHL. With more experience, more offices and more commercial flights a week than any other operator, nobody knows China like we do. Not just the geography but the people and their way of working. So if you're doing business in China, remember there's one network with all the right connections.
Call 800 4004 now and ask about our fantastic "takeaway" offer.
Offer valid only in UAE from 15th October to 31st December 2005.
Don't miss out, call NOW.

Internet

Other options → **Internet Cafes [p.223]**
Internet [p.68]

Internet services are available in many internet cafes throughout Bahrain at a cost of about BD 1 per hour. Many hotels also offer in-room internet facilities to guests. There is little, if any, censorship on internet sites. Emails for the local server in Bahrain end in .com.bh. Most subscribers use the Batelco system, which has a varying list of tariffs depending on the option chosen. The options vary from straightforward dial-up with a BD 5 set-up fee and a BD 3 monthly charge, to unlimited broadband at a BD 10 set-up fee and a BD 30 monthly charge. Note that if you are in an apartment your charges will increase to BD 50 for the monthly charge for unlimited broadband. There are levels of access in between these two and Batelco now supplies a reasonable summary of these options at its site, www.batelco.com.bh. You do however have to register with Batelco to get internet access and there is no straightforward 'dial and surf' option available

Websites

There are a number of websites giving general and specific information on Bahrain. The main ones are given in the table on the page opposite.

Annual Events

Bahrain is host to many conventions and high level meetings but has limited recurring annual events. The main two are National Day (16 December) and the Bahrain Formula 1 Grand Prix, which is held during the first quarter of the year. For 2007, it takes place from the 13th to the 15th of April.

Various celebrations take place on National Day, including sporting, cultural and leisure activities. The day ends with an address by HH King Hamed at the National Stadium, accompanied by various national displays and a massive fireworks display.

The Bahrain F1 Grand Prix, the only one in the region, is the highlight of the sporting calendar in Bahrain. This international, world-class event lasts three days, Friday to Sunday, and attracts people from all corners of the world. The Bahrain authorities relax visa requirements for the event and make every effort to streamline the organisation and ensure the success of the race, although track-side facilities still leave much to be desired. The circuit, which first opened for the 2004 event, also hosts a number of other racing events throughout the year. Full details can be obtained on the circuit's website (www.bahraingp.com.bh).

Manama at Night

Websites

Business/Industry

www.aiwakuwait.com	Aiwa Gulf – Complete Search Engine For & About Gulf Countries
www.ameinfo.com	Middle East Business News
www.bahrainchamber.org.bh	Bahrain Chamber of Commerce
www.bahraincustoms.gov.bh	Information on custom rules and tariffs
www.bahrainstock.com	Information on Bahrain Stock Exchange
www.bbbforum.org	British Business Forum Bahrain
www.britishcouncil.org/bahrain	British Council
www.gulfdirectory.com.bh	The Gulf Directory – Business to Business Directory of the Gulf
www.tradearabia.com	Trade Arabia – Business, News and Information

Embassies

www.embassiesabroad.com	Embassies In Bahrain and Bahrain embassies abroad
www.embassyworld.com	Embassies abroad

Bahrain Information

http://english.daralhayat.com	Dar Al Hayat - London based Arabic Newspaper
www.accessgcc.com	Info about everything in Bahrain
www.arab.net/bahrain/index.html	Loads of Bahrain info
www.bahrain.gov.bh	Bahrain Government Information site
www.bahrainguide.org	The vistor's complete guide to Bahrain
www.bahrainthismonth.com	Bahrain This Month magazine
www.bahraintoday.net	News from Bahrain
www.bahraintourism.com	Bahrain Official tourism site
www.bahraintribune.com	English-language newspaper
www.bahrainyellowpages.com.bh	Bahrain Yellow Pages
www.capital.gov.bh	Capital Governorate
www.explorer-publishing.com	Our site!
www.gulf-daily-news.com	Bahrain English-language newspaper
www.gulfweeklywordwide.com	The definitive What's On in the GCC
www.hejleh.com/countries	The Country & People of Bahrain
www.inet.com.bh	Inet – highlights, newstrack, local buzz
www.miceonline.net/bahrain/intro.htm	MICE Bahrain info
www.middleeastmediaguide.com	Middle East Media Guide
www.newarabia.net	Info on Hotels, Restaurants, Business
www.northern.gov.bh	Northern Governorate

Hotels/Sports

Hotel details listed in General Information [p.22], and sporting organisation in Activities

Snip snip snip!

Red tape – it's that boring bureaucratic stuff that makes you want to cry, with queues, forms, documents, dead-ends, and a whole lot of wasted time. From visas and licences to housing and driving, this vital guide cuts through the paperwork.

Supported by

HADEF هادف الظاهري
AL DHAHIRI وشركاؤه
& ASSOCIATES
ADVOCATES AND LEGAL CONSULTANTS

betterhomes

Residents

EXPLORER

Residents

Highlights...

Housing
[p.54]

Moving house can be a major headache, especially in a foreign country, but fear not – our comprehensive housing section will guide you through all those accommodation conundrums. In addition to advice on rental procedures and avoiding property pitfalls, there's an overview of all the main residential districts and a Setting Up Home section to help you settle in without too many headaches.

Bahrain is the financial centre of the Gulf and in many respects of the entire Middle East. It was also the first country in the region to discover oil. Before oil was found, Bahrain was a major trading post. As a result, it is in some ways a more mature country than its richer neighbours. The Bahrainis are well educated and most of the senior positions in both the public and private sector are filled by qualified Bahrainis. This has had an impact on the expatriates who used to fill the majority of jobs in the country.

However, expatriates are still very much part of Bahrain, but as would be expected, there is a certain amount of red tape to plough through before you are up and running as a new resident. The good thing is that your employer will know the ropes and most of the formalities will just happen behind the scenes during your first few weeks here, allowing you to spend time on finding a house and arranging transport.

The process of obtaining work permits, residence visas and identity cards is a somewhat laborious one and you will find that without these formalities completed it will be difficult to start feeling at home. The one thing you can prepare for before you arrive is to arm yourself with a sheaf of passport sized photographs on a white background. There are many places you can get this done in Bahrain if you haven't brought any, but you will probably go through at least twenty photos in your first month. All new residents have to go through the process and it is best to accept that things here just take time.

The following information is meant only as a guide to help you get yourself set up in your new home in the sun. Our best advice though is to get a professional to deal with all government visa requirements, as queuing in government offices all morning will give you the wrong impression of one of the friendliest countries in the region. Normally this will be done by your employer, but otherwise ask your employer who they use as there are a number of agents in Bahrain who will be able to queue for you, for a modest sum.

In The Beginning...

Residents of the GCC countries (Saudi, UAE, Kuwait, Qatar, Bahrain and Oman) do not need visas to enter Bahrain. However, all non GCC nationals must be sponsored to stay and work in Bahrain. The majority of expatriates coming to the country are sponsored by their employer for the purpose of work and residence. Most people are recruited from overseas and your employer will have arranged for your entry visa and formalities to be completed before you arrive. The process should be as follows, but remember it is very unlikely that you will have to do this yourself, and in fact you cannot actually apply for a work permit unless you are a Bahraini. Your employer obtains a work permit for the position that you are to fill. He then obtains what is called a No Objection Certificate (NOC). This enables you to enter the country on a valid visa. Your employer should send you a copy of the NOC before you arrive. The original is held at the airport by the Immigration department who issue an entry visa on the back of this document.

Before the residence permit can be granted, all expatriates must undergo a medical examination at a state medical centre. This is required regardless of whether you have undertaken a medical before arriving in Bahrain, and is a state rather than a company requirement so you may find that you need to undergo a second medical to comply with your individual company requirements. The medical normally involves a chest x-ray, eye test and a very brief examination by a doctor. Your employer will arrange this medical for you and you are advised to go with someone (preferably a Bahraini who knows the ropes) who can take you through the process. It can be somewhat overwhelming for the uninitiated as there may be many hundreds of people wandering around trying to find out where to go. Blood tests, however, are not taken.

Once you are in Bahrain and have completed the medical check, you will then be issued with what is known as a CPR (Central Population Register) card, which details your name, profession, sponsor and address. At the same time, you are issued with a multi-entry visa (which allows you to leave and enter the country without any further form filling), and a work permit. The latter two are stamped in your passport and are valid for two years.

However, sometimes there hasn't been enough time to get the NOC before your arrival. If this is the case, and you come from the European Community, USA, Canada, Australia, New Zealand, Japan or Hong Kong, you will be able to obtain a visit visa on arrival valid for up to three months depending on your nationality. If you are not from these countries but have been a resident of one of the Gulf Cooperation Council (GCC) countries for at least 6 months you can still get a visa on arrival, the length of which depends on your nationality. Your sponsoring employer can then transfer this visit visa into a permanent visa once you have arrived, although there is an additional cost of BD60 to be paid, which your employer normally covers.

The peaceful side of Bahrain life!

Your sponsor is responsible for renewing your residence visa and work permit at the end of the two years and you should make sure this process starts before the expiry of your original permits as you will otherwise have to pay a late renewal fee. Your CPR card cannot be issued without a copy of a lease agreement or electricity bill and so you may need to use your employer's address to obtain your first CPR card.

If you are a national of the European Community, USA, Canada, Australia, New Zealand, Japan or Hong Kong, your spouse and children can travel with you when you first arrive. However when considering this, remember that if you are being put up in a hotel when you first arrive you will be very cramped until you are able to move into your own residence. If your family haven't travelled with you initially, or if they don't hold the above listed nationalities, you can apply for visas and residence permits for your spouse and children once your own formalities have been completed. You can't sponsor your parents or other relatives, except on short stay visas.

Under new regulations, you can now be self sponsored as a resident if you own property in one of the designated areas open to expatriate

purchasers. This does not, however, entitle you to work in Bahrain. Alternatively if you set up a business here you can be sponsored by that business without a Bahraini sponsor. Once all of your formalities are completed you can apply for a residence permit for your spouse and children. This residence permit will not permit your spouse to work. For this he or she will need to obtain a work permit from their prospective employer and you will need to obtain an NOC from your own employer allowing your spouse to work. This is different from the formal NOC that you will receive to obtain a visa to enter the country.

Essential Documents

The most essential document that you must have is, of course, your passport. It is a good idea to keep copies of this document to ease delays which may otherwise occur when you are asked for a copy. Once you have your CPR card it is also a good idea to make copies of this as you will frequently be asked for a copy when you hire a car, join a gym or make any semi-formal application. Again passport sized photographs will be required for almost every activity you can think of; you just cannot have too many.

There are photo shops all around Bahrain which can take your pictures at a low cost. Some stores now keep a record of your photo electronically so that you can come back and get reprints done when you need them. On occasion you may be required to obtain a salary certificate from your employer stating that you work for them and confirming your salary details. In addition you may need a specific NOC from them to open bank accounts or obtain a driving licence. These do not follow any particular format and your employer should be able to give this to you straight away should you be asked for it.

If you are taking a professional position be sure to bring your original degree certificates, professional certificates and any other certificates relevant to your position with you. If these are not in English or Arabic you will need to get them translated, notified and certified preferably by your embassy, or if not by a translation house in Bahrain. Berlitz seems to be accepted for almost any language for this purpose. In addition, ensure you have an up-to-date CV which is relevant for the position for which you are being employed. Your CV and certificates may be submitted to the Ministry of Labour for the purpose of obtaining your work permit, and whether they were required the first time or not they may be required when you renew your work permit. Any company information you

They Mean the World to You

We understand the importance of making your relocation experience as smooth as possible. After all, we're not just relocating your possessions, we are helping to relocate the most precious things in your life. Crown Relocations is a leading provider of domestic and international moving and settling-in services with over 100 locations in more than 45 countries. **Well Connected. Worldwide.™**

Dubai
Tel: (971) 4 289 5152
Fax: (971)4 289 6263
Email: dubai@crownrelo.com

Abu Dhabi
Tel: (971)2 674 5155
Fax: (971)2 674 2293
Email: abudhabi@crownrelo.com

Bahrain
Tel: (973)17 227 598
Fax: (973)17 224 803
Email: bahrain@crownrelo.com

Egypt
Tel: (202) 580 6628
Fax: (202) 580 6601
Email: cairo@crownrelo.com

Kuwait
Tel: (965) 299 7850
Fax: (965) 299 7800
Email: kuwait@crownrelo.com

Qatar
Tel: (974) 462 1115/1170/1439
Fax: (974) 462 1119
Email: doha@crownrelo.com

Turkey
Tel: (90) 212 347 4410
Fax: (90) 212 347 4413
Email: istanbul@crownrelo.com

Please Visit **www.crownrelo.com**
for details.

bring to Bahrain will need to be attested by the foreign office of your country and then stamped by the Bahraini embassy in your home country.

Documents

Entry Visa

Other options → Visas [p.17]

You should ensure that you enter Bahrain with the correct visa. If you are working you should have an NOC that will be linked to your work permit and so your visa will allow you to work. Family members accompanying you will need an NOC for residence. Transit and visit visas do not normally allow you to take up employment subsequently, although a fee (BD60) can be paid if you come to Bahrain looking for employment. You can transfer your visa status at the Immigration Ministry in Hoora, but you will need your work permit and NOC in place to be able to do this. You can only transfer your visit visa to a residence visa through your employer. The exception to this is if you have purchased qualifying property in Bahrain for which special residence visas are now issued. The developer of your new property will be able to help you complete the formalities to obtain this visa.

Visa on Arrival

Citizens of Andorra, Australia, Austria, Belgium, Brunei, Canada, China, Denmark, Finland, France, Germany, Greece, Hong Kong SAR, Iceland, Ireland, Italy, Japan, Liechtenstein, Luxembourg, Malaysia, Monaco, Netherlands, New Zealand, Norway, Portugal, San Marino, Singapore, Spain, Sweden, Switzerland, Turkey, United Kingdom, United States Of America and Vatican City receive an automatic visa on arrival in Bahrain.

Health Card

Your CPR card acts as a health card and you need to show this card before obtaining medical treatment at any of the state hospitals. The state hospitals are good but you are advised to take out medical insurance in addition to this which will allow you to attend any of the many private hospitals and medical centres in Bahrain. Your employer may well have a

Don't Leave it at Home!

Make sure you always carry your CPR card as this will ensure you are always treated straight away. If you don't have medical insurance it is also a good idea to have a credit card with you in case you are taken to a private hospital.

private medical scheme which will normally provide you with a pass card allowing direct billing to the insurance company for any medical services you receive.

Residence Visa

Other options → Visas [p.17]

Work Permit

You must have a work permit to work in Bahrain. As the number of qualified Bahrainis increases, these are becoming tougher to get as employers are limited to the proportion of expatriates they employ. As a general rule, Bahrainis should make up fifty per cent of the total work force.

To obtain a work permit you must first be offered a position with a Bahraini company who will take on the role of sponsoring you. It is then the responsibility of your employer to obtain a work permit which you must have before you start work. Often your offer letter will be subject to a work permit being granted, but it is rare that an employer makes an offer without already having a work permit as he is able to obtain these up to one year before he assigns them to an individual. You must check that your work permit is for the position that you are actually filling. Often an employer will have a spare work permit for a different position and whilst this may not present any problems in the first instance, you may find that you have difficulties renewing the work permit after two years, especially if you are not qualified for the position to which your permit relates.

You are able to obtain your own work permit only if you own your own business in Bahrain and there are now many categories of companies that can be 100 per cent foreign owned. As an owner or part owner of a company in Bahrain you are automatically entitled to a residence permit. Your company is also allowed a certain number of work permits automatically. You can take one of these permits if you are working in the company rather than just owning it.

Other than your passport and photographs, you will only need a copy of your CV to obtain your work permit. This is to ensure that you are suitably experienced for the position to which your work permit relates. It is also wise to have with you originals and copies of your educational certificates, as these are sometimes required. You will definitely need these if you are taking up a professional role or are starting up your own business.

Residents

Documents

Sponsorship by Employer

Whilst obtaining a work permit and residence visa all seems rather complicated it should not cause you any inconvenience personally, as all aspects of this process are the responsibility of your employer. They will have their own department that deals with the Ministries on these matters, or they will outsource the work to one of the many agencies which specialise in carrying out this work. Even if you set up your own business you are advised to use an agency to complete these formalities for you as they can often get things done much faster than you would be able to on your own. They normally charge between BD10 and BD20 depending on which permits need to be obtained. Only a Bahraini national can actually make an application for a work permit, so even if you have your own business, you need to employ an agency or grant power of attorney to a Bahraini national to deal with the Ministry of Labour.

Residence Visa

Once you have a work permit you can obtain your residence visa which runs concurrently with your work permit. There are two types of residence visa, one for those who come to Bahrain for employment and are sponsored by their employer, and one for residence only, i.e. as dependants of expats who are employed in Bahrain. It is now possible to obtain a residence visa if you buy freehold property in one of the designated areas where expatriates are entitled to own homes. These are the recently developed areas such as Amwaj, Durrat Al Bahrain, and Bahrain Financial Harbour. This residence visa will not allow you to work but will allow you to sponsor your spouse and children under the age of eighteen. If you subsequently take up employment you will still need to obtain a work permit through your employer in the normal manner, but of course this your employer's responsibility.

Family Sponsorship

When you have your work permit and residence visa, and your CPR card, you can apply for residency for your spouse and children. You cannot obtain residency for other family members, who are restricted to short term visit visas. Should one of your children be born in Bahrain, you need to obtain an NOC from your employer stating that they will sponsor the new family member. This is just a formality which you can complete while you are arranging for your child's birth certificate and passport. It is normally difficult for expatriate mothers (or even Bahraini mothers married to expatriates) to sponsor their children. If at all possible this should be carried out by the father.

If you arrive in Bahrain as a spouse and are therefore on a non-working residency visa, but subsequently you decide to take up work, you will need to obtain a work permit from your employer, which will be their responsibility. However, you normally remain sponsored by your spouse's employer, who will issue you with an NOC which you must give to your prospective employer to enable them to obtain a work permit for you.

Labour Card

You do not receive a Labour card in Bahrain although this is common in other GCC countries. You will receive a work permit which is stamped in your passport detailing who you work for and the validity of the permit. This lasts for two years. You will also be issued with a Central Population Registry (CPR) card.

Central Population Registry (CPR) Card

Your CPR card is the most important card you will have in Bahrain. You will be asked for it almost wherever you go; in fact you are often asked to leave it at an office reception desk in exchange for a visitor ID card. You will also need it, and copies of it, when you rent a house or apartment, hire or buy a car, open a bank account or complete any official transaction. You are advised to keep a copy of your CPR with you at all times and you should also carry your original with you at all times. In many ways the CPR card works as an identity card. It states your name, your address, your employer and sponsor, and is linked to other documents such as your driving licence.

Your employer or sponsor will apply for your CPR card for you (the form is in Arabic and English, and can be completed in either language), once you have received your work permit and residence visa. You will need a copy of your lease agreement or electricity bill together with two passport photographs on a white background. You can obtain a temporary card if you do not yet have an address at this stage, but you should try to hold off getting the card until you have at least your lease agreement, as changing the card later is just as difficult as obtaining it the first time. You should be able to get a lease agreement as soon as you have found your future home, even if you do not move in for a few months.

Your spouse and children also need to have CPR cards and your employer will be able to arrange this as soon as their residence permits are completed and stamped in their passports. Your CPR card is valid for three years and you should change the card if your address changes or if you change your employer. You will also need your CPR card to obtain medical attention at one of the public hospitals or clinics in Bahrain, so it really is important that you carry it with you at all times.

Free Zones

At present there are no free zones in Bahrain. However the new developments of Bahrain Financial Harbour and proposed new city developments in the south of Bahrain may have some special dispensation granted to them to attract overseas investors and employers.

Certificates & Licences

Driving Licence

Other options → Transportation [p.78]

If you are staying in Bahrain for an extended period you can drive on your international licence until you obtain your residence visa and your CPR card. Your CPR card is similar to an ID card and you will often be asked to provide it as a means of identification. To obtain your Bahrain driving licence you need copies of your CPR and your present driving licence together with the originals of these documents. You must take these and two photos to the Traffic Department in Isa Town. Here you will have an eye test, and if you need glasses for the eye test you must make sure that you are wearing them in the photos that you provide, or your application will be rejected.

When you get to the Traffic Directorate you must go to the second building; the first is for traffic offences. Once in the building there are good directions in English to the driving licence application section. Here you can fill in the application form and you will be directed through the rest of the process. Your application will be processed immediately and you should be able leave with your new licence.

If you already have a GCC licence, but have an original licence from the UK, other European

countries, the USA or Australia, you can drive on your GCC licence until you receive your residence visa and CPR card. You can then follow the same procedure as above but you will need a letter from your sponsor stating that they have no objection to your obtaining a Bahrain licence. Getting the licence should only take a few hours and your employer will normally arrange for someone to take you to the Traffic Directorate to achieve this. There are no separate queues for women but the numbering queue system means it really is first come first served.

Unfortunately, licence holders from other countries must take a Bahrain driving test. This can be organised by going to the National Driver Training Centre (NDTC) in A'ali. You must book a course of lessons however confident or experienced you are. Your instructor will be booked at the training centre and he will arrange for your actual test.

The driving licence is valid for five years. If you are waiting for your CPR card you can drive on an international driving licence until it is ready. Make sure you get the licence stamped. This can be done by your car rental company or by the Traffic Directorate. Always carry your driving licence with you when driving and remember that if you have an accident, however small, you must obtain a police report at the scene. If you are asked to pay BD5 the accident was not your fault, DB15 and it was!

Driving Schools

There is only one driving school in Bahrain, the National Driver Training Centre (NDTC) in A'ali (1764 2106), which is administered by the Traffic Directorate of the Ministry of the Interior. The minimum age for applicants is 18. The course costs BD3 per hour, and lasts a minimum of 18 hours, of which 8 hours are conducted inside the NDTC and the other 10 hours on the road. Learners have occasionally complained that their driving instructors have delayed sending them for a driving test. If you feel that this is happening, you should

> ### GCC easy as ABC
>
> *If you want to drop in on your neighbours then make sure you go prepared - with an Explorer guide! Be it for shopping in Dubai, a luxury holiday in Abu Dhabi, a get-back-to-nature trip to Oman, a long weekend to Qatar or a slice of eventful history in Kuwait the Explorer residents' guides will give you the inside scoop on the GCC.*

bring it to the notice of the administrators of the NDTC. A word of warning! If you fail the driving test, you have to start all over again and take a full course of lessons.

Liquor Licence

Other options → Alcohol [p.158]

There is no system of liquor licences in Bahrain. Alcohol is permitted but it can only be purchased at off-licences by non-Muslims, although no ID card is needed to prove this. Alcohol is freely available in the many restaurants, bars and hotels, where there is no restriction on the purchaser.

Birth Certificate & Registration

The process of registering the birth of your child is surprisingly simple. Before leaving the hospital where your child is born, ensure that you receive a Notification of Birth form, which can be completed in English or Arabic. You need to fill in the details and it is countersigned and stamped by the hospital. This should then be taken to your nearest Health Centre. The hospital can tell you which one to go to, as it depends on the details on your CPR card.

You should take the Notification of Birth form, together with the parents' passports and CPR cards to the Health Centre. There is a desk at the Health Centre which deals with new births. Normally a Bahraini birth certificate, which is also in English and Arabic, can be issued in about a week and costs under BD1. If it is urgent you can ask for an urgent turnaround and pay a little more. Once you have your baby's Bahraini birth certificate you can take this to your own embassy who will provide you with a birth certificate from your country. At the same time you should be able to obtain a passport for your child. You will then need to obtain a residence permit for your child through your employer. You should also check your country's regulations regarding children born overseas. In Britain, for example, children whose parents were born overseas are not entitled to British passports unless they are born in the UK.

It always causes some amusement when parents see the stamp in their baby's passport which says that he/she is not allowed to take up employment. There are no fixed time limits on applying for a birth certificate, but you are advised to get it completed as soon as possible as your child is effectively living in the country illegally until the residence permit has been granted and your fee may go up if you leave this for more than a month.

It should also be noted that in order to register a birth you need to show a marriage certificate, and that it is in fact against the law to have a child out of wedlock in Bahrain. As far as the actual birth is concerned, some private hospitals may turn a blind eye and not require proof of married status, but government maternity hospitals may insist on the full formalities and report any such births to the police.

Marriage Certificate & Registration

A surprising number of expatriates get married in Bahrain. The process is really determined by your own country's requirements, as the Ministry of Justice in Bahrain requires an NOC from your embassy. Your embassy will have their own regulations as to what you need to undertake to obtain this. It will normally require a residency period of 21 days in order for marriage banns to be issued. You can have these issued in your own country first but it's best to check with your embassy for up-to-date information.

If you wish to have a civil marriage you will need to take the NOC from your Embassy and an NOC from your employer/sponsor to the Ministry of Justice in the Diplomatic Area. Your CPR cards will of course also be required, as they always are.

Muslims can marry in the House of Judgement at the Ministry of Justice. In addition to the requirements above you will need a letter from the father of the bride. Other religious ceremonies can be arranged by contacting the relevant church or temple, but you will still need the above mentioned documents to conduct the civil aspect of the marriage. The fees for the marriage will depend on your embassy charges, possibly on your nationality and on the amount charged by the institution carrying out the ceremony.

Roman Catholics can marry at the Sacred Heart church on Shaikh Isa Al Khabeer Avenue, and Anglicans at St Christopher's Cathedral opposite the Police Fort. There are two Hindu temples, one in the Manama souk and the other, which is dedicated to the Goddess Durga, is out in the desert beyond Alba, south of Sitra. There are also three Sikh Gurudwaras in Bahrain. For a Hindu wedding, no court documents are required. It doesn't have to take place in a temple, but can be performed anywhere. Basically all that is needed is for the banns to be read at the Indian Embassy for the requisite period of time, and then the necessary ritual is carried out in front of relatives on both sides, officiated by the Pundit. The marriage is then registered at the Indian Embassy. There is no fixed charge for the wedding, although donations to the temple and the Pundit are expected.

Death Certificate & Registration

Should you have the misfortune of suffering the death of a friend or family member you should immediately contact a hospital. The deceased will be taken to the hospital where an official Notification of Death form will be issued to you. If the police have been involved, for whatever reason, the public security doctor should also issue you with this form. Make sure it is stamped by the hospital or public security doctor. This form, together with the passport and CPR card of the deceased, should then be taken to your local Health Centre who will arrange for the Death Certificate to be issued. The informer will also need to take along their own passport or CPR card. You can then take this certificate to your own embassy who will provide you with the relevant documents for your country. Your embassy will also assist you with the formalities of repatriation of the deceased, although you will be responsible for all charges. There is no fee for a death certificate if undertaken within 48 hours of the death, otherwise it is 400 fils. The relevant embassy will advise on the procedure for cancelling visas and passports.

Since Islam requires that a dead Muslim must be buried before sundown on the day of death, an autopsy is not required unless there are suspicious circumstances. There is no donor card system in Bahrain as transplants are unacceptable to most Muslims. However, within the past year, two kidney transplants have been carried out on Bahraini patients following the death of the Asian donor in a road accident.

Should the body of the deceased need to be embalmed for repatriation, the authorities at Salmaniya Hospital should be contacted. There are two Christian cemeteries in Bahrain, but only the one at Salmabad is still used. St Christopher's Cathedral charges BD120 for the burial.

Work

Working in Bahrain

Bahrain still has a large population of expatriate workers (according to a 2004 estimate, 44% of the population in the 15 to 64 age group is non-national). This is despite strenuous efforts by the Government to increase the level of Bahrainis employed. The Economic Development Board, led by His Highness The Crown Prince, is spearheading the drive to make Bahrainis the first choice for employers, but he publicly recognises that expatriates are still very much needed by Bahrain in all areas. Therefore there are still considerable opportunities for well qualified expatriates to take up employment in Bahrain. What is noticeable though is that the remuneration for expatriates has not kept pace with pay scales around the world, a reflection of the fact that Bahrainis really are competing for jobs.

English is the business language in Bahrain but Arabic is becoming more widespread especially in the financial services industry with its concentration on the Saudi market. Generally however expatriates are not expected to speak Arabic but it is good to try to pick up a certain amount if only to enable you to greet and thank people.

The expatriate workforce is spread throughout the whole economy. The financial sector is now predominantly Bahraini but there is still a large number of expatriates working in this field, helped by the fact that Bahrain has well over one hundred financial institutions. The large family companies also rely heavily on expatriate workers although they are working hard to increase the number of Bahrainis employed. The major industrial companies are predominantly Bahraini staffed, except for some of the senior specialist roles. The construction and garment industries are probably the fields which are most heavily reliant on expatriates. However these positions are very poorly paid and are therefore not attractive to Bahrainis.

The benefits expatriates receive as part of their remuneration vary considerably and are really up to the individual to negotiate. You should expect at least four working weeks' holiday a year. In expat contracts this is often phrased as 30 calendar days. Do not be misled by this, as you will have to count weekends as part of your holiday allowance. So if you take a holiday on Wednesday and report back to work on Monday you will be deemed to have taken five days from your holiday entitlement.

Most senior expatriates will be given housing and car allowances. You should, if you can, try to view property within your allowance to establish whether you feel this is sufficient. Property options vary considerably in price and many rents have increased dramatically over the last few years as workers from Saudi base their families in Bahrain.

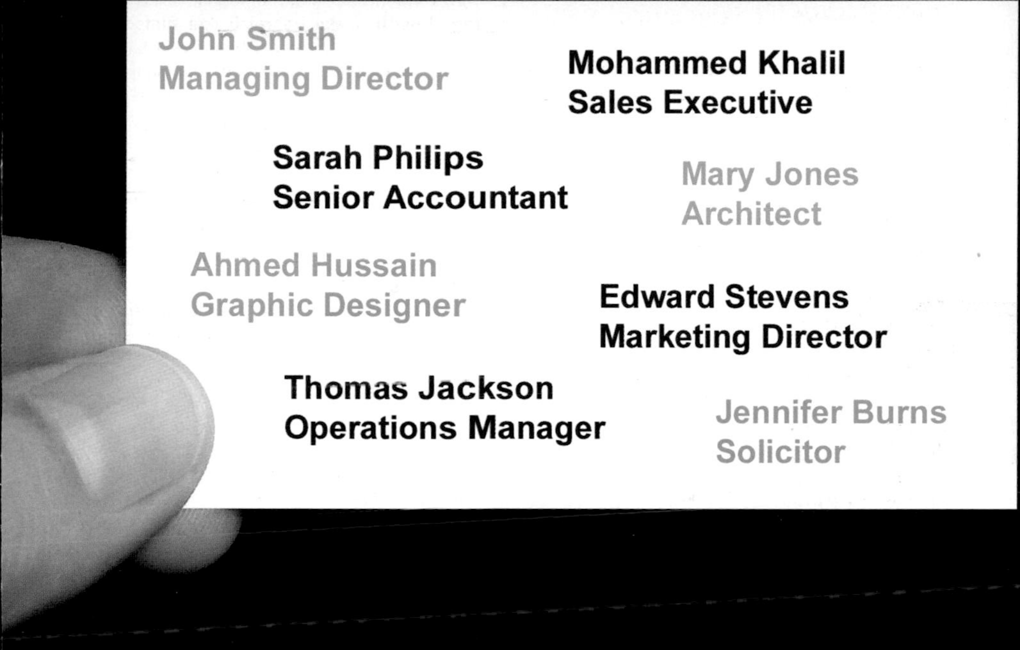

John Smith
Managing Director

Mohammed Khalil
Sales Executive

Sarah Philips
Senior Accountant

Mary Jones
Architect

Ahmed Hussain
Graphic Designer

Edward Stevens
Marketing Director

Thomas Jackson
Operations Manager

Jennifer Burns
Solicitor

Employment Plus

What do you want your business card to say? With Bahrain's premier recruitment agency the possibilities are endless...

With a broad range of well qualified candidates and excellent career opportunities, Employment Plus is designed to help you succceed.

Apply online or call today.

Employment Plus
P.O.Box 3106, Manama
Kindgdom of Bahrain

Tel: +973 17214000
Fax: +973 17214333

eplus@batelco.bom.bh

www.speedymotors.com

Working Hours

Bahrain has a mixed working week. The government works from around 07:00 to 14:00 Saturday to Wednesday. The quasi government industrial companies work from around 07:00 to 15:00 Saturday to Wednesday. The private sector tends to work five and a half days a week from 08:00 to 13:00 and then from 15:00 to 18:00, with a half day on Thursday. The financial institutions and those companies dealing in the international market, however, work from Sunday to Thursday. A standard working week in the private sector is forty five hours, although more and more companies are reducing this to forty. The Labour Law stipulates a maximum working week of forty eight hours.

Holidays vary from company to company but there is a legal minimum of twenty days holiday per year. Most companies, however, give a minimum of one calendar month including weekends. Expatriates are normally encouraged to take this leave in one block although there is no legal requirement for the leave to be taken in this way.

Bahrain has fifteen days of public holidays a year. The actual dates of many of the religious holidays are announced by the government in the local press, as their exact date depends on the new

moon being observed, signifying the start of the new month. Most private companies do not recompense staff should the official public holiday fall on a weekend, although it is becoming a more accepted practice now that government staff are compensated for this.

Finding Work

You are not advised to come to Bahrain looking for work. Of course it is possible to find work here but contacts are everything and without them you will find it difficult to find a suitable position within the duration of your visit visa. Most foreign workers are recruited through agencies and you should look for an agency in your country specialising in the Gulf region. Most local recruitment companies are focused on local recruitment and do not tend to recruit extensively overseas. Word of mouth is probably the most effective recruitment method although companies are beginning to understand the value of using the services of a recruitment company in order for them to obtain the best choice of potential employees. There are a number of recruitment companies operating in Bahrain now and most have a website which details positions available and a CV registering service. You are advised to contact all the agencies as they tend to concentrate more on filling vacancies rather than on finding jobs for individuals. There are also many overseas agencies who work in the region and they often handle the more senior positions. The application process is normally a rather drawn out affair, but you should try to get a visit to Bahrain included in the process if you can so, that you can get a taste of the country before you uproot your family.

A Working Holiday?

Working in Bahrain is no longer a pleasant sojourn on a holiday island. Generally you will find the working environment to be similar to that in your own country. Also remember that Bahrain is a very small place. It is likely that if you know someone here, they will know someone who knows someone who is looking for someone just like you.

Downtown Bahrain

Recruitment Agencies	
ABC	1722 6777
Azrek Search Associates	1771 4709
Clarendon Parker	1731 0064
Employment Plus P.47	1721 4000
Focus	1753 4044
JHC Recruitment	1753 0077

Voluntary & Charity Work

There are many opportunities to do voluntary work in Bahrain but you will need to be resident here before you can become involved. Once you are resident and you find that you have time available to give to a charitable organization, one of the best routes is to join one of the local Rotary clubs, (see Business Groups & Contacts below), or one of the Clubs & Associations, [p.149]. Many of these undertake extensive charitable work and you should be able to find an opportunity to help relatively easily.

The Bahrain Society for the Prevention of Cruelty to Animals (BSPCA) (1759 3479), is always looking for volunteers to help out at their animal shelter and in their second-hand clothes shop. They are also desperate for dog-lovers willing to walk the dogs on a regular basis. The RIA Institute, for autistic children, welcomes helpers with experience in this field. The Indian Ladies Association organises many charitable events, and always rallies round to give immediate aid in emergency situations to help those made homeless by fires, or injured in accidents. There is also a 24-hour helpline for people who are depressed or needing help. The advisors are all volunteers and the group welcomes new recruits, particularly those with experience of this kind of work. You can also contact St Christopher's Cathedral or the Sacred Heart Church to find out how you can become involved in their charity events. The American Women's Association (1775 6075) also organises charity events and welcomes new members of any nationality.

Business Groups & Contacts

The Rotary clubs in Bahrain are probably the quickest way to network with the business community. There are three clubs, Adliya, Manama and Salmaniya, and they meet once a week at the Diplomat Hotel, Gulf Hotel and the Golden Tulip respectively. Otherwise business groups tend to be focused on particular nationalities and so you should contact your embassy or consulate to find out what groups are active that would enable you to network effectively. The Bahrain British Businessman's Forum for example is open to all those who are involved in business in Bahrain but has an emphasis on British business. Embassies often arrange trade delegations where local businessmen are invited to meet the visiting delegates, so registering with your embassy is a good idea.

You should remember that Bahrain is a Muslim Arab country. As such its business etiquette is sometimes a little frustrating when you first arrive. Patience and the ability to drink tea will help you relax into the Bahraini way. You should always make sure that you are punctual for all your meetings as arriving late is considered to be very bad mannered. However do not assume that your meeting will start at the appointed time, or that it will not be interrupted.

Many businesses are still run by families and so the senior family member will almost constantly be required to approve each decision that is made in the company. This means that there may be a constant flow of people arriving at his desk asking for signatures. Alternatively you may find that phone calls are taken when you are mid-meeting. You should not take this the wrong way, as he is often unwilling or unable to cut himself off from his colleagues. Of course you should ensure your mobile phone is switched off during meetings.

Start and end your meetings with a firm handshake, unless you are meeting with a woman, when you should not offer your hand unless she first offers hers. Most Muslim women will not touch the hand of a man other a family member. They are not being rude, and you should not embarrass them (or yourself) by offering your hand. Most meetings will start with a general discussion before you get down to business. Business cards are expected and an exchange of cards will assist both parties in pronouncing the other's name. In formal meetings you will often be served Arabic coffee. This is an acquired taste, but it is served in very small cups so you should be able to finish one cup whatever your taste buds are telling you. If you don't want a second cup make sure that you tilt the cup back and forth to the waiter, as he will otherwise automatically give you a refill.

Business Councils & Groups	
Bahrain British Business Forum	1722 8364
Bahrain Business Men Association	1722 9009
Bahrain Business Women Society	1772 1188
Bahrain Chamber of Commerce and Industry	1722 9555
Bahrain Economic Society	1772 3444
Bahrain Engineering Bureau	1727 1718
Bahrain French Business Club	1726 1632
Bahrain Inst Of Banking & Financial	1772 8008
Bahrain Investors Centre	1756 2222
Rotary Clubs	3939 4522

Finally, you should remember that the Bahrain business community is a small one and that Arab families tend to be very large. As the old saying goes, throw a stone and you hit half the country. Be very careful what you say about anyone else, unless you are really sure that this will not cause offence. Even competing large family groups have connections through marriage, and as an expatriate your view will not normally be welcome.

You can find the Bahrain British Business Forum (BBBF) at www.bbbforum.org, or you can contact them by phone on 1722 8364, or by e-mail on bbbforum@batelco.com.bh. The Rotary Clubs can be contacted by phone on 3939 4522. Information on the Rotary clubs is also available at www.arab.net/bahrain/links.

Employment Contracts

You should always get the terms of your contract in writing before you start your new job. Often however, you will not be provided with an official contract until you have completed the statutory probation period of three months. This probation period allows the employer or employee to terminate the employment with one day's notice. You should not be unduly concerned by this as your employer will have paid for your flight out and so it is in his interest to keep you in the new position. Even if you only have an offer letter when you take up employment, make sure that you get a copy of the contract that will be signed after the three months. In general, no contract can include terms more onerous on the employee than the conditions laid out in the Bahrain Labour Law. If your contract omits benefits included in the Bahrain Labour Law you are still legally entitled to them, but their omission would suggest that your employer may try to avoid them. The Bahrain Labour Law specifies the minimum level of conditions or benefits and most companies will offer considerably more than this minimum.

The contract that you receive can be in Arabic or English. If you do not read Arabic you should obtain a copy of the contract in English. Be aware that if you are given an English translation, the Arabic contract may be interpreted differently, and so you are advised to ask for an English contract with an Arabic translation and then find a sympathetic Arabic speaker to check it at the earliest opportunity. The most important aspect of the contract is of course your monthly salary, housing and car allowances. In addition the contract should state what annual leave entitlement you have, and specify your annual leave flight. Be sure that your place of origin is also included correctly as this will determine the destination that your employer is bound to provide you with flights for each year. The contract does not need to say anything else, as the terms of the Labour Law are relevant by default. Of course, should you get more benefits, these should be included in the contract, and most sophisticated institutions will have their own detailed contract.

Maternity leave is not included in the contract as a standard, but is provided for under the Labour Law, whereby women are entitled to 45 days paid leave and 15 days unpaid leave. In addition, breast-feeding mothers are entitled to one hour off each day as long as this is taken at the beginning or end of the day.

Full details of the Labour Law can be found on the Labour Ministry's website: www.bah-molsa.com/english. This details all the minimum standards that employers should adhere to. It also sets out the laws on working hours, holidays, end of service indemnity and annual leave flights. Should you encounter difficulties with your employer you must consult a lawyer. The Bahrain courts are effective in dealing with employee issues and if you feel you have been wrongly dismissed your only solution is to file a case against your employer. Of course it is often better to negotiate a settlement with your employer, who will normally prefer to settle the issue amicably.

If you do go to court you will find that the initial hearing will be undertaken quite swiftly. However, the system falls down if one party does not turn up to court or asks for an extension. You may then find that you will have a long delay before your case is settled and an appeal system can drag this out even further. As you need a sponsor to stay in the country you may find it difficult to pursue the case when you are outside Bahrain. To find alternative employment, you need to have your work permit and residence permit cancelled by your existing employer, and even then you may have difficulty in obtaining further employment in Bahrain without obtaining an NOC from your existing employer. So try and settle things amicably.

There are fledgling unions in some of Bahrain's large quasi-government companies such as Alba and Bapco, but since these have a very high percentage of Bahraini employees, they are unlikely to have the best interests of expat workers at heart. No information is available regarding expat labour unions.

'Banning'

The NOC

The NOC is one of the most difficult aspects of changing employment in Bahrain. In theory you do not need one to take up alternative employment. In practice you do, and your previous employer can make your life very difficult by not providing you with one. If your employer refuses to give you an NOC, make sure that they cancel your residence permit and work permit in your passport. You can be held liable for the pro rata cost of your recruitment if you leave within the first two years, and for the pro rata cost of government fees if you leave after this period. Once you have agreed a final settlement and your permits have been cancelled, you will have fourteen days in which to leave the country. Your new employer should be able to arrange an extension, but they may still wish you to leave the country.

There is continued confusion in the Ministries regarding the NOC and expatriates constantly write to the newspapers asking for clarification. The simple reality is that you should try to work out your contract or work permit duration, and then you should give as much notice as possible and do whatever you can to get an NOC from your ex employer. The NOC has to be signed by the individual in the company who is registered with the Ministry of Commerce as an authorised company signatory.

It is hoped that the revision to the Labour Law presently being considered will change this problem so that expatriates can change jobs freely in practice as well as in theory. The downside is that the cost of the work permit will increase significantly and you may be faced with having to repay some of these costs, but at least you won't feel like an indentured labourer.

Meetings

Meetings in Bahrain tend largely to follow the culture of the people involved in the meeting. When the majority of the people are Bahrainis, or other Arab nationals, they are on the long side. The Bahraini culture is rooted in hospitality, and business meetings follow a more leisurely path than one would be used to in the west. Conversation often starts in a non-specific way, and greetings and general chat often make up the first ten minutes or so. This doesn't mean that the participants aren't switched on to the purpose of the meeting, just that they approach it in their own manner. Often, western expatriates comment that one of the first things that they had to get used to with regard to meetings is adding on the 'ten minute tea factor' and once you get used to it and learn to be calm and patient, it becomes an enjoyable norm. As you would expect, the greater the diversity of nationalities, the less the meetings adhere to the Bahraini format.

Often meetings are not one-on-one, unless there is a very specific purpose and its clear that no one else is needed. Two representatives of each party is more common. Business cards are widely used and are exchanged at the beginning of the meeting. Many meetings are still done in person, and in a small-sized country this doesn't pose too much hassle. However, conference calls are becoming more common, particularly in the banking sector or in meetings which involve conferencing parties in other parts of the world.

Bahrain is trying to increase its reputation as a destination for seminars and conferences, and a number of hotels have good conference facilities. These attract international business people, mainly from within the region although interest from further afield is constantly building.

Company Closure

There are always risks with joining a new venture, but some of the best opportunities arise from start-up companies. In addition, Bahrain has a rapidly expanding economy and the large amount of available investment funds in the region mean that there is a proportionately large number of start-ups. If you are unlucky enough to find that your company is facing closure, you should be paid all of your remaining salary and allowances, holiday pay and end of service indemnity (sometimes known as gratuity) before you leave the country. Be sure that you press for this as once your residence and work permits have been cancelled you will only have a certain amount of time left in Bahrain. The Ministry of Labour should be contacted if you believe that you are not being paid what you are due.

As a last resort you can file a case against the company to ensure that it is not wound up and liquidated before your claim is heard. It is rare however for employers not to pay the dues of their employees. The end of term indemnity is paid to all expatriates at the end of their service in a particular company and is due once you have stayed with the company for three years. Any period of employment of between three and five years will earn you an end of service indemnity of one half of your final monthly salary for each completed year of service. After five years this increases to one full month's salary for each completed year, paid at the rate of your final salary.

Financial & Legal Affairs

Bank Accounts

There are a number of international banks operating in Bahrain including Citibank, HSBC and Standard Chartered. They all have a number of branches in the town centre, Diplomatic Area and the Seef Area. The local banks, however, offer a good alternative and when choosing a bank it is worth considering who your employer banks with. You will often not only be charged a fee of BD3, but there may also be a delay of up to three days before your salary is credited to your account if it is with a different bank from that of your employer. The major local banks include Al Ahli United Bank, Bank of Bahrain and Kuwait, and National Bank of Bahrain. All these banks, local and international, offer standard savings and current accounts and of course offer many investment options. Most of these banks also have internet banking options and some form of tele-banking, although the branch network is still the most common form of banking. If you maintain a minimum deposit in your account of BD50 there are normally no charges that you will face, unless paying for a particular service. A higher deposit will sometimes assure you of a status account. This enables you to jump queues and have a more personal service. For transferring money abroad, the exchange houses will normally offer a slightly better rate. The downside is the parking problems involved in getting close to one of the exchange houses.

The banks all follow slightly different times but are generally open from 08:00 until 12:30 and then from varying times in the afternoon or evening depending on the branch location. HSBC has a branch in Adliya which is open from 07:00 until 19:00 seven days a week. Dedicated parking makes this branch an easy one to deal with.

Cost of Living

Apples (per kg)	BD0.500
Bananas (per kg)	BD0.350
Bottle of house wine (restaurant)	BD8
Bottle of wine (off-licence)	BD4
Burger (takeaway)	BD2.400
Bus (10km journey)	BD0.150
Camera film (Kodak 36 exposure)	BD1
Can of dog food	BD0.400
Can of soft drink	BD0.150
Cappuccino	BD1.100
Car rental (per day)	BD1000
Carrots (per kg)	BD0.400
CD album (single cd)	BD7
Chocolate bar	BD0.200
Cigarettes (per pack of 20 Rothmans)	BD0.550
Cinema ticket	BD2
Dozen eggs	BD0.600
Film developing (colour, 36 exp)	BD4.100
Fresh beef (per kg)	BD1
Fresh chicken (per kg)	BD0.750
Fresh fish (per kg)	BD0.800
Golf (18 holes - visitor's weekend rate)	BD38
Golf (18 holes - mid-week and night golf)	BD27.500
House wine (glass)	BD2.500
Large takeaway pizza	BD4.500
Loaf of bread	BD0.500
Local postage stamp	BD0.110
Milk (1 litre)	BD0.450
Mobile to mobile call (local, per minute)	BD0.055
New release DVD	BD15
Newspaper (international)	BD3
Newspaper (local)	BD0.200
Orange juice (1 litre)	BD0.450
Pack of 24 aspirin/paracetamol	BD0.500
Petrol (litre/gallon)	BD0.100/0.600
Pint of beer	BD1.600
Postcard	BD0.110
Potatoes (per kg)	BD0.200
Rice (per kg)	BD0.250
Salon haircut (female)	
(including styling and blow dry)	BD4
Salon haircut (male)	BD0.600
Shawarma	BD0.250
Six-pack of beer (off-licence)	BD4.200
Strawberries (per punnet)	BD0.400
Sugar (2kg)	BD0.500
Taxi (10km journey)	BD5
Text message (local)	BD0.035
Tube of toothpaste	BD0.600
Water 1.5 litres (restaurant)	BD0.200
Water 1.5 litres (supermarket)	BD0.150
Watermelon (per kg)	BD0.150

Financial Planning

Saving money for the house back home has always been one of the perks of living in Bahrain. If you are careful and don't have too active a nightlife almost everyone can save money in Bahrain. Taking the advice of financial planners is, as in the rest of the world, a potentially risky option. There are many excellent Independent Financial Advisors operating in Bahrain but of course there are also the slightly less scrupulous operators. If you are saving a reasonable amount it is definitely worth talking to one, but do make sure that they are licenced by the Bahrain Monetary Agency, and be aware that even if they are part of a global operation they may be able to operate in Bahrain without all the built-in safeguards you may find back home. Generally, residents opt for opening offshore accounts connected to their own countries as this enables them to safeguard their savings. There are savings schemes run by a number of banks in Bahrain offering cash prizes in the manner of the UK premium bonds, but otherwise expatriates tend to repatriate their savings in some manner on a regular basis. The property boom that has hit the Gulf over the last few years has produced an alternative for the richer expatriates who for the first time can now invest in property in a number of areas in Bahrain (see Purchasing a Home [p.61]).

> ### Pay Up or Else!
>
> *It is illegal in Bahrain to bounce a cheque. You can be fined or indeed face a custodial sentence. So be sure you have funds in your account before you write a cheque. Neither the recipient of the cheque or your bank will consider this an oversight' as they might elsewhere.*

Financial consultants in Bahrain include Middle East Consultancy (1721 3223) and Mudhaffar Public Accountants (1722 3034). There are also several Financial Information Services listed as having offices in Bahrain, including AP Dow Jones, and Reuters Middle East.

Taxation

The only tax that you will be aware of paying in Bahrain is the Municipality tax charged at ten percent of your home rental cost. Therefore if you rent a flat for BD350 per month you will find a charge of BD35 added to your electricity and water bill each month. You pay this tax and your utilities bill as one payment. There are taxes on alcohol and there is a government levy of five percent charged on purchases from the five star hotels. There is as yet, however, no income tax to worry about.

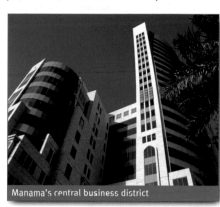
Manama's central business district

Legal Issues

Bahrain's law is based on Sharia law. However it is less strictly enforced than in some other Gulf countries. The courts in Bahrain are generally considered fair and well run, with the major complaint being the delay in proceedings being finalised and the slight disparity in sentences, slapping someone with a wet fish being the latest heavily fined misdemeanour to catch the headlines.

Bahrain is by statute a constitutional democracy. In reality Bahraini democracy is in a transitional phase and has made great strides in involving the people in the government of the country. This transition is expected to continue in future years as the democratically elected bodies grow in maturity and are able to take on more direct responsibility which at present is still held by the appointed Ministers. The Judicial system is by royal decree an independent body separate from the Government. Generally you should expect the laws and courts to treat you in the same manner as your home country. The local proceedings are in Arabic, and so if you find yourself going to court, even for a minor offence, you should try to get yourself a lawyer or an interpreter, although the judges will make an effort to speak English if they can.

It is illegal to drink and drive in Bahrain. If you are caught and are lucky enough not to have killed anyone, you will face at least a BD500 fine and often the withdrawal of your driving licence. You may also have up to three days in jail waiting for your case to be heard. It goes without saying that drugs are not welcome in Bahrain and abusers of this law will be heavily fined and/or jailed. Generally, when an expat is convicted of a criminal offence they face a heavy fine and/or a jail sentence followed by deportation.

Understandably, Bahrain does not want to import criminals so the courts are fairly tough in enforcing this. Minor traffic offences will get you fined, unless you are a repeat offender. Be aware that if you repeatedly get caught speeding you could face a jail sentence. Family law in Bahrain still comes under Sharia Law although there is a significant movement pressing for a separate code to be drawn up to deal with family issues such as divorce. Muslims can get divorced in Bahrain but under Sharia Law rather than under a separate family code.

Law Firms

Law Firms	
Al Mahmood & Zu'bi	1722 5151
Baker & McKenzie	1753 8800
Dr Husain Al Barharna	1753 6066
Elham Ali Hassan	1753 3317
Hassan Radhi	1753 5252
Haya Rashed Al Khalifa	1753 7771
Qays H Zu'bi	1753 8600
Rashid A R Ebrahim	1753 0274
Salwa Ahmed Al Khalifa	1753 0352
Seyadi	1721 5151
Sheik Ahmed Zaki Yamani	1721 1433
Trowers & Hamlin	1753 0082

Housing

Your major choice when you decide where to live is whether to look for an apartment or a villa. Apartments are generally in the Manama area and its suburbs, while villas are situated right across the country. If you chose a villa you will also have to choose an individual villa on its own, or a villa in a compound. Most expatriates choose a compound villa with its added security and facilities, which often include a swimming pool, tennis and squash courts and a children's play area. Many apartment blocks also include a swimming pool and some even have roof top tennis courts. Almost all apartment blocks and compounds have some form of security and prices for both apartments and villas vary considerably according to the age and state of repair of the building, and the facilities provided.

Renting in Bahrain

There are now opportunities for expatriates to purchase property in Bahrain, although this is only possible in certain newly developed areas. As these developments are still in their infancy, they will not be ready for people to move in to for some time. Renting therefore is currently the only real option for expatriates.

There is no fixed rule as to how your contract deals with the matter of an accommodation allowance. There are companies that will specify a house or a selection of houses for you to live in. This is normally because they are involved in the property rental business and you will often end up with a good deal, if this is the case. However, for most expats the most pressing task when they arrive is to find a home which fits their budget. With the spiralling cost of accommodation, many firms now consider an overall package when they are making you an offer of employment. What this means is that they will arbitrarily allocate the total cash to be paid to you each month to cover salary, housing and a car. You just receive on total amount and can choose how you spend it; a one-bedroom flat and a Ferrari, or luxury mansion and a rust bucket.

If you are renting an apartment you will often find that your rent is termed as all inclusive. You should check exactly what this means. It should include the Municipality tax, as well as electricity and water, and satellite television charges. However, sometimes it is only some of these. Remember the Municipality tax is ten percent of your rental charge, so it makes a considerable difference to your overall cost. Villa rents are very rarely all inclusive, and you will normally have to pay for your electricity, water and Municipality Tax on top of your rental charge. Most reasonable apartments have a limited amount of dedicated parking but you should make sure you understand what this means before you sign up. Parking is an increasing problem in Bahrain, and struggling back with the weekly shopping and not being able to park outside your apartment is not fun, particularly when the temperature is in the upper 40s and the level of humidity feels as though you are having a sauna bath.

Rental contracts tend to be for two years with a break clause after one year. You should try to get your lease to include a reasonable notice period after the first year, for example three months, as you will often find that you want to relocate once you have settled down in Bahrain. The frequency of rental payments varies from landlord to landlord but you should never be required to pay more than three months in advance, and once you have been in a property for over a year you should be able to negotiate for monthly payments. Of course you can try and negotiate a rental reduction if you pay a year's rental in advance, but this is not likely to be significant. Normally you can pay by passing a cheque to the landlord every quarter and this is probably better than making a bank transfer, as there will be less chance of the record of your payment going astray.

The construction boom in full swing

Rental agreements sometimes have a clause allowing the landlord to increase the rent after the first year or two years. It is unlikely however that the landlord will enforce this if you are a good tenant and he wants to keep you, unless of course you are now paying considerably under market rates. Generally, no deposit is taken by the landlord for damages or maintenance. Ask your potential neighbours what the maintenance is like in your chosen location, as landlords can vary significantly in the level of service they provide their tenants. A speedy air conditioning repair will make a big difference to you in the height of the summer. Your biggest electricity cost will be air conditioning and you will find that badly maintained units consume an incredible amount of power to keep you cool.

The place to look for shared property, apartments and villas is the classified advertisements section of the Gulf Daily News. Here you will find all of the agents advertising and individual advertisements for rooms to share or for individual houses. You don't have to use an agent. You can literally just drive around and ask the doorman or watchman at compounds to show you any empty units. The

benefit of this is that you save the landlord the commission paid to the agent. The downside is that you can take a very long time driving and looking at unsuitable accommodation, and may miss the home of your dreams because you did not find out that it was coming up for rental. The agents tend to be good. If you don't like the one you have, then get another, or get a few. You are earning them their commission and they tend to treat you accordingly. Be happy to be driven around by the agent if you have just arrived, as this may save some considerable time. You can always go back and have a look at the area on your own later.

Individual houses often just have a sign on the exterior wall saying 'For Rent', and a telephone number. If you are interested in an individual villa this can be an effective way of finding a home, especially if you know the area you would like to live in. If you do find your villa on your own, be sure to mention the lack of agency fees in your negotiation of the rent, and be aware that it is unlikely that the watchman at a compound or block of apartments actually knows the correct price of the property. He is equally likely to give you a higher as well as a lower figure.

The important term you will come across is semi-furnished. This means that you will have most kitchen white goods provided, for example fridge and cooker, and that you will have air conditioning units and curtains. There will not be any actual furniture in the house. Unfurnished means that you get none of the above. Fully furnished should mean that you are provided with absolutely everything, from knives and forks to stereo systems. Most property is advertised as semi-furnished.

Real Estate Agents

Most people find their property through an agent. The best place to look for one is the classified section of GDN, where you will find all of the agents advertising particular properties, but don't feel you only have to speak to an agent who is advertising something you are particularly interested in. Word of mouth is the other method of establishing who to use. Ask your work colleagues to recommend an agent. Many people use an agent so that they can move to a new house every few years, and so know who is good at finding that particular apartment or villa or you are looking for. Also, don't necessarily be taken in by websites. Most property goes before it has a chance to hit a website, and the best agents are often one-woman bands.

Real Estate Agents

Real Estate Agents	
Al Dahiya Const & Real Estate	1772 5572
British Guides	3925 4100
Carlton Properties	3969 6372
Century 21	1721 2000
Cluttons	1722 7667
Deewania	1729 3553
Fortune Property Management	3974 4662
Landmark	3963 3885
Marketing Plus	3955 1130
Projects Properties	1772 5772
Purple Properties	3962 9209

The Lease

The lease you are given should be in English. Don't accept a lease in a language that you do not understand as there may be interesting interpretations. You normally need a copy of your CPR card and a salary letter from your employer, so that the landlord can be assured that the property is within your means. Also make sure you are clear as to the notice period after the first year of occupancy. Does the lease start again or can you give three months notice at any time after the first year? As long as you stay for a year, landlords may be willing to have a reasonable notice period click in after this period.

Main Accommodation Options

Sharing

Sharing tends to be done amongst friends or by families sub-letting one room. The Gulf Daily News lists rooms available on this basis.

Apartments

Apartments tend to offer the best value for money, but as would be expected, prices can still vary significantly. You can get a basic apartment for BD100 a month or pay BD1,700 to stay in the Sail Tower connected to The Ritz Carlton, and there is everything in between. Of course the facilities and amenities change as you go up the scale. At the top end you will have a swimming pool, squash court, gym, shaded parking and satellite television. Most newer apartment blocks are located in Juffair or Seef, while the older ones tend to be in the centre of Manama. Many flats on offer in Exhibition Road

have tiny rooms and no parking, and the whole area gets extremely crowded and rowdy in the evenings, particularly at the weekend, when tourists flock across the Saudi causeway.

Villas

Villas are either individual or in a compound. There are many older compounds where you can get excellent value for money and a lot of character, if you are prepared to put up with seventies-style bathroom and kitchen suites. Almost every compound will have at least a swimming pool. The best have squash courts, a gym, a children's play area and even bowling alleys. Individual villas are often slightly cheaper than equivalent houses in compounds and may have a small pool at the most.

Serviced Apartments

Serviced apartments are getting more popular as their numbers grow. These are often but not always attached to hotels and offer a great

Housing Abbreviations

Housing Abbreviations	
BR	Bedroom
C.A/C	Central air conditioning (usually included in the rent)
CC	Carpets & curtains
D/S	Double storey villa
Ensuite	Bedroom has private bathroom
Ext S/Q	Servant quarters located outside the villa
FF	Fully furnished
Fully fitted	Includes appliances (oven, refrigerator, washing machine)
GG	Garage & garden
Hall flat	Appt has entrance hall (ie, entrance doesn't open directly onto living room)
L/D	Living/dining room area
LD	living & dining rooms
Pvt garden	Private garden
S/Q	Servant quarters
S/S	Single storey villa
SF	Semi-furnished
Shared pool	Pool shared with other villas
SP	Swimming pool
UF	Unfurnished
W.A/C	Window air conditioning (often indicates an older building)
W/robes	Built in wardrobes (closets)

The Best Choices

For over 30 years, Gulf Hotel has brought diversity in cuisines. With 11 outlets, the hotel is a showcase of tastes for the most discriminating palates at Royal Thai, China Garden, Sato, La Pergola, Zahle, Takht Jamsheed, Al Waha, Fusions, Sherlock Holmes, Al-Andalus & Palace.

BAHRAIN
Hotels Company

شركة
فنادق البحرين

MEMBER OF
WORLDHOTELS
DELUXE COLLECTION

GULF HOTEL
Bahrain
WHERE SERVICE COUNTS

فنـدق الخليـج
البحـرين
الخدمة التي يعتد عليها

P.O. Box 580 Manama, Kingdom of Bahrain
Tel: (973) 1771 3000 • Fax: (973) 1771 3040
e-mail: ghbc@batelco.com.bh – www.gulfhotelbahrain.com

alternative if you are not staying for long or want to be flexible. Rental periods can be anything from one day to one year. The rates vary according to the length of your stay. The facilities tend to be good and you should also have a regular cleaning service.

Residential Areas

Other options → Exploring [p.87]

Making the decision on where to live really hinges on whether you want to live in town or out of town. In Bahrain, saying out of town means only a ten minute drive away, so you won't feel like are living in the provinces if you live out of town. Finding out the lowdown on different areas and their pros and cons can be difficult, try asking friends or work colleagues for their opinions as this will probably be your best source of unbiased advice.

Other than agents, there are presently only two official sources for real estate information: the Gulf Daily News or Arabian Homes. The latter is really a better option for individual houses and for those able to purchase property. Otherwise you have to rely on your own knowledge or that of an agent.

Juffair   Map Ref → 14-D3

Juffair is the centre of apartment living. Located opposite the Gulf Hotel and the Grand Mosque, the area is all reclaimed land and most of it did not exist 15 years ago. It now has a certain maturity about it, however, and although some areas may still seem like a building site you can now find apartment blocks which are in fully developed areas, rather than the surrounding plots being under development. This is a point worth considering. If you rent an apartment in a block which has a vacant lot next to it, your life for months could become a miserable hell of early-morning cacophony, with the pile-drivers starting up at 06:00, including on Friday mornings, and some construction companies work far into the night. There is a full range of prices in this area for apartments and there is also a small number of individual villas. The potential downside of Juffair is its proximity to some of Bahrain's more exotic nightspots.

Hoora   Map Ref → 12-C4

Hoora is situated between Exhibition Avenue and the Corniche. There is a good mix of apartment blocks here offering a good range of prices. Those closest to the embassies at the top end of Hoora tend to be more pricey. Hoora is incredibly convenient for getting to work in the Diplomatic

Area and also to the nightlife of Exhibition Avenue. The traffic at weekends and in the evenings though can be a little trying, but this is compensated for by the five-minute commute to work. There are no villas in this area.

Adliya   Map Ref → 14-B2

Adliya is Bahrain's restaurant area and so is busy in the evenings, but in a slightly more dignified manner than Exhibition Avenue. Adliya has a few expensive compounds and some great value-for-money apartment blocks. It is a pleasant place to live with easy commutes to the town centre, shopping, expatriate clubs and restaurants and bars. If you are going to live in town then Adliya is a good choice, although there is less rental accommodation available than in Juffair.

Um Al Hassam   Map Ref → 14-C4

Um Al Hassam is Adliya's poor relative. Somewhat dishevelled in appearance, Um Al Hassam is actually a pleasant place to live. There are not many apartments or villas here, but the ones you find have a pleasant atmosphere about them. You are very close to the action of Adliya but feel that you are somewhat off the beaten track, and prices tend to be lower. There are also a few excellent restaurants in Um Al Hassam itself.

Muharraq   Map Ref → 2-B4

Muharraq is the island to the north of Bahrain Island and houses Bahrain's airport. Few expatriates live in Muharraq, it being a predominantly local area, but there are a number of individual villas on the way out to Hidd. Things will change, however, as the Amwaj Islands become inhabited. The Amwaj Islands are to the north of Muharraq on fully reclaimed land. The project has been going on for some years and construction has now started on villas and apartment blocks. Amwaj is one of the few areas where expatriates can buy property and its proximity to the airport will be very attractive to airline industry workers and frequent travellers alike. There are plans for theme parks and golf courses on Amwaj and it could well become one of Bahrain's premier residential areas in a few years time. Most of the property has been sold but there are opportunities to buy new from the original investors, and to buy leases in some of the condominiums being constructed.

Manama Central   Map Ref → 4-B2

The centre of Manama, including the souk area, is home to many less well-off expatriates. There is a

Bahrain housing options

constant bustle in this area and you either love it or hate it. The properties, however, tend to be old and slightly run, down but with this comes lower prices. Along the corniche on the city side, there are a few apartment blocks which are relatively new but although offering great views, they have little in terms of facilities.

Seef/Sanabis   Map Ref → 3-E1/11-A4

Seef and Sanabis run either side of the main highway leading into Manama from Budaiya and Saudi Arabia. Sanabis is still a Bahraini village but the once empty land between it and the highway is now being filled with new luxury apartment blocks. Seef, with its shopping malls and commercial area is the Mayfair of Bahrain. There are a number of luxury apartment blocks and even a few individual villas, but prices are high in Seef, even higher than across the road in Sanabis. Both areas are also home to a number of prestigious serviced apartment blocks, and so are ideal if you are new to Bahrain and want to be close to the offices and malls of the area. Be warned however that despite the massive improvements in the road system around Seef and Sanabis over the last few years, the area comes to a stand still in the evenings and at weekends as the many tourists from Saudi Arabia soak up the pleasures of Bahrain's cinemas and malls.

Budaiya Highway   Map Ref → 3-A2
and Budaiya   4-B2/3-A2

Beyond Seef and going out to the 'country' is the Budaiya Highway. There are many compounds to be found on the side roads to this busy four lane highway. Many of these compounds are relatively old but tend to be well-maintained. This is Bahrain's green belt and if you are missing the greenery from home then this is where you should be. Many villas in the compounds in this area have quite extensive gardens and the common areas are full of mature trees. There are also several newer compounds in this area and so the prices vary quite considerably. You need to remember that you pay for the greenery, so you may find that an older villa in this area is more expensive than a comparable one in certain areas of Saar. Budaiya is right at the end of the Budaiya Highway and is a little local village, but there are compounds in all the villages up to Budaiya. If you are going to browse on your own, this area and Saar are the easiest to do without an agent, but you still might miss the real gems. There are supermarkets and schools in this area, making it a favourite amongst expatriate families.

Saar   Map Ref → 3-B4

Saar is in some ways Budaiya's overspill, but the compound area in Saar is now probably larger than that in Budaiya. Most of Bahrain's new compounds and individual villas are being built in Saar. There are still a number of older compounds in the area and so you should be able to find a villa that matches your budget. The area's proximity to the Saudi causeway has forced prices up considerably in the last few years though, as expatriates from Saudi have relocated their families here. Saar is home to the Dilmun Club, the Rugby Club, a cinema and good supermarkets. There are also a number of excellent schools in this area and the area vies with Budaiya as the senior expatriates' area of choice.

Hamad Town, Riffa,   Map Ref → 5 E4 (and
Isa Town and A'ali   Map 7)/6-A3/5-E1/5-D1

These areas are not heavily occupied by expatriates and although there are a few compounds, especially in A'ali and Riffa, as well as individual villas, the distance from the centre of town puts off most expatriates from living here. Consequently, the prices are considerably lower for exactly the same facilities as you would find in the more popular areas.

Awali   Map Ref → 8-A2

Awali is Bahrain's oil city of old and was once the place everyone wanted to go to, but as Bahrain's dependence on oil and expatriate oil workers has declined, so has Awali. It is still a unique place in Bahrain with well-trimmed hedges, many trees, and rows of identical houses. It is a bit of a trek to get anywhere from Awali (at least half an hour's drive), but if you want peace and quiet, it has a lot to offer. You hear birds in Awali rather than traffic, and the air seems somehow cleaner. It is still mainly reserved for BAPCO workers but some villas are rented externally. Awali Hospital is very popular with expatriate families and there is a thriving Junior School. The small commercial area boasts a supermarket, laundry and dry cleaners, a tailor and a travel agent. The BAPCO club has top-class facilties, including restaurants, sports facilities and a swimming pool. Full membership of the club is restricted to BAPCO employees and their families, but anyone can use the restaurants and coffee shop.

Durrat Al Bahrain   Map Ref → 1-C4

Durrat Al Bahrain is right at the south eastern tip of Bahrain. It is a set of reclaimed islands on which will be built some 4,000 homes and apartments. A major highway is being constructed to link the area to the rest of Bahrain. Expatriates can buy property here but there are many phases to be completed before the construction is finished. Prices look as though they are going to be high however, and may be beyond the reach of most expatriates; and then there's that half-hour drive (in reality more like one hour, by the time you have tackled the gridlocked nightmare of the Sitra causeway).

Other Rental Costs

All expatriates are required to pay a BD100 deposit for their electricity and telephone services. There is no getting around this, but you are given a certificate which you can redeem when you leave the country, and it is transferable from property to property. Generally other than electricity, water and telephone, the only further cost you should encounter is the ten percent Municipality tax which is levied on the rental value of your home. You pay this as part of your electricity bill which arrives monthly. You are advised to get your electricity bill addressed to your PO Box number, as otherwise you may come across the bills well after they are due lurking underneath a bougainvillea shrub in the garden having been thrown over the wall by a careless postman.

You should not be charged extra for the maintenance of your house, but some compounds require you to take on the services of a gardener. This will only be when you have a reasonably sized garden and the BD20 you might pay is well worth it considering the continuous work required to keep that beautiful lawn in pristine condition. You should never have to pay a search fee to an agent for showing you a house or apartment, and your agent should make this clear to you from the outset. However, if you sign a lease through an agent, you will have to pay a fee to them so make sure you know what this is before enlisting their services.

Purchasing a Home

Expatriates can now purchase both property and land in Bahrain. You are entitled to own the full freehold title, and ownership grants you and your spouse residency in Bahrain. However, you are only entitled to buy in certain areas, currently restricted to the new development areas of Amwaj, Bahrain Financial Harbour, Seef (with certain restrictions) and Durrat Al Bahrain. At the time of writing none of these areas have occupied

apartments or villas, but are nearing completion in certain parts of Amwaj.

The real estate market in Bahrain has exploded over the last five years, and because of its infancy, it really is too early to say whether investing in property in Bahrain makes sense. Certainly, early investors in Amwaj have made money already on their uncompleted houses, but what will happen to prices once all these new houses come on to the market is still unknown. The developers of each of the sites where expatriates are allowed to purchase property have their own sales offices dealing with sales and purchases.

Mortgages

Mortgages are a new entity in Bahrain and an even newer concept for expatriates. The developers of each of the sites allowing ownership to expatriates have set up relationships with individual banks, normally Islamic Banks, to offer mortgages on the properties they are selling. You will normally have to pay a fairly decent deposit (30%) before you are granted a mortgage, and then the amount available to you is a multiple of your monthly salary. The rates do not compare to the rest of the world so don't expect to have a range of mortgage offers.

Also be aware that many banks will only give mortgages to employees of certain respected companies, and the National Bank of Bahrain and HSBC only deal with Bahraini house purchasers. Things will begin to change as the property market matures, but at present you may be better advised to re-mortgage your property at home and pay for your Bahrain property in cash.

Other Purchasing Costs

The fees you need to pay in purchasing a house are at this stage individual to each development. Some of these have fixed service/maintenance charges. If you purchase through an agent rather than directly from the developer, you may be faced with a one percent fee, although this depends on whether the agent is acting for a reseller or for the developer directly.

Real Estate Law

At present you are only able to buy through one of the developers of the new residential areas in Bahrain. These companies have their own contracts relating to the sale and purchase of properties and land, and you are advised to appoint a lawyer to ensure that you are protected. This is especially important as these properties are mostly yet to be built. Individual properties in the unrestricted areas will come with freehold, which means that you own the title for the land the property occupies. Condominiums and apartment blocks are devising some form of stratum title allowing owners of condos and apartments to own a part of the freehold of their building. No such buildings have yet been completed in Bahrain, so how this will actually work is yet to be seen. It is not necessary to redraft your will when you purchase property, as your property will form part of your normal estate to be treated under the laws of your country of domicile.

Setting up Home

Moving Services

One of the delights of living in Bahrain is that you will never have to pack up your home. For a fee of BD100-300 you can obtain the services of one of many packing and moving companies based here. They will pack up your entire house, transport it to your new house (or pack it in a container if you are moving overseas), and then unpack it into your new house. These companies are real professionals and are very unlikely to break anything, but if you do have expensive items you should take out extra insurance to cover breakages, as this is not normally covered in your packing and moving fee. You should always make sure that you have a full inventory of items packed and the total number of boxes. The packing company will deal with all customs requirements on your behalf, if you are moving outside Bahrain. If you are coming to Bahrain, whoever is transporting your goods will have a clearing agent in the country who will contact you when your possessions have arrived, and they will take you to the customs office to clear them. Shipping your possessions is much cheaper

Removal Companies

Ahmadi Packing & Forwarding	1727 6199
Al Mulla Cargo	1729 2924
Allied Pickfords	1773 5355
Crown Relocations P.41	1722 7598
Gulf Agency Company P.63	1781 4500
Gulf Packing Company	1774 9040
Pic Pac International	1772 7332

than air freighting them and the service can be remarkably quick. Sea freight from the UK can take as little as three weeks, time you can be using to find your ideal home.

Furnishing Accommodation

Other options → Second-Hand Items [p.177]
Home Furnishings & Accessories [p.170]

Homes in Bahrain come fully furnished, semi-furnished or unfurnished. Most expats take a semi-furnished property unless they are in Bahrain for a short period. Semi-furnished means that you are provided with air conditioners, most kitchen white goods, and curtains. You don't actually get any furniture. Whether you get all the white goods you require will vary from landlord to landlord, but if you have to buy some of your own, you should expect a slightly lower rent. Make sure you know exactly what you get before you move in, and check that everything really works. It is surprising how many years some of these items keep on being repaired before they are eventually replaced.

Unfurnished means without the above features, while fully furnished should include absolutely everything you need to move into your new home. There are many furniture shops in Bahrain. Most of these are situated in Shaikh Salman Highway which leads from the Salmaniya roundabout (known as the Dairy Queen roundabout) to Isa Town. You should also look out for house sales advertised in the Gulf Daily News, but if you intend going to one, get there early as competition for second-hand furniture is intense. You will also find advertisements for second-hand furniture and household goods displayed on the notice boards of the main supermarkets, Jawads, Al Jazira and Al Osra in Adliya and Budaiya/Saar. Furniture allowances are rarely given in Bahrain, but when they are, you are normally given a fixed amount that will be amortised over two or three years. After this period you may have a second smaller allowance, again amortising over two or three years. If you leave before this period you will normally have to repay the cash value of the allowance you have received as unsurprisingly the banks that offer their top employees furniture allowances don't want the second hand furniture once they have left.

Once you are settled, you may find that your enormous new home requires a lot more furniture than you originally thought. You can get custom-made furniture in Bahrain which is often well priced and of good value. Word of mouth tends to be the

GAC Bahrain International Moving
Quality, Reliability, Flexibility

Relocation in itself is a challenge. And we believe that you already have enough to do without worrying about your forthcoming move. That's why when it comes to moving your home or office, GAC treats each item with care and every move with pride.

With more than 30 years of experience in moving household goods in and out of the Middle East, GAC provides comprehensive, high quality door-to-door services for any relocation need. Moves are professionally planned, starting with a free initial survey and recommendations on the most efficient shipment mode. All necessary services, including professional export packing, custom built crating, forwarding and secure storage facilities, are also provided.

 **www.gacworld.com**

GAC Bahrain   P O Box 412, Manama, Kingdom of Bahrain
Tel: +973-17-814 500   Fax: +973-17-827 928   Email: moving.bahrain@gacworld.com

way these small companies make their contacts, so ask your neighbours if they can recommend someone as companies often specialise in building furniture items for particular compound villa styles. For custom-built fitted wardrobes and bookshelves, contact Anthony on 3907 3152. He also makes furniture to order and his workmanship and prices are excellent. You should, however, give very clear instructions and diagrams of what you want, and supervise the work closely so as to nip errors in the bud and prevent them from blooming into disasters. For more functional, less fancy carpentry, try Ramesh on 3908 5202. He can provide you with a whole wall-full of sturdy built-in bookshelves (three metres high by four metres wide) for BD150, which includes wood, labour and finishing. Gulf Antiques in Adliya (1771 7700) advertises custom-made fake antique furniture, which sounds rather nasty and is probably expensive, though obviously not as expensive as real antiques.

For kitchen appliances, Géant, Al Moayyed Electronics and Rouben's Store near the Bab Al Bahrain, and Equinox in Exhibition Avenue, all stock a wide range of brands, including Phillips, Westpoint, Ignis, Philco, Hitachi and Toshiba. All offer reasonable prices, particularly at sales time. All deliver, but unless you live on one of the old established compounds you will have to draw a map for the delivery team. You can try to pin them down as to what time they will deliver, but they will invariably fail to stick to the agreed time, and will often have to phone you several times en route to get precise directions. As the driver is unlikely to have either good English, or a knowledge of the area where you live, this can try your patience to the utmost, but if you want your stuff delivered it's vital to remain calm. If all else fails, find out where the driver is, tell him to stay there and then drive out to find him and lead him back to your home.

Household Insurance

Unfortunately Bahrain is not as safe as it once was. Although security has been greatly enhanced in both compounds and apartment blocks you are advised to get some level of household insurance, although thefts are still considered rare. You should assess the level of cover you need, but be sure to list high value items separately and those which are easily transportable, such as DVD players, etc.

Household Insurance Companies

Al Ahlia Insurance	1722 5860
AXA Insurance P.81	1758 8222
Bahrain Kuwait Insurance	1754 2222
Bahrain National Insurance P.238	1758 7400
Gulf Union Insurance	1725 5292
Oryx Insurance Services	1723 2632
Protection Insurance Services	1721 1700

Laundry Services

There are numerous laundry and dry cleaning companies in Bahrain and in most residential areas in town they can be found on every other street. You can, as you would imagine, get clothes repaired, washed, ironed and dry cleaned at very good prices.

Domestic Help

Other options → Entry Visa [p.42]

One of the luxuries of living in Bahrain is the ready availability of excellent home help. Most expats resort to the services of at least a part-time housemaid. You have a choice at present in Bahrain either to hire directly through an agency, or to recruit locally from the large pool of people whose previous employers are leaving. If you want to recruit locally, look on the supermarket advertising boards or ask your neighbours if they know of anyone leaving who can recommend someone, as this is often the best method of getting someone reliable. It is also easier to recruit someone locally, as you will have the opportunity to interview them face to face. Agencies will give you large files full of potential maids, but you will find it difficult to choose and face what amounts to a lottery in making your selection.

If your maid comes from an agency, you will have to pay fees to the agent of about BD200, as well as the relevant costs for obtaining a work permit and for bringing your maid to Bahrain. The expected salary can be as low as BD50 per month, plus board and lodging. For this money, your maid

Domestic Help Agencies

Abha Manpower	1723 3983
Al Fahad Services & Manpower	1724 6664
Al Jabor Manpower Services	1727 4161
Al Shoala Public Relations	1726 4001
Jakarta Manpower Services	1771 5558
Mansoori Manpower	1726 2676
Tylos Manpower	1725 6664

should not have to pay for anything for herself as you should provide everything, including food, clothing, toiletries and lodging. If you recruit locally you will normally have to pay in excess of BD100 per month plus board and lodging, but will have the advantage of knowing that your maid knows Bahrain and probably has friends here. Of course this will increase her outgoings, which is one reason why you will have to pay more. You should be aware, however, that maids fresh out from India, Sri Lanka or the Philippines may suffer dreadfully from homesickness, particularly if they have left their children behind with their families at home, as is often the case. If you want to rely on part-time assistance you will find a ready source advertised in the local supermarkets. Placing an advertisement in the Gulf Daily News will also bring you a considerable response for both part-time and full-time positions. The going rate for hourly workers is BD1 per hour.

Babysitting & Childcare

Bahraini residents tend to use their housemaids or nannies to act as baby sitters. There are no other real options other than friends and families. There is no organised child minder system operating in Bahrain. You can look at the advertisements in the supermarkets around the country for staff who are looking for part-time work, or you might find that a neighbour has a live-in housemaid who you would be happy to use. As might be expected, it is difficult to assess the qualifications of most staff working in homes with children in Bahrain.

If you go to an agency you can normally find out whether they have worked with children before or whether they have children of their own. Often you will find out that the lists of CVs you are offered include people with high levels of qualifications but they may not be in child care. The agencies, however can recruit specialised staff for you if you want to have a properly trained child carer or nanny. Bahrain is a very child-friendly country but there are still very few public crèches in shopping centres or gyms. Many of the malls have a children's play area but these need supervision. Hotels do not normally provide a baby sitting service and so if you require this you must talk to the hotel management personally to try to arrange it, as it will not be a standard service. There are a large number of pre-schools and kindergartens but these tend to open in the mornings only.

Domestic Services

You will find that the maintenance office of your landlord should cover most of your urgent requirements. If you want something specially done then you should probably still speak to your landlord's maintenance team, as they will be the best people to put you in touch with a specialist. If you are still stuck, then have a look at the classified ads in the Gulf Daily News. Under Services, you will find plumbers, carpet shampooers, swimming pool and building maintenance companies, pest control services, electricians, TV antenna and satellite dish erectors, washing machine repairers, etc. In the Yellow Pages there are all of the above, plus furniture designers and custom builders, furniture manufacturers, upholsterers and second-hand furniture shops.

Pets

If you have all of the right certificates and vaccinations, bringing your pet to Bahrain is relatively simple. Bahrain has signed up to the PETS scheme, allowing micro-chipped and vaccinated pets to travel between member countries without being quarantined, so well before you want to leave you should visit your own vet to enrol your pet in the scheme. This will involve your pet having a microchip implanted beneath its skin, a vaccination against rabies and other up-to-date vaccinations. There is also a requirement for a blood test to demonstrate that the animal is not infected with rabies. Once the certificate is issued, it is normally valid for up to six months. With your certificate and vaccination records you can either contact a reputable vet in Bahrain or approach the Government vet directly. Dr Aziri, the government vet, can be contacted on 1764 3373. He will be able to provide you with an import licence, which you will need before embarking from your country of residence. He will also be able to confirm that your pet is suitable for bringing to Bahrain.

The process operates in the reverse for leaving to another PETS registered country, but you should check out the exact requirements for your particular country. A good website to visit is www.defra.gov.uk/animalh/quarantine. You will also need an export certificate and again the government vet should be contacted for this. You should also check well in advance with your airline, as some airlines will not take pets on board. There are a few good boarding kennels in Bahrain which are not cheap, but at least you can be assured your faithful friends are being well cared for.

Pets Boarding/Sitting

Dr Nonie Coutts	Adliya branch	1724 5515
(Kennels, Cattery & Vet)	Saar branch	1769 1397
Saar Kennels		1779 2064

There are a surprising number of cats and dogs kept as pets in Bahrain. Bahrainis tend not to have dogs in the house, but cats are quite popular. Unfortunately too many people have left Bahrain without caring what became of their pets and there are now quite a large number of strays, so you are advised to make sure your pets wear a collar with your details attached. Many landlords will have restrictions on pets so make sure you check this out before you sign your lease. Exercising your dogs is best done along one of Bahrain's waterfronts. In town the corniche around the Diplomatic area is good for a walk and in Budaiya and Duraz there are beach fronts where you can walk. The limited parks in Bahrain are not really ideal places to take your dogs as they are designed for children to play in. You will also find that many local people and Asians are literally terrified of dogs. If workmen come to your house and hear your dog barking, may refuse to set foot through the gate until you have managed to reassure them that the dog is safely locked in a room and can't get at them.

Animal Rescue

The BSPCA is a local charity which faces the daunting task of looking after Bahrain's unwanted pets. You should visit the kennels in Saar if you are thinking of getting a dog or cat. They often have puppies and kittens, as well as well-loved older animals whose owners couldn't take them home with them when they left Bahrain. The centre relies entirely on donations and volunteers to carry out its excellent work. They also have a thrift shop off Budaiya Road where you can donate goods to be sold. The BSPCA can be contacted on 1759 1231. If you are leaving Bahrain and simply cannot, for whatever reason, take you

Veterinary Clinics

Dr Nonie Coutts	Adliya branch	1724 5515
	Saar branch	1769 1397
Modern Animal Health Centre		1759 0908
The Veterinary Services Establishment		1769 2975

pet home with you, the BSPCA will normally accept your pet and try to rehouse him. A contribution to his upkeep will enable the centre to hold your pet for longer if they are unable to find him a home at once.

Utilities & Services

Electricity & Water

The electricity and water supplies in Bahrain are controlled by the Ministry of Electricity & Water. Once you move into your new home your landlord should arrange for your electricity and water to be connected in your name. However, you may need to do this for yourself. If this is the case, arm yourself with your CPR card, several photos just in case, and a copy of your rental agreement, and take this to one of the Ministry's offices. The easiest one to go to is next to the old Bahrain Chamber of Commerce Building and the National Bank of Bahrain Tower, just off Government Avenue. You can park either in the main Bab Al Bahrain car park or alternatively, you can go to the Investors' Centre in the Seef Mall. You need to go to the back suite of offices and there you will find a Ministry of Electricity & Water desk. Make sure that you have the exact address on your lease agreement. If in doubt ask your landlord for an address card.

As an expatriate you will be required to make a BD100 deposit to have your supply connected, but once you have done this you should be connected very quickly. The BD100 is refundable when you cancel your supply. If you move, you can transfer the deposit over to your new residence. The electricity supply in Bahrain is 220/240volts and the sockets are identical to the three point British system, although any appliance you buy here is almost guaranteed to come with a two point plug. Adaptors are easy to come by in the local supermarkets. Your bill will vary tremendously depending on the season and how cool you like your home to be. If you have a large villa and like to keep your garden green, expect to pay over BD100 a month in water and electricity charges. There is a stepped scale to the charges, so the more you use the more expensive the rate.

Be aware that water can be more expensive than electricity, and with water being a scarce resource you may find you are visited by a Ministry official if your usage is deemed excessive. You are not advised to drink the tap water unless you live in Awali, but water bottled in five gallon containers are easily available from supermarkets, and once you are settled you can have these delivered weekly to your house. Aquacool (1778 4101) make regular deliveries and charge BD1 for five gallons of water. You have to pay a small deposit for the first set of containers they supply, and then put the empties out every week in exchange for full bottles. You can also buy books of BD1 coupons from them to stick in the neck of each empty bottle, so that you don't have to get up at the crack of dawn to pay the delivery man. Many people invest in a water cooler which dispenses water directly from these five gallon bottles.

Tune It Up or Turn It Down?

If you think that your electricity charge is high, investigate whether your air conditioners have been serviced recently, as old air conditioners are very inefficient. Alternatively just turn down the A/C when you go to the office.

Sewerage

Sewerage should be dealt with by your landlord. The central areas of town all have mains sewers. In some of the compounds out towards Budaiya separate septic tanks are still used but these should be emptied and dealt with by your landlord. If you rent a newly-built individual villa in a new residential area, you may have to wait several years before the approach road is laid down with tarmac, and the mains sewerage connected.

Gas

There is no mains gas in Bahrain unless you live in Awali. Instead, several companies supply bottled gas which is used for heating water and cooking. Electric cookers are for some reason rare in Bahrain, so make sure you check that the gas cooker supplied by your landlord is in good working order, as these are often veteran appliances. The gas bottles can be delivered to your house and cost only a few dinars. Bahrain Gas charges a deposit of BD30 for the gas bottle, and BD3 for refilling it. Nader Gas has similar charges. Both will come out to deliver gas at short notice in an emergency, but you need to check the office opening hours to be sure of being able to contact them.

Rubbish Disposal and Recycling

The rubbish collection system is similar to that in mainland Europe. There are large bins on street corners to which you must take your rubbish. These bins are emptied regularly by an independent contractor which operates the rubbish disposal and street cleaning system in Bahrain. If you wish to recycle some of your rubbish, take it to one of the main supermarkets in Bahrain which have recycling drop-off bins. These are available at Jawads and Al Osra in Budaiya/Saar. Dumping has long been a problem in Bahrain, and many sites that look like official landfill sites are in fact illegal dumping areas, so make sure you use a legal site. Normally your landlord can arrange to have large amounts of waste collected for you.

Telephone

Bahrain's landline telephone network is run by Batelco, which is effectively a government monopoly but is listed on the Bahrain Stock Exchange. Getting a new line has become much simpler in recent years with Batelco at last beginning to understand the meaning of customer service. There are a number of service centres you can visit to get your phone connected. The easiest two are situated in the GOSI complex off Exhibition Road or the Bahrain Commercial Centre in between the Bab Al Bahrain Souk and the municipal car park. These centres can deal with all your requests. There are also a growing number of smaller Batelco shops where you can get all kinds of services. These are situated in most of Bahrain's malls and residential areas, including Seef Mall, Bahrain Mall and Alawi Mall. The Malls tend to be open all day, as are the GOSI centre and the Bahrain Commercial Centre. You can also call Batelco on 1788 1881, or visit their website at www.batelco.com.bh.

Local calls are not free in Bahrain but they are not expensive. 21 fils gets you three minutes of local calls to a fixed line call and one and a half minutes to a mobile. Off peak hours for international calls are from 19:00 to 07:00. There are no off peak hours for local calls. When your phone is connected, you will have to pay an installation charge of BD20 and a line charge of BD1.160 per month. As an expatriate you will also be required to make a BD100 deposit for international calls. This is refundable once you leave Bahrain or cancel your phone line. Batelco now offers all the standard telephone features you would expect including Caller ID, SMS, faxmail and call forwarding.

Mobile Telephones

When it comes to your mobile phone you have a few more choices. Firstly there are two suppliers, Batelco and MTC Vodafone, and secondly you can chose pre-paid or post-paid. As expected, the rates on these services continue to change as the two suppliers become more competitive. Both have shops in all the malls, the airport and in most of the residential districts, so you can easily pick up their latest leaflet offering a range of different post- and pre-pay options and make your choice. The pre-paid option is called using a SimSim card in Bahrain, as opposed to using a Sim card for post-paid.

Getting a pre-paid SimSim card and number is very easy and can be done in minutes. It is available to non-residents and only requires you to bring your passport or CPR card. Again, the rates change frequently for this service, but you can often get started for as little as BD10, including a certain amount of call credits. Call charges for mobiles tend to vary according to which package you have chosen and the peak hours can also change according to your package. If you are a heavy user you can pay a higher fixed charge every month, and receive lower call charges and a higher free call number of units. These packages change relatively often however, so you should keep an eye open for the latest offers.

Mobile Phone Providers		
Batelco P.IFC P.v P.69		1788 7022
MTC Vodafone P.31 IBC		1758 8118

Internet

Other options → Internet Cafes [p.226]
Websites [p.34]

Batelco is currently the only residential supplier of internet services in Bahrain. A number of new companies have recently obtained licences and are expected to start offering services during 2006, but as yet none have given a definite time for when operations will commence. Getting connected to the internet with Batelco involves the same process as getting your phone line connected. Any of their offices can take your subscription for the internet, but the easiest are GOSI Centre off Exhibition Road

or the Bahrain Commercial Centre in between the Bab Al Bahrain Souk and the municipal car park. There you have the full range of Batelco's services under one roof.

Options vary from straightforward dial up, with a BD5 set-up fee and a BD3 monthly charge, to the unlimited use broadband at a BD10 set-up fee and a BD30 monthly charge. Note that if you are in an apartment your charges will increase to BD50 for the monthly charge for unlimited broadband. There are levels of access in between these two and Batelco now supplies a reasonable summary of these options on its website, www.batelco.com.bh, or call 1788 1881 for more information. You do however have to register with Batelco to obtain internet access and there is no straight dial and surf option available.

There are many Internet Cafes around Bahrain, from coffee shops to specialised computer shops. Many can be found in Adliya, or try Cinnabons in the Diplomatic area. Hotels are beginning to offer WiFi services but these are not yet common. Internet charges are normally about BD1 per hour.

Bill Payment

You will be sent your phone bill every month and will have a grace period of a week in which to pay. If you are late in paying you will be repeatedly reminded by telephone. There are many ways to pay. You can go to any Batelco or MTC Vodafone shop, pay through your bank's ATM machine, or by phone with a credit card, and if your bank offers telephone banking, you can pay directly using this service. The easiest way for Batelco users is to use one of their automated pay machines which are springing up around the country. Here you just type in your phone number, swipe your credit card, and it's done. You can also check your balance and buy SimSim pre-pay cards through this machine. The Batelco shops have these machines and they are also found in supermarkets and malls. Both Batelco and MTC Vodafone have automated bill inquiry services which you can access by dialling customer services: Batelco: 1788 1111; MTC Vodafone: 3610 7107.

Postal Services

Other options → Post & Courier Services [p.30]

There is a postal service in Bahrain and for international mail it is very good, but virtually everyone in Bahrain gets a PO Box as the home

delivery system may often result in you finding those important documents lurking under the bougainvillea in your garden, weeks after they arrived. Getting a PO Box is a very simple business. Just go to your most convenient post office (there is also one in the Bahrain Mall) with your CPR card. The process is immediate and the annual cost is just BD13. You will receive two keys for your box and you are able to check it at any time the post office is open, and most post offices have boxes which are accessible even when the post office is closed. Most expatriates rely on their mail being delivered to their place of work, using their company PO Box, but check with your company that this is acceptable before you distribute its PO Box to your family and friends.

If you are sending gifts home you may find it cheaper and more secure to use one of the many courier companies in Bahrain such as DHL or FEDEX. Alternatively you can take out insurance, or register the package you are sending.

The Postal Directorate comes under the jurisdiction of the Ministry of Transportation, and the switchboard number is 1753 4534. There is a registered local and international delivery service known as Barid Mumtaz, which is supposed to be an express service, but there are frequent letters of complaint in the GDN about late delivery.

Television

There are many TV channels available in Bahrain. However, there are only a couple of local channels, both of which start broadcasting in mid-afternoon. They are probably not the most frequented channels and most expatriates pick up one of the many satellite deals available. The local channels are Bahrain 55 and Channel 38. Both broadcast programmes in Arabic and English.

Satellite TV & Radio

There are a number of satellite TV options available in Bahrain. The most popular are FirstNet, Orbit and Showtime, which mainly show British and American entertainment, Pehla which is aimed at an Indian audience and Al Awael for Arabic channels. The cable network Bahrain Radio & Television also offers various TV packages. It is possible to get the DSTV channels from South Africa, but this is rather expensive unless you really must have those six sports channels. The packages of programmes vary from company to

company and you can choose different packages from the same provider depending on whether you want news, films, sport , dramas or soap operas. Choosing the sports channels tends to push the cost up but most bars show the premier sports action. If you enrol in any of the satellite packages you should be able to obtain a decoder and dish for free as long as you stay with the satellite provider for a fixed period. As you would expect, these deals come and go and so you should check out all the companies offering satellite services before making your final choice.

> **Back to Reality**
>
> *If you're a reality TV junkie then you will love Star World, available on FirstNet. From American Idol to The Simple Life and For Love or Money to The Apprentice you can expect to get your fill of cliff-hanger, nail biting reality drama. The good news is the sport on ART, also on Firstnet, has excellent coverage of the football to keep him in-doors happy too!*

The available radio channels are a little disappointing if you are looking for British Radio; you can only get it on short wave. Music channels are aplenty, however, and remember that you can get most radio channels through the internet if you have a fast enough connection. You may find that your property is unsuitable for a satellite dish without some reinforcement being made. This will normally be at your own cost but landlords generally have no problems with satellite dishes being erected.

It is best to do your homework before you choose your satellite provider as they all offer different channels, which can be annoying – you may well end up with three satellite dishes on your roof!

Pehla, FirstNet, Al Awael and Showtime are available from Satlink Limited, while Pehla, FirstNet, Al Awael, Showtime and Orbit are also available from Al Mufeed. The Bahrain Radio & TV package is a cable network which includes a selection of programmes from all the satellite networks, installation of equipment for an initial fee of BD 18.500 and a monthly payment of BD 13.500.

The Gulf Daily News classified ads section is also currently advertising French, Italian, German, Turkish, Greek, Chinese and European TV channels for BD 65, but the company name isn't given.

Satellite/Cable Providers

Satellite/Cable Providers	
Al Mufeed	1771 2571
Bahrain Radio & TV	1768 1777
Satlink Limited	1771 3333

General Medical Care

The general level of health care in Bahrain is good. Of course many expatriates prefer private hospitals to the public hospitals, but in a real emergency you are advised to go to the country's largest government-run hospital, Salmaniya, which has all the services you would expect of a top hospital. Your problem as a non-Arabic speaker will be getting yourself understood in an emergency, although most hospital staff speak English. Private hospitals used most often by expatriates are Awali Hospital, International Hospital of Bahrain, American Mission Hospital (AMH), the Bahrain Defence Force Hospital (BDF) or Bahrain Specialist Hospital. They all have GP services that expats can use.

The public hospitals can be used by expatriates and locals alike, but you must make sure that you have your CPR card with you. Although of course the public hospitals should treat you immediately, there have been stories of delays when expatriates did not have their CPR cards with them. Whether these are true or not, it is another good reason why you should always have your CPR card, or at least a copy of it, with you at all times.

You should, as an expatriate, try to take out personal medical insurance. Your employer may provide this, but it is by no means standard in Bahrain. Having medical insurance enables you to have treatment at the hospital of your choice, but should also allow you to be treated outside the country if your condition is serious. There are many international companies you can get cover from, as well as well-respected local companies.

American Mission Hospital

Government Hospitals

East Riffa Maternity Hospital	1777 1258
Geriatric Hospital	1732 0969
Jidhafs Maternity Hospital	1755 0022
Muharraq Maternity Hospital	1732 2911
Psychiatric Hospital	1728 8888
Salmaniya Hospital	1725 5555
Sitra Maternity Hospital	1773 0758
Western Region Maternity Hospital	1763 1627

Private Hospitals

American Mission Hospital	1725 3447
Awali Hospital	1775 3333
Bahrain Defence Force Hospital	1776 6666
Bahrain Specialist Hospital	1781 2000
Dr Tariq Hospital	1782 2822
Ibn Al Nafees Hospital	1782 8282
International Hospital	1759 8222
Noor Specialist Hospital	1726 0026

There are many pharmacies that open 24 hours a day. Some work on a rota system, with those open on any particular day listed in the GDN, while some others are also open 24 hours a day, every day, and are also listed in the GDN. Most pharmacies can give you basic medicines for colds, etc. If you go to a hospital to visit a GP, which is normal for expatriates here, the hospital usually has its own pharmacy, making it easier for you to reclaim your expenses if you are covered by insurance.

Government Health Centres/Clinics

A'ali	1764 0323
Al Hoora	1729 0611
Al Razi	1725 8801
Bilad Alqadim	1740 3392
Budaiya	1769 5697
Dair	1733 2021
East Riffa	1777 0422
Hamad Kanoo	1777 0181
Hamad Town	1741 2343
Ibn Sina	1753 5220
Isa Town	1762 5400
Jau & Askar	1784 0261
Jidhafs	1755 3932
Muharraq	1732 0039
Naim	1727 4362
Sitra	1773 1753

Private Health Centres/Clinics

American Mission Hospital	1725 3447
Awali Hospital	1775 3333
Bahrain Defence Force Hospital	1776 6666
Bahrain Specialist Hospital	1781 2000
International Hospital	1759 8222

Residents

Health

In an emergency, call 999 for an ambulance. You need to decide which hospital to go to. Often you are best served by going to the hospital you are used to, but remember some of the smaller private hospitals have a very restricted A&E department during the night, so if your condition is serious you should probably go to Salmaniya Hospital in Manama.

Dermatologists

Al Arrayed Khalil Clinic	1727 2323
Al Matrook Samira	1772 0110
Ghalia Dawaigher Clinic	1727 0911
Mahmood Al Fadhil	1723 0240

Maternity

Other options → **Maternity Items [p.173]**

Many expats give birth in Bahrain, although some prefer to go back home to be near their families, or to see a particular doctor/hospital. From a safety or comfort point of view however, Bahrain offers a range of hospitals which are all perfectly acceptable. In fact many expats choose to stay in Bahrain so as not to uproot their older children from school/friends, retain the domestic help which they gladly use, and fly their families over from home, which ends up being a cheaper and more comfortable experience. The only time when it is definitely preferable to have your baby in your home country is when its nationality may be at risk from your giving birth abroad. For example, if you were born outside your home country it may preclude your child from getting your nationality. If you are in doubt, check with your embassy about nationality laws.

If you decide to have a baby in Bahrain, the first thing to do is to find a doctor and hospital that you feel comfortable with. The state hospitals (Salmaniya and BDF) are well-equipped and a good choice if you think that you may have a difficult birth, or you are concerned about emergency procedures. However, the private hospitals are often more comfortable. Each one has its own culture, so you need to visit them and ask around, to make up your mind as to which is best for you. All hospitals offer pain relief, including epidurals, although you will find some doctors or midwives more pro-natural birth than others; good to keep in mind when making your enquiries. The American Mission Hospital offers water births, but home births are not usual in Bahrain any more.

Private hospitals allow husbands or birthing partners into the delivery room with the mother,

Maternity Hospitals & Clinics

American Mission Hospital *Private*	1725 3447
Awali Hospital *Private*	1775 3333
Bahrain Defence Force Hospital *Private*	1776 6666
Bahrain Specialist Hospital *Private*	1781 2000
Dr Tariq Hospital *Private*	1782 2822
Ibn Al Nafees *Private*	1782 8828
International Hospital *Private*	1759 8222
Noor Specialist Hospital *Private*	1726 0026
Salmaniya Hospital *Government*	1725 5555

provided that the labour is proceeding normally. This applies for caesarian sections too, unless its an emergency C-section where the mother has to go under general anaesthetic. The state hospitals, however, do not allow husbands or families in the delivery room, although they are welcome in the maternity ward.

The cost of maternity and delivery in Bahrain varies, so check around to see what is offered by the different hospitals. Most private hospitals have ante-natal and delivery packages, but note that there are often some hidden costs. For example, few packages cover consultations before 12 weeks, and pain relief is usually charged separately, as are costs for the baby, once born. Most expatriates are either on health insurance packages or have their medical costs covered by their employers. However, although most health insurance packages cover maternity services, some have a qualification period of up to a year and many do not cover the full cost of delivery, particularly C-section deliveries.

Sheikh Isa Bin Salman Causeway

Gynaecology & Obstetrics

Afaf Al Hamer	1753 3555
Bahrain Gynaecology & Infertility Ctr	1723 2444
Fekria Mustafa	1727 9619
Rajab Khalil Ebrahim	1772 9408

Paediatrics

All the main hospitals, both private and Salmaniya, have resident paediatricians. It is a case of personal choice at the end of the day. Ask your friends who they recommend. Generally, these services are very good in Bahrain and people actively come here because of the ease of dealing with child issues! Your visits should be covered by your medical insurance, but be aware that conditions arising in the first twelve days from birth are generally considered maternity issues and if you are not covered for maternity costs your child may not be covered in its first twelve days, so check your policy carefully. The list below contains those paediatricians who have their own surgeries or clinics outside of these hospitals.

Paediatrics

Abdulnabi Abdulla Hussain Alsaif	1726 1333
Ahmad Mahmood A Rahim	1733 0360
Al Shefaa Paediatric Specialist Centre	1725 3111
Ali Mansoor	1733 2390
Bastaki Mohammad Abdulla	1777 7990
Ebrahim Khan	1726 3223
Mohammad Alsaee	1724 6246
Mohammad Najeeb Samiei	1772 0523
Nadia Shirawi	1725 0124
Nageh Al Bagali	1778 2887
Saheera Mohammad Al Durazi	1759 1819
Yousif Akbar Jawad	1771 5515

Dentists/Orthodontists

There are many dentists in Bahrain, and if you are used to paying the high dentist's charges in the west, it is an ideal place to get that treatment you have been putting off. Unlike other medical treatment, expatriates seem to be happy to use the smaller clinics for dentistry, although all the main private hospitals have excellent services and facilities as well. Cosmetic dentistry is also available in Bahrain and generally the service and treatment is considered to be excellent.

Dental Clinics

Al Re'aya Medical Complex	1723 0008
Al-Alawi Dental Centre	1725 5657
American Mission Hospital	1725 3447
Dr Ebtisam Al Dallal	1724 6500
Dr Munem Haffadh	1731 1180
Gulf Dental Speciality Hospital	1774 1444
Hamad Town Dental Clinic	1741 0400
Manama Dental Clinic	1754 0101

Opticians

Opticians are plentiful in Bahrain and can be found in malls, hospitals and clinics right across the country. Prescription lenses, sunglasses and contact lenses are all easily available. You do not need an eye test to get a driving licence, except at the Licensing department itself. But remember that if you need glasses to read the number they give you, make sure you are wearing them in the photos you take with you. You also have an eye test when you have your medical shortly after arrival in Bahrain, so make sure you are wearing your glasses or lenses for that too. Laser treatment can be obtained at many of the hospitals and clinics, but you are advised to ask around before you make your decision about where to go.

Opticians

Al Noor Opticals	1721 2153
Al Razi Optical Centre	1726 3763
Al Wazzan Ahmad Abdulaziz	1722 8989
Arabian Opticals	1725 5575
Bahrain Optician	1754 0522
Buhijji Optics	1721 6406
Delmon Optics	1729 4898
Ehsan Optics	1721 3478
New Optical House	1721 3085
Palace Optics	1728 0933
Perfect Eye Optician	1755 4341
Yateem Optician	1725 3397
You Will See Optical	1731 1913

Hairdressers

Hairdressers abound in Bahrain. You can get a 500 fil cut or a BD20 cut, and everything in between. Most of the top hotels have their own barbers and hairdressers. If you ask around you may be able to find stylists who can come to your home, or work from home. Prices do not necessarily determine the quality of your cut, but even at the five star hotels prices start at below BD5 for men, more for ladies. Out in the streets, men can get a decent enough cut even cheaper at a barbers for BD1 or less. Treatments and colouring at the hotels tend to be more expensive, so a number of people get the haircut in one location, and have their highlights put in somewhere else.

Hairdressers

Al Anaqa Salon	1733 4486
Ann Beaty Salon	1768 1952
Black & White Salon	1727 6777
Cartel Salon Ladies	1772 8990
Classic	1725 4632
Dunya Salon Ladies	1729 2344
Four Seasons Ladies	1723 2667
Green Salon	1771 5350
Gulf Hotel	1771 3000
Hair Club	1772 7121
Iqbal's Gents Salon	1771 0800
Jedayel Beauty Salon Ladies	1729 4008
Ladies Corner Salon	1777 5106
Le Soleil Salon Ladies	1772 3757
Majestic Men's Salon	1725 0909
Mexico Salon	1771 4771
Mona Liza Ladies	1771 2203
New Dinars Salon	1725 7546
Novel Beauty Salon	1779 1222
Prestige Gent's Salon	1771 5717
Rainbow	1727 1052
Scissors Salon Ladies	1725 9629
Sheba Beauty Salon	1774 2992
Style Beauty Salon	1727 1516
Valentino	1722 6043

Cosmetic Treatment & Surgery

There is only one hospital offering cosmetic surgery in Bahrain listed in the Yellow Pages. People generally leave the country to have more obvious and serious operations done, like nose jobs and tummy tucks, probably more from a vanity perspective so people don't see them while they are recovering, than from a safety point of view. Cosmetic surgery can be obtained in India for a fraction of the cost of a comparable operation in the west, but there have been the occasional horror stories of people waking up one kidney short.

Alternative Therapies

Alternative therapies are becoming increasingly popular here in Bahrain. The major beauty salons and spas, such as the Ritz Carlton and Jacque Dessange, are probably the most popular with the western expat community. Most alternative therapies are on offer, sometimes for extremely high prices. Choose from aromatherapy, rebalancing, thalassotherapy, body polishing, salt scrub, body wrapping, slender wraps, invigorating Oshadi envelopment, restorative mud envelopment, detoxifying with seaweed algae, hot stone massage, Ayurvedic treatments and skin hydrating. The Ritz Carlton even offers special spa packages for couples who cannot bear to be away from each other. The usual beauty salon treatments are also available including tanning, wax treatments and massage from all corners of the world, including Bali, Sweden and Thailand. Reflexology is a growing interest here and is offered at some of the bigger salons. Check the local supermarket notice boards and you may be lucky enough to find someone to manipulate your feet in the comfort of your own home. Even smaller pokey-looking beauty salons offer massage, usually at excellent prices.

Alternative Therapies

Bahrain Wellness Resort	1779 5962
Bahrain Meditation Centre	1771 2545
Betsy's Day Spa	1772 0026
Bodyline Spa	1779 3932
Jacques Dessange	1771 3999
The Ritz-Carlton	1758 0000

Back Treatment

The Physiotherapy Centre (09:00 to 20:00) behind Tropicana Motel (1772 2012) charges BD50 for a course of 6 sessions or BD 10 per session. This includes examination by an osteopath, treatment by a physiotherapist and massage.

At Bahrain Wellness Resort (1779 5961), the Spinal Care Course includes diagnosis, herbal medicine, massage and exercise. Courses of daily sessions last for one, two or three weeks, depending upon the severity of the problem, and charges vary according to the treatment prescribed. As an example of the Resort's charges, a one-hour full body Ayurvedic massage, including head and face, followed by a 15-minute session in a steam chamber, costs BD12.

Rehabilitation & Physiotherapy

For treatment after injury, the government and private hospitals all have their own physiotherapy departments. There are also several private establishments offering courses of treatment, including some of the spas which offer Alternative Therapies listed above.

Rehabilitation & Physiotherapy

Bahrain Physiotherapy Centre	1762 1818
Bahrain Sports Medicine Association	1771 6889
Physical Therapy & Rehab Centre	1725 2004
Specialized Physiotherapy Complex	1723 1000
Sports Medicine Centre	1768 1101
The Modern Physiotherapy Centre	1777 3399
The Physiotherapy Centre	1772 2012

Counselling & Therapy

In addition to the Psychiatric Hospital located at the government-run Salmaniya Hospital, the main private hospitals, such as the American Mission Hospital and the International Hospital of Bahrain, have psychiatric clinics. There are also two private psychiatrists with their own clinics.

Counsellors/Psychologists	
American Mission Hospital	1725 3447
Dr Abdulsalam Hamza Khashaba (Psychiatric Clinic)	1727 0221
Dr Shubbar Al Qaheri Clinic	1772 2265
International Hospital of Bahrain	1759 2222
Salmaniya Hospital	1725 5555

Support Groups

There are several support organizations in Bahrain, many of which cater mainly for the large Asian expat community. As well as the churches, such as the Sacred Heart Church and St Christopher's Cathedral, there are the AA and Alanon, which meet every day, the Be-Free Anti Child Abuse and Neglect Project, The Indian Ladies Association (ILA), the Interdenominational Women's Fellowship, the American Women's Association (AWA) and Tots and Toddlers at the British Club.

The Migrant Workers' Protection Society (MPWS) is always looking for volunteer helpers and fund-raisers. They have recently raised enough money to open a shelter for runaway housemaids who have left their employers because of alleged physical or sexual abuse. For more information, contact Marietta on 3945 2470, Florina on 3913 4027, Mehroo on 1724 2563 or Manijeh on 3984 7953.

A 24-hour telephone helpline, something along the lines of the Samaritans in the UK, is operated by a group of ladies, most of whom are members of the ILA. They currently have 22 volunteers speaking English, more than 10 regional Indian languages, Urdu, Sinhalese and Tagalog. 40% of their calls relate to labour and immigration issues, 21% to medical and psychological problems, 28% marital and domestic problems and eight percent concern parental issues. They listen to callers' problems and help them to find their own solutions, and can also refer callers with specific problems to people such as medical and legal professionals, embassies and other relevant authorities. 90% of their callers are Asian, with Indians being the largest group, but they also have calls from Filipinos, Sri Lankans, Pakistanis, Bangladeshis and other Asians, and occasionally from Americans, British and other European nationalities. For more information contact 3987 3357, 3965 6410 or 3987 0815. You can also email helplinebah@yahoo.com, and all correspondence is kept strictly confidential.

Education

For expatriate,s education in Bahrain can be expensive as they cannot attend the public schools. That said, the private schools in Bahrain are first class with students from all nationalities often getting top awards back in their home countries. One thing you must do once you know you are coming to Bahrain is to get your child registered, as a number of schools fill up very early and you may find that you are on a waiting list for some time. If you arrive half way through a school year there will almost certainly be a school you will be happy with even though it may not be your first choice. Just make sure you register for the next year as soon as possible. The situation has been aggravated in recent years with the influx of expatriate families from Saudi's eastern province relocating their families to Bahrain. The schools have responded and many are undergoing expansion plans to deal with the additional numbers.

There is a wide range of schools in Bahrain dealing with most curriculums. These include British, American, Pakistani, Indian, French, Philippine and Bangladeshi. There is no concept of catchment areas in Bahrain, although if you are going to rely on a school bus you should check out the routes they operate on.

Generally, your chosen private schools in Bahrain will follow the curriculum that your child would otherwise follow at home. The British curriculum schools follow GCSEs and A levels and the American schools follow an American High School Certificate. Your child's schooling therefore should be comparable to what they would be doing in your home country and so of course they can, to a certain degree, slot back into the home system should you leave. If you do have to move back to your home country, or on to another country, make sure you get a report and introduction letter from your child's school as this can assist in getting them into school straight away even if it is during a term.

The schools in Bahrain all operate on the Saturday to Wednesday timetable which can cause problems as most international businesses operate from Sunday to Thursday. Term timetables tend to be very similar to the country whose curriculum is being followed.

Pre-school

Nurseries & Pre-Schools

There are many nurseries, kindergartens and pre schools in Bahrain; the difficulty is in choosing one that is right for your child. Many nurseries take children from as young as 15 months, and your child's ability to use the bathroom is not considered to be an issue here. You can choose from English only, Arabic only, or a combination of both languages of instruction for your little one. In the same way, you can choose one or two mornings a week, or full time from 8am to 12pm, depending on your needs.

Waiting lists for some of the more popular schools are a sure thing, so as soon as you see that little blue line on the pregnancy testing kit, it is advisable to put your name down for a place. This simple request can often cost up to BD30 and is often non-refundable. Nevertheless, it is the only way to go if you want a place for your toddler at the more

popular schools, especially in the Budaiya area. As with many other issues, your personal choice of nursery may not suit someone else, and although asking around is a good way to get information, a visit to the pre-school during school hours is the best way to go. Five days a week, 08:00 to 12:00, can cost up to BD450+ per term. There are a number of schools where it is rumoured that the 'teachers' are not qualified. Expat mothers tend to be recruited for these schools. Of course some of these ladies can be excellent teachers, but do make sure you know exactly who will be looking after your children before you sign up. Although all the schools are registered and monitored by the Ministry of Education, some schools may still try to save on their costs by recruiting this way. Some nurseries offer drop-off facilities if you really have no other cover, but you may be better borrowing a neighbour's nanny if this is the case.

Nurseries & Pre-Schools

Al Dana Nursey	Salmaniya	1777 0423
Al Emam Bin Mohammad Saood Kindergarten	East Riffa	1733 6624
Al Falah School	Muharraq	1772 2144
Al Fateh English Pre School	Gudaibayah	1764 4336
Al Maaly Gate Pre School	Sitra	1740 5433
Al Majid Private School	Bilad Al Qadim	1741 2744
Al Nasseria School	Hamad Town	1773 6773
Al Noor International School	Sitra	1772 0527
All Kids Kindergarten	Mahooz	1725 7745
Bangladesh School	Salmaniya	1779 1491
Budaiya Pre School	Budaiya	1771 0720
Creativity Model Pre School	Adliya	1771 3483
Dilmun School	Adliya	1725 1124
Gulf Kindergarten	Salmaniya	1724 1193
Hala Kindergarten	Salmaniya	1777 4504
Happy Childhood Kindergarten	East Riffa	1769 4947
Lilliput	Budaiya	1769 4356

Residents

Education

Primary & Secondary Schools

The private primary and secondary schools in Bahrain are generally considered excellent, with many of the top schools getting into the top ten percent of the league tables of schools in the home country of the curriculum they are following. Of course this has something to do with smaller classes, the right sort of peer pressure and possibly the lack of distractions for teenagers. Teachers are usually recruited from overseas and are all well qualified with experience of teaching their curriculums. There are no entrance exams for schools in Bahrain but some do have waiting lists, so put your child's name down for your chosen schools as soon as possible. The schools in Bahrain all have some recreational space outside, but as you would expect of a country with Bahrain's climate, these are somewhat limited.

Many schools use the facilities of clubs such as the Rugby Club for athletics and football, as they do not have sufficient grass facilities themselves. The schools themselves tend to be reasonably modern and the top schools will compare well with similar schools back home in regard to drama, music, science, etc. The schools start early and almost all at the same time, 07.45. Most of the schools are in Isa Town, in what has become Education Valley. The wisdom of having all the schools in one area is questionable, particularly when you are stuck in a massive traffic jam trying to drop your children off. Most schools finish in the early afternoon with lunch being taken at around 11:00. The American and British schools are the most expensive with fees going up to in excess of BD5,500 per year per child. There are cheaper schools, and these are sometimes chosen in preference to the largest schools because of their particular reputation in certain areas. The top schools are St Christopher's and The British School for the UK curriculum, and Bahrain School and Ibn Khuldoon for American and International Baccalaureate curriculums.

Primary & Secondary Schools	
Abdul Rahman Kanoo School	1787 5055
Al Mahd Day Boarding School	1779 2422
Al Majid Private School	1740 5433
Al Manar Private School	1725 0026
Al Noor International School	1773 6773
Al Raja School	1725 4414
AMA School of Basic Education	1759 3858
Arabian Pearl Gulf School	1740 3666
Asian School	1772 8857
Bahrain School	1772 7828
Bayan School	1768 2227
British School	1771 0878
Dilmun School	1771 3483
Ecole Francaise	1732 3770
Gulf International School	1729 0209
Habara School	1727 1737
Ibn Al Haitham Islamic School	1727 1694
Ibn Khuldoon national School	1778 0661
Indian School	1768 4166
Modern Knowledge School	1772 7712
Nadeem International School	1772 8886
New Indian School	1762 2350
New Millenium School	1727 2700
Pakistan School	1768 2304
Pakistan Urdu School	1768 7921
Shaikha Hessa Girls' School	1775 6111
St Christopher's School	1778 8108
The Children's House	1769 9844
The New Horizon School	1726 2139

University & Higher Education

Bahrain is not yet the place to send your child to university. Although there are a growing number of private universities in the country, they still tend to be one or two faculty operations with very few facilities for any extra-curricula development. Other than the state university, Bahrain University, there are no university campuses and until this is changed you will be depriving your children of the great experience that going to university at home will be. If you really insist on your child attending a local university, you can normally get a visa on an educational basis and the institution your child is attending should be able to arrange this for you. The entrance requirement for the universities is not high and payment of the fees will normally secure

University Education

your child a place. However, the likely lack of international recognition for a local university degree is something you need to consider.

Universities	
Ahlia University	1729 8999
AMA International	1723 3688
Gulf University	1762 0092
NYIT	1782 5070
Royal College of Surgeons in Ireland	1758 3500
University College Bahrain	1779 0828

Special Needs Education

The RIA Integration school (1771 6871) specialises in helping children with autism and other communication difficulties to get into the main stream schools, which they achieve with some success. The Hope Institute (1768 0815) caters for physically challenged children. An alternative would be to hire your own teachers and carers on a part-time basis, which can sometimes be done at a manageable cost.

Learning Arabic

Other options → Language Schools [p.150]

Learning Arabic in Bahrain is best achieved by marrying an Arab and living with your spouse's family. Otherwise you will struggle. There are some excellent Arabic tuition providers but the opportunities to practise your new skills in a country where most of the service personnel are not Arabs, are small. Picking up and learning vocabulary is therefore difficult. That said, all expatriates living in Bahrain should make an effort to learn a few basic phrases, and your efforts will be rewarded with a smile from your Bahraini hosts.

Learning Arabic	
Berlitz	1782 7847
Discover Islam	1753 7373

Transportation

Other options → Getting Around [p.25]
Car [p.26]

Transport in Bahrain is all about private cars and where to park them. You really must have a car here as the taxi system is far from satisfactory. The road system has almost kept pace with the ever increasing numbers of cars, but there are still bottle necks at certain junctions at peak hours. That said, your commute to work will never be more than half an hour, except perhaps during the holy month of Ramadan, when the change in the Government hours means that almost everyone is setting out at the same time in the morning.

Six-lane highways connect most of Bahrain, and so getting from A to B even for a new resident is relatively simple and it is very difficult to get lost for more than a few minutes. It's comforting to know that if you drive in any direction for more than 15 minutes you're sure to come to a recognizable small town, or failing that, the coast. Cars are cheap new and even cheaper second-hand where great bargains can be had, as people regularly upgrade their one-year-old cars to get the latest full option model. It is also easy to lease cars for the day, week, month or year. Parking, however, is difficult in places like the Diplomatic area, where there are many office blocks, so try to get your employer to allocate you a reserved parking space. Other traffic hotspots are the Seef area and Exhibition Road at the weekends, when the influx of visitors from Saudi is at its peak. People drive very fast in Bahrain, and undertaking at speed is a normal occurrence. The high level of road accidents is almost totally attributable to high speeds.

Vehicle Leasing

You must have a residence visa to own a car. The other option, which is very popular, is to rent a car on a long term lease, normally monthly. The rates for leasing in this way are very reasonable and you should be able to get a good car for around BD150 per month. You can lease for any period you want, from a day to over a year, but generally the rates flatten out at monthly rates. Daily leasing comes in at around BD12 per day, with weekly rates starting at around BD70. To lease a car all you need is your driving licence, a credit card and your passport. Any of the reputable leasing companies in the table below can arrange for a car for you almost immediately and they can often deliver the car straight to you, or pick you up from your hotel. In addition to these, most of the main car dealers now also arrange leasing directly.

Vehicle Leasing Agents

Adams Rent A Car	1729 2235
Al Bader Car Hire	1727 6087
Al Dhahiya	1724 6582
Al Fajer Rent-A-Car Est.	1732 2999
Al Hamra	1725 9400
Al Jahara	1777 2453
Al Meer Rent-A Car	1724 4410
Al-Arwali Car Hiring Est.	1726 1881
Al-Mahara Car Hiring	1733 6498
Al-Thawadi Car Hiring	1777 3066
Avis Rent-A-Car	1753 1144
Bahrain Car Rental	1729 2012
Budget Rent A Car	1753 4100
Delmon Rent-A-Car	1772 7900
Europcar Interrent P.79	1732 1249
Express Rent-A-Car	1723 4111
Hertz Rent-A-Car	1732 1358
United Car Hiring	1778 4164

Buying a Vehicle

To buy a car in Bahrain you must have a residence visa. Once you have this the process is very simple. Agree your price and go to the Traffic Department in Isa Town together with the seller. You will need your CPR card and the seller should have the insurance certificate, and ownership card. A simple form then needs to be completed and signed by both parties and your new ownership can be registered at once. You are advised to go with the seller, as sometimes signatures change and you may find that the form is rejected as the seller's signature does not match the one used when he originally purchased the car.

Almost every car manufacturer is represented in Bahrain, from Daihatsu to Maserati. A lot of the wealthier Bahrainis update their car as new models are released, so Bahrain is an excellent place to get a one to two-year-old car. In addition, with the general movement of expats, good quality slightly older cars are also readily available. If you want a new car, these are often cheaper than back home, and many of the dealers offer lease or lease-to-buy options, making the cars even more affordable.

Before you buy, remember you should consider how easy it will be to sell your car should you leave. Toyota and other Japanese cars are much loved in the Middle East for their affordability and reliability, so you will never have a problem selling the car on when you leave. This is also true for most of the SUVs which are ever-popular, even

though they are rarely taken off-road. Secondhand cars are often advertised by expats on the supermarket notice boards, and this is a good place to start with. Alternatively, the Gulf Daily News and the Arabian Motors magazine both advertise used cars.

If you buy from a dealer (or from an individual, for that matter) make sure you get the car checked out by the agent before buying. In a country as small as Bahrain, they will normally be able to tell you whether the car has been regularly serviced, or has been involved in an accident. The cost for this check is only around BD10 and could save you considerable problems in the future. Many of the new car dealers have now also opened their own used car centres, where you can get dealer warranted second-hand cars. One of the more popular showrooms is on the Budaiya Highway just past the turning for Janussan. Here Bahrain Auto Services and Hudson Motors display a range of premium and middle range cars respectively. They normally sell for the owners, taking a commission on the sale, and have a good reputation.

Importing a car into Bahrain privately can be done, however it is almost never cost effective. Exporting a car when you leave can be a more financially rewarding exercise, but in both cases you will have to pay customs fees. Exporting to or importing from another GCC country is very expensive, as you will need to pay export and import fees, and you will almost certainly be able to find a car similar to yours at a similar price to yours, should you sell it locally before moving. If you decide you do want to export or import your car, you should contact one of the relocation companies, see Removal & Relocation Companies [p.62], who will be able to sort out the paper work and custom fees which will be levied on an arbitrarily decided value of the car.

Vehicle Insurance

You must have at least third party insurance for your car in Bahrain. However, the car is insured in Bahrain and not the driver, so as long as they are qualified, anyone can drive your car and be insured without you having to adjust your insurance policy. Car insurance is based on the value of your car, and of course premiums are higher for high performance cars. In addition, the rates change according to whether you have extra services, such as a car replacement service if your car is off the road. Basic third party car insurance for a twelve month period

Enjoy your drive with AXA

Motor Perfect Insurance

Call 17 588 222 for peace of mind

Get on the road with AXA's unique comprehensive motor packages. Motor Perfect Insurance gives you extra services and benefits like a no claim bonus, roadside assistance, free 13th month coverage, off-road cover for 4x4 vehicles and much more.

AXA
INSURANCE

www.axa-gulf.com

— Be Life Confident —

starts at under BD100 for a car under BD2,000 in value, and rises from there. You can shop around for insurance in Bahrain, with some of the smaller un-heard-of agents giving excellent rates. However, check what your insurance company's policy is on repairs and when you might not be covered. Many companies, for example, will not allow a dealer to repair you car if it is over a certain age, unless you can prove that you always get the car serviced by the dealer. Also, some policies will state that the car is only insured if you are on the highways of Bahrain, so you will be excluded if you are off-road, or taking your car for a spin around the Formula One circuit. Most insurance cover is invalid if the driver has been drinking alcohol.

Vehicle Insurance Companies

Axa Insurance **P.81**		1758 8222
Bahrain National Insurance **P.238**		1758 7300
Gulf Union Insurance & Reinsurance Co		1725 5292
Protective Insurance Services		1721 1700

Registering a Vehicle

New cars will be delivered to you ready registered, and the dealer will take your details and a copy of your CPR card to get this done. After that you need to register your car every year. If it is a new car you can do this by picking up a car registration form at any post office. You can submit this directly to the post office or send or deliver it to the Traffic Directorate in Isa Town. If applying by post, you will be sent back your registration card by post within a few weeks, together with the registration certificate to be placed on your front windscreen. Once your car is over four years old, you will need to take it for an inspection before it can be registered. This is a very simple process which takes place at the Traffic Directorate in Isa Town. You won't even have to get out of your car, as they normally just check that the brakes and the lights work. Once you have passed

Used Car Dealers

Al Khalil Car Exhibition	1755 3396
Al Moayyed Trade In Centre	1773 9311
Al Zarqawi Secondhand Car	1727 7919
Bahrain International Car Centre	1778 5558
Basma Buying & Selling	1734 2130
First Motors	1762 3909
Gulf Second Hand Car Exhibition	1725 2355
Majestic Car Centre	1767 3667
National Motor Co	1745 7100
Riviera Car Centre	1755 4922

New Car Dealers

Aston Martin	Montana Motors	1766 9999
Audi	Behbehani Brothers	1770 2111
BMW	EuroMotors	1775 0750
Ferrari	EuroMotors	1775 0750
Ford	Almoayyed Y.K. & Sons	1773 7373
Honda	National Motor Company	1745 7100
Hyundai	First Motors	1762 3909
Jaguar	Mohammad Jalal & Sons	1725 2606
Jeep	Behbehani Brothers	1773 5000
Kia	AA Bin Hindi	1740 8000
Land Rover	EuroMotors	1775 0750
Lexus	Ebrahim K Kanoo	1773 0730
Maserati	EuroMotors	1775 0750
Mercedes Benz	S A Al-Haddad & Bros	1778 5454
MG	EuroMotors	1775 0750
Mini	EuroMotors	1775 0750
Mitsubishi	Ahmed Zayani & Sons	1770 3703
Nissan	Almoayyed Y.K. & Sons	1773 6060
Opel	Mannai Motors	1773 2255
Peugeot	Mohammad Jalal & Sons	1725 2606
Porsche	Behbehani Brothers	1753 1503
Renault	Almoayyed Y.K. & Sons	1773 1999
Rolls Royce	EuroMotors	1775 0750
Saab	Mannai Motors	1773 2255
Toyota	Ebrahim K Kanoo	1724 1001
Volvo	Al Jazira Motor Company	1773 6222
VW	Behbehani Brothers	1770 1333

this test, you will be given a form which you can take to the registration department across the car park, and your new registration certificate will be produced while you wait. If your company has a driver, you can easily get him to do this for you. He can then bring back the paperwork for you to sign, it can be submitted to the post office, and your new certificate will be posted to you.

Traffic Fines & Offences

Bahrain has become more sophisticated in recent years in respect of traffic offences. There are now a large number of speed cameras which are regularly moved, as well as traffic light cameras. The fines for speeding, or jumping red lights vary from BD15 to an appearance in court and a much higher fine. Multiple offenders can even find that they are jailed. Be aware of the cameras at traffic lights, as the car in front of you may suddenly screech to a halt on an orange light to avoid the chance of jumping the red light. Parking tickets are normally BD10 per ticket and will appear as a rather small piece of official-looking card on your side window. You can pay all your fines when you reregister your

Residents

Transportation

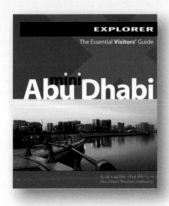

Made with hand luggage in mind

Don't be fooled by their diminutive size, these perfectly pocket proportioned visitor's guides are packed with insider info on travel essentials, shopping, sports and spas, exploring, dining and nightlife.

car. You may find that you have fines that you were unaware of , so make sure you have a few extra dinars with you to pay your parking or speeding fine when you go to register your car.

It is illegal to drive in Bahrain under the influence of alcohol and the minimum fine for drink driving is BD500. There is no set limit, so if you are involved in an accident and have had even one drink you will be deemed to be driving under the influence. Pre-booking a taxi with Speedy Motors or Bahrain Limo allows you to arrive home safely and could also save you a great deal of money in the long run.

There are all sorts of rules in Bahrain about tinted windows, but they are clearly not obeyed by most of those who have them. There are limits to the degree of tint for the size of car, and the windscreen must not be tinted. Your car dealer will show you what the regulations are, and it is illegal to have a darker tint than that specified, despite the fact that so many cars appear to have almost totally black windows.

Breakdowns

If you have a breakdown in Bahrain you will not be too far from help, even if you are in the very south of the country. The breakdown services here are quick and cheap, charging BD5 for a call out and pick up of your vehicle, if they cannot fix the problem on the spot. It is a good idea to carry water with you during the summer, just in case you have a long wait, but you should not carry petrol due to the high temperatures Bahrain experiences. Of course, carrying your mobile phone with you when travelling is very sensible, as even in Bahrain you could be some way from the nearest house or public telephone. Someone will normally stop to help you, particularly if you are female.

Recovery Services/Towing (24 hour)	
AA P.85 ▸	1768 2999
Classic Marketing Company	1774 0707
Gulf Assist	1721 5214

Traffic Accidents

Other options → Car [p.26]

Crashed cars in Bahrain are a regular sight. Accidents are almost always caused by speeding drivers, so not only do you need to drive with due care and attention, you also need to be highly aware of other road users and what they are doing around you. If you do have an accident, try to establish exactly what happened and if necessary take photographs. Of course, if there is someone injured you should call 999 straight away. However, for most minor accidents you need to call the traffic police on 199. You will find that most drivers will not move their cars after even the smallest of accidents until after the traffic police have arrived. The traffic police will determine who caused the accident and complete an accident report. You will be charged BD5, or BD15 if you are deemed to have caused the accident. It is imperative that you get this report, as without it you cannot get your car repaired or claim on your insurance.

You are allowed to leave the scene of a minor accident and go either to the small accident centre behind the Bahrain Mall in Sanabis or the Traffic Directorate in Isa Town, but both of you must go and you may find the other party does not show up. If you are happy that the other party will go to one of these centres, then you can avoid the long wait for the traffic police and will also prevent a traffic jam building up behind you. If there is a dispute, try and get a witness from a nearby car who may have seen the accident. You should always travel with your driving licence, insurance certificate and car registration card, and the traffic police will want to see these documents. There is no points system in Bahrain to be applied against your driving licence, but the courts will ban you for at least three months if you are a persistent offender.

Repairs (Vehicle)

Following an accident you need a copy of the police report before any garage will agree to take your car in for repairs, no matter how minor the repair may be. You can have paintwork touched up, but once you have any form of impact, even if no other cars are involved, you will need to have the police report. Where you can take your car for repairs will depend on your insurance company. The cheaper policies will not allow you to take the car to a dealer unless you can prove that this is where you always take your car, and even then they may require quotes from another garage which they will have the right to insist that you use. So check out your insurance policy on these points before you sign up. The small garages, however, are normally perfectly competent in carrying out repairs and will be able to buy genuine parts from your dealer.

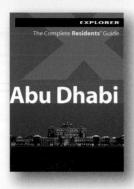
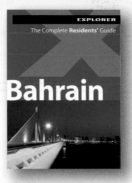
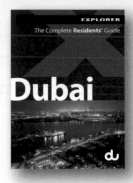

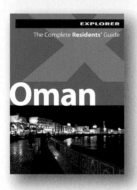

Exploring

Exploring

Highlights...

Feel the Need, the Need for Speed [p.132]

The Bahrain International Circuit brought Formula One to the Middle East for the first time in 2004, and when it's not hosting the F1, itself one of the highlights of the sporting calendar in Bahrain, it is the perfect place for speed demons looking for the thrill of the track. If you fancy yourself behind the wheel you can race your own car or get some guidance from the only BMW Performance Centre located outside of Europe. Check out www.bahraingp.com.

Arabian Adventures

Make the most of your weekends and hop on a plane, or in the car, to Bahrain's neighbouring countries for a different view of the Gulf. Be it shopping in Dubai, luxury living in Abu Dhabi, the colourful heritage of Kuwait, the magnificent mountains of Oman or the rapid developments of Qatar, there's more to these countries than you might imagine. And of course, don't forget to take along a copy of the relevant Explorer to be your guide while you're there!

Heritage Hotspot [p.97]

Despite its diminutive size, Bahrain has an impressive history stretching back many thousands of years – some people believe that Bahrain may have even been the Garden of Eden, with its abundance of fresh water and lush green palm trees. Plenty of this rich heritage still remains with archaeological sites, art galleries, forts, heritage sites, historic houses, museums and mosques to visit all over the island.

Exploring

Bahrain is an archipelago of 33 small islands covering about 665 square kilometres between the east coast of Saudi Arabia and the west coast of Qatar. Most of the islands are low-lying, uninhabited, rocky ledges. The main islands – Bahrain, Sitra, Muharraq, Arad and Hidd – are joined by causeways. The islands are home to just under 700,000 people, including about 240,000 expatriate workers and their families. Bahrain Island is joined to Saudi Arabia by a 27 kilometre causeway which was opened in 1986. Another causeway linking Bahrain to Qatar is in the planning stage.

The name Bahrain means 'two seas' and refers to the sea which surrounds the islands, and to the abundance of fresh water springs, many of them welling up from under the seabed. It is said that pearl fishermen on the old pearling dhows knew the location of these springs and would dive down with goatskin bags to collect fresh water.

Most of Bahrain is low-lying; the highest point is Jebel Dukhan (Smoke Mountain), which is only 137 metres above sea level. Apart from the fertile northern coastal strip, most of Bahrain Island is barren desert.

Bahrain was once known as the land of a thousand palm trees, although these are now sadly depleted because of the rapidly falling groundwater level, and the ever-increasing development of roads and housing. Because of its strategic position on the Arabian Gulf trade route, and its abundance of fresh water, Bahrain has for centuries been visited by travellers. Bahrainis are used to welcoming people to their shores, and Bahrain is still known as the land of golden smiles, which reflects the friendly, tolerant nature of the Bahraini population.

Since the discovery of oil in 1932 and the decline of the pearl fishing industry, Bahrain has concentrated on petroleum processing and refining, and during the past decade has become an international banking centre. Diversification into other manufacturing and processing industries, such as aluminium smelting and the production of related aluminium products, has also taken place.

> **GCC easy as ABC**
>
> *If you want to drop in on your neighbours, then go prepared. Be it for a shopping spree in Dubai, a luxury holiday in Abu Dhabi, to find tranquility in the wilderness of Oman or to see the colourful heritage of Kuwait, don't leave Bahrain without an Explorer!*

Bahrain is a popular destination for business travellers and for weekend visitors from across the Saudi causeway, but is not, as yet, on the map for tourists from Europe or the USA. The tourism infrastructure is still in its infancy and many of the tourist attractions are woefully lacking in the amenities western visitors expect to find, such as tour guides, information booklets, places to buy souvenirs or refreshments, and even toilets.

Manama is a busy, cosmopolitan city, with a traditional souk area, high-rise buildings, modern shopping malls and an almost unlimited choice of international cuisine. Adliya and Umm Al Hassam are particularly famous for their wide variety of restaurants. The new Financial Harbour, which is still being developed, will have futuristic multi-storey buildings, changing the face of Manama forever. There are still some old buildings left, but many of the old windtower houses have been pulled down, or left to fall down, to make way for modern apartment blocks.

View across to Manama

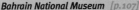

Exploring

Bahrain Visitor's Checklist

Other options → Key Bahrain Projects [p.6]

The following is our list of 'must dos' to help you make the most of your time in Bahrain. Although it is a small country, there is still a fair amount of heritage; with enough forts, museums, old houses and mosques to delight culture vultures. There are also plenty of other attractions to suit other tastes such as the high speed thrills at the Formula One race track, shopping in modern malls and traditional souks, boat trips to remote islands and a variety of fun for kids. So sit back, read on and tailor your own memorable tour of this fascinating island.

Bahrain Fort [p.102]

Bahrain Fort, (Qal'at Al Bahrain or the Portuguese Fort), is the most important archaeological site in Bahrain. Extensively restored during the past 50 years, this impressive edifice is well worth a visit. Watch out for the amazing painted village by the entrance.

Beit Al Qur'an [p.107]

This modern building near the Manama/Muharraq Causeway houses a lovely collection of rare Islamic manuscripts, books and prints. On site there is also a mosque, a library, a lecture hall and a school for Islamic studies.

Arad Fort [p.100]

This 16th century Portuguese fort is located on Arad Island just across the bay from Bahrain Airport. Lovingly restored using traditional local materials, the fort is worth a visit. During the winter months, local handicraft stalls are set up in the courtyard.

The Oil Museum [p.108]

This small museum at the foot of Jebel Dukhan offers a fascinating insight into the history of oil exploration in Bahrain. There are several interesting working models, mineral samples, many old photographs and comprehensive explanations of all the exhibits.

Riffa Fort [p.102]

Perched on the edge of the escarpment, Shaikh Salman Bin Ahmed Al Fateh Fort, built in the 19th century, overlooks Hunanaiyah Valley. On a clear day there's a spectacular view across the valley all the way to Jebel Dukhan, the highest point on the island.

The Tree of Life [p.96]

One of the best-known natural wonders of Bahrain, an enormous acacia known as the Tree of Life, stands alone in the midst of what is otherwise a virtually barren desert, its age and source of water both a mystery.

Bahrain National Museum [p.107]

Well worth visiting, the museum holds wonderful collections in its nine halls, including natural history, reconstructed grave mounds, documents and manuscripts, trades and crafts, customs and traditions, as well as exhibitions on Dilmun, Tylos and Islam.

Al Areen Wildlife Park [p.116]

Check out this great collection of birds and mammals. Kids especially will love the ducks, pelicans and flamingoes, as well as the young camels and giraffes. Keep your eyes peeled for a clutch of huge ostrich eggs in the shade of a shrub.

Al Fateh Mosque [p.113]

Don't miss the chance of visiting Bahrain's largest mosque, which can accommodate 7,000 people at prayer time. Guides are on hand to show you around this beautiful building and abayas are provided for ladies to wear during the visit.

Bahrain Int'l Circuit [p.132]

Visit Bahrain's new Formula One circuit, the only one in the region, which hosted its first event in 2004. Take a tour of the site, try a spin around the track or enjoy some of the other high octane activities available in bikes, cars and 4WDs.

The Souks [p.94]

Browse through Manama Souk and haggle over local craft items, fabrics, toys, and of course, gold. Soak up the bustling atmosphere and revel in the exotic sights, sounds and aromas. Don't miss Muharraq Souk, Isa Town Souk, the Gold Souk and Gold City.

Art Galleries [p.99]

Bahrain boasts an abundance of galleries showing works by local artists. Arabesque Art Gallery, for example, offers oil paintings, watercolours and etchings, antique maps and hand-produced silkscreens on quality hand-made paper.

Kids' Stuff

Go bowling or ice-skating at Funland on the Manama Corniche. When it gets too hot for trips to forts or the desert, take the kids to an indoor theme park such as Foton World in Bahrain Mall or Chakazoolu in Dana Mall, or visit the Water Garden and paddle a pedal boat.

Traditional Handicrafts [p.106]

Visit villages where local handicrafts are made; the potters at A'ali, cloth weavers at Bani Jamrah and basket weavers at Barbar. All handicrafts are also on display at Al Jashrah Handicraft Centre or the Craft Centre in Manama with jewellery, iron, wood and Arabic Calligraphy.

Boat Trips [p.112]

Get away from it all with a boat trip to Bahrain's islands. Go dolphin watching from Bahrain Yacht Club, enjoy birdwatching and watersports off the remote Hawar Islands or enjoy a continental lunch or dinner while cruising the coastline in a luxury dhow.

The Bahrain-Saudi Causeway

Drive out across the 27 kilometre Bahrain-Saudi Causeway to the halfway point and have a meal in the Tower Restaurant, which has fantastic views of the sea and the two coastlines. A great place to enjoy the sunset if you time it right!

Hawar Islands [p.97]

If you really need a break, how about a daytrip to the Hawar Islands or an overnight stay at the Hawar Island Hotel? Boats leave at 10:00 every morning for the 45 minute journey to the islands and the price includes a buffet dinner at the hotel.

Central Market [p.188]

Visit the Central Fish Market early in the morning for the bewildering variety of fresh fish and seafood. Then check out the kaleidoscope of colours, shapes and sizes of fruit and veg from all over the world at the Vegetable Market, all cheaper than in the supermarkets.

Riffa Golf Club [p.96]

Fancy a round of golf? Riffa Golf Club has special rates for visitors, and there is a range of suitable clothing for hire. There are also two excellent restaurants that are open to non-members.

Beaches [p.109]

Bahrain's natural beaches are in short supply and at the few public beaches ladies usually bathe fully clothed. You can, however, visit artificial beaches at hotels and clubs, where the beach and the water are both sure to be clean, and refreshments are on hand.

Shisha Cafes [p.225]

There are many shisha cafes in Bahrain, but one of the best is the Verandah Gallery Cafe. You can enjoy the traditional water pipe, choose a meal from the cosmopolitan menu or browse the collection of bric-a-brac and curios from many parts of the Arab world.

Historic Houses

Although many of the traditional windtower houses have gone, you can still see one or two in the Awadiya and Dhuwawdah areas of Manama and on Muharraq Island. Shaikh Isa Bin Ali House, Bait Sayadi and Al Jasrah House are all well worth a visit.

The main areas of Manama are the Diplomatic Area, Exhibition Road, Adliya, Seef, Manama Souk and Juffair.

The Diplomatic Area   Map Ref 12-C2

The Diplomatic Area is characterised by high-rise buildings housing embassies, hotels, banks and government offices.   The area is extremely congested during weekdays and finding a place to park is a major problem. As a result, you'll see double parking (and sometimes triple parking) on many of the side streets. There is a large car park south of the Golden Tulip Hotel, to the west of the Diplomatic Area, but all the covered parking places belong to banks and other companies located in the Diplomatic Area. The remaining parking slots fill up very quickly every morning, so you'll be very lucky to find an empty slot later in the day.

The government buildings, such as the Ministry of Finance & National Economy, the Bahrain Monetary Agency (which houses the Currency Museum), the Ministry of Justice & Islamic Affairs and the Ministry of Housing, all have their own covered parking areas, but you'll have quite a job persuading the soldiers who guard these buildings to let you park there, even if you have a valid reason for visiting the building. The embassies of Saudi Arabia, Kuwait, Turkey, Germany, Sweden and Norway are also located in the Diplomatic Area, with the embassies of Oman, Jordan, France and Korea within easy walking distance beyond the Beit Al Qur'an along the Al Fateh Highway. BNP Paribas, United Gulf Bank, the Bank of Bahrain & Kuwait, TAIB bank (which has a small art gallery on the ground floor) and Al Baraka Islamic Bank are also found here.

As well as the Golden Tulip and Sheraton Hotels to the west of the area, the Crowne Plaza Hotel, where the Bahrain Conference Centre is located, and the Diplomat Radisson SAS Hotel are on the north-eastern side, while the more down-market Sheza Tower Hotel is to the south. As well as the hotel restaurants and coffee shops, Costa Coffee on the ground floor of the Al Rossais Tower, Curry Country on the ground floor of the Hawar Building, Cinnabon Coffee shop and the Sunset Restaurant, which is a corner sidewalk cafe opposite the Crowne Plaza Hotel, are convenient for office workers to grab a bite to eat at lunchtime.

For those foolhardy enough to brave the traffic on the King Faisal Highway, Gulfashan Restaurant has recently opened at the eastern end of the King Faisal

Corniche. In addition, there are several shawarma and juice kiosks dotted among the skyscrapers. Bearing in mind that the Diplomatic Area covers only about one square kilometre, there's not much in the way of greenery, apart from the odd palm tree outside one or two of the ministries. There is a paved area with a fountain in front of the Investcorp building, but that's it as far as beautification is concerned.

Exhibition Avenue   Map Ref 12-C4

Exhibition Avenue, which was once a single lane road without pavements on reclaimed land, has burgeoned into a major hotel, shopping and fast-food area that has become very popular with visitors from Bahrain's closest neighbour. Unfortunately, this influx of pleasure-seekers from across the causeway has resulted in nose-to-tail traffic cruising the area every evening and all weekend. Even more unfortunately, the road is no longer safe for women to walk along after nightfall. Recently there have been several instances of women being subjected to verbal and even physical abuse. Petty theft and vandalism are also on the upsurge in the area, with cars being broken into and robbed.

There are numerous two and three-star hotels in this area, such as the Relax Inn Hotel, Casanova Hotel, Grand Hotel and the unpronounceable Crwan Plaza and Frsan hotels, as well as blocks of what are variously described as 'luxury', 'luxurious' or 'luxorius' serviced apartments. Many of the hotels have nightclubs in which statuesque blonde dancers and singers from Eastern Europe perform and are hugely popular with visitors from across the causeway. Exhibition Avenue itself has three main

Exhibition Road

Exploring

Manama – Main Areas

roundabouts, two of which sport large, modernistic, triangular structures with a clock on each face, while the third has an extremely ugly fountain consisting of a series of reddish-brown basins from which water drips to the lowest level.

On the corner of Exhibition Avenue and Tarafa Bin Al-Abd Road there is a profusion of fast-food outlets, such as Pizza Hut, Burger King, Yum Yum Tree and McDonalds. There are also many other restaurants, cafes and coffee shops, as well as a couple of 24 hour supermarkets and cold stores, video rental shops, hairdressing salons, computer shops, travel agents and mobile phone companies.

Adliya   Map Ref 14-B2

Adliya is famous for having dozens of restaurants serving food from all over the world and a wealth of oriental carpet shops. Although small, it is a popular area in which many western expats live. Adliya High Street, one end of which is commonly known as Shawarma Alley because of the numerous fast-food outlets there, used to be popular with young Bahrainis showing off their cars and is still quite congested in the evening, although much of this kind of traffic has long since moved to Exhibition Road.

There are 12 oriental carpet shops in less than 300 metres along this road, with another in the parallel road behind the supermarket. There is a bank, a pharmacy, a laundry and dry cleaners, more fast-food outlets such as Fuddruckers at the western end of the street, as well as Mansouri Mansions, which is a small hotel. There are also two boozeramas (outlets which are licensed to sell alcohol) in the side streets, African & Eastern and Bahrain Mercantile & Marine. They are open from 11:00 to 19:00, except on Fridays and during Ramadan. Singapore Flower, which has a huge range of plants and fresh flowers flown in daily, is at the western end of Adliya High Street.

In Adliya you can find Cico's, the best (and probably the oldest) Italian restaurant in Bahrain, Casa Mexicana, Senor Paco's and Coco's, as well as several Thai and Chinese Restaurants, coffee shops and cafes. In a side street off Shawarma Alley is Mezzaluna, which is located in a stunningly decorated, old Bahraini house. The main dining area is in the courtyard of the original one-storey building, over which a glass roof has been constructed, with fold-away blinds to protect diners during the heat of the day. The decor is ochre with purple, crimson and maroon light fittings made of sculpted fabric, including an enormous chandelier with rope tassels suspended from the roof. The

small dining rooms round the sides of the main dining area are decorated in blazing shades of purple, turquoise and scarlet, and furnished with zebra-striped or leopard-patterned sofas. The pièce de résistance, however, is the ladies' toilet, which has harlequin-patterned ochre and crimson walls, purple fabric light fittings and elegant basins. The food? With decor like this, who cares? The menu is a bit pretentious, (mostly French/Italian but with surprising combinations of flavours), and the food a bit pricey, but the service is impeccable.

Nearby is Monsoon, housed in a beautiful Thai-style wooden building with a high-pitched roof supported on massive wooden pillars. The main dining area is on a raised platform surrounded by a small moat in which frangipani flowers and bougainvillaea float, outside the veranda doors is a pond into which oriental statues pour water. There is also a teppanyaki counter. The cuisine is oriental and the food is delicious and not too expensive (though the restaurant belongs to the same company that owns Mezzaluna, as well as other restaurants in the area). Not far away, in Umm Al Hassam, is the Hong Kong restaurant, one of the best Chinese restaurants in Bahrain.

Seef   Map Ref 3-E1

Seef is the newest area of Bahrain, being built entirely on reclaimed land. Several large shopping malls are located there and the first skyscraper office block is already open for business. The Ritz Carlton Hotel & Spa is on the northern edge of the area and the Blue Elephant, a luxury Thai restaurant, has opened near the hotel.

The largest shopping mall in Bahrain, Seef Mall, was opened in 1997. It has over 220 shops, two foodcourts, two cinema multiplexes with 16 cinema screens, and Magic Island, an indoor theme park with fairground rides and attractions for children of all ages. The mall covers 100,000 square metres and attracts over 80,000 visitors every week. It is the most popular venue for 'hanging out' in Bahrain, so is full of Bahraini and expat teenagers strolling along and eyeing up the competition, particularly at weekends. The largest stores are Marks & Spencer, Debenhams and Bhs. A word of warning; the main parking area on the northern side of the mall is the most popular, but it has only one exit, so it can take quite a long time to get out of it at the weekend.

Al Aali Shopping Complex, next door, is smaller and much less popular, though it is becoming more so with the opening of THE One, as well as several upmarket boutiques. Don't miss the Al Taweesh

Souk wing, an elegant, beautifully designed area in which you will find the Bradran Persian carpet store and Al Bindaira Cafe, which has a cosy seating area upstairs on a bridge overlooking the souk, as well as a shisha area on the ground floor. Across the Shaikh Khalifa Bin Salman Highway, though not strictly in the Seef area, are the Bahrain International Exhibition Centre and two more huge shopping malls, Bahrain Mall and Dana Mall. Bahrain Mall houses the Géant hypermarket, while Dana Mall has the Giant hypermarket... a coincidence? You can buy almost anything in Géant, much of it at reasonable prices. Dana Mall also has a Cineplex with 12 cinema screens and Chakazoolu, a two-storey indoor theme park for kids.

Manama Souk   Map Ref 11-E3

Manama Souk is a rabbit warren of narrow, covered alleyways inland from the Bab Al Bahrain, or Gateway of Bahrain. The sea originally came right up to the Bab and trading dhows used to tie up to the jetty there. Now the sea is some distance away and is retreating even further with the land reclamation for the new Financial Harbour project.

Opposite the Bab Al Bahrain is the main post office, and for connoisseurs of public statuary there are a couple of very nice life-size camels and their driver resting in the shade of a palm tree on the small roundabout at the entrance to the Regency InterContinental Hotel carpark. The main carpark between the Regency and the post office is always full at weekends, but if you join the queue waiting to enter, a member of the fiercely competitive flock of car cleaners will rush out to offer to park the car for you and clean it for BD1.

A visit to the souk is a must. You can still see old shopfronts with mouldering old wooden shutters and handprints on the walls where the builders smoothed out the plaster. You can find everything there, from domestic appliances to fabric, furniture, toys, woven baskets, and of course, gold. How about an alarm clock in the shape of a mosque which tells you when it's prayer time? Does a watch with Arabic numerals take your fancy, or a walking stick with a brass eagle's-head handle? If it looks as though you are a serious shopper, elderly souk porters pulling low two-wheeled carts will offer to carry your purchases.

Most items will be a lot cheaper than in the shopping malls and can be haggled over, but the main reason for visiting the souk is to revel in the sights, sounds and smells. The spice souk is a riot of colour and aromas. Follow the sound of the tinsmiths hammering on their wares to see cooking pots and utensils of every size, some big enough to cook a camel in! You will also see tin trunks painted with scenes of Mecca in garish hues of pink, green and blue. The cloth souk has a kaleidoscopic array of fabrics, many designs suitable only for making panto dame costumes.

In the square in front of the Sahara Hotel, old ladies wearing batoola face masks used to sit under sunshades on the pavement selling embroidery, and in one of the side streets leading off the square, donkeys, goats, sheep and caged birds were once sold. Here you can still hire a pick-up truck in which to carry your purchases and a couple of labourers to load and unload the truck. Shop till you drop and then pop into the Adhari Hotel to rest your weary legs and have a fresh fruit juice.

Juffair   Map Ref 14-D3

Another area which has mushroomed over the past decade is Juffair, with many high-rise apartment complexes and hotels built on reclaimed land. The Grand Mosque is located in Juffair and a magnificent new library is being built beside it. This group of connected buildings is richly decorated in Islamic style, with the main building having a curved outer wall surmounted by enormous half-dome structures facing the Al Fateh Highway. The original little village of Juffair, with its crowded narrow streets of shabby old houses, is now completely dominated by the huge buildings which have grown up beside it.

The Juffair Dome, in which local teams play basketball, is at the northern end of Juffair Village, while to the east and south of the village are several old one-storey buildings which were once part of the British forces' base when Bahrain was a British Protectorate, before declaring independence in 1971. Bahrain School, until recently a joint venture between the American forces and Bahrain, and the American Naval Support Group are also located in this area, which borders the Mina Sulman container port. The high-rise residential area is very popular with British, American and Asian families and American service people, while the large villas and compounds on the eastern coast house mainly Bahraini families and expat businessmen and their families.

As well as the hotel restaurants and coffee shops, there are one or two cafes, but very few shops, apart from those in the large grey building with fake windtowers beside the Al Fateh Highway. This building has taken a long time to construct (in fact, the southern end of the building still appears to be unfinished) and even longer to fill with shops. Xerox is one of the companies that can be found here.

Other areas of Manama worth visiting are Naim, Awadiyah and the area south of Awadiyah between Shaikh Isa Avenue and Al Ma'arif Avenue.

Naim   Map Ref 11-D4

Central Market is situated in Naim and the fish and vegetable markets are well worth a visit for an experience of local colour and aroma! Go early in the morning before the fish market gets oppressively hot and smelly. Wear serviceable shoes as the floors are always awash. The market traders are a jolly crowd and enjoy a good haggle. There are a couple of large discount stores in the area, which sell an amazing variety of cheap bric-a-brac, and Marina Mall, which has clothes and shoe shops, a large furniture store on the upper floor and a shop which sells all sorts of items with which to adorn your home, such as vases, wind chimes, mirrors and ornaments.

Down from the famous landmark, the Pearl Fountain Roundabout, and on the other side of Suwayfiyah Avenue opposite Marina Mall, there is a supermarket and filling station. Behind the supermarket are two boozeramas (outlets licensed to sell alcohol), Gulf Cellar and Bahrain Mercantile & Marine. They are open from 11:00 to 19:00 except on Fridays and during Ramadan. From the central bus station in Naim you can travel in air-conditioned buses to most inhabited areas of Bahrain for around 500 fils, but the buses are few and far between and the routes confusing.

Awadiyah   Map Ref 12-B3

Awadiyah is just north of the American Mission Hospital and is one of the last areas where you can see old windtower houses, although they are disappearing fast. Visit La Fontaine Centre of Contemporary Art, which is housed in a restored windtower building. Unfortunately, the architect has added several European-style features, but the beauty of the original house can still be seen.

The American Mission Hospital, which recently celebrated its 100th anniversary, has an interesting exhibition of old photographs of Bahrain. There are pictures of the early American missionary doctors and their patients, as well as photographs of old buildings and previous rulers of Bahrain. The exhibition is on the first floor in the corridor leading to the Ear, Nose and Throat department. Behind the Family Bookshop, which is on Isa Al Kabeer Avenue, there is a very large old

Bahraini family house with a beautiful blue-painted gateway leading into a courtyard in which large palm trees can be seen, and not far from there is a large, modern mosque with unusual square balconies on the two minarets.

South of Awadiyah   Map Ref 12-A4

Off Shaikh Isa Avenue, south of the American Mission Hospital, is an area where many Asian expats live and work, so there are several really cheap restaurants serving excellent food from different parts of India.

In one of the vegetarian restaurants near the Middle East Hotel you can order a vegetarian thali with freshly fried puri for only 800 fils, and waiters keep coming to refill the dishes for as long as you are able to keep eating. Bachelors sit downstairs and there is a family room upstairs. Cutlery is available on request and there are washbasins at the side of the restaurant where you can wash your hands before and after your meal. Some restaurants have lunch deals which provide Indian labourers with a midday meal every day for a month for only BD 10.

Several Asian social clubs, such as the Indian and Pakistani Clubs, are located on Shaikh Isa Avenue, and the Awal and Al Hamra cinemas show Arabic, Hindi, Malayalam and sometimes English films.

Isa Town

In response to the growing national population and a higher standard of living, the government began a programme of urban development in the early 1960s, with Isa Town (or Madinat Isa) as one of its first projects. Around 6,000 homes, both houses and apartments, were built and handed over to Bahraini families. Just off the east coast of the island, this is still a densely populated residential area, with some shops, schools and leisure facilities.

West of Isa Town is A'ali, home to the traditional potteries, and further west the ancient burial mounds. The birthplace of the former Amir, Sheikh Isa Bin Sulman Al Khalifa, is in the village of Al Jasra over near the west coast. There is also an interesting heritage museum with workshops nearby. From Al Jasra you can drive out across the Bahrain/Saudi Causeway for a meal in the Tower Restaurant half way across. If you time it right you can watch the sun setting over the shoreline of

Saudi Arabia only 13 kilometres away. Telephone 1769 0674 for more information.

Riffa

Situated in the middle of Bahrain island, Riffa is a large, residential district, that is divided into West Riffa, East Riffa and Riffa. West Riffa is a particularly desirable place to live, with lush green areas and plenty of large dwellings. Many members of the royal family live around here.

You won't be able to miss the imposing Riffa Fort. Constructed in the early 19th century, the fort has been renovated and offers great views across the Riffa Valley.

Riffa Golf Club has special visitors' golf rates ranging from BD 16 for Night Golf (9 holes) to BD 38 for Weekend Golf (18 holes). Golf clubs, carts, shoes and clothes can be hired reasonably cheaply. There are also two restaurants, which are open to non-members for lunch and dinner. Telephone 1775 0777 for more information.

Riffa Golf Club

Awali and Jebel Dukhan

Just to the south is the smaller neighbourhood of Awali, which is next to the Riffa and Awali golf clubs. To the south is Bahrain's highest point, Jebel Dukhan. The Oil Museum is also here, at the site of the country's first oil well.

Just west of Jebel Dukhan is the Bahrain International Circuit, the home of Formula One. The circuit hosted its first event in 2004 and you can visit the website at www.bahraingp.com to take a

Tree of Life

virtual tour of the circuit. You can also arrange to visit the circuit for a guided tour of the VIP tower and the grandstands, followed by a drive around the track. Telephone 1745 0000 for more information.

One of the best-known natural wonders of Bahrain is the Tree of Life, an enormous acacia which grows alone in the otherwise barren desert southeast of Jebel Dukhan, its source of water a mystery. It features in all government tourist information, on maps and in books about Bahrain. It is on the logo of the American Mission Hospital and several other companies.

Many Bahrainis believe the tree to be around 4,000 years old and are very proud of it, though few have ever actually driven out into the desert to visit it. In fact, the tree is estimated to be about 400 years old, much older than the normal 150 year lifespan for this type of tree. The route to the tree is signposted from Al Muaskar Highway, but after you pass Riffa Golf Club the signs are few and far between. If all else fails, follow the small green signs for the Shaikh Isa Air Base. The route is quite depressing as it goes past a sprawling scrap metal yard and eventually turns off at a group of ugly corrugated iron shacks.

The huge tree is very impressive but has suffered greatly from the attention of its fans and is covered in graffiti and carvings. Many of the branches have been broken or cut off and the area is littered with plastic bags, bottles and cans. Perhaps it would be better not to go right up to the tree, but to continue on down the road towards the air base and then turn left up a narrow road to the eastern escarpment. From there you can see just how remarkable the tree is, as there are no other trees visible as far as the eye can see.

Sitra

Sitra is an island off the north-east coast, now permanently linked to the main Bahrain island by a number of bridges. Predominantly an industrial area, it has a port and oil and petrochemical processing facilities. The southern tip is where you should head to though; here you'll find beaches, the Bahrain Yacht Club, and Al Bandar Resort with its health club, dive cente and watersports facilities.

Hamad Town

A 'new town', officially inaugurated in 1984, Hamad Town (or Madinat Hamad) occupies a rectangle of land in the Western Region, approximately 10km by 2km. The town was built primarily to accommodate the growing national population, and to this day it is still inhabited mostly by local families. To cater for the residents, there are a number of facilities including shops, schools, restaurants, mosques, and recreation centres.

Muharraq

Muharraq is another island off the north-eastern tip of Nahrain island. It is connected by three main causeways. Bahrain's international airport occupies the top half of the island, while the southern portion is home to the Khalifa bin Salman Port and the dry docks.

Visitor attractions include the historical Sheik Isa's house and the Pearl Merchant's house (Beit Siyadi). With some fine examples of old Arabian architecture (including a few remaining windtower houses), narrow lanes, and traditional shopping areas, Muharraq seems a world away from the modern Bahrain visible just across the water.

Muharraq

Hawar Island

For those that have always dreamt of stepping ashore a fantasy desert island, Hawar Island could be just the place. Lying 20km south-east of Bahrain island, it is in fact much closer to the State of Qatar than Bahrain (indeed, 'ownership' of the island was hotly debated for many years.) Possibly the biggest attraction here is the Hawar Resort Hotel, with lots of recreational, dining and entertaiment facilities – especially watersports. The resort operates a regular shuttle service between the island and Ad Dur on the mainland. The thrilling trip takes 45 minutes by speedboat.

Museums, Heritage & Culture

The imprint of Bahrain's incredible recorded history, which stretches back over 5,000 years can be seen in the many archaeological sites found all over the islands. Some even believe that Bahrain may have been the Garden of Eden, with its abundance of fresh water and lush green palm trees; it certainly must have seemed so to weary travellers plying ancient trade routes through the Gulf region. Bahrain still welcomes travellers with tolerance and an easygoing charm. Bahrainis are proud of their rich heritage and delight in sharing it with visitors. In this section you will find details of the major archaeological sites, art galleries, museums and heritage sites in Manama, Muharraq and Al Jasrah village, including sites which are on the itineraries of the tour operators listed in the Tours and Sightseeing section, such as the National Museum, Beit Al Qur'an, the Grand Mosque, Forts, Historic houses and Craft centres.

Archaeological Sites

There is a wealth of archaeological sites all over Bahrain Island, many dating back four or five thousand years. Early excavations were carried out by amateur archaeologists and explorers nearly a hundred years ago, but within the last 50 years, modern professional archaeologists have uncovered much of the past history of Bahrain, notably the Danish Expeditions, whose work is described in Geoffrey Bibby's book, *Looking for Dilmun*. Over the ages, Bahrain has been called Dilmun, Tilmun, Tylos, Awad, Samak and Awal, names that can be seen on the shopfronts and hotel signboards of Bahrain today. Archaeological sites can be visited at any time and there is no entry fee. However, there aren't any information leaflets, toilets, souvenirs or refreshments available.

Al Khamis Mosque

Location → Off Shaikh Salman Highway · Al Khamis	na
Hours → Visit at any time	
Web/email → na	Map Ref → 3-E3

This mosque is the oldest in Bahrain and is thought to have been built 1,300 years ago by the Ummayed Caliph Omar bin Abdul Aziz. The two minarets were added later, one during the 12th century and the other in the 16th century. The site is well looked after, but once again there is no information available, or any other facilities. The mosque, which is located beside Shaikh Isa Bin Salman Highway, opposite Khamis Police Station, has been extensively renovated with one of the minarets being taken down and rebuilt completely a few years ago.

Al Khamis Mosque

Barbar Temple

Location → South of Barbar Village	na
Hours → Visit at any time	
Web/email → na	Map Ref → 3-B1

Barbar Temple, which was excavated in the 1950s and 60s, dates back to around 2200BC. There are several levels of development including a sacred well from the second temple era, which is thought to be the legendary abyss of subterranean waters of Enki, the God of Spring Waters. The remains are remarkable in that the structures are made of large stone blocks fitted together without plaster. Many objects retrieved from the site can be seen in the

Bahrain National Museum, including several of the famous Dilmun seals, which were found in the well itself. Barbar Temple is situated on the outskirts of Barbar Village, which is on the northern coast. The area is surrounded by a wire fence and guarded by a soldier. There are two noticeboards giving general information in English and Arabic at the entrance to the site. The temple is well signposted from the Budaiya Road.

Barbar Temple

Ein Umm Al Sojoor

Location → East of Diraz Village · Barbar	na
Hours → Visit at any time	
Web/email → na	Map Ref → 3-B2

This ancient sweetwater spring is located off the Budaiya Road to the east of Diraz Village. There is a wire fence and the ubiquitous soldier guarding it, but the site looks as though it has not been visited for a long time. There is water in the well, but it looks stagnant and has rubbish floating in it. There is thought to have been a small well-temple here during the Dilmun era and two headless statues of stone animals were found at the site when it was first investigated.

Saar Settlement

Location → West of Saar Village	na
Hours → Visit at any time	
Web/email → na	Map Ref → 3-C4

It is advisable to visit this major archaeological site west of the present-day Saar Village during the winter months from January to April, which is when a team of British archaeologists usually arrives in

Bahrain to work on the site. At other times of the year the settlement is deserted (apart from the soldier guarding the wire fence, of course!), though it is possible to enter the site and wander around at any time. There were plans at one time to open a visitors' centre and museum, but they have not yet materialised. The settlement dates from 2000BC and one can see the remains of many small houses built on either side of the main road which leads up to the temple, and along the side streets. A great number of objects such as fish and animal bones, shells and seeds have been found at the site, along with pieces of pottery and Dilmun seals. It is thought that an inlet from the west coast may have stretched as far as the settlement during the time that it was occupied. The site is not signposted, though it appears on some maps as Ancient Saar.

The Burial Mounds

Location → South of Saar Village & West of A'ali Village
Hours → Visit at any time
Web/email → na   Map Ref → 3-B4   na

One of the most remarkable sights in Bahrain is the vast area of burial mounds near A'ali Village (known as the Al A'ali Burial Mounds), at Hamad Town and at Sakhir. The mounds were built during the Dilmun, Tylos and Helenistic periods and are anything from two to four thousand years old. The largest burial mounds, which are known as the Royal Tombs, are found in and around A'ali Village, where the traditional pottery kilns are located. In fact, many of the old wood-burning kilns have been built right into the mounds. The mounds originally extended all the way from Saar down to Zallaq, but thousands of them have been destroyed to make way for new roads and houses.

Burial Mounds

There are no guides or leaflets at the burial mounds, so it's a good idea to follow up with a visit to the Hall of Graves at the National Museum, where actual grave mounds have been rebuilt, showing the different methods of construction, the way in which the bodies were placed in the graves and the articles that were buried with the dead.

Art Galleries

Other options → Art Supplies [p.159]
Art [p.159]

There is a thriving contemporary art movement in Bahrain, with many of the artists finding inspiration from works of art and sculptures from the Dilmun era. Some local artists, such as Abdul Wahab Al Koheji, Abdulla Al Muharraqi and Rashid Al Oraifi, have opened their own galleries. Art classes are provided by several of the galleries and art groups.

Abdulla Al Muharraqi

Location → Nr A'ali walking track · A'ali
Hours → Telephone for an appointment
Web/email → na   Map Ref → 5-D1   3966 0688

One of Bahrain's best-loved and internationally famous artists, Abdulla Al Muharraqi has opened a gallery in A'ali. He points out that most of his paintings have been sold, but about 70 paintings from his private collection are on display in the gallery. To view these paintings, it is best to make an appointment. He plans to add a collection of his cartoons, which appear regularly in local publications making witty and pertinent comments on local and international political issues. His son Khalid is rapidly earning an international reputation for his stunning 3D designs on the internet. You can check them out on his website: www.muharraqi-studios.com.

Arabesque Art Gallery

Location → Off Umm al Hassam Ave
Hours → 08:00 - 19:00 Fri closed
Web/email → www.arabesque-gal.org   Map Ref → 4-C3   1772 2916

Located in a modern building in Umm Al Hassam, the gallery's antique brass and iron studded door opens on a huge array of paintings, the majority of which are the work of one of Bahrain's best-known artists, Abdul Wahab Al Koheji, who works in the mediums of oil on canvas, watercolour and etching. There is also a series of hand-produced silkscreens, printed on hand-made paper. The inspiration for many of these designs was the old home of the former ruler Shaikh Isa Bin Ali in Muharraq. The gallery also houses a large collection of antique art of the Middle East, including lithographs and engravings by the Victorian artist David Roberts. Antique maps of Arabia are also on display. A certificate of authenticity is provided with all antique art sold. The artist is often on hand to offer advice in the picture framing section, and he oversees all framing work. The gallery holds regular exhibitions by visiting artists and also runs a series of extremely popular art classes.

The gallery has a shop in the A'ali Shopping Complex which is open from 10:00 to 22:00, seven days a week.

Bahrain Arts Society

Location → Nxt to Lanterns Restaurant | 1759 4211
Hours → 08:00 - 12:45 16:00 - 18:00 Thu am & Fri closed
Web/email → www.bahartsociety.org.bh | Map Ref → 3-E2

The Arts Society holds art exhibitions, art courses, workshops, lectures and other cultural events at the gallery. Members of the society include many of Bahrain's best-known artists such as Abdulla Al Muharraqi and Abbas Al Mosawi.

Dar Al Bareh (Gallery and Cafe)

Location → Rd 2705 · Umm Al Hassam | 1771 3535
Hours → 08:30 - 23:00 Fri 17:00 - 21:00
Web/email → na | Map Ref → 4-C2

Dar Al Bareh Gallery has a display of pottery, paintings and sculpture by local artists. The gallery offers classes in decorative painting, furniture painting and wall effects painting, and sells a complete range of painting materials. The shop upstairs also sells items which make ideal gifts. The cafe is peaceful and pleasant, and has an interesting menu, including selections from the Health Bar.

La Fontaine Centre of Contemporary Art

Location → 92 Hoora Ave · Ras Romman | 1723 0123
Hours → See below
Web/email → www.lafontaineartcentre.com | Map Ref → 4-C1

This art gallery is located near the centre of Manama in an old windtower house lovingly restored over a period of six years by Jean Marc Sinan, French artist and architect. The centre holds regular exhibitions of paintings, sculptures, photographs and architectural designs by international contemporary artists. In addition to the gallery, the centre houses La Fontaine Spa, which offers a wide range of beauty treatments, and a first-class restaurant serving French cuisine. During the cooler months, regular film evenings are held in the central courtyard of the building.

Timings: 12:00 - 15:00, 19:30 - 22:30, Fri 19:30 - 22:30, Sat 12:00 - 15:00

Rashid Al Oraifi Museum

Location → Building 374, Road 214 · Muharraq | 1733 5616
Hours → 08:00 - 13:00 16:00 - 20:00
Web/email → na | Map Ref → 2-B4

Leading Bahraini artist Rashid Al Oraifi was the first Bahraini to open his own gallery in his home country. He has now opened a museum and art gallery to display works of art and sculptures from the Dilmun era. The gallery also houses a collection of Al Oraifi's own paintings that are inspired by the Dilmun period. More of Al Oraifi's paintings are on display in his gallery, which is in the Bahrain Commercial Complex behind the Sheraton Hotel.

Forts

There are two forts on Bahrain Island and one on Arad Island. The forts are very interesting and have been extensively renovated, often using traditional materials. Unfortunately, there are no guides to show visitors around the forts and information leaflets (in English and Arabic only) are brief and in short supply. None of the forts have detailed maps of the interior layout, or any information about the way in which different rooms and areas within the forts were used. There are no souvenir shops, or places where you can buy refreshments, so you should take water with you. Only the Bahrain Fort has toilets and they are located in a block on the seaward side of the moat, so it's quite a trek to reach them.

Arad Fort

Location → West of Arad Village | na
Hours → See below
Web/email → na | Map Ref → 2-C4

Built at the end of the 15th century, when Bahrain was occupied by the Portuguese, the fort was designed to defend the invaders against the local

Bahrain Fort

population and the Ottomans in Saudi Arabia. The fort is interesting because of the use of traditional local materials in its restoration, such as coral stone (in which small sea shells are embedded), lime, gypsum and date palm trunks. Its location on the edge of the bay opposite Bahrain International Airport is quite picturesque, but although it is signposted from Al Hidd Highway, there is no indication of which way to go after that. After leaving the highway, you should take the first right turn at the small roundabout and follow the road round to the left. The entry fee is 200 fils, but quite often the ticket kiosk is empty and there is nobody to check or collect tickets in the fort itself. During the winter months, handicraft stalls are set up in the courtyard between the fort and the sea, and sometimes cultural events are staged in the same area. At the water's edge is a small coffee shop with benches outside for shisha smokers.

Timings: Sun - Tue 08:00 - 14:00, Wed & Thu 09:00 - 18:00, Fri 15:00 - 18:00. Closed Sat.

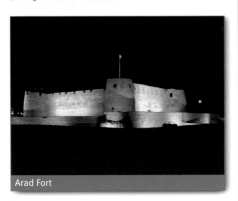
Arad Fort

Bahrain Fort

Location → Nr Karbabad Village |na
Hours → 08:00 - 13:00
Web/email → na   Map Ref → 3-D1

The site of the first professional archaeological dig in Bahrain in 1953, the impressive 16th century Portuguese fort is built on the remains of several previous settlements, going back to the Dilmun era around 2800BC. There are beautiful views of the sea and surrounding landscape, and interesting contrasts between the ancient structure of the fort and the distant skyscrapers of the Seef district. The interior of the fort is a maze of rooms on many different levels. Some of the rooms have photographic displays of the different stages of renovation of the fort, unfortunately without captions. There are several large, informative notices dotted around the area, but no information booklets in English showing detailed plans of the interior of the fort. Entry is free and the fort is open from 08:00 to 13:00 every day including Friday. Follow the signs to Karbabad Village. The small village at the entrance to the fort is remarkable in that the houses are covered in brightly coloured murals. Every inch of space, including the water tanks on the roofs, the TV dish aerials and the air-conditioning units, has been painted. Well worth a photo or two!

Shaikh Salman bin Ahmed Al Fateh Fort

Location → Nr Hunanaiyah Valley |na
Hours → See below
Web/email → na   Map Ref → 6-A4

From its spectacular vantage point on the escarpment above Hunanaiya Valley, the 19th century Shaikh Salman bin Ahmed Al Fateh Fort (also known as Riffa Fort) looks down on a modern housing development of whitewashed houses. The fort contains many small rooms, the walls of some of them showing the handprints of the workmen who smoothed the plaster finish. A general leaflet listing five heritage sites in English and Arabic is available, but the information is somewhat sparse and the attendant who collects your entry fee of 200 fils may not be able to answer any questions about the fort. The small mosque adjoining the fort is not open to the public. The fort is open from Saturday to Tuesday from 08:00 to 14:00, on Wednesday and Thursday from 09:00 to 18:00 and on Friday from 15:00 to 18:00. Access to the fort is from Riffa Avenue and the route is well signposted.

Al Fateh Fort

Exploring

Museums, Heritage & Culture

Heritage Sites - City

Other options → Museums - City [p.106]
Mosque Tours [p.113]
Art [p.159]

The Bab Al Bahrain was originally built in 1945 to be used as government offices. At that time the building was actually on the seafront. A short distance to the west along Government Road, is the old Law Court building, which was built in 1937. For the past 10 years or so, the Heritage Centre Museum was housed in this building, but it is now used by the Ministry of Justice. There is also a Currency Museum in the Bahrain Monetary Agency building in the Diplomatic Area. As described in the section on the main areas of the city, there are still a few old windtower houses in the Awadiya District.

Opposite the Gulf Hotel, Gudabiya Palace is also known as the Guest Palace because visiting heads of state often stay there. The palace is surrounded by beautifully landscaped gardens which can be seen through the ornamental gates and railings, but it is not open to visitors. Teams training for the annual marathon relay race, which is held in November, often jog round the Guest Palace because the pavement outside its perimeter fence measures three kilometres, the distance each runner has to complete in the race.

The Old Palace at the end of Bani Otbah Avenue (which is commonly known as Old Palace Avenue) was built by Shaikh Hamad Bin Isa Al Khalifa in the 1940s. It has not been lived in since 1968, when the ruling family moved to the new palace in West Riffa. The Old Palace was renovated a decade ago and is occasionally used for official events, but it is not open to visitors.

They don't build dhows in the dhow builders' yard by the Pearl Roundabout in Naim any more. Why not? Because the seashore has moved several hundred metres away, so they can't launch the dhows once they have been built. There is still one forlorn dhow languishing on its props, and piles of dhow-material tree trunks (traditionally imported from India), but the dhow builders have all moved to Muharraq, as have the fish-trap makers. The area is still worth a visit, however, because of the blacksmiths' workshops, where everything from birdcages and ornamental railings to bed frames are hammered out over primitive open fireplaces. There are also tinsmiths' workshops displaying tin trunks, ovens, cooking pots and utensils.

A new heritage centre, to be called the Safina (ship) Traditional Project, is planned for the area, according to a recent report in the *Gulf Daily News*. The centre will have workshops for model-dhow makers, blacksmiths and tinsmiths, and there will be a museum, a heritage library, restaurants and shops.

There is still a dhow builders' yard in Muharraq. Turn right onto Khalifa Al Kabir Highway from the old Muharraq Causeway, then turn off to the right just before the traffic lights to the airport and Al Hidd Highway. You'll find two or three dhows under construction and the fish-trap makers working in one of the yards along the seashore. The dome-shaped wire fish traps are woven by hand on a circular wire frame base, the weaver standing inside the trap until the dome is finished, at which point he crawls out through the trap entrance.

This is also where the big sailing dhows from India unload and load, though they are few and far between nowadays; you'll probably have to look at them through the chain-link fence, because you won't be allowed into the dockside area. A new port for the fishing fleet is in the final stages of construction, the official sign on one side of the gateway proclaiming it to be Muharraq Fisheries Port, and the equally official sign on the other side saying that it's the Muharraq Fishermen Port. You can still see a sizeable fleet of dhows anchored off the King Faisal Highway in the vicinity of the old Manama Dhow Port, but

Dhow building

they will soon have to move because of the development of the new Financial Harbour. There are also many dhows anchored near the Gulf Petrochemical Industries plant off Sitra Island and you can often see a flock of flamingos wading in the shallows there as well.

Bab Al Bahrain

Location → Opp PO, Government Rd · Manama	1721 1595
Hours → 08:00 - 13:00 16:00 - 20:00	
Web/email → na	Map Ref → 4-B1

The Bab Al Bahrain (which means the Gateway of Bahrain) was originally built in 1945. It was designed by Sir Charles Belgrave (the British Political Advisor to the Emir) to be used for government offices and at that time was right on the waterfront. Trading dhows from all over the Arabian Gulf, and from Oman and India, used to tie up to the jetty to unload their cargoes, which were then carried directly up into the souk. Now the sea is some distance away and is retreating even further with the land reclamation for the new Financial Harbour project. The Bab, which was extensively renovated in the late 1980s, now houses the Tourist Information Office and a shop selling local handicrafts, guidebooks, maps and postcards.

Bab Al Bahrain

Currency Museum

Location → Monetary Agency Bldg · Manama	1753 5535
Hours → 07:30 - 13:30 Fri & Sat closed	
Web/email → na	Map Ref → 4-C1

This beautiful little museum is located on the first floor of the Bahrain Monetary Agency in the Diplomatic Area. The Currency Museum exhibits ancient Arab gold and silver coins, including one of the nine rarest Islamic currency coins in the world and a couple of cabinets of banknotes. There is a comprehensive guide book in fairly accurate English as well as Arabic, which shows the two faces of each of the coins in the collection, alongside a note giving details such as the Empire, date, size and weight of each coin. Entrance is free. Unfortunately, several factors give one the impression that not many people visit the museum. Firstly, there is nowhere to park, unless you can persuade the soldier at the gate to let you into the car park reserved for the building. Secondly, the young men at the reception desk don't appear to know anything about the museum. You have to hand over some form of identification in exchange for a clip-on pass, which allows you to go up the stairs.

The only person who knows anything about the exhibition is Hisham, whose phone number is 1754 7766. If Hisham is not available, there doesn't seem to be anyone else who can show you around. Recommended for ardent numismatists only, perhaps? If you want to go, phone in advance, ask Hisham to arrange a parking space for you, and enjoy your visit!

Heritage Sites - Out of City

Other options → Museums - Out of City [p.107]
Tours & Sightseeing [p.111]

Three important historic houses are open to the public, two in Muharraq and one in Al Jasrah Village. Shaikh Isa Bin Ali House in Muharraq is located on Shaikh Abdulla Avenue and Bait Sayadi, or the Pearl Merchant's house, is nearby. Both houses were built in the early 19th century, as was Bait Al Jasrah, the birthplace of the late Emir, Shaikh Isa Bin Sulman Al Khalifa. Also in Jasrah Village is Al Jasrah Handicrafts Centre, which was opened in 1990.

Visit the Muharraq Souk and wander through a maze of narrow lanes where you can see old houses and buy fabric or traditional Bahraini sweets. Traditional crafts such as pottery, cloth and basket weaving, and rug and tapestry weaving are still carried out in Bahraini villages, and one can see dhow builders' yards near the shore in Muharraq. For a vivid slice of Bahraini life as it is now lived, visit the bustling Isa Town Souk (also known as the Persian Market) on a Thursday morning. You can buy anything and everything

Sheikh Isa House

there, including very cheap and cheerful china, caged birds, chickens, furniture and an astonishing array of second-hand rubbish.

Weaving

Al Jasrah Handicraft Centre

Location → Al Jasra Village	1761 1900
Hours → 08:00 - 14:00	
Web/email → na	Map Ref → 5-A1

At Al Jasrah Handicraft Centre you can see different handicrafts such as cloth weaving, palm weaving, pottery and furniture making being practised in separate rooms. The centre runs handicraft courses to train Bahrainis in the traditional crafts and there is a shop that sells examples of their work. Entrance is free.

Al Jasrah House

Location → Al Jasra Village	1761 1454
Hours → 08:00 - 14:00	
Web/email → na	Map Ref → 5-A1

Al Jasrah House, the late Shaikh Isa's birthplace, was built of local materials in 1907 and consists of several small rooms which still have the original furnishings. One of the rooms was used to drain juice from dates which were stacked in palm baskets to become ripe. Entrance is 200 fils.

Bait Sayadi

Location → Nr Shk. Isa Bin Ali House · Muharraq	1733 4945
Hours → See below	
Web/email → na	Map Ref → 2-A4

Bait Sayadi (also known as the Pearl Merchant's House) is particularly interesting because of its height, the intricate external and internal decoration

and stained glass windows. One of the rooms has a mirrored ceiling. The house belonged to a pearl merchant in the 19th century and was renovated in 1974. Unfortunately, the house is now closed for extensive reconstruction, but since it is only just round the corner from Shaikh Isa's house, it's worth visiting, if only to take a photograph of the building.

Shaikh Isa Bin Ali House

Location → Shaikh Abdulla Avenue · Muharraq	1733 4945
Hours → See below	
Web/email → na	Map Ref → 2-B4

This could be one of the highlights of your tour; Shaikh Isa Bin Ali House, which was built in 1800 and used as a residence until until the early 1900s. The house, which has three internal courtyards and 29 rooms on the ground floor, is most notable for its functioning windtower, an early form of air conditioning.

Stand in the room below the tower, and even on the hottest days you can feel the cool air being pulled down through the triangular channels into the room. There are large wooden shutters which can be closed across the base of the tower during the winter, to keep the cold air out. It also has typical one-metre thick walls and small door openings designed to protect the interior from heat in the summer and cold in the winter.

The courtyards are surrounded by archways and the house was built using traditional materials such as sea rock, plaster, lime and palm trunks. Some of the upstairs rooms are beautifully decorated with carved gypsum panels and stained glass panels above the doors and windows. The house was restored in 1976, using the same materials as were used in the original construction. The entrance fee is 200 fils and there is a good leaflet in English and Arabic with plans and photographs of the different areas of the building.

Timings: 08:00 - 14:00, Wed & Thu 09:00 - 18:00, Fri 15:00 - 18:00

Museums - City

Other options →

Art [p.160]
Heritage Sites - City [p.103]
Mosque Tours [p.113]

There are two main museums in Manama: the Bahrain National Museum and Beit Al Qur'an. Both are within easy walking distance of most of the major hotels in the city (during the winter months when it's not too hot) and should be on every visitor's must-see list. To do the National Museum justice, you will need to spend several hours there, so put aside at least a day in which to appreciate the exhibits and gain an understanding of the fascinating history of this unique land and the lives of its people over the past 7,000 years.

Bahrain National Museum

Location → Nr Shaikh Hamad Causeway · Manama | 1729 2977
Hours → See below
Web/email → www.bnmuseum.com   Map Ref → 4-C1

Situated beside the harbour at the Manama end of the Shaikh Hamad Causeway to Muharraq, the museum is housed in a series of low, modern, rectangular buildings and was opened in 1988 at a cost of BD 13 million. Take the last road to the right off the Al Fateh Highway before the turning to the causeway. You will see the famous Sail Monument (irreverently known by some as the Flying Diapers) on your left as you turn. There is a large carpark, and the entrance to the museum is across a spacious courtyard in which modern sculptures are displayed. Different types of local boats (dhows) are moored in the small lagoon behind the museum. Entrance is 500 fils for adults and children are admitted free of charge.

There is an excellent guide book to the museum which is available at the Bab Al Bahrain tourist shop and in the museum itself. It gives a floor plan of the museum and has coloured photographs and short informative articles about the main exhibits. Children especially will love the Hall of Customs and Traditions and the Hall of Trades and Crafts, where life-size models of people are displayed in realistic settings, showing how life in Bahrain was lived in pre-oil, pre-air-conditioning times.

Excavations at Bahrain Fort

Children will also thrill to the exhibits in the Hall of Graves, where skeletal remains of people are laid out in reconstructed burial mounds in the positions in which they were found during excavation.

One exhibit in particular which will appeal to children's sense of the macabre is the remains of two tiny children buried in an earthenware jar. A special section of the Hall of Graves gives a fascinating insight into how people lived all those millennia ago. A study of their skeletons has shown their gender, age and height, as well as the type of food they ate and the diseases from which they suffered. Don't miss the natural history exhibition, which features examples of the mammals, birds, reptiles, amphibians, insects, molluscs, minerals and fossils found in Bahrain. Pop into the Museum shop before you leave. There you can buy traditional handicrafts, books, films, postcards and souvenirs of your visit.

Timings: 07:00 - 14:00 Wed & Thu 08:00 - 14:00, 16:00 - 20:00 Closed Mon

Beit al Qur'an

Location → Nr Diplomat Htl · Manama | 1729 0101
Hours → 09:00 - 12:00 16:00 - 18:00 Thu pm & Fri closed
Web/email → www.beitalquran.com   Map Ref → 4-C1

This modern concrete building is situated on the Shaikh Hamad Causeway Road, opposite the Diplomat Radisson SAS Hotel, and is remarkable for its rather ugly, squat shape and strangely thin minaret tower. When you get closer to the building, however, you begin to appreciate the beauty of the smooth concrete walls and the wide band of engraved Arabic calligraphy which decorates them. Beit al Qur'an, or House of the Quran, displays rare Islamic manuscripts and works of art, including beautiful hand-calligraphed Qurans decorated with intricate Arabesque and geometric designs. The building also contains the Al Rahman Mosque, a library, a lecture hall and the Kanoo School for Islamic Studies. Entrance is free, but donations are welcome. Visitors should dress conservatively; don't wear shorts and ladies should cover their arms.

Museums - Out of City

Other options → Heritage Sites - Out of City [p.104]
Tours & Sightseeing [p.111]

The Oil Museum is the only museum located outside Manama, apart from the Rashid Al Oraifi Museum and Art Gallery in Muharraq.

The Oil Museum

Location → Nr Jebel Al Dukhan	1775 3475
Hours → 10:00 - 17:00 Open Thu, Fri only	
Web/email → na	Map Ref → 8-A4

You really must make the effort to visit this interesting little museum. It's a long way out of town, in the midst of the Bahrain oil fields at the foot of Jebel Dukhan (also known as the Mountain of Smoke, because of the mist in which it is sometimes shrouded). If you've never seen an oil field, with rust-coloured pipelines of every diameter zigzagging across the desert, the trip is interesting. The whole area smells of crude oil, or as one writer put it, the smell of money. The turn-off for the museum is signposted from Zallaq Highway.

If you don't have your own car, the easiest way to visit this area is by hire car. It is definitely not a good idea to go by taxi; you will find that many local taxis have meters that are not working or hidden behind tissue boxes, and quite often drivers who are unable or unwilling to travel outside the city. Perhaps the best way to visit this museum, however, is to take one of the commercial tours.

Theoretically the museum is open from 10:00 to 17:00 on Thursdays and Fridays, but it is advisable to phone before you set out, just to make sure. Inside there is a fascinating collection of objects related to oil exploration and a wonderful photographic history of the early development of the oil industry in Bahrain. There is a working model of an oil rig and several display cabinets of geological samples. One of the most interesting exhibits is a home-made, gas-powered fan, with beaten copper blades. It must have been awfully hot living in a tent in the middle of the desert back in the early 30s! All the exhibits are well documented and there is a small covered carpark outside the museum beside which you can see Oil Well Number One, the first well which started pumping out oil in 1932.

Parks & Beaches

Bahrain is sadly lacking in beaches and beach parks. There are small gardens dotted around the city and in some of the villages. These generally have a few trees, swings and other playground equipment, but they are usually dilapidated and neglected. Adhari Park was once the best outdoor theme park with many fairground-type attractions such as a giant swing boat, bumper cars and slides. It also had a little train running on a track around the park. Unfortunately, the park was neglected and eventually closed. It is now being rebuilt at a cost of over BD 9 million. The new park, which is due to open in December 2006, will have a rollercoaster, a water park, children's play areas, a mini-golf course, a bowling alley, a games arcade, family recreation facilities, a shopping mall and a museum. There are also plans for a Desert Spa and Resort near the Bahrain International Circuit in Sakhir. The Spa, which will open in 2008, will cost over BD 37 million and will include over 70 villas for rental, retail facilities, a water park and restaurants.

Underwater Explorer

For an underwater adventure you'll be sure to remember, the UAE has many interesting dive sites and areas for snorkelling that can be combined with a weekend of off-roading and camping. For more information on various underwater adventures grab a copy of the Underwater Explorer.

Beach Parks

Other options → Parks [p.111]

As there are very few public beaches, there are no beach parks as such, though there is an unfenced

Bahrain/Saudi Causeway

park which extends the length of Al Fateh Highway from just south of the Marina Club to within about a kilometre of Al Fateh Grand Mosque. This park is commonly known as the Manama Corniche. The area is very popular with local and Asian families and with young people. There are kiosks selling icecream, sweets, snacks, toys and balloons. There are swings and small roundabouts for the kids to play on.

Sometimes during the winter months there are people offering rides on ponies, donkey carts and a camel at the end nearest the Grand Mosque, although it has not been possible to verify whether or not this is a regular occurrence. A new restaurant has just opened at the southern end of the corniche and the Funland Bowling Centre and Ice-Skating Rink is also found in this area. There is no beach, only a sea wall and rock breakwater. There is also a rapidly diminishing area of park alongside the King Faisal Highway, which is being swallowed up by the land reclamation being carried out for the new Financial Harbour district and the Lulu Island project.

There is a small outdoor playground called Kids' Kingdom in this area, with a bouncy castle, a huge, blow-up Titanic slide and various other amusements. Pull off the highway on the right before you come to the flyover which goes to Seef district. Visitors can also use the Marina Club outdoor pool and beach for BD 1 per visit, and the Health Club for BD 5.

Marina Club

Location ➜ Off Al Fatih Highway · Hoora | 1729 1527
Hours ➜ Timings on request
Web/email ➜ www.bahraintourism.com   Map Ref ➜ 12-D2

The Marina Club offers use of all club facilities, including the Health Club, for a one-off payment of BD 50 and a yearly single membership fee of BD 225. You can also get membership for six months from July to December for BD 112.500. As well as the Health Club, facilities include restaurants, an indoor pool for ladies only, an outdoor pool and a beach. There are also squash and tennis courts and beach sports equipment is available. Non-members can use the outdoor pool and the beach from 08:00 for BD 1 per visit and the Health Club for BD 5 per visit. Island Tours run a dolphin-watching trip, an island trip and an evening cruise from the Marina Club. See further details in the Boat Trips section (p.112).

Beaches

Other options ➜ Parasailing [p.133]
Beach Clubs [p.142]
Parks [p.111]
Swimming [p.135]

Considering that Bahrain is a group of small islands, you would have thought that there would be an abundance of beaches suitable for bathing. You would have thought wrong! Bahrain has very few pleasant bathing beaches. This sorry situation is due to a number of factors; the sea around Bahrain is very shallow and the shoreline stony; many of the beaches which were once passable have been swallowed up by land reclamation; and illegal dumping of industrial and domestic rubbish is rampant. Two of the few remaining public bathing beaches are described in detail below. The best beaches, which are mostly man-made, belong to clubs and hotels. Most have club membership fees and some allow access to temporary visitors. Bahrain residents who have boats usually go out to small offshore islands and sand bars, and some tour companies offer similar boat trips.

Al Dar Island

Location ➜ Off the east coast south of Sitra | 3988 3757
Hours ➜ 09:30 - 17:30   Thu & Fri 10:00 - 16:30
Web/email ➜ na   Map Ref ➜ 6-E3

For a more lively beach experience, visit Al Dar Island off the east coast of Bahrain. This tiny man-made island resort was opened about 10 years ago and is very popular with young Bahrainis. Sea taxis are available from the Sitra Fishermen Port (that's what the sign says) and cost around BD2.500 for the 10 minute trip. Phone the island and the boat will be sent to take you over. There is a sandy beach and a restaurant in which alcohol is available. Parasailing, waterskiing, fishing trips, banana-boat rides and pedal boats can all be booked on the island. Sea swimmers are warned to be careful, as there is a very strong current at certain states of the tide.

Al Jazayer Beach

Location ➜ On the west coast, about 8 km from Awali | na
Hours ➜ Open at all times
Web/email ➜ na   Map Ref ➜ 9-A4

Situated on the west coast of Bahrain, several kilometres south-west of Al Areen Wildlife Park, Al Jazayer Beach is one of the few swimming beaches open to the general public. The beach runs alongside a landscaped (but neglected) garden and has several small dilapidated beach chalets with bamboo-slatted walls, wooden roofs and power points. The huts can be rented at BD 3 for 24 hours.

There are sweetwater taps and shower heads at intervals along the beach, a few sunshades and a basketball net. There is a small shop which sells sweets, icecream, beach toys, cigarettes and basic foodstuffs. There is ample room for parking, though there are reports of vehicles being broken into or vandalised during the night. There are two large notices beside the shop, one in English and one in Arabic, exhorting members of the public to refrain from causing a nuisance by playing loud music and behaving in an inconsiderate manner. There is a new toilet block near the shop. The beach is very popular with local and Asian families, and groups of young men.

Many people stay overnight at weekends and cook over open fires on the beach. Ladies go into the sea fully clothed. Unfortunately, the beach itself is not very clean, the water is very shallow and it has rubbish floating in it. Plans are afoot to build new huts which will be segregated into separate areas for families and young men.

ASRY Beach

Location → South of Hidd before ASRY at harbour entrance	na
Hours → Open at all times	
Web/email → na	Map Ref → 1-C1

Just before the Arab Ship Repair Yard at the entrance to Bahrain Harbour there is a small sandy beach with stone seats, sunshades, litter bins and showers. Like Al Jazayer Beach, the shoreline is stony and the beach is not very clean. The swimming area is marked by buoys. Ladies go into the sea fully dressed. The beach is an interesting area in which to sit and watch ships entering and leaving the busy harbour, but the sea is probably quite polluted by oil and garbage thrown from ships.

Bahrain Yacht Club & Marina

Location → Nxt to Al Bander Resort	1770 0677
Hours → 08:00 - 24:00	
Web/email → www.bahrainyachtclub.com.bh	Map Ref → 6-E4

If you go on a dolphin-watching trip with the Bahrain Yacht Club you are entitled to use the club facilities for the rest of the day. The club offers a private beach (man-made), a swimming pool, restaurants, bars and a coffee shop. There is also a fully-equipped diving and sailing school. Single membership is BD 150 a year, or BD 180 if paid in two instalments of BD 90. The dolphin trip costs BD 6 for adults and BD 3 for children under 13 years old.

Novotel Al Dana Resort

Location → Sheikh Hamad Causeway	1729 8008
Hours → 10:00 - 21:00	
Web/email → www.novotel-bahrain.com	Map Ref → 4-C1

The only city beach resort in Bahrain, the Novotel offers the Curves sports and leisure facility, a large outdoor pool and a small private man-made beach. Watersports equipment available for hire on the beach includes jet skis, water skis, windsurfers and kayaks. Jet skis are not available on Sundays and Mondays. Single annual membership fees are BD 400 for gold membership, which gives access to all the facilites, including the beach. Non-members can have access to the pool and beach, but not the health club; the fee is BD 6 per day for adults and BD 3 per day for children.

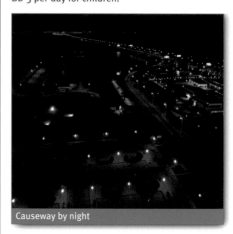

Causeway by night

The Ritz Carlton Bahrain Hotel and Spa

Location → Seef	1758 3380
Hours → 06:30 - 20:00	
Web/email → www.ritzcarlton.com	Map Ref → 3-E1

The hotel has one of the best beaches on the island in a man-made lagoon surrounded by lush landscaped gardens. The 600 metre private beach sweeps round the lagoon with its own island and private marina. As one would expect from a luxury five-star hotel, the annual club membership fees are very high. There's a BD 150 joining fee and single membership fees range from BD 400 for silver membership, which is only valid on weekdays, to BD 750 for platinum membership, which includes access to the Spa Health Club (ladies only). Temporary single membership for a minimum period of 2 weeks ranges from BD 28 to BD 42. One-day entry fees are BD 18 for a couple, and BD 25 for a family with two children.

Parks

Other options → Beaches [p.109]

Unfortunately, the only park worth visiting in or outside the city is the Water Garden in Ghufool. There are some gardens, such as Salmaniya and Al Andalus Gardens, but they are generally only used during the winter months by Bahraini and Asian families. Salmaniya Garden has a delightful, though neglected, perimeter fence which features small metal figures of ladies with prams and people playing games. The garden has a few trees and rather tired grass, but not much else, and Al Andalus Garden is in a similar condition.

Western expat families usually go to clubs, such as the Yacht Club, Dilmun Club and British Club, or have membership at the Ritz Carlton Hotel and Spa. It is unlikely that anyone goes to Al Areen Wildlife Park just to sit on the grass near the reception area; once you've paid to go in, you might as well take the bus tour. People are not allowed to drive their cars or walk around the park, but are restricted to the reception area.

The Water Garden	
Location → Shaikh Salman Highway · Ghufool	na
Hours → na	
Web/email → na	Map Ref → 4-B2

The oldest park in Bahrain is the Water Garden, which is located in the Ghufool District off Shaikh Salman Highway. This park is very popular with local and Asian families, but it does not have a swimming pool. There is a big lake and a smaller pool surrounded by pathways and trees, kiosks selling ice cream, popcorn and toys, and several sideshows for children, such as swings, roundabouts, bumper cars, a swing boat and a train that runs around the lake. Most of the sideshows cost around 400 or 500 fils a go. Entrance is 500 fils and you can hire a pedal boat for BD 1. Unfortunately, the upkeep of this park is not always that great and at times you may find the toilets are dirty and see rubbish floating in the lake.

Other options → Activity Tours [p.112]
Weekend Breaks [p.117]

There are several types of tours offered by tour operators in Manama, Muharraq and further afield. History tours usually take in Bahrain Fort, King Fahad Causeway and the Burial Mounds. Heritage tours include the National Museum, The Forts, Shaikh Isa's House and Muharraq Souk. Desert trips take you to the Tree of Life and the Oil Museum. Craft trips go to Bahrain Craft Centre, Al Jasrah Craft Centre, basket and textile weavers and pottery makers. Shopping tours go to Manama Souk, the Gold Souk, and the two main shopping malls, Seef Mall and Al Aali Shopping Complex. Islamic tours visit the Grand Mosque, Beit al Qur'an and Al Khamis Mosque.

One of the most endearing aspects of Bahrain is the proliferation of bizarre monuments and water features which decorate the city and surrounding areas. These do not feature on tour operators' itineraries, but for people with their own transport, and some time to spare, the following sights are well worth seeing.

First, the artificial waterfall at the junction of the Airport Road and Al Hidd Highway (Map Ref 2-C4) – the waterfall is sometimes decorated with statues of small deer and sometimes with small boys cooling off in the pools. Second, the statue of a disgruntled looking falcon on the opposite side of the Airport Road from the waterfall. Third, the weird statue of a rabbit/fish-like thing on the Marina Corniche (Map Ref 4-C2).

Fourth, the Budaiya Castle, which is an enormous turreted, battlemented private palace beside the sea beyond Budaiya Village. There is also an unusual mosque with a multitude of white fibreglass domes on its roof in the same area (Map Ref 3-A2). Fifth, a Nodding Donkey oil pump painted to look like a giraffe (Map Ref 6-B4). There used to be another pump painted to look like a black and white striped hoopoe, but that has been removed to make way for a gigantic structure being erected near the entrance to the Sakhir Race Track, the purpose of which has not yet been revealed (Map Ref 8-E2).

Last but by no means least is the most bizarre structure of all, the 'brick on a stick', which can be seen on the large roundabout at Nuwaidrat Village on Shaikh Jaber Bin Ahmed Al Subah Highway. This is a large rectangular rock supported on a 3 metre steel pole. It is in fact a fountain, but the true significance of the structure is not clear until you see it working, which only happens infrequently.

Exploring

Tours & Sightseeing

Remember the old fairground rifle range target of a ping-pong ball bouncing on a jet of water? The architect was obviously bored and decided to create a visual joke (Map Ref 6-C3).

Aali pottery

Activity Tours

Other options → Tours & Sightseeing [p.111]

There are no activity tours available in Bahrain, although sailing courses, diving courses and diving trips can be arranged through the Bahrain Yacht Club. Yacht Club details are provided in the Boat Tours section.

Boat Tours

Several organisations offer boat tours such as dolphin-watching trips, lunch and dinner cruises, and swimming and snorkelling trips, in addition to the regular speedboat journey to the Hawar Islands. The uninhabited, outlying Hawar Islands are home to many species of seabirds, including a huge breeding colony of Socotra cormorants, greater flamingo, ospreys and sooty terns, but with plans to increase tourist activity in the area, one wonders for how much longer the birds will be left in peace. The islands, which were once described by an over-enthusiastic government official as 'The Maldives of the Gulf' are, in fact, flat barren treeless deserts. There is nowhere to go outside the hotel grounds, so one tends to laze in the pool soaking up the peaceful atmosphere (and any beverage that comes to hand).

The Bahrain Yacht Club (1770 0677) runs three dolphin-watching trips every day. Weather permitting, boats leave the club at 10:00, 12:00 and 14:00. The trip costs BD 6 for adults and BD 3 for children under 13 and lasts about an hour and a half. The boat holds 12 passengers and is partly shaded. Make your booking by phone a couple of days before you want to go, but be warned! There is a minimum charge of BD 24 per boat, so it's a good idea to phone the day before you go in case they have nobody else booked for the trip. The fee entitles you to spend the rest of the day enjoying the club facilites, which include an outdoor pool, a private beach (man-made), restaurants, bars and a coffee shop.

Island Tours offers three types of boat trip which leave from the Marina Club: dolphin watching, a lunchtime island trip and an evening cruise. The dolphin-watching trips leave at 10:00, 12:00 and 14:00 every day and last for two hours. The charge is BD 8 for adults and BD 4 for children, and soft drinks are provided. The company uses two boats, one large one with a sunshade and one small boat without shade for smaller parties. If you suffer when exposed to too much sunshine, check which boat will be used for your trip. The lunchtime island trip leaves at 12:00 and lasts for four hours.

The company's air-conditioned, luxury, 51 foot yacht, the Island Mermaid, takes you out to Jarada Island, where you can swim or ride on a jet ski, which is carried on board. Tickets cost BD 25 for adults and BD 12 for children and the price includes a light lunch and unlimited soft drinks, though there is also a cash bar for those who fancy something a bit stronger. There are ladies and gents toilets.

GCC easy as ABC

If you want to drop in on your neighbours, then go prepared. Be it for a shopping spree in Dubai, a luxury holiday in Abu Dhabi, to find tranquility in the wilderness of Oman or to see the colourful heritage of Kuwait, don't leave Bahrain without an Explorer!

The evening cruise leaves at 18:00 and lasts for two hours. The price of BD 10 for adults and BD 5 for children includes snacks and soft drinks, and a cash bar is also provided. Private charters are also available for birthday parties and corporate meetings. Phone 1729 4439 for bookings and more information.

Dadabhai Travel can arrange dhow trips for BD 10 for adults and BD 5 for children, based on a minimum of 15 passengers. Trips, which are available on request, include a continental lunch or dinner. Phone 1722 6650 for bookings and more information.

Boats to the Hawar Islands leave the Al Dur Jetty at 10:00 each morning. Coach transfers can be arranged from the Hawar reservation office on the Marina Corniche to the jetty. The return trip costs BD 12 per passenger. The sun-shaded, 24 seater boats are fast and very noisy with two 225 hp engines on the back.

After a bumpy 45 minute ride you are met at the Hawar Resort Jetty and taken on a five-minute journey round the lagoon to the hotel, where you are greeted with a welcome drink of orange juice. A buffet lunch is served at 12:30 (get there early, as there is a limited choice of food and it runs out fairly quickly if there's a big crowd). The staff are friendly, but the hotel is a bit on the shabby side. There is a small pool with a slide and another pool with a much bigger slide in the children's playground half way round the lagoon. Jet skis, pedalo boats and canoes can be hired. Boats return to the mainland at 17:30.

Room rates are BD 54 for two people per night on weekdays and BD 68 for two people per night at the weekend. Two slightly more luxurious suites, which can accommodate four people, are also available. They have two bedrooms, two bathrooms and toilets, and a sitting room with direct access to the poolside and beach area. The weekday rate is BD 140 per night and the weekend rate is BD 180 per night. Phone 1729 0377 for bookings and more information.

Bus Tours

Other options → Walking Tours [p.28]

There are no regular bus tours around the city, except tour buses picking people up from hotels and the airport and taking them to the various tourist attractions.

City Tours - In Manama

Two of the tour operators which offer organised city tours are Dadabhai Travel and Oasis Travel.

Dadabhai's Shopping Tour visits Manama Souk, the Gold Souk, Seef Mall and A'ali Mall. The tour takes three hours and ranges from US$29 per person (for two to five people), down to US$19 per person for 25 or more people. They also have what they call a City Tour, which not only goes to Bahrain Fort but also to King Fahad Causeway and the Camel Farm. The tour takes two and a half hours and ranges from US$32 per person (for two to five people), down to US$19 per person for 25 or more people. Phone 1722 6650 for more information.

The Oasis Travel & Tourism Excursion Programme for 2006 includes a half-day Culture & Tradition Tour every day except Friday and Saturday, which takes in Al Khamis Mosque, Bait Al Qur'an, Muharraq Souk, Sheikh Isa's House, Beit Sayadi (which is closed for reconstruction) and Arad Fort. Their half-day Fascinating Capital Tour (every day except Monday and Friday) visits the Fish and Vegetable Markets, the Al Fateh Mosque, the National Museum, the Bab Al Bahrain and the Manama Souk. Tours cost BD 20 per person for adults (for a minimum of four people), and BD 10 per child (4 - 12 years old). Telephone 1781 3713 for more information.

Dolphin & Whale Watching

The Bahrain Yacht Club (1770 0677) runs three dolphin-watching trips every day. Weather permitting, boats leave the club at 10:00, 12:00 and 14:00. The trip costs BD 6 for adults and BD 3 for children under 13, and lasts about an hour and a half. The boat holds 12 passengers and is partly shaded. Make your booking by phone a couple of days before you want to go, but it's a good idea to phone again the day before you go to check if anybody else has booked, as there is a minimum charge of BD 24 per boat. The fee entitles you to spend the rest of the day enjoying the club facilites, such as an outdoor pool, a private beach (man-made), restaurants, bars and a coffee shop.

Island Tours offers three types of boat trip which leave from the Marina Club: dolphin watching, a lunchtime island trip and an evening cruise. The dolphin-watching trips leave at 10:00, 12:00 and 14:00 every day and last for two hours. The charge is BD 8 for adults and BD 4 for children, and soft drinks are provided. The company uses two boats, one large with a sunshade and one small boat without shade for smaller parties. If you suffer when exposed to too much sunshine, check which boat will be used for your trip. Phone 1729 4439 for bookings and more information.

Mosque Tours

Other options → Museums - City [p.106]

Al Fateh Mosque, commonly known as the Grand Mosque, is on the seaward side of Al Fateh Highway opposite the Gudabiya Guest Palace. This enormous building with its huge dome and two minarets can accommodate 7,000 worshippers in

Exploring

Tours & Sightseeing

the main prayer hall, balconies and courtyard. The mosque houses the Ministry of Islamic Affairs, a library and a conference centre. Non-Muslims can visit at any time, except during prayer time, from Saturday to Wednesday between 09:00 and 17:00, provided they are suitably dressed. Nobody wearing shorts is admitted. Ladies can borrow an abaya to wear when entering the prayer hall.

Knowledgeable, courteous guides are available to conduct you around the mosque, which is a beautiful example of Islamic architecture. The gigantic dome is, in fact, made of fibreglass, but it blends in perfectly with the pale stonework of the building. An outstanding feature of the prayer hall is the main chandelier which looks like a gigantic, iron wheel rim suspended from the roof by chains. Also notice the wonderful ironwork lanterns hanging outside the entrances. Contact Farahat Al Kindy on 1772 7773 or 3947 4091, or by fax on 1772 9695 for more details. There are no tours available at Al Khamis Mosque.

Islamic Architecture

Tour Operators

As Bahrain is such a small country and the number of tourist sites limited, there are not many tour operators. The four main tour operators are Al Gosaibi Travel, Dadabhai Travel, Sunshine Tours and Island Tours. A few independent operators also offer

guided tours. Some offer tours during the winter months only. Some offer tours for a while and then close down due to lack of custom, opening again later when there is a demand for their services. Al Gazal Desert Camp is one such company. When contacted, their representative said that the camp had been discontinued and he seemed unsure as to when they would start it again. Tours can be booked from most hotels, or tour operators can be contacted direct by telephone. Most tour operators will collect passengers from their hotels.

Other tour operators include Al Reem, Oasis Travel & Tourism and Gulf Tours.

Al Reem (listed in the telephone directory as Al Reem For Environmental & Consultation Eco Tourism) appears to be affiliated to Dadabhai Travel. They have a charming website (www.alreem.com) – what it lacks in the correct use of English it more than makes up for with beautiful colour photographs and detailed descriptions of all their birdwatching and nature tours. They advertise a six-day birdwatching package which includes a return economy air fare on KLM, but they don't say where the trip originates. Day trips include a five-hour trip on Thursdays and Saturdays around all the main natural habitats on Bahrain Island to see birds, butterflies, reptiles and wild plants, and an eight-hour bird-watching trip on Fridays to some of the outlying Hawar Islands. According to the website, both trips need a minimum of 10 people, although if you call the agent directly you may find they are more flexible.

The Oasis Travel & Tourism Excursion Programme for 2006 includes a half-day Culture & Tradition Tour every day except Friday and Saturday, which takes in Al Khamis Mosque, Bait Al Qur'an, Muharraq Souk, Sheikh Isa's House, Beit Sayadi (which is closed for reconstruction) and Arad Fort. Their half-day Fascinating Capital Tour (every day except Monday and Friday) visits the Fish and Vegetable Markets, the Al Fateh Mosque, the National Museum, the Bab Al Bahrain and the Manama Souk. Oasis Travel also has tours to Al Areen Wildlife Park, the Jebel, Oil Museum and Tree of Life, as well as visits to the handicraft centres and burial

Off-Road Explorer

Experience the UAE's delights off the beaten track. Designed for the adventurous, a brilliant array of outback route maps, satellite images, step by step guidance, safety information, details on flora and fauna, and stunning photography make this outdoor guide a perfect addition to your four wheeler.

mounds. They say that all their excursions are accompanied by German, English and Arabic-speaking guides.

Gulf Tours advertises land tours to archaeological sites, sea trips around the coastline of Bahrain Island with a buffet lunch, and a trip out to the restaurant on the King Fahad Causeway.

Tour Operators	
Al Gosaibi Travel	1721 2333
Al Reem	1771 0868
Bahrain International Travel	1722 3315
Dadabhai Travel	1722 6650
Farid	3955 2910
Gulf Tours	1731 1885
Hawar Resort	1729 0377
Oasis Travel & Tourism	1723 1900
Sunshine Tours	1722 6204

Other Attractions

Amusement Centres

Other options → Amusement Parks [p.116]

There are several indoor amusement centres in the city. All the big malls in the Seef area (except A'ali Mall) have indoor theme parks and there are play areas at Fuddruckers in Adliya and Sanad. On a more serious, but equally enjoyable note, the Children & Youth Science Centre in Umm Al Hassam is a delightful hands-on science museum.

Chakazoolu	
Location → Dana Mall · Sanabis	1755 8585
Hours → 10:00 - 10:00	
Web/email → na	Map Ref → na

An indoor theme park on two floors with rides, bumper cars, a roller coaster, games and places to buy food. Entry is free, but you need to buy a rechargeable card (minimum charge BD 2.000) to use the games and rides. If you buy a card for BD 5.000, you get another BD 2.000 free. Video games cost 250 fils a go.

Foton World	
Location → Bahrain Mall · Seef	1755 6112
Hours → 10:00 - 24:00	
Web/email → na	Map Ref → na

Foton World in Bahrain Mall is an indoor theme park that has small boat rides, bumper cars, a roller coaster, games and places to buy food. Entry is free and children can enter alone and remain unattended. Games and rides cost 400 to 500 fils.

Funland Centre	
Location → Funland Centre · Hoora	1729 2313
Hours → 10:00 - 23:00	
Web/email → funlandcenter.tripod.com	Map Ref → 12-D3

Funland on the Marina Corniche has a bowling alley with 18 lanes and a full-size ice-skating rink. The centre is open for bowling from 09:00 to 01:00 and for skating from 09:00 to 23:30. The prices are BD 2.500 for two hours of ice skating, which includes hire of skates. There is a concession of BD 2 per person for a group of 10 or more people, but you need to book in advance. Bowling costs BD 1 per game from Saturday to Wednesday and BD 1.600 per game on Thursday and Friday.

Magic Island	
Location → Seef Mall · Seef	1758 2888
Hours → 10:00 - 24:00 Wed & Thu 10:00 - 01:00	
Web/email → na	Map Ref → na

Magic Island is an indoor theme park in Seef Mall with over 120 different games and attractions including a Chamber of Horrors, a Roller Coaster Simulator and a Roller Blade Arena. Open from 10:00 to midnight every day (except for Wednesdays and Thursdays when it stays open for an extra hour). Entrance is free, but you have to pay for each ride. Charges range from 200 fils to BD 1.500. Children can enter and remain in the park unattended, but there is a height limit on some of the rides, like the Roller Coaster Simulator.

Playland	
Location → Above Fuddruckers · Adliya	1774 2266
Hours → 10:00 - 22:00	
Web/email → na	Map Ref → 4-C2

Playland, above Fuddruckers in Adliya, is an indoor centre with games, climbing frames and a ball pool. Each ride costs 100 fils.

The Children & Youth Science Centre	
Location → Nr Kuwait Ave · Umm Al Hassam	1772 1132
Hours → 07:00 - 14:00 Wed/Thu 16:00 - 19:00 Fri closed	
Web/email → na	Map Ref → 4-C3

On a more serious but highly enjoyable note, the Children & Youth Science Centre in Umm Al Hassam is a hands-on science museum for children. The staff are friendly and helpful, and children are encouraged to experiment and learn about science through playing with the colourful exhibits. Entry is free.

Amusement Parks

Other options → Water Parks [p.116]
Amusement Centres [p.115]

At present there are no major outdoor amusement parks, but see the Parks & Beaches section for information about the development of Adhari Park. There is a small amusement park at Kid's Kingdom on the King Faisal Corniche.

Kid's Kingdom

Location → King Faisal Corniche · Manama | 1722 7476
Hours → 16:00 - 22:30   See below
Web/email → na   Map Ref → 11-D3

The outdoor part of Kid's Kingdom has a mini chair-o-plane, bungee bouncers, a bouncy castle, a giant blow-up Titanic slide and other attractions. The park is open from 16:00 to 22:30 from Saturday to Tuesday, 16:00 to 24:00 on Wednesday, 16:00 to 01:00 on Thursday and 15:30 to 22:30 on Friday. Entry is free, but there is a charge for each of the rides. Children cannot be admitted without an adult, or left unattended.

Nature Reserves

Although Al Areen Wildlife Park is the only nature reserve in Bahrain, several of the small rocky islands in the Hawar group are breeding sites for sea birds such as flamingo, osprey and Sooty Falcon, and the world's largest breeding colony of the Socotra cormorant. For tours of these areas, see details listed in the Tour Operators section (p.114).

Al Areen Wildlife Park

Location → Nr Bahrain International Circuit | 1783 6116
Hours → 08:00 - 17:00   Fri 14:00 - 17:00
Web/email → na   Map Ref → 9-D2

Al Areen Wildlife Park, south of the Bahrain International Circuit, is the only Nature Reserve in Bahrain. Unfortunately, there is still a considerable amount of mistreatment of animals in Bahrain, evidenced by frequent newspaper reports from the Bahrain Society for the Prevention of Cruelty to Animals. The Park is open from 08:00 to 17:00 and from 14:00 to 17:00 on Fridays. Follow the signposts for the Circuit, then follow the signs to Al Areen. The park covers more than eight square kilometres and has an impressive collection of birds and mammals, many of which are native to the Arabian Gulf region. Tickets cost BD 1 for adults and 500 fils for children and the tour is excellent value for the money.

The area around the reception buildings is beautifully landscaped with mature trees, lawns, flower beds, ponds and ornamental water features. There are covered seating areas and walkways, and many of the larger trees and shrubs are labelled with information plates. There are several species of water fowl such as ducks, pelicans and flamingos in the rather stagnant-looking ponds near the reception area and at the Water Birds Park half way round the tour, where there is a collection of more exotic birds such as Sacred Ibis, Swans, and Crowned and Paradise Cranes.

In the small cafeteria, a continuous film loop with an Arabic commentary and English subtitles gives information about the park and the wildlife in it. There is a gift shop containing small tanks of tropical fish and very small cages containing birds for sale, local pottery, some Arabic books on wildlife and one very expensive English book, but there are no maps of the park, or information leaflets about the animals. The tour takes 45 minutes and starts every hour, on the hour, in an air-conditioned bus with a driver and tour guide, who gives a running commentary in Arabic and English during the tour.

There are several herds of different varieties of gazelles, oryx, wild sheep and goats in large enclosures, and a group of young giraffes in a pen. Ostriches roam the park area freely and can be seen everywhere sheltering in the shade of large acacia bushes. There is also a mosque and a Falcon Clinic where injured or sick birds are treated.

Water Parks

Other options → Amusement Parks [p.116]

There is only one public water park in Bahrain. Another has recently opened beside the Shaikh Khalifa Bin Salman Highway south-west of Jidhafs, but it has not only proved difficult to find its name, but also how to get to it, since there is no turning off the highway in that area. The Hawar Resort Hotel (www.hawaresort.com) has two swimming pools; the main pool has a normal slide which is used by kids and adults, while the other is located in a kid's playground and has

Exploring

Other Attractions

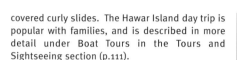

covered curly slides. The Hawar Island day trip is popular with families, and is described in more detail under Boat Tours in the Tours and Sightseeing section (p.111).

Al Qassari Water Park

Location → Nr Al Khamis Mosque · Jidhafs	1740 0739
Hours → See Below	
Web/email → na	Map Ref → 4-A3

Al Qassari Water Park has recently reopened after being partly destroyed by fire during the civil unrest in the mid-90s. It is located on the right of Shaikh Salman Highway, on the bend just before you reach the traffic lights at Al Khamis Mosque. There are three swimming pools, a large one for adults and two smaller ones for children. Attendants on duty at each pool and it is possible to arrange swimming lessons. The shower blocks and toilets are clean. Ladies do not generally go into the pools, but tend to sit around the children's pools. However, a separate ladies' pool will be opened in the near future. Icecream, cold drinks and sandwiches are on sale. The entry fee is BD 1 for a two-hour session. There are five sessions throughout the day from 10:00 to 12:00, 13:00 to 15:00, 15:00 to 17:00, 17:30 to 19:30 and 20:00 to 22:00. Phone for further details.

Weekend Breaks

Other options → Hotels [p.22]
Tours & Sightseeing [p.111]

The only weekend break available in Bahrain is a trip to the Hawar Islands, a group of 16 small islands near the coast of Qatar, which is covered in the Boat Tours section (p.112). Camping out in the desert is a possibility, although all of Bahrain Island south of the Tree of Life is a restricted area and everything north of that is criss-crossed by oil pipelines. The Sakhir area near Jebel Dukhan is very popular with Bahraini families during the spring, before the weather gets too hot. People with boats sometimes anchor off outlying islands for the night, but tour companies don't organise overnight trips.

Weekend Breaks outside Bahrain

If you fancy getting away from Bahrain for a few days there are many interesting and varied opportunities just a short hop away in neighbouring GCC countries. The local operators, including Gulf Air, Qatar Airways, Oman Air, Kuwait Airways, Emirates and Air Arabia, offer regular flights throughout the region, plus you may find a flight with one of the international carriers who often make stopovers. Depending on your nationality you may be eligible for a visa on arrival in certain GCC countries. Just remember, if you are in Bahrain on a visit visa and you leave, you will need another one to get back in. However, access is a little easier now the government allows 33 nationalities to obtain visas on arrival.

For those who want a complete change of scene, weekend trips to Dubai and Salalah are available and can be booked through a travel agent or with the relevant airline; apparently the price is the same whether you book through an agent or with the airline directly.

Emirates Holidays offers a three-night package to the gleaming metropolis of Dubai, which includes economy class airfare from Bahrain to Dubai and back, three nights bed and breakfast, airport assistance and transfers from airport to hotel by private car, room tax and service charges. The price ranges from BD 126 for a single room at the Pearl Residence, to BD 498 for an Arabian Deluxe room at the Al Qasr Madinat Jumeirah, but varies depending on the time of year.

Oman Air Holidays has a tempting package of three nights in Salalah which includes economy class airfare from Bahrain to Salalah and back, three nights bed and breakfast, transfers from airport to hotel, hotel taxes and service charges. The price ranges from BD 134 for a single room at the Majan Hotel, to BD 334 at the Grand Hyatt. Optional services include car rental and sightseeing tours.

Trips to Thailand, India, Egypt, Jordan, Cyprus or Turkey are a possibility, of course, if you don't mind going on a three-hour (or longer!) flight for only a three-day break. Gulf Air offers package deals to all these destinations, but they are usually for a minimum of five nights.

Kuwait

While Bahrain is quite a popular spot for residents of Kuwait the visa versa may not be as appealing (no alcohol don't forget), however, the colourful and somewhat tainted heritage of this small yet rich country it is still worth a weekend break. Kuwait may be one of the world's smallest countries, but its 500km coastline has endless golden beaches that remain refreshingly tranquil. From the Grand Mosque to the Kuwait Towers there are many architectural splendours to take

Exploring

Weekend Breaks

snaps of while Al Qurain House, which still shows the scars of war with its immortal bullet holes, gives you a fascinating insight into the troubled times of the Iraqi invasion. There is also Green Island, an artificial island linked by a short bridge and home to restaurants, a children's play area and a great alternative view of Kuwait's shoreline.

If you have a Bahrain residency visa you may be able to get a transit visa for Saudi, allowing you to drive to Kuwait. The drive takes about four hours but some delays may be experienced at the border, and women, who should be covered, are not allowed to travel alone or with a man to whom they are not related. You may therefore prefer to fly. For more information and inspiration, check out the *Kuwait Explorer* from Explorer Publishing.

UAE

Often described as the city of gold, a shopper's paradise and one of the best nights out in the Middle East, Dubai is by far the favourite destination in the Emirates. There's so much to see and do you're unlikely to fit everything into one weekend, but some visitor 'musts' include exploring the creek and the historic souks, enjoying the thrill of a desert safari, doing some serious shopping and then treating yourself to some hard-earned pampering at one of Dubai's luxury spas. The range of eating, drinking and dancing options is also worth the airfare alone!

Don't forget the other emirates though, including Abu Dhabi, Sharjah and Fujeirah. There's bags of culture and heritage to discover, no end of golden sandy beaches and the east coast has some great snorkelling and diving sites. To help you make the most of any trip to the Emirates, don't miss the *Dubai Explorer*, the *Abu Dhabi Explorer*, the *UAE Off-Road Explorer*, and the *UAE Underwater Explorer* – all from Explorer Publishing.

Qatar

Qatar once had something of a sleepy reputation, but things are changing fast and the amount of development and investment in the country means it is becoming increasingly popular with visitors. With an attractive corniche, world-class museums and cultural centres and plenty of hotels with leisure and entertainment facilities, the capital Doha makes a perfect weekend retreat from Bahrain. The inland sea, or Khor Al Udaid, in the south of the country also makes a great day trip, usually as part of an organised tour. The *Qatar Explorer* from Explorer Publishing has details of all these activities and many more.

Oman

There are countless reasons to visit Oman and with frequent flights from Bahrain there's really no excuse not to. The Gulf of Oman's rich sea life, the historic buildings, the wildlife and the variety of unspoilt landscapes including vast dramatic deserts, rugged mountains and lush green wadis and valleys, are all things that you will remember fondly. The fascinating sights and sounds of the capital Muscat will provide more than enough to keep any weekend visitor busy, but Oman has much more. You should also consider exploring the Mussandam Peninsula with its amazing dive sites, the historic mountain towns and villages with stunning scenery, the turtle beaches in the east and the blissful summer rain in the southern Dhofar region. For more information on all these areas and details of all there is to see and do, grab a copy of the *Oman Explorer* from Explorer Publishing.

Travel Agencies

Other options → Tour Operators [p.114]

As mentioned previously, the only weekend break available in Bahrain is a trip to the Hawar Islands Resort. This has to be booked through the Hawar Reservations office in Manama, not through a travel agent. Of course, weekend breaks in Dubai are popular and these can be arranged through any of the travel agents on the list.

Travel Agencies	
Al Bader Travel	1721 3333
Al Mannai Travel	1727 6664
Al Reem	1771 0868
Algosaibi Travel	1721 2333
Bahrain International Travel	1722 3315
Cleopatra Travel International Co.WLL	1727 7900
Delmon Travel	1721 1345
Emirates Holidays	1758 8707
Galaxy Travel & Tourism	1771 3003
Gulf Tours	1731 1885
Kanoo Travel	1722 0220
Manama Travel	1722 2633
Oasis Travel & Tourism	1727 2211
Oman Air Holidays	1722 5383
Sunshine Tours	1722 3601

Exploring

Weekend Breaks

ABU DHABI
Experience The Magic

Abu Dhabi offers all the attractions of a top class
international resort ... plus a taste of something
extra. It combines year-round sunshine and
superb facilities for leisure and recreation with
the spice and mystique of an Arabian adventure.
Abu Dhabi is a dynamic 21st century city with
unspoiled beaches, the tranquility of the desert,
rugged mountain scenery and lush green oases.

هـيـئـة أبـوظبـي للسيـاحـة
Abu Dhabi Tourism Authority

P O Box 94000 Abu Dhabi, United Arab Emirates, Tel +971 2 4440444, Fax +971 2 4440400
info@abudhabitourism.ae

Activities

EXPLORER

Activities

Highlights...

Down the Club

More than in other Gulf countries, social life in Bahrain revolves around its 'clubs'. These vary from the smaller sports oriented clubs, focusing on sports like sailing and rugby, to grand beach clubs at five star hotels. Nearly all offer a range of sporting facilities as well as a beach, pool, gym, activities and often bars, restaurants and social events organised for its members. See Sports Clubs [p.144] and Clubs & Associations [p.149].

Hello Sailor!!

Being an island nation, sailing is a popular weekend pastime for many people in Bahrain. There are many small islands just a short sail away which make great places to get away from it all. You can discover remote beaches where the shallow waters are packed with marine life; perfect for diving, snorkelling and fishing. Sailing clubs also act as social clubs, for both individuals and families, to meet people and enjoy a variety of activities and events.

Newcomers to Bahrain may be surprised by the sudden transition from summer to winter and back again. It usually happens overnight and temperatures can leap or plummet between 10 and 15 degrees Celsius. In the summer months, activity is restricted to indoor, air-conditioned facilities such as the EZ FIT sportsplex where cricket lovers can play indoor league or to outdoor, floodlit venues such as the Riffa Club where golf-crazy aficionados swarm to the course as soon as the sun goes down. The winter is much like any other place in the Arab world where temperatures are comfortably within an 18 to 25 degree range so that outdoor sports and activities can be enjoyed at anytime of the day. Most of the Sports and Social Clubs have their own individual sports sections which cover anything from sailing, horse riding, football and rugby to cricket, netball, tennis and diving.

With Bahrain being an island, it's hardly surprising that sailing is one of the most popular sports activities going. The Bahrain Yacht Club has over 130 berths and 600 members who regularly head for the water at the weekend. Bahrain is surrounded by numerous small islands, some of which are only visible at low tide. These islands are therefore washed clean every day and many boat owners head for these pristine islands as the tide goes out and spend as much time there as they can before the tide comes in to reclaim them. Dolphins are regular visitors to Bahrain and a number of organizations have taken the opportunity to provide Dolphin Watch Boats for the interested clients.

Bahrain has a small but diverse population with numerous cultures which cater for their needs in many ways whether it be sporting, social, artistic or intellectual. Whatever your interests are, chances are that there is an organization, club or society in Bahrain which will be able to fill your leisure time with fulfilling and worthwhile activities.

Aerobics

Other options → Sports & Leisure Facilities [p.142]
Dance Classes [p.149]

Aerobics is a great way to burn some calories, get fit and have fun at the same time. Covering a whole range of exercises these days, aerobics can be enjoyed in most of Bahrain's local Sports Clubs or hotels, both in the gym and in the water.

World Beat Fitness Centre	
Location → Bldg 1762 · Janabiyah	1761 2576
Hours → See below	
Web/email → www.worldbeatfitness.com	Map Ref → 5-B1

Located in Janabiya, this jewel of a work-out studio does it's best to avoid the conventional approach to staying fit and so keeps guests interested. The courses here are infused with a healthy dose of edgy kookiness but still follow the basic Nia, Yoga, Pilates and Aerobics fundamentals. The music is loud, the atmosphere is fun and for a little while you may even forget that you're doing any work. Buy a monthly pass or just pay the walk-in fee. Women work out in the mornings and in the afternoons and evenings the classes are mixed.

Timings: 08:00 - 13:00 & 15:30 - 21:00, Mon & Wed 08:00 - 13:00 & 15:30 - 20:00, Thu 0830-1300, Closed Fri

Badminton

Badminton is a minority sport which is played in most of the 'clubs' here on an ad hoc basis. If you are interested in playing Badminton on a social level, it might be a good idea to ring up one of the clubs or, if you are a competitive player, give the Badminton & Squash Federation a ring.

Bahrain Badminton and Squash Federation	
Location → Various locations	1729 2662
Hours → Various timings	
Web/email → na	Map Ref → na

The Association, under the chairmanship of Dr Salaman Rashid Al Zayani, is responsible for the registration of Badminton Clubs and the organisation of Leagues and competitions both here and abroad. Contact them on the above number for more details of competitions in Bahrain.

BAPCO Club	
Location → Nr Riffa Golf Club	1775 3666
Hours → 08:00 - 24:00	
Web/email → na	Map Ref → 8-A2

The Badminton Club meets at 16:00 on Saturdays and Tuesday and open Badminton is held on Mondays. Contact the club for more details.

British Club

Location → Kanoo Ave · Adliya	**1772 8245**
Hours → See below	
Web/email → www.britishclubbahrain.com	Map Ref → 14-C4

Originally known as the Gymkhana Club, the firmly established British Club offers a wide range of sporting activities, including regular sessions of badminton every Tuesday from 17:00 - 20:00. For more information call the club or check out their website.

Basketball

Basketball is the most popular game in Bahrain, although soccer gets the most attention. There are 12 teams in the National League here with teams such as Muharraq, Ahli and Manama employing overseas players, including Americans, and coaches are from other countries in the Gulf. Matches are played at the Youth Dome in Juffair. For more details, call the Bahrain Basketball Association (1774 1010).

> **Oops!**
> Did we miss anything out? If you have any thoughts, ideas or comments for us to include in the Activities section, drop us a line, and if your club or organisation isn't in here, let us know and we'll give you a shout in the next edition. Visit www.Explorer-Publishing.com and tell us whatever's on your mind.

Boat & Yacht Charters

Other options → **Dinner Cruises [p.222]**
Dhow Charters [p.126]

Boat charters are available in Bahrain, although most companies prefer to provide a skipper for the occasion. If you are a certified sailor and show your credentials then most companies will be happy to offer you a sailing boat. Charters are usually by the day or half day and the hire of larger boats usually also includes food and beverages.

Bahrain Yacht Club & Marina

Location → Nxt to Al Bander Resort · Sitra	**1770 0677**
Hours → 08:00 - 24:00	
Web/email → www.bahrainyachtclub.com.bh	Map Ref → 6-E4

The BYC was founded in 1968 as a breakaway group from the RAF Sailing Club. It has a 130 berth marina at Sitra and is a fully recognized Royal Yachting Association Training Centre. Boat hire can be arranged through the club by ringing John or Margaret on the above number.

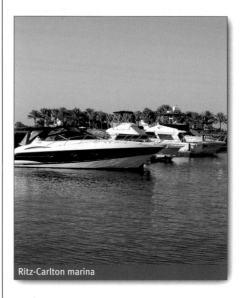
Ritz-Carlton marina

Island Tours

Location → See below	**1771 0088**
Hours → Timings on request	
Web/email → www.islandtours.com.bh	Map Ref → 14-B2

The 'Island Mermaid' is a 51-foot tour yacht berthed at Marina Club on which is offered dolphin watching tours, island trips and an evening cruise. Private charters are available on request.

Zallaq Sailing Club

Location → End of Zallaq Highway · Zallaq	**1783 6078**
Hours → Call for timings	
Web/email → na	Map Ref → 7-B3

The Zallaq Sailing Club is part of the BAPCO Club and have their own centre out at Zallaq complete with a clubhouse. For boat charter details, call the above number.

Bowling

Bowling is big in Bahrain with regular popular tournaments sponsored by Batelco that draw competitors from all over the Gulf. Most tournaments are held at the Funland Centre. All competitions are organised by the Bahrain Bowling

Association (1782 2077), www.bowling.com.bh. For the social bowler, there are a good number of well-maintained centres in Manama, see below for more details.

Al Bander Hotel & Resort

Location → Nr Bahrain Yacht Club · Sitra	1770 1201
Hours → See below	
Web/email → www.albander.com	Map Ref → 6-E4

The Resort has a fully-computerised six lane bowling alley along with billiard and snooker tables, darts and also video games. The bowling alley can also accomodate groups with packages ranging from 4-24 bowlers. Opening hours are 16:00 - 23:00 Saturday to Tuesday, 16:00 - 02:00 on Wednesday and 12:00 - 02:00 on Thursday, Friday & Public Holidays .

Bahrain Bowling Centre

Location → Seef Mall · Seef	1758 2464
Hours → See below	
Web/email → na	Map Ref → 3-E1

A compact bowling alley, but clean and well organised with 12-lanes. It is worth checking before you go as it is often booked for private events. The alley is open from 16:00 - 23:00 between Saturday and Tuesday, 16:00 - 02:00 on Wednesday and 12:00 - 02:00 on Thursday, Friday and Public Holidays.

BAPCO Club

Location → Nr Riffa Golf Club	1775 3666
Hours → 08:00 - 24:00	
Web/email → na	Map Ref → 8-A2

The BAPCO Club has a six lane bowling alley in Awali and the times for bowling are: Wed 08:00 - 17:00, Thu & Fri 09:00 - 23:00 & Sun 08:00 - 23:00.

Funland Centre

Location → Al Fateh Corniche · Hoora	1729 2313
Hours → 10:00 - 23:00	
Web/email → http://funlandcenter.tripod.com	Map Ref → 12-D3

Funland Centre has an 18 lane Bowling Alley and is open 7 days a week, 10am till Late. Games cost BD1.000 Saturday to Wednesday and BD1.600 per game on Thursdays and Fridays.

Boxing

EZ FIT Sportsplex

Location → Budaiya Rd · Budaiya	1769 2378
Hours → 08:30 - 24:00	
Web/email → www.ezfit.biz	Map Ref → 3-E1

Boxing is just one of the many sports pursued at the EZ FIT Sportsplex and details about the boxing programme can be obtained by ringing Chris on the above number.

Camel Rides

Believe it or not, Bahrain is not the best place to see camels. A few can be found near the Tree of Life and desert tours can take you up close. If you are looking for camel rides or just want to be photographed on one, the open area along the Marina Corniche between Al-Fatih Mosque (14-D2) and the Dolphin Park (12-D4) is the place to go.

Camping

Other options → Outdoor Goods [p.174]

Whether on the beaches or in the desert of Bahrain, camping is a great way to get away from it all for a while and is also the best way of getting clear views of the starry Arabian night skies, away from the dazzling lights of the city. There are no official campgrounds in Bahrain, so it's just a case of pitching up well away from habitation and making sure you're not on private land. Although there are no companies offering camping trips as an activity yet, the EMK group provides services for large groups of campers at their fixed campsite. Contact them on 1773 0558 or at emkgroup@batelco.com.bh for further details.

Cricket

Cricket has been alive and well in Bahrain for many years and is played by expats from Pakistan, England, India, Australia and many other countries. Although the number of cricket grounds has unfortunately diminished with the voracious appetite of the construction industry, apart from the Pakistan Club, the Indian Club (only usable by their own players), The Young Goans Club and the Awali Club, there are very few pitches left.

Activities

Bowling · Cricket

However, it is possible to see cricket being played all over Bahrain every Friday afternoon and you should be able to get yourself a game. The Bahrain Cricket Association is improving the quality of cricket in Bahrain and as a member of the Asian Cricket Association it has introduced coaching courses for players and umpires. It also organises and selects national teams to play in tournaments throughout the Gulf.

Awali Cricket Club

Location ➜ North Awali | 1775 6959
Hours ➜ Call for timings
Web/email ➜ na   Map Ref ➜ 8-A1

Awali Cricket Club play their matches at the Awali Oval in pleasant surroundings. Probably the most sought after team to play for, players are largely expats from England, Australia, Pakistan and India, amongst other countries. They play in all seasons regardless of weather and the pavilion also provides refreshments. Call the above number for games to join.

EZ FIT Sportsplex

Location ➜ Budaiya Rd · Budaiya | 1769 2378
Hours ➜ 08:30 - 24:00
Web/email ➜ www.ezfit.biz   Map Ref ➜ 3-E1

The EZ FIT Sportsplex in Budaiya is the venue for the Bahrain Indoor Cricket League and you can also organise social games for your friends or company.

Cycling

Other options ➜ **Sporting Goods [p.178]**
Mountain Biking [p.133]

Cycling is a well supported sport in Bahrain and the Bahrain Cycling Association are actively involved in improving the quality of cycling in the Kingdom with the sponsorship of Batelco. The BCA welcome cyclists to train with their national team and compete in local competitions. The national clubs are restricted to U19's and they have plans for a continental team as well. Solitary weekend cyclists can often be seen along the backroads of Sakhir

Off-Road Adventure

Outdoor types should get their hands on the UAE Off-Road Explorer. In addition to the 18 exciting off-road routes through deserts, mountains and wadis, this book has plenty of info and advice on the best places to pitch your tent in the Emirates.

and down towards Shaikh Isa Air Base and there are a number of clubs you can attach to if you're keen. Contact Khalid Hamad at bahraincycling@hotmail.com for more details.

Bahrain Cycling Association

Location ➜ Various locations | 1766 0956
Hours ➜ Call for timings
Web/email ➜ na   Map Ref ➜ na

The Bahrain Cycling Association is responsible for creating the BCA/Batelco League and organising time-trials and road races in Bahrain. It also selects and funds the national teams in various competitions within the Gulf. If you are keen on cycling in Bahrain, call Mr. Nasser Fakhroo, the General Secretary

Dhow Charters

Other options ➜ **Dinner Cruises [p.222]**
Boat & Yacht Charters [p.124]

Dhows trips to the islands can be arranged with most tour operators, (see p.111), or through Gulf Discovery at the Novotel Hotel (see below), the Marina Club or Bahrain Yacht Club.

Gulf Discovery

Location ➜ Novotel Al Dana Resort | 3648 6428
Hours ➜ See below
Web/email ➜ na   Map Ref ➜ 4-C1

Gulf Discovery offer dhow cruises from the Novotel Hotel beach on request, leaving at 09:15 and returning at 17:00, costing BD20 for adults and BD15 for children. The star of their fleet is the recently converted 60-foot 'Scaramouch', which can accomodate 25 passengers. Tours are tailored to customers' preferences and they offer charters for everything from scuba diving, fishing and dolphin watching to excursions to places such as Jaradah Island and sunset cruises.

Diving

Other options ➜ **Snorkelling [p.135]**

The history of diving in Bahrain is amongst the most ancient and lucrative in the world, with over 4200 years in the 'pearl diving' trade. As a result of this massively historic tradition in diving there is a wide range of wrecks dotted about the reefs and the coasts of Bahrain. The temperature of the sea encourages diving most of the year, ranging from a comfortable 20C to 34C in summer. Wetsuits are worn from November to April, while lycra suits are usually sufficient during the summer - although you have to be pretty brave to bear the conditions to get out to the dive sites in roasting 40C+ temperatures.

The visibility in the waters is very good for offshore dives, averaging around 25 metres although it understandably reduces to 5 metres inshore. There is also a wide range of wildlife including rays, moray eels, crayfish, trigger fish, clown fish, turtles and sturgeon on the reef and mackerel, cobia, tuna and barracuda, as well as over 200 species of fish and around 30 species of coral. Popular dive spots include the pearl diving sites where there is the chance of finding a pearl yourself!

Aqua Hobbies

Location → Palace Rd · Ras Romman	**1729 3231**
Hours → Call for timings	
Web/email → www.aqua-hobbies.com	Map Ref → 12-B3

For tourists and visitors, Aqua Hobbies hire out equipment and conduct dive trips, so just show your PADI card and you're away!

Aquatique

Location → Government Ave · Naim	**1727 1780**
Hours → See below	
Web/email → www.pearldive.com	Map Ref → 11-E3

Aquatique offers a full range of snorkelling and scuba-diving trips and instruction from basic pool lessons through to professional training and are a PADI 5 star instructor development centre. For day trips, present your PADI card and Aquatique can provide all the equipment. Trips leave the Marina Club at 08:30, returning at 15:00 and BD35 gets you 2 dives. Contact the number above or 3967 1748.

Bahrain Yacht Club & Marina

Location → Nxt to Al Bander Resort · Sitra	**1770 0677**
Hours → 08:00 - 24:00	
Web/email → www.bahrainyachtclub.com.bh	Map Ref → 6-E4

The scuba diving section of the Bahrain Yacht Club is a well-established and fully accredited branch of the British Sub Aqua Club. They have the full range of scuba equipment that may be rented by members or used by beginners or qualified visitors. Diving is more or less guaranteed for every week of the year.

Fishing

Other options → Boat & Yacht Charters [p.124]

Fishing is another big sport in Bahrain as can be witnessed by the number of fishermen hanging out lines from the Sitra causeway. However, the best fishing is found out at sea, so most fishermen get out in their boats as often as they can. The shallow waters around the island teem with Spanish Mackerel but hamour is to be found out in the deeper holes in the reef areas. Most of the inner reefs have been fished out now so most fishermen go out 5-10kms and go trawling with rapellas or fish with live bait and sinkers for sharri, barracuda, kingfish and needlefish.

Bahrain Yacht Club & Marina

Location → Nxt to Al Bander Resort · Sitra	**1770 0677**
Hours → 08:00 - 24:00	
Web/email → www.bahrainyachtclub.com.bh	Map Ref → 6-E4

Fishing is a popular sport at Bahrain Yacht Club and there can be anything up to 200 people out in their boats at any one time. During the Annual Fishing Competition there is usually around 50 boats out in the water. Anyone who is interested in deep water fishing should go along to the Yacht Club for more information and to find out when it is possible to get a lift out on one of the boats.

Traditional fishing

Football

Bahrainis are football mad and there is a National League with two divisions which provide a good standard of play. At the time of writing, Bahrain ranked 53rd in FIFA's top nations of football. They got through the preliminary 2006 World Cup round before being knocked out by Trinidad & Tobago and came fourth in 2004 in the Asian Cup. Social football can be found at most of the Sports and Social Clubs.

Bahrain Football Association

Location → Nr National Stadium	1768 5775
Hours → 08:00 - 12:00 17:00 - 20:00 Fri & Thu pm closed	
Web/email → na	Map Ref → 6-A2

The Bahrain Football Association was founded in 1957 and was affiliated to FIFA in 1966. They are responsible for running the domestic and international programme for the Kingdom and for information on upcoming matches, call 1772 9563.

Dilmun Club

Location → Off Janabiyah Highway · Saar	1769 0926
Hours → See below	
Web/email → www.batelco.com.bh/dilclub	Map Ref → 3-B4

If you're a fan of 5-a-side football, then this is the place for you. Games are played three times a week, usually in the evening, and coaching can also be arranged with Andy Richard on 3925 8771.

EZ FIT Sportsplex

Location → Budaiya Rd · Budaiya	1769 2378
Hours → 08:30 - 24:00	
Web/email → www.ezfit.biz	Map Ref → 3-E1

Indoor football can be played at the EZ Fit Sportsplex where you can rent the hall for a social game with your friends or you can enter your team in the indoor league.

Golf

For the Golf enthusiast, there are three courses in Bahrain that offer the opportunity for anyone who wants to play, be it on a regular or casual basis. Two of the courses are 'Brown' courses complete with portable turf and mirage-type water hazards while the other one is the Real McCoy with green grass fairways, green greens and wet water hazards. The former two are The Awali Golf Club and The Bahrain Golf Club while the green course is located at the Riffa Golf Club. All the clubs offer refreshments and The Riffa Golf Club also has a first class restaurant.

Awali Golf Club

Location → Awali	1775 6770
Hours → 07:00 - 19:30	
Web/email → na	Map Ref → 8-B1

Awali Golf Club, situated next to East Riffa Air Base, was the Middle East's first golf course and is now home to Bahrain's Open Golf Championship, which is held here annually. Members carry a pad of articial grass around the course which can only be used within the boundaries of the fairway. Visitors are welcome and can play 18 holes for BD7.500 and refreshments are available at the clubhouse.

Bahrain Golf Association

Location → Hamamla Camp	1761 1136
Hours → Various timings	
Web/email → na	Map Ref → 5-B2

The Golf Association is responsible for sanctioning the various tournaments played in Bahrain and also the selection of the Bahrain Amateur Golf Team, which has been the strongest team in the Gulf for a number of years now. For any information on golf in Bahrain, give them a call.

Bahrain Golf Club

Location → Nr Riffa Fort · East Riffa	1777 8620
Hours → Call for timings	
Web/email → na	Map Ref → 6-A4

The Bahrain Golf Club is situated quite close to the Sh. Salman Bin Ahmed Al Fateh Fort in East Riffa and is another challenging sandy course which can be played every day of the week except Monday. The club offers potential members a free introductory round.

Riffa Golf Club

Location → East of Awali	1775 0777
Hours → 08:00 - 21:00	
Web/email → www.riffagolfclub.com	Map Ref → 8-A1

This Par 72 Championship golf course with five lakes and more than 600 date palms is a popular choice for golfers due to its extensive 6,187 yard of fairways and pristine greens. The course also runs a golf academy with three PGA golf pros and state-of-the-art computerised swing analysis equipment plus shops, brasserie, restaurants and conference rooms.

Hashing

Other options → Running [p.134]
Pubs [p.231]

The Bahrain Hash House Harriers (BH3) was started by expats here in 1972 and ran until 1979 when it gradually changed its philosophy and eventually became the Bahrain Running Club. However, Hashing still continues in Bahrain under its original tenet, which is to promote physical fitness among its members, to get rid of weekend hangovers, to acquire a good thirst and to satisfy it with beer, as well as persuade the older members that they are not as old as they feel.

Bahrain Hash House Harriers	
Location → Various locations	1786 2620
Hours → Call for timings	
Web/email → na	Map Ref → na

The Bahrain chapter of the Hash House Harriers meets on Mondays at 5pm and runs are followed by the inevitable barbecue and liquid refreshment. All comers are welcome, just ring 1786 2620 for directions to the next meet.

Hiking

Other options → Outdoor Goods [p.174]

Bahrain is basically very flat with nothing in the way of uplands that can compare to the mountainous terrain of Oman, for example. However, there are a few small jebels (mountains) in the south of the island below Sakhir, including Jebel Dukhan, the highest point in Bahrain at 134m. As a result, there are no organised hiking clubs, although some people gather informally at the weekend for treks into the desert and low hills. If you are keen to meet like-minded people and want to know more about the various trails on offer, with the expat community being

Trekkers Unite

If you fancy yourself as a bit of a trek-head then you simply must grab a copy of the Oman Trekking Explorer, with 12 spectacular hiking routes in handy cards with detailed maps as well as a trekking handbook.

as small as it is in Bahrain, just ask around and you should be able to get in contact with hikers through friends of friends of friends ...

Horse Riding

Apart from the numerous stables run by Bahrainis, there are several stables frequented by the expat community. All offer lessons in dressage and show jumping at Intermediate and Advanced levels and Beginner lessons for all ages. They also offer livery for private horses and hacking, while some specialise in pony club, polo and cross country. Anyone with some riding experience can participate in dressage, show jumping, endurance and cross country. Spectators can watch all of the above plus Flat Racing, which is literally 'The Sport of Kings' in Bahrain and races are held every Friday in the winter season from October to May.

Al Abid Private Riding Centre	
Location → Hamad Town	3968 3334
Hours → Call for timings	
Web/email → na	Map Ref → 7-D2

Located just outside Hamad Town, this boutique stable teaches everything from grooming to horsemanship. Lessons by appointment only.

Awali Riding Club	
Location → South-West of Riffa Golf Club	1775 6525
Hours → 07:00 - 19:00	
Web/email → na	Map Ref → 8-A2

The Awali Riding Club is a branch of the BAPCO Club and has 50 registered riders. For more information on what the club offers and how to join, contact Mike Ragel on the above number.

Bahrain Royal Equestrian & Endurance Federation	
Location → Nr BAPCO Club	1775 4300
Hours → Various timings	
Web/email → na	Map Ref → 8-A2

BREEF are responsible for the registration of all showjumpers and riders in the Kingdom and organises the Showjumping season. They also run the Flat Racing season which takes place every Friday from October to May.

Dilmun Club

Location → Off Janabiyah Highway · Saar | 1769 3766
Hours → 15:00 - 19:00 20:00 - 23:00 Fri closed
Web/email → www.batelco.com.bh/dilclub   Map Ref → 3-B4

Horse Riding is a very popular activity at the Dilmun which has a pony club and lessons for Tiny Tots.   There are private lessons, shared lessons, group lessons, accompanied hacks and horse hire for unaccompanied hacking. For more details, contact Hilary Picton on the above number or mobile 3960 4268.

Gulf Air Riding School

Location → Gulf Air Club · Salmabad | 1778 0087
Hours → 09:00 - 22:00
Web/email → na   Map Ref → 3-E4

Located at the Gulf Air Club near Zayed Town, this riding school is a good place to go if you are looking for a casual ride and want to hire a horse for the day. Contact the school for more details.

Shakoora Riding Centre

Location → Off Budaiya Highway · Budaiya | 1759 1103
Hours → 08:00 - 12:00 15:30 - 19:00 Mon & Fri closed
Web/email → www.thingstodobahrain.com   Map Ref → 3-A2

Located in Budaiya and considered one of the best in the Kingdom, this school offers qualified riding instruction for beginners and advanced riders in dressage and showjumping for children and adults. You can learn to ride, hire a horse or stable your own as they cover everything from Hacking to Show Jumping and Dressage and the services these require. Contact Samia Al Saffar for more information.

The Country Club

Location → Off Al Nakheel Highway - Nr Jannusan | 1759 3593
Hours → 08:00 - 20:00
Web/email → na   Map Ref → 3-C1

The stables at The Country Club provide one-hour guided trail rides, half hour and one hour private lessons and one hour group lessons. Prices vary for members and non-members. Further details can be obtained from the Country Club at the above number.

Ice Skating & Ice Hockey

Funland Centre

Location → Al Fateh Corniche · Hoora | 1729 2313
Hours → 10:00 - 23:00
Web/email → http://funlandcenter.tripod.com   Map Ref → 12-D3

Ice skating at the Funland Centre costs BD2.500 for two hours, including skates. With ten or more skaters it costs BD2.000 per person, but you have to make reservations first.   Kids also play ice hockey on Wednesday evenings from September to May. Surprisingly, there are no adult teams and no organised league.

Jet Skiing

Other options → Beach Clubs [p.142]

Jet-skiing is enjoyed by a large number of people in Bahrain, with beaches such as at Bahrain Yacht Club and the Marina Club being popular places for jet-ski owners to launch their crafts. If you don't have your own, most of the beach hotels such as the Ritz Carlton, the Novotel, the Al Bander Resort and Hawar Island Resort have jet-skis for hire.

Karting

Karting is a popular sport in Bahrain and is actively supported by Sheikh Salman bin Rashid Al Khalifa who sponsors the Unstoppabulls, a Bahraini based motor racing team.   The Bahrain International Circuit, which hosts the Formula 1 Grand Prix at Sakhir every April, has four separate tracks already and has plans for a new karting track to be constructed.   This will include an international standard karting track with workshops and facilities for spectators. More information about karting in Bahrain can be obtained from the Bahrain National Kart Association (1761 2992).

Gulf Speed One

Location → Nr Citibank · Seef | 3944 4137
Hours → 15:00 - 23:00
Web/email → na   Map Ref → 3-E1

Situated in Seef near Citibank and Ahli United Bank, Gulf Speed One has a modern track with a range of karts. Sessions cost between BD2 and BD10 depending on your choice of kart.

Rally Town

Location ➜ Nr Shk Isa Bin Salman Highway	1761 2992
Hours ➜ 15:00 - 23:00	
Web/email ➜ na	Map Ref ➜ 3-C4

Located in Janabiyah, Rally Town offers Go Kart racing for all ages, with faster karts available for adults and kids over 14 years of age and 5 feet or taller. Costs are BD2.000 for a single engine kart and BD 2.500 for a double engine kart. There is also a mini golf course which costs BD 1.000 per hour, a pool table, arcade games, a snack bar and a party room.

Silver Go-Kart Circuit

Location ➜ East of Sh. Salman Flyover · Tubli	1778 0011
Hours ➜ 14:00 - 22:00 Thu 14:00 - 23:00	
Web/email ➜ na	Map Ref ➜ 4-A4

Located in Tubli Bay, this circuit has battery operated cars, kiddie rides, karting, twisty trucks and dune buggies. Entrance is free and karts cost BD1.000 for ten laps.

Kayaking

Other options ➜ Tours & Sightseeing [p.111]

The waters around Bahrain are shallow and warm, so kayaking is the perfect way to get around and visit some of the other islands within the archaepeligo. Some expats do have their own, but for those that don't, kayaks are available to hire from most of the beach hotels or beach resorts. Prices are around BD4 per hour for two people.

Kitesurfing

Other options ➜ Beaches [p.109]

Kitesurfing is arguably the number one activity on the water around Bahrain these days. It's taken about two years to get the infrastructure organised but now, with The Skate Shack at the centre of the sport, kitesurfing is up, up and away. Being an island, Bahrain has no problems offering venues for the sport.

However, recent construction developments has started to cut down the number of places to go. The Anwaj Islands, behind the International Airport, is currently one of the favourite locations and it looks as though the new development on the island may give the go ahead for the sport to take place there. For more information on kitesurfing in Bahrain, contact the Skate Shack (1769 7176) or visit their website www.skate-shack.com

Martial Arts

Bahrain Karate Centre

Location ➜ World Beat Fitness Centre · Janabiyah	3947 7709
Hours ➜ See below	
Web/email ➜ www.bahrainkarate.com	Map Ref ➜ 5-B1

This school offers the most traditional Japanese Shotokan karate in Bahrain, teaching it in its original form and in perfect surroundings as the WBF centre is well equipped with good wooden flooring and proper airconditioning. Junior classes are from 16:00 - 17:00 and 17:00 - 18:00, for children aged 6 to 13 on Saturdays, Mondays and Wednesdays. For people older than this are the senior classes from 18:30 - 20:00 on Mondays and Wednesdays. Fees are BD25 per month and the instructor Phil Dutton, a 6th Dan, takes them through classes, in preparation for exams run by the British Martial Arts Association.

Oops!

Did we miss anything out? If you have any thoughts, ideas or comments for us to include in the Activities section, drop us a line and if your club or organisation isn't in here, let us know and we'll give you a shout in the next edition. Visit www.Explorer-Publishing.com and tell us whatever's on your mind.

GoJu Karate Club

Location ➜ Nr Salmaniya RA · Salmaniya	3965 9510
Hours ➜ 18:00 - 19:30 Sun, Tue & Thu	
Web/email ➜ na	Map Ref ➜ 13-D2

This club is run by Mohammed Mashal who teaches the whole philosophy of dedication, meditation and discipline. Particular emphasis is placed on children's classes, ranging from 6 year olds and upwards. Classes cost BD15 per month.

Hoi Jeon Moo Sool

Location ➜ Budaiya Rd · Budaiya	1769 2629
Hours ➜ 15:30 - 23:00 Fri closed	
Web/email ➜ http://hoijeonmoosool.free.fr	Map Ref ➜ 3-E2

Master Kang Kyo Sik is a Korean martial arts master who lives and breaths Hoi Jeon Moo Sool and offers a variety of martial arts coaching. Fees are BD25.000 per month for three hour long sessions per week and transportation is provided.

Marina Club

Location → Off Al Fatih Highway · Hoora | 1729 1527
Hours → Timings on request
Web/email → www.bahraintourism.com   Map Ref → 12-D2

Non-members can make use of the facilities at the Marina Club for BD5 per day and programmes include taekwondo and karate. For more details of their martial arts, call the club. Separate facilities are available for men and women.

Master Khan's Fighting Arts Academy

Location → Al Hala Club · Muharraq | 3996 6139
Hours → 19:00 - 21:00   Sat, Mon & Wed
Web/email → www.mkfaa.com   Map Ref → 11-B2

The Bahrain branch of this BMAA approved school is led by Ashraf Ali Ghansar (IV Dan Black Belt) and is a great place for beginners to learn or for those wanting to learn a new style. A whole host of courses is on offer enabling everyone to get involved and get the most out of themselves, whatever their personal goals. These include The Little Warrior Program for children from 3 to 6 years old, Children's Taekwondo Program for 7 to 14 year olds, Kyuk Too Ki (Korean Kickboxing) for students over 15, Kick Aerobix, which combines aerobics, kickboxing & music, a Self Defence programme and Khan Do Kwan, a program designed by Master Javed Khan for all to participate in.

Zen-Do Bahrain

Location → Shk Mohd Bin Essa Compound · Jasra | 1761 1909
Hours → 09:30 - 20:30   Thu & Fri closed
Web/email → www.zendobahrain.com   Map Ref → 5-B2

Zen-Do Bahrain is a complete kickboxing school that teaches a martial art encompassing mind, body and spirit where the goal isn't just punching and kicking techniques but also to impart life lessons. It is run by Suhail Algosaibi and has nearly a decade of experience in self-defence classes. The team of four instructors, two part time and two full time, is led by the black belt and there are four unique courses for children under 18.

Moto-Cross

Other options → Motorcycling [p.133]

2005 saw the first ever Bahrain Motocross Championship which was organised by the Bahrain Motorcycle Club at the purpose-built dirt track off the highway to the Saudi Causeway. Only eight bikes took part but over 1000 spectators came and went during the course of the afternoon, so it looks as though motocross could be about to take off in Bahrain. For more information about practice sessions and race schedules with the BMC, please contact Isa Al Awadhi 3969 3837 or Samer Al Arayed on 3946 1999.

Motor Sports

The people of Bahrain are mad about motor sports. Since the inaugural Formula 1 Grand Prix in April, 2004, the whole Kingdom has jumped on the band wagon and now races of all kinds can be watched at the Bahrain International Circuit. Two local drivers, Shaikh Salman bin Rashid Al Khalifa and Hamad Fardan are well on the way to becoming the first Arab Formula 1 drivers in sports history. Both have recently won races during the Formula BMW Asia Championship and have really put Bahrain on the motor racing map.

Bahrain International Circuit (BIC)

Location → Gulf of Bahrain Ave · Sakhir | 1745 0000
Hours → Call for timings
Web/email → www.bahraingp.com   Map Ref → 9-D1

In addition to holding the first Formula 1 races in the Middle East, the last year has seen the BIC grow in many directions. The circuit has hosted a variety of races, corporate activities and functions. A national drag championship has been initiated and BIC will soon host the BAPCO Caterham Challenge. In addition, the Formula BMW Performance Centre has been set up and recently held its first Formula BMW Race Professional course with a view to educating Bahraini drivers and giving them a real chance to become international Formula 1 drivers.

Bahrain Motor Club

Location → Various locations | 1768 6295
Hours → Call for timings
Web/email → na   Map Ref → na

The Bahrain Motor Club was founded in 1980, since when, interest in motor sports in Bahrain has grown tremendously. To find out more about the activities the club is involved in; be it rallying, Formula 1, karting, car racing or drag racing, contact the number above.

Motorcycling

Other options → Moto-Cross [p.132]

Motorcycles are a rare sight in Bahrain except at the weekends when a couple of loosely knit social groups get together; The Bahrain Bikers Group and the Harley-Davidson Bahrain Chapter (see www.hogbahrain.com for contacts). One other club is Bahrain Motorcycle Club (See Moto-Cross p.132), which is more interested in off-road competitions.

Mountain Biking

Other options → Cycling [p.126]

Mountain Biking is something you don't see much of in Bahrain due to the fact that there aren't really any mountains. The island is only about 48km long, so you can easily cycle the entire length in a day, and the highest point is at Jebel-Al Dukhan standing at only 134m. The Skate Shack (1769 7176) www.skate-shack.com, sells decent brands of bikes and accessories, and you may find other bikers there.

Netball

Bahrain Netball League	
Location → Various locations	1779 5167
Hours → 17:30 - 21:30 Tue	
Web/email → na	Map Ref → na

There are currently about fifteen teams in the Bahrain Netball League playing matches at the Bahrain Rugby Club, British Club and the Dilmun Club. The various clubs contribute teams to the league and each team plays two matches every Tuesday night at different locations during the season which goes from October to April. At around Christmas time the league splits into two divisions and starts playoffs for the championships. For more details about netball in Bahrain, phone Julie Berquist on the above number.

Bahrain Netball Club	
Location → Off Janabiyah Highway · Janabiyah	1769 5809
Hours → See below	
Web/email → na	Map Ref → 3-B4

Netball is played through the winter from the second week in September with matches played on Tuesdays, mini league matches from 16:30 - 18:00 and adult matches from 19:30 - 21:00. Bahrain Rugby and Netball Club has four adult teams, three teams for 9-14 year olds, two teams for under 9's and practice sessions are on Sundays at 19:00 for adults and at 17:00 on Thursdays for youngsters.

EZ FIT Sportsplex	
Location → Budaiya Rd · Budaiya	1769 2378
Hours → 08:30 - 24:00	
Web/email → www.ezfit.biz	Map Ref → 3-E1

EZ FIT Sportsplex is the only place you can play indoor netball, with a new indoor netball league started up recently and coaching is also available. For more information, call the centre's number above or call Mel (3983 4431).

The British Club	
Location → Kanoo Ave · Adliya	1717 2845
Hours → See below	
Web/email → www.britishclubbahrain.com	Map Ref → 14-C4

There are currently two adult teams at The British Club which take players from 14 or 15 years of age. Training takes place on Sunday nights through the season which begins in September and continues through until April. You don't have to be a competitive player to attend the training. If you just want to enjoy some fitness training and ball throwing give it a go and join in the sessions.

Parasailing

Parasailing is available in Bahrain at The Ritz Carlton Hotel (1758 0000), The Al Bander Resort (1770 1201) and the Marina Club (1729 1527) as part of their watersports programmes.

Rugby

Bahrain Rugby Club	
Location → Off Janabiyah Highway · Janabiyah	1769 5809
Hours → See below	
Web/email → www.bahrainrfc.com	Map Ref → 3-B4

The Bahrain Rugby Club has two full-sized grass rugby pitches and a clubhouse which houses a bar, restaurant and a swimming pool. The season runs from September through to May although many navy games are played through the summer months and the club players train each week even through summer. You must be a member of the club to play there and full membership costs

Motorcycling · Rugby

BD125 per year. The First XV team play in the Gulf League and produce a quality of rugby that is highly regarded by both players and spectators. Teams and businesses can also hire the pitches at a fee of BD40 per pitch. Opening hours are from 09:00 with varying closing times each day depending on games or whether the club has an evening planned.

Running

Other options → **Hashing [p.129]**

Bahrain Cross Country Road Runners

Location → Various locations | 1768 9320
Hours → Call for timings
Web/email → www.bahrain-roadrunners.com   Map Ref → na

BCCRR has been in existence for over 27 years and during that time it has developed a comprehensive running calendar. They are responsible for organising all cross-country and road running events in Bahrain, including the Annual Marathon. An 8km Summer Series is held every week and usually starts from Awali and the organisation also run biathlons. More information can be obtained from Adnan (Chairman) on the above number or Joyce Boswell on 3946 5378.

Sailing

Other options → **Boat & Yacht Charters [p.124]**

Bahrain Sailing Club

Location → Al Jazayer Beach | 1783 6078
Hours → 08:00 - 22:00
Web/email → na   Map Ref → 9-B3

Situated out at Al Jazayer beach on the west coast, Bahrain Sailing Club is a neat little complex equipped with swimming pool, restaurant, beach, a two-storey accommodation building where you can book in for the night or a week, and all the facilities for water-based sports. Day visitors are charged a nominal BD1 per person. The Club is hosting this years Al Bareh International Regatta when sailors from all over the Gulf will compete.

Finding Nemo
Whether it's clown fish or manta rays that float your boat you'll find them all in the Arabian Gulf and the Gulf of Oman. To help you along the way just pick up a copy of the Underwater Explorer for the best dive sites and tips on what there is to sea and when to see it!

Bahrain Sailing School

Location → Near Al Fateh Mosque · Juffair | 1731 0252
Hours → Call for timings
Web/email → www.bhseasports.com   Map Ref → 14-D1

This organisation opened in 1997 and teaches sailing to boys and girls from 7 to 15 in a fleet of Optimists and Lasers at its base near the Marina Club and Al Fateh Mosque. The school also works with national and international schools, the Scouts and Bahrain University. If you're interested in learning, get in touch for more details.

Bahrain Yacht Club & Marina

Location → Nxt to Al Bander Resort · Sitra | 1770 0677
Hours → 08:00 - 24:00
Web/email → www.bahrainyachtclub.com.bh   Map Ref → 6-E4

Sailing at the Bahrain Yacht Club is made up of two aspects that are closely linked. The first is their full social cruising programme, the second is their exciting racing programme and many members participate in both. For nine months of the year the racing programme is highly active, with sailors battling it out in two major regattas and up to eighteen races a year across the autumn, winter and spring. Races are held just outside the club itself, with distances between five and twelve nautical miles.

Zallaq Sailing Club

Location → End of Zallaq Highway · Zallaq | 1783 6078
Hours → Call for timings
Web/email → na   Map Ref → 7-B3

The Zallaq Sailing Club is affiliated to the BAPCO Club and maintains a number of Kestrels boats. They have a clubhouse down by the beach at Zallaq and it is a very pleasant little setup.

Sailing options

Snooker

Snooker is quite popular in Bahrain and there are a number of snooker halls. Bahrain plays in the Gulf league and there are many talented local players including Habib Subah, who was awarded a concessionary place on the 2005/06 World Tour by World Snooker. Bahrain was also the venue for the 2005 World U21 Snooker Championship. If you're just interested in a social game of snooker, then you will find a table at any of the clubs and hotels in Bahrain. For more information on competitions, contact Shaikh Abdula bin Abdulraham, President of the Bahrain Snooker Association, (1785 8818) or email: subah.habib@bmb.com.bh

Bahrain Snooker Centre (BSC)

Location → Awal Cinema Building · Awadiya	1724 8024
Hours → 16:00 - 24:00	
Web/email → na	Map Ref → 12-B4

The Bahrain Snooker Centre can be found in the Awal Cinema Building in the heart of Manama and offers six snooker tables which are very often booked so to be sure of a table get down there early or book.

Jimmy's Snooker & Billiard Club

Location → Nr Post Office · Adliya	1771 6147
Hours → 15:00 - 03:00	
Web/email → na	Map Ref → 14-B2

Jimmy's has eight snooker tables and seven billiards Tables and it will cost you BD1.500 for every hour you play. Jimmy's is open seven days a week.

Snorkelling

Other options → Diving [p.126]

The warm shallow waters around Bahrain are an ideal place to learn to snorkel and boat trips to outlying islands are popular weekend excursions. Snorkelling is gaining in popularity here in Bahrain and diving companies and clubs, as well as beach resorts and hotels offer snorkelling equipment.

Aquatique

Location → Government Ave · Naim	1727 1780
Hours → See below	
Web/email → www.pearldive.com	Map Ref → 11-E3

Please see Aquatique's entry under Diving [p.127].

Squash

Other options → Sports & Leisure Facilities [p.142]

Squash players have no worries when it comes to finding places to play in Bahrain with almost all sports clubs and major hotels having their own courts. There are not many squash leagues in operation within the Kingdom as yet, except the Duffer's league organised by Michael Brian (1761 1096) but things are changing with competitions such as the 2004 Bahrain WISPA Open which was held in the Al A'ali Mall in Manama. Further details on squash venues and competitions can be obtained from Mohamed Abdulla Janahi - Secretary General of the Bahrain Badminton and Squash Federation on 1729 2662.

Al Bander Hotel & Resort

Location → Nr Bahrain Yacht Club · Sitra	1770 1201
Hours → See below	
Web/email → www.albander.com	Map Ref → 6-E4

Lessons are available from professional coaches either for those new to squash, or for more experienced players looking to brush up their existing skills or improve their technique. For the casual player the resort has two air-conditioned courts available for hire from 08:00-21:00, although reservations are required. For more details of classes or schedule information, dial extension 341.

The Country Club

Location → Off Al Nakheel Highway · Nr Jannusan	1759 3593
Hours → 08:00 - 20:00	
Web/email → na	Map Ref → 3-C1

The Country Club is a great place to go for a casual game of squash and they also provide many other facilities within their complex including tennis and racquetball courts.

Swimming

Other options → Beaches [p.109]
Sports & Leisure Facilities [p.142]

Swimming in Bahrain is very popular, particularly during the summer months - it's just a question of where. One of the problems of swimming in the sea is that the water is usually very shallow and there are few beaches worth visiting. Beach clubs have their own beaches and often their own swimming pools as well. Most clubs also have swimming coaches so that non-swimmers can learn to swim in safe hands. Many of the major hotels have pools which can be accessed on a casual basis with prices varying from BD1 to BD8. In addition to these, most compounds also have swimming pools so, if you make the right friends, swimming won't be a problem.

Bahrain Swimming Association	
Location → Damascus Rd	1768 0867
Hours → Call for timings	
Web/email → na	Map Ref → 6-A1

The Bahrain Swimming Association is responsible for testing and certifying all coaches in Bahrain and also for organising swimming competitions within the Kingdom. For details on swimming events call the number above.

Dilmun Club	
Location → Off Janabiyah Highway · Saar	1769 0926
Hours → 15:00 - 19:00 20:00 - 23:00 Fri closed	
Web/email → www.batelco.com.bh/dilclub	Map Ref → 3-B4

The Dilmun Club offers expert swimming tuition from a choice of coaches. Call the club for more details of what they offer. Also available are Swim Fit classes for Mums and Toddlers, with Kirsty Mitchell (3966 0853).

Table Tennis

Other options → Sports & Leisure Facilities [p.142]

Al Bander Hotel & Resort	
Location → Nr Bahrain Yacht Club · Sitra	1770 1201
Hours → Call for timings	
Web/email → www.albander.com	Map Ref → 6-E4

There are a variety of health and fitness classes at Al Bander including the facilities to play Table Tennis for 30 minutes at a rate of BD1.000.

Ramada Hotel Bahrain	
Location → Bani Otbah Ave · Adliya	1774 2000
Hours → Call for timings	
Web/email → www.ramadainternational.com	Map Ref → 14-C2

The Oasis Fitness Mini Gym at the Ramada Hotel has tables where you can sharpen up your reflexes

& concentration with a game of table tennis. Call for bookings and more details.

Tennis

Other options → Sports & Leisure Facilities [p.142]

Bahrain Tennis Club	
Location → Nr Bahrain School · Juffair	1772 9561
Hours → Call for timings	
Web/email → na	Map Ref → 14-E3

Bahrain Tennis Club offers tennis coaching for adults and children of all ages and abilities, right from beginner level, by their own qualified coaches. For more details on courses, contact the club.

Bahrain Tennis Federation	
Location → Beh Football Stadium	1768 7236
Hours → Call for timings	
Web/email → www.bahraintennis.com	Map Ref → 6-A2

As the national body of tennis in Bahrain, the Federation has a 6 court complex near the National Stadium for games and is the source of all information you'll need on the sport. Check out the Federation's website or call the above number.

Dilmun Club	
Location → Off Janabiyah Highway · Saar	1769 0926
Hours → 15:00 - 19:00 20:00 - 23:00 Fri closed	
Web/email → www.batelco.com.bh/dilclub	Map Ref → 3-B4

Tennis is a very popular activity at the Dilmun Club with regular tables and competitions taking place. Tennis coaching can be obtained from Dan Barrie on 3969 7114.

Volleyball

Bahrain Volleyball Association	
Location → Villa 131, Rd 2803 · Adliya	1725 5254
Hours → 01:00 - 00:00 Call for timings	
Web/email → http://volleyb.tripod.com	Map Ref → 14-A3

The Bahrain Volleyball Association has developed enormously since the 1950's and is now responsible for the organisation of the Bahrain Volleyball League, the Beach Volleyball league and the selection and participation of National teams for the Arab Volleyball Championships every year in which Bahrain perform at the top level. Further details on this sport can be obtained from the Association on the above telephone number.

Hawar Resort Hotel

Location → Hawar Resort Bahrain · Hawar Island | **1784 9111**
Hours → Call for timings
Web/email → www.hawarresort.com   Map Ref → na

The Hawar Resort offers many various beach, outdoor and indoor ball games and activities for hotel guests and day visitors to the island, including beach volleyball.

Water Sports

Al Bander Hotel & Resort

Location → Nr Bahrain Yacht Club · Sitra | **1770 1201**
Hours → See below
Web/email → www.albander.com   Map Ref → 6-E4

For adventurous thrill seekers the Al Bander Resort provides boats and equipment for water skiing, wind surfing, knee-boarding and sailing. Banana tube ride, rowing boats, canoes, pedalo rides, boat trips and fishing are also available. For more information and rates of individual activities, contact the resort.

Bahrain Yacht Club & Marina

Location → Nxt to Al Bander Resort · Sitra | **1770 0677**
Hours → 08:00 - 24:00
Web/email → www.bahrainyachtclub.com.bh   Map Ref → 6-E4

The Bahrain Yacht Club offers lots of water based activities and is far more than just a sailing club. The club is popular with families, with attractive

Racing off Manama

pricing for membership and services and many water activities all year round including wakeboarding, waterskiing and fishing. Sailors are of course well catered for and they organise several regattas ranging from small club events to the Cable & Wireless Inter Gulf Open Regatta.

The Ritz Carlton Bahrain Hotel and Spa

Location → Seef District · Seef | **1758 3380**
Hours → 06:30 - 20:00
Web/email → www.ritzcarlton.com   Map Ref → 3-E1

The Ritz Carlton has its private beach around a lagoon with it's own marina from where they offer watersports such as waterskiing, windsurfing, fishing and boat trips. All boats and equipment are provided. Contact the hotel for more information.

Well-Being

If it's 'well-being' you're after, you have no excuse for not achieving it here in Bahrain! There are an abundance of spas, salons, gyms, clubs and fitness centres offering the entire spectrum of services for your well-being. You can indulge yourself at a very expensive five star spa or pamper yourself with regular treatments from one of the very reasonably priced smaller salons. Services on offer include all the usual beauty treatments; manicures, pedicures, facials, every type of massage, nail services, hair removal, weight loss and detoxifying treatments to name but a few! Then there are the range of exercise options such as yoga and pilates.

Beauty Salons

Other options → Hairdressers [p.73]
Perfumes & Cosmetics [p.176]

Beauty is big business in Bahrain! Everyone likes to look their best and there is every service you could wish for to help achieve this. As well as a multitude of hair stylists and general beauticians to suit all price ranges, there are specialists providing manicures, pedicures, henna, waxing, threading and hair removal. All of the major hotels have beauty salons, usually popular with the expats but more expensive than the smaller salons. If you go to an Arabic women's salon in Bahrain, remember not to take your husband anywhere near it as they have a very strict policy of not allowing men in the establishment at all.

Activities

Volleyball -Beauty Salons

The traditional practice of painting henna on the hands and feet, especially for weddings or special occasions, is still very popular with Bahraini nationals. For tourists, a design on the hand, ankle or shoulder can make a great memento – they are available quite cheaply and the intricate brown patterns fade after two to three weeks.

Beauty and Nail Salon

Location → Nr Seashell Hotel · Saar | 1771 7323
Hours → 10:30 - 20:30   Fri closed
Web/email → na   Map Ref → 12-D3

Beauty & Nail Salon offer the usual range of beauty treatments for hair, body, relaxation and therapy and they are particularly specialised in artificial nails.

Beauty Spot

Location → Nr Batelco Compound · Jasra | 1761 1888
Hours → 09:00 - 19:00 09:00 - 21:00 Wed & Thu
Web/email → www.beauty-spot.net   Map Ref → 5-B1

Beauty Spot can be found close to Batelco in Hamalaya. As well as the usual range of hair and beauty treatments they also offer a foot spa and slimming treatments.

Elie & Jean

Location → Ritz Carlton Hotel & Spa · Seef | 1722 7300
Hours → 09:30 - 13:00 15:00 - 20:00 Fri closed
Web/email → na   Map Ref → 3-E1

Elie & Jean's two salons are located at the Ritz Carlton and the Regency Intercontinental Hotel (1722 7777). These salons are hugely popular and you will definitely have to make an appointment before you go. The haircutting, styling and coloring, in particular, are very professional and the prices reflect this. It's a busy, buzzing place and if you have any problems with your hair, it is a good place to get expert advice.

Fantana Salon

Location → Budaiya Highway · Saar | 1759 1775
Hours → 09:00 - 19:00   Fri 09:00 - 12:00
Web/email → na   Map Ref → 3-C2

The Thai ladies at Fantana go out of their way to give the best possible service. All the usual beauty treatments are on offer, at very reasonable prices.

Jasmin Salon

Location → Exhibition Rd · Hoora | 1771 7242
Hours → 09:00 - 20:00
Web/email → na   Map Ref → 12-C3

For a full range of hair treatments, including hair straightening and styling, then pay a visit to Jasmin Salon.

Le Soléil Salon

Location → Nr Bahrain School · Juffair | 1772 3757
Hours → 09:30 - 19:30
Web/email → na   Map Ref → 14-D3

Le Soleil prides itself on its serene atmosphere and has an environment of deep calm mingled well with its informed and skilled service. Many services are on offer including beauty treatments, hair styling (including braids and 'Up-Dos'), plus they have a Moroccan Bath as well as various body treatments.

Novel Beauty Salon

Location → Off Saar Ave · Saar | 1779 1222
Hours → 09:00 - 18:00   Fri closed
Web/email → na   Map Ref → 3-B3

A very popular beauty salon with friendly, efficient staff and reasonable prices. You can go all out with a dry hair cut, manicure and pedicure for about BD10 or they offer a full range of beauty treatments and have one of the best magazine selections in town!

Stephen Grant

Location → Delmon International Hotel | 1722 4077
Hours → 09:00 - 18:00   Fri closed
Web/email → na   Map Ref → na

Stephen Grant is a well known personality in Bahrain and his salon is very popular. From time to time there are special deals on beauty packages. Clarin's products are used for facials and if you need an instant tan, they supply tropical air brush tanning.

The Best Beauty Salon

Location → Off Budaiya Highway · Budaiya | 1759 1996
Hours → 09:00 - 19:00   Fri 09:00 - 12:00
Web/email → na   Map Ref → 3-A3

The Best Beauty Salon offer all the usual beauty treatments and are very good with babies' and young children's haircuts.

Health Spas

Other options → **Massage [p.140]**
Sports & Leisure Facilities [p.142]

Banyan Tree Al Areen Desert Spa and Resort

Location → Nr Al Areen Wildlife Sanctuary | **1755 8455**
Hours → Call for timings
Web/email → www.banyantree.com/bahrain   Map Ref → 9-D2

This is the first venture in Bahrain for the Singapore-based chain of luxury spas, and one to watch out for. It is the most extensive spa in the Middle East, offering a huge range of body and beauty treatments in luxurious surroundings including twelve spa treatment rooms, self scrub cabin, grotto steam cabin, ice igloo, garden hammam, herbal steam room, brine cavern and an assortment of 'experience' showers!

Bodyline

Location → Off Budaiya Highway · Saar | **1779 3932**
Hours → 07:00 - 21:00   Fri 10:00 - 18:00
Web/email → na   Map Ref → 3-B2

Beauty and body treatments are offered in a beautifully designed spa that features a Moroccan Bath, fully equipped gym, indoor swimming pool and squash court. There is also the option of pilates, aromatherapy massage and Thai massage plus they provide health foods to go - catering for all the body's needs, both external and internal.

Future Shape

Location → Garden City · Budaiya | **1759 4459**
Hours → Call for timings
Web/email → na   Map Ref → 3-D2

As well as Future Shape's array of exercises, keep-fit classes and programmes with the latest up-to-date techniques taught by experienced teachers, you can also get their particular specialty, a pampering head and facial massage, and they do lots more of the usual beauty treatments as well.

Images

Location → Sheraton Bahrain Hotel & Towers | **1752 4570**
Hours → 07:00 - 21:30
Web/email → na   Map Ref →

Images Salon at the Sheraton Bahrain Hotel & Towers provides a complete range of facilities including a fully equipped gym, pool and a steam and sauna room. The range of beauty treatments encompasses 'aromassage', swedish massage, therapeutic massage, facials, reflexology and waxing. Spa timings run according to gender with ladies having focus in the the mornings and afternoons from 09:00 - 18:00, while men are catered for in the afternoon/evenings from 11:30 - 20:30. There are also separate state-of-the-art ladies' and gents' gyms.

Jacques Dessange

Location → Nr Al Bustan Hotel · Adliya | **1771 3999**
Hours → 07:00 - 21:00
Web/email → na   Map Ref → 14-B2

Jacques Dessange in Adliya offers total pampering and has something to suit everybody in their luxurious ladies spa, salon and health club. There is a spacious, fully-equipped gym including exercise machinery designed with women in mind and there are also a range of massages available including aromatic oil massage (with inclusive foot massage), full body massage and Thai massage.

La Fontaine Center of Contemporary Art

Location → Beh Raja School · Awadiya | **1723 0123**
Hours → 09:00 - 18:00   Fri closed
Web/email → na   Map Ref → 12-B3

This spa, set in a historic house in Hoora, is architecturaly harmonious with interior designs promoting an atmosphere of peace and tranquility. On the grounds there is a restaurant, art gallery and a pool to add tranquility to the Spa's offerings of full beauty treatments and specialist massages. Particularly impressive is the state-of-the-art women-only spa with its exclusive Jean Marc Sinan skin care line, body treatments, the latest performance slimming technology (Ultrasonolipolysis), along with the pilates method of exercises, aroma therapy, weight loss and detoxifying treatments.

Pineapple Spa

Location → Batelco · Adliya | **1771 2000**
Hours → 07:00 - 21:00   Fri 09:00 - 17:00
Web/email → na   Map Ref → 11-B4

The Pineapple Spa offers a great range of massages, facials and beauty treatments (particularly good is the threading). It also offers hairdressing and a gym.

Activities

Health Spas

Royal Spa

Location → Ritz Carlton Bahrain Hotel & Spa · Seef	1758 6808
Hours → 09:00 - 21:00	
Web/email → na	Map Ref → 3-E1

The Royal Spa is located in the five star Ritz-Carlton Bahrain Hotel and Spa where you can 'exchange pressure for pleasure'. So if five star treatment and total indulgence are what you are after, this is the place to go. Their various holistic, traditional or contemporary techniques care for the whole being of a person and all treatments are available for men and women, including a particularly impressive range of massages. ESPA & Guinot treatments and products are also available.

TJ's Health & Beauty Spa

Location → Nr Ramada Hotel · Adliya	1771 0429
Hours → 09:00 - 22:00	
Web/email → na	Map Ref → 14-C2

TJ's Health and Beauty Spa offers a fitness centre, facials, hair styling and Chinese massage.

Massage

Other options → Sports & Leisure Facilities [p.142]
Health Spas [p.139]

For sheer indulgence and pampering, or just for health and therapeutic reasons, you can't beat a good massage. There is a great selection available in Bahrain and it is simply a matter of deciding what type of massage you require, then booking yourself an appointment. You can experience a five star, totally pampering full body massage, therapeutic massages, reflexology, aromatherapy massages, sports therapy massages or perhaps an Oriental Chinese style massage (see below for more details). You can even organize a massage for your baby! Whatever type you choose, the results should reduce any anxiety and worries and give you an enhanced sense of well being.

For more places offering massage, please refer to: Bodyline, Jacques Dessange, La Fontaine Spa, Pineapple Spa, Royal Spa, TJ's Health & Beauty Spa in Health Spas [p.139].

Chinese Ladies Massage Centre

Location → Off Highway 35 · Zinj	1723 2381
Hours → 10:00 - 22:00	
Web/email → na	Map Ref → 13-D3

You don't need to go to the Far East to experience Oriental massage and reflexology, just try out some of the really authentic Chinese treatments here in Bahrain. Also if you have problems with your feet then this is the place to go, as they claim to be able to take in anyone even with dry, rough, cracked heels and have them leave with baby soft tootsies!

Pilates

Other options → Yoga [p.140]

Pilates has been around for about 70 years and even the All Blacks, the New Zealand Rugby Team, have used it as part of their training. It is a safe and sensible exercise system that tones the body, builds body strength and helps you look and feel your best.

Increasing in popularity all the time, there is a range of places in Bahrain where you can take pilates classes, such as Bodyline [p.139], La Fontaine Spa [p.140] and Royal Spa [p.139], listed in Health Spas, and World Beat Fitness Centre [p.142] listed in Yoga.

Yoga

Other options → Pilates [p.140]

Bahrain Wellness Resort

Location → Off Budaiya Highway · Seef	1779 5961
Hours → See below	
Web/email → na	Map Ref → 3-D2

The centre offers mixed Yoga classes on Saturday and Wednesday from 19:00 to 20.30 and ladies only classes on Sunday and Tuesday from 10:00 to 12:00. All classes are taught in a unique wellness resort where you will find all that is required for a healthy body, a sound mind and a peaceful soul. Their team of health practitioners can also help and encourage you to follow a natural, healthy life style. Other courses include Ayurveda & Naturopathy.

The British Club

Location → Kanoo Ave · Adliya	1717 2845
Hours → See below	
Web/email → www.britishclubbahrain.com	Map Ref → 14-C4

The British Club runs yoga classes three days a week on Monday, Thursday and Friday, from 16:30 to 17:30 where you can learn this ancient practise developing breathing, stretching and a form of exercise to strengthen you from the inside out!

La Fontaine Center of Contemporary Art

World Beat Fitness Centre

Location → Bldg 1762 · Janabiyah   1761 2576
Hours → See below
Web/email → www.worldbeatfitness.com   Map Ref → 5-B1

World Beat, an immaculate little studio located in Janabiyah, has brought innovation and edge through the choice of courses with a selection of fitness classes including yoga, pilates, aerobics, youth and adult focused courses like karate, various forms of dance and their speciality of NIA (Neuromuscular Integrative Action), a dynamic workout which blends dance, martial arts and yoga. Mixed Yoga classes are held on Sunday and Tuesday from 19.30 to 21:00 and ladies only classes on Wednesday morning from 10.30 to 11.30.

Sports & Leisure Facilities

Bahrain boasts a whole host of sporting and leisure facilities. While the majority of facilities are located in clubs and hotels, there are also plenty to be found on beaches, in shopping malls and in purpose-built sports centres and neighbourhood gyms.

Clubs and hotels are generally more expensive to use so casual visits can work out better for your pocket. However, if you're planning on being in Bahrain for the long haul, it's advisable to check out the major Beach Clubs p.142 and Sports Clubs p.144 as these establishments often become the hub of life in more ways than one.

Beach Clubs

Other options → Health Clubs [p.143]
Beaches [p.109]

Beach clubs offer a similar range of facilities to health clubs (see below) but with the additional bonus of beach access. They are very popular, especially with families, and for some are the centre of life at the weekend in Bahrain. You can swim, play sports or just lounge in the sun in a peaceful environment. Most also offer some excellent food and beverage outlets, so people tend to stay for the day.

Generally beach clubs require you to be a member to make use of their facilities, although many also have day guest rates. However, due to the scarcity of good beaches in Bahrain, there are few clubs owning their own beaches.

For listings of the facilities at Bahrain's beach clubs and their rates, see the Club Membership Rates and Facilities Table below.

Club Membership Rates & Facilities

Beach Clubs			
Seef	The Sports Club	Ritz-Carlton	17580000
Al Hoora	The Marina Club	Corniche	17291527
	Curves	Novotel	17298430

Health Clubs			
Diplomatic Area	Golden Tulip Sports Club	Golden Tulip Hotel	17523570
	Image	Sheraton Hotel	17524570
	Le Mirage	Diplomat Hotel	17531666
	Nautilus	Crowne Plaza	17531122
	Regency Fitness Centre	Intercontinental Hotel	17208355
Juffair	Health & Recreational Club	Gulf Hotel	17726185
Muharraq	Fitness Centre	Movenpick	17460000
Seef	Health Centre	Mercure	17584400

classes varying from aerobics to yoga, while some also have swimming pools and tennis or squash courts. Many of the beach clubs also offer some sports and gym facilities so are worth considering if you want the added bonus of the beach.

Remember that when using the changing rooms of your health club, some people may feel uncomfortable if you do not use the private cubicles. Respect the modesty that prevails in any Islamic country and always remain as covered up as possible. For listings of Bahrain's main health clubs, see the Club Membership Rates and Facilities Table below.

Sports Centres

EZ FIT Sportsplex

Location → Budaiya Rd · Budaiya | 1769 2378
Hours → 08:30 - 24:00
Web/email → www.ezfit.biz | Map Ref → 3-E1

This place has a great setup with two indoor courts where you can play football, cricket, netball and tennis. There are also three workout rooms; the Burn Room containing 10 exercycles, three walking machines and a rowing machine, the Random Room where there is a wide range of resistance stations and the Shape Room where you can exercise by

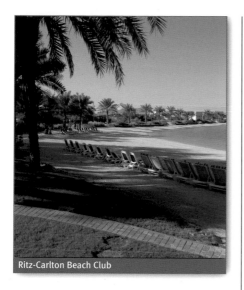

Ritz-Carlton Beach Club

Health Clubs

Other options → Sports Clubs [p.144]
Beach Clubs [p.142]

Most health clubs, which are usually associated with the Clubs or the major hotels, offer workout facilities such as machines and weights, plus

Membership Rates					Gym						Activity				Relaxation				
Male	Female	Couple	Family	Non-Members (peak)	Treadmills	Exercise bikes	Step machines	Rowing machines	Free weights	Resistance machines	Tennis courts	Swimming Pool	Squash courts	Aerobics/Dance Exercise	Massage	Sauna	Jacuzzi	Plunge pool	Steam room
550	550	650	700	–	7	4	6	3	✔	16	4	✔	1	✔	✔	✔	✔	✔	✔
225	225	–	275	–	8	1	1	3	✔	16	2	3	3	✔	✔	✔	✔	✔	✔
320	320	400	–	6	3	2	1	1	✔	5	–	✔	–	✔	–	✔	✔	✔	✔
185	185	448	600	6	6	6	4	1	✔	4	✔	✔	✔	✔	✔	✔	✔	–	✔
345	345	430	510	3.5	5	4	1	2	✔	20	–	✔	–	–	✔	✔	–	–	✔
212	212	275	275	5	5	4	1	–	✔	20	2	✔	2	✔	–	✔	✔	–	✔
150	150	250	380	5	5	5	2	1	✔	15	1	✔	2	–	✔	✔	✔	–	✔
180	175	240	–	4	2	2	1	1	✔	5	–	✔	–	–	✔	✔	✔	–	✔
345	305	400	460	3	3	1	2	1	✔	9	2	✔	–	–	✔	–	–	–	–
160	160	200	230	5	4	2	1	1	✔	10	2	✔	–	–	✔	✔	✔	–	✔
258	258	330	358	5	4	2	2	–	✔	15	2	1	1	–	✔	✔	✔	–	✔

yourself or in group situations. The sportsplex also provides classes in Gymnastics, Martial Arts and Fitness and Body Transformation. There is also a creche for participating parents, a cafe which stresses the importance of nutrition, physiotherapy consultation and activities for the disabled.

Sports Clubs

Other options → Health Clubs [p.143]
Beach Clubs [p.142]

Bahrain is unique in the Gulf in that many expats have been living here for years and now there are second and third generation families residing here with some of the first generation actually retiring here. During those years, the sporting and social life of many families has revolved around the 'clubs'. These clubs provide just about all requirements for families or single people in terms of recreational and social activities. The 'Big Six' are listed below with all the facilities and activities which they provide, so whatever you're interested in, be it horse riding, sailing, rugby or canasta, check out which one's for you.

Bahrain Rugby Club

Location → Nr Dilmun Club · Saar | 1769 5809
Hours → Call for timings
Web/email → www.bahrainrfc.com   Map Ref → 3-B3

Facilities here include two full-sized pitches, a temperature controlled swimming pool, tennis & netball courts, cricket nets, roller blading and skateboarding area and a kid's play area. Activities include rugby, football, netball, tennis and swimming. The club also has a wonderful restaurant and a bar which is always well stocked and well patronaged. Entertainment is provided at the club with many of the visiting artistes to the island often popping in to perform. For more information, contact the manager, Annie Harris on 3922 3446.

Bahrain Yacht Club & Marina

Location → Nxt to Al Bander Resort · Sitra | 1770 0677
Hours → 08:00 - 24:00
Web/email → www.bahrainyachtclub.com.bh   Map Ref → 6-E4

The BYC was founded in 1968 as a breakaway group from the RAF Sailing Club. It has a 130 berth marina at Sitra and is a fully recognized Royal Yachting Association Training Centre. Primarily attracting members for their sailing facilities and events, the club offers tuition for both children and adults in a variety of crafts, but also has its own beach, a swimming pool, a restaurant open seven days a week (catering primarily to lunchgoers and is particularly welcoming to visitors on Fridays with a casual entrance fee of BD1), a coffee shop open all day and a diverse social programme covering events and regattas throughout the year. It has also now launched a Dolphin Watching service with 3 boats departing at 10:00, 12:00 and 14:00 every day.

Costs: Membership Fees: Family; BD250. Single; BD150.

BAPCO Club

Location → Nr Riffa Golf Club · East of Awali | 1775 3666
Hours → 08:00 - 24:00
Web/email → na   Map Ref → 8-A2

The BAPCO Club is one of the oldest clubs on the island and was built during the heyday of the oil industry. It continues to serve the needs of its members and facilities at the club consist of a cricket oval, tennis and squash courts, a sailing club, a golf club, swimming pools and a theatre. The clubhouse contains an enormous dining hall/ballroom, a restaurant, coffee shop, meeting rooms, six lane bowling alley and various TV rooms. Some of the clubs belonging to BAPCO require extra membership fees.

Dilmun Club

Location → Off Janabiyah Highway · Saar | 1769 0926
Hours → 15:00 - 19:00 20:00 - 23:00 Fri closed
Web/email → www.batelco.com.bh/dilclub   Map Ref → 3-B4

The Dilmun Club was founded in 1974 and is one of the most popular clubs on the island. The club caters for the needs of individuals, couples and families with a wide range of sporting activities and facilities for all ages. On the social side, the Dilmun Club constantly strives to seek new and innovative forms of entertainment ranging from live bands and quiz shows to themed dinner evenings and food promotions. The Sports Bar regularly shows major sporting events on large screen TVs and the restaurants serve up a never-ending stream of delicious food, particularly during the Friday Brunch. On the sports side, the club boasts squash courts, outdoor courts for tennis, netball and football, a swimming pool for the toddlers and one for adults, a riding school, a dive club and a golf club. The club also maintains a well-stocked English language library and various clubs such as Mahjong, Bridge and Sewing are very active here.

Membership fees: Married - BD155; Single - BD135; Joining Fee - BD15

The British Club

Location → Kanoo Ave · Adliya
Hours → See below
Web/email → www.britishclubbahrain.com | 1717 2845
Map Ref → 14-C4

The British Club is one of the oldest and among the most popular clubs in Bahrain. Founded in 1935, it was originally known as The Gymkhana Club, and has since gone from strength to strength, currently boasting a membership of over 1500. The club offers a safe, friendly atmosphere for individuals and families to relax in and has a wide range of facilities. These include a swimming pool, squash courts, a first class restaurant, tennis courts, coffee shop, refreshment areas and one of the main attractions, a gym which is fully equipped with state-of-the-art equipment, and fitness sessions held on a regular basis.

Oh Man!
Oman has a plethora of breathtaking beaches that no-one should miss out on. Just grab a copy of the Oman Explorer and discover a whole new coastline right on your doorstep.

Membership Fees: *Family - BD160, Single - BD115. Monthly; Family - BD16, Single - BD13.*

The Country Club

Location → Off Al Nakheel Highway - Nr Jannusan
Hours → 08:00 - 20:00
Web/email → na | 1759 3593
Map Ref → 3-C1

Only 15 minutes from Manama and set in over 20,000 square metres of picturesque, shaded landscaped gardens, the Country Club offers a complete range of recreation and leisure. Amongst the facilities is a swimming pool, the latest computerised cardiovascular and exercise equipment from Nautilus and qualified instructors to help with your fitness programme. Sports on offer include tennis, squash and racquetball with professional coaching, and horseriding at The Country Stables, where there is instruction, livery and Arabian horses available for guests use. Little ones are accommodated by a giant playhouse, swings, see-saws, paddling pool and creche which all ensure energetic youngsters are free from boredom.

Membership Fees: *Family - BD260, Single - BD200, Joining Fee - BD50.*

Expand Your Horizons

If you are looking to expand your horizons on a physical, cerebral or aesthetic level you would do well to check out the clubs (see Sports Clubs on p.144) first of all as they organise courses, programmes and classes to satisfy the needs of their members which are continually changing. If you can't find your particular interest there, there are many other organisations and groups in Manama that specialise in their own fields and can be found listed below for a wide range of interests.

Art Classes

Other options → **Art Galleries [p.99]**
Art & Craft Supplies [p.159]

Arabesque Art Gallery

Location → Off Umm Al Hassam Ave
Hours → 08:00 - 19:00   Fri closed
Web/email → www.arabesque-gal.org | 1772 2916
Map Ref → 4-C3

The Arabesque Gallery run art classes at their studio in Umm Al Hassam during the winter months, which are usually beginner's classes in water painting or oil painting. A course lasts around a month for four sessions, each lasting two and a half hours, and cost BD30 for the whole course. Children's workshops are also held in the school breaks during the winter months. For further details contact Ann.

Bahrain Arts Society

Location → Nr Burgerland · Budaiya Ave
Hours → Call for timings
Web/email → www.bahartsociety.org.bh | 1759 4211
Map Ref → 3-E2

Bahrain Arts Society offers art classes for children and adults including drawing, painting and Arabic caligraphy. The courses are split into three age categories; 5-10 year-olds, 11-15 year-olds and 16 and over. Days, timings, days and costs of classes vary. For more information, please contact Naziha.

Dar Al Bareh Gallery and Cafe

Location → Nr Carlton Hotel · Adliya
Hours → 08:30 - 23:00   Fri 17:00 - 21:00
Web/email → na | 1771 3535
Map Ref → 14-C3

This Art Gallery provides classes in basic decorative painting, furniture painting and wall

Bahrain's Painted Village

effects painting as well as provisions for a complete line of painting supplies.

Ballet Classes

Other options → **Dance Classes [p.149]**

Bahrain Ballet Centre

Location → Nr Iranian Embassy · Budaiya | 1769 3232
Hours → 14:30 - 19:00 Fri closed
Web/email → na | Map Ref → 14-A4

The Ballet Centre specialises in teaching children and teens and preparing them for grades and majors examinations. Children from the age of three years and up are taught the The Royal Academy of Dance (RAD) syllabus, classes are held every day and begin with the little ones at 15:00. Monthly fees start at BD10 for the toddlers up to BD13 for the older children.

Belly Dancing

Other options → **Dance Classes [p.149]**

If you wish to experience the visual delights of belly dancing performed by genuine Arabian dancers, you will find regular performances at hotels and night clubs, which are usually well advertised in the local media. If you are more interested in learning yourself, then try the courses available at Bahrain Ballet Centre [p.149] or the World Beat Fitness Centre [p.149].

The Water Garden (p.111)

Birdwatching Groups

Al Reem Ecotours

Location → Off Exhibition Rd · Hoora | 1771 0868
Hours → Timings on request
Web/email → www.alreem.com/ecotourism | Map Ref → 14-C1

Al Reem Environmental Consultation and Ecotourism offer tours to some of Bahrain's most hidden away natural areas, including birdwatching packages to see Bahrain's resident and migratory bird populations. For more information, check out their website.

Bridge

Bahrain Bridge Club

Location → Nr Petrol Station · Adliya | 1771 3080
Hours → See below
Web/email → na | Map Ref → 14-B3

The Bahrain Bridge Club has been running since 1985 and meets every Monday night at 19:30 where between four and seven tables are filled, each needing a minimum of four people. Also, every Tuesday morning, there is one for the ladies at 09:00. New players are always welcome, for further information contact the number above.

Bahrain Bridge Committee

Location → Nr Mansouri Mansion · Adliya | 3968 7190
Hours → Call for timings
Web/email → na | Map Ref → 14-B3

This Committee, associated to the Bahrain Mind Sports Association, has been running for 20 years, with over 60 members, and new people are always warmly welcomed. It is situated in Adliyah near Mansouri Mansion and its members meet on a weekly basis. For more details, contact Rizwan Mumtaz, Honourary Secretary of the Committee, on the number above.

Oops!

Have we missed you out? If you'd like a free entry for your club or organisation, or have any other ideas or comments for us on the Activities section, drop us a line and we'll include you in the next edition. Visit www.Explorer-Publishing.com to tell us whatever's on your mind.

Activities

Art Classes · Bridge

Bahrain Mind Sports Association

Location → Yateem Centre · City Centre
Hours → Call for timings
Web/email → www.geocities.com/alafoo   Map Ref → 12-A3

1724 2641

The Bahrain Mind Sports Association is an umbrella organisation, founded in 1984, for more cerebral gaming pursuits and maintains a substantial following. Apart from Bridge, they also run Chess and Scrabble sessions. For further information on each section contact: Chess; Khalid Al Awadi on 3946 8715, Bridge; Rizwan Mumtaz on 3968 7190, Scrabble; Roy Kietzman on 3963 9324.

Chess

Other options → Scrabble [p.151]

Bahrain Mind Sports Association

Location → Yateem Centre · City Centre
Hours → Call for timings
Web/email → www.geocities.com/alafoo   Map Ref → 12-A3

1724 2641

Please see the entry for Bahrain Mind Sports Association in Bridge [p.149].

Clubs & Associations

Clubs & Associations	
Alliance Française de Bahrain	1768 3295
American Association of Bahrain	1727 6431
American Women's Association	1775 6075
Australasian Association of Bahrain	3920 6432
Awali Ladies Association	1767 8947
Bahrain Business Women's Society	3960 3603
Bahrain Caledonian Society	1752 8111
Bahrain Contemporary Art Association	1772 8046
Bahrain Kannada Sangha	1727 1257
Bahrain Keraleeya Samajam	1725 1878
Bahrain Round Table	3936 0785
Bahrain Society for the Prevention of Cruelty to Animals	1759 1231
Bahrain Welsh Society	3960 0287
Bangladesh Club	1724 4242
Children and Mothers Welfare Society	1725 2637
Indian Fine Arts Society	1723 0279
Indian Ladies Association	39250604
International Ladies Group	1772 9128
Kerala Arts and Cultural Association	1724 0161
The Awali Caledonian Society	1775 4136
The Irish Society	1779 0403

Dance Classes

Other options → Belly Dancing [p.148]
Music Lessons [p.150]

Bahrain Ballet Centre

Location → Nr Iranian Embassy · Budaiya
Hours → 14:30 - 19:00   Fri closed
Web/email → na   Map Ref → 14-A4

1769 3232

The Bahrain Ballet Centre offers a whole host of dancing courses including the Mediterranean's most alluring dance, Salsa, for which there are classes at 19:30 on Tuesdays run by Latin Fever. There are also lessons for Ballet - both youth and adult sessions, Belly Dancing, as well as Oriental dancing. Contact the centre for futher details.

Caledonian Society

Location → BAPCO Club
Hours → 08:00 - 24:00
Web/email → www.bahraincaledoniansociety.com Map Ref → 8-A2

1775 3666

If you would like to get involved in the fun, social activity of learning Scottish Dancing, lessons are held at the BAPCO Club every Monday at 19:30. There is also the chance to show off your skills at the societies' two main annual events, the St Andrew's Ball in November, celebrating Scotland's patron saint, or the Burns Supper in January, a tribute to the Nation's favourite poet, Robert Burns. Both events centre around a common theme, good dinners and plenty of Scottish dancing!

British Club

Location → Kanoo Ave · Adliya
Hours → See below
Web/email → www.britishclubbahrain.com   Map Ref → 14-C4

1717 2845

The British Club offers several different styles of dancing including the popular Line Dancing, every Sunday and Wednesday 09:30 - 11.30, as well as Salsa Dancing and Ballroom Dancing. For further information contact the club.

World Beat Fitness Centre

Location → Bldg 1762 · Janabiyah
Hours → See below
Web/email → www.worldbeatfitness.com   Map Ref → 5-B1

1761 2576

The World Beat Fitness Centre is a jewel of a studio located in Janabiya. Dance and movement classes such as Belly Dancing, jazz dancing, Ballroom and Latin dancing are held here along with plenty of activities for children.

Timings: Sat, Sun & Tue 08:00 - 13:00, 15:30 - 21:00, Mon & Wed 08:00 - 13:00, 15:30 - 20:00, Thu 08:30 - 13:00, Fri closed.

Drama Groups

Manama Theatre Club

Location → Various locations	**1777 6489**
Hours → Call for timings	
Web/email → na	Map Ref → na

The Manama Theatre Club has been putting on plays for the Bahrain public since the amalgamation of the Manama Players and the Bahrain Theatre Group in the mid-80s. Theatres are hard to come by in Manama so the club quite often moves from stage to stage. Recent productions have been performed at the British Club and The Awali Hall, with most productions being lively and very entertaining. The chairman of the Club, Brig Rooke, has been involved for a number of years and has a passion for theatre which carries the club through thick and thin and keeps the audiences coming back for more. Newcomers to the club are always welcome, either on stage or behind the scenes.

Language Schools

Other options → Learning Arabic [p.78]

Alliance Française de Bahrain

Location → Nr Bahrain University	**1768 3295**
Hours → 09:00 - 13:00 15:00 - 19:00	
Web/email → www.afbahrain.com	Map Ref → 5-E1

The Alliance Française is a non-profit organisation supported by the French Government, with the goal of promoting French Language and Culture. The Alliance in Bahrain is an International French Institute and offers a complete range of courses from complete beginners to advanced levels, for both adults and children, in group classes or private lessons. Degrees offered: DEL/DALF - TEFL.

American Cultural & Educational Center

Location → Nr Al Fateh Grand Mosque · Juffair	**1772 3037**
Hours → Call for timings	
Web/email → www.acec.edu.bh	Map Ref → 14-D2

The ACEC is run by the US Embassy and offer all types of English classes for non-native speakers. For

more information contact Fatema Hashem, the RLO Assistant, by telephone or at hashemf@state.gov.

Libraries

Other options → Books [p.160]
Second-Hand Items [p.177]

Alliance Française de Bahrain

Location → Nr Bahrain University	**1768 3295**
Hours → 09:00 - 13:00 15:00 - 19:00	
Web/email → www.afbahrain.com	Map Ref → 5-E1

Alliance Française have their own library and resource centre in Isa Town. The library consists of over 5000 books and a video library of French films and documentaries on contemporary France. For more information visit their website.

British Council Library

Location → Off Shaikh Salman Highway	**1726 1555**
Hours → 14:30 - 19:30	
Web/email → www.britishcouncil.org	Map Ref → 4-A2

The British Council has a library and multimedia centre with over 9000 books, including children's books, English language teaching and self-study materials, a management library and reference resources. Books can be borrowed by members while encyclopaedias, atlases and references are available for reference in the library only.

Manama Public Library

Location → Off Al Ghous Highway · Muharraq	**1732 0017**
Hours → 07:30 - 21:00 Thu 07:00 - 12:30 Fri closed	
Web/email → www.education.gov.bh	Map Ref → 1-C1

Bahrain's public library is situated in Manama City and contains books in both Arabic and English. For more information check out their website.

Music Lessons

Other options → Singing [p.151]
Dance Classes [p.149]

Bahrain Ballet Centre

Location → Nr Iranian Embassy · Budaiya	**1769 3232**
Hours → 14:30 - 19:00 Fri closed	
Web/email → na	Map Ref → 14-A4

The Bahrain Ballet Centre offers piano lessons. Contact the centre for futher details.

Bahrain Music Institute

Location → Kuwait Ave · Adliya | 1772 1999
Hours → 08:30 - 12:30 15:30 - 19:30
Web/email → www.bahrainmusic.com | Map Ref → 14-B4

The Bahrain Music Institute was established in 2000 and offers training in piano, keyboard, guitar, oud, violin, flute, drums, clarinet, saxophone and vocal music and theory. Instrumental Music classes last for 50 minutes while Vocal Music lessons last 25 minutes.

Costs: *Registration Fee; BD.10. Courses between BD.24 to BD.50 per month depending on the course and the number of classes per month.*

Classic Institute of Music

Location → Juffair Ave · Juffair | 1772 8791
Hours → 09:00 - 19:30
Web/email → na | Map Ref → 14-D3

Lessons are available on piano, guitar, flute, clarinet, organ, lute, violin, oboe, vocals and music theory. Call for details of registration and costs of lessons.

Photography

Bahrain Photography Club

Location → Various locations | 1759 0551
Hours → Call for timings
Web/email → na | Map Ref → na

Bahrain Photography Club is part of Bahrain Arts Society and was the first photograph association in Bahrain, established in 1985 for the exchange of ideas and technical experience and to provide a creative atmosphere. The club also joined the International Federation of Photographic Art in 1985 as its first Arabic member and was appointed as continental representative in the Middle East in 1987. The club has also participated in many international competitions, exhibitions and conferences.

Oops!

Have we missed you out? If you'd like a free entry for your club or organisation, or have any other ideas or comments for us on the Activities section, drop us a line and we'll include you in the next edition. Visit www.Explorer-Publishing.com to tell us whatever's on your mind.

Scrabble

Other options → **Chess [p.149]**

Bahrain Mind Sports Association

Location → Yateem Centre · City Centre | 1724 2641
Hours → Call for timings
Web/email → www.geocities.com/alafoo | Map Ref → 12-A3

Please see the entry for the association under Bridge [p.149].

Singing

Other options → **Music Lessons [p.150]**

Manama Singers

Location → St. Christopher's Cathedral · Salmaniya | 3904 7734
Hours → 19:30 - 21:30 Tue
Web/email → www.stchcathedral.org.bh | Map Ref → 14-A1

Manama Singers meet weekly at the Alun Morris Hall by the Cathedral. Under the leadership of Alistair Auld, the singers present wonderful concerts, each seeming to outdo the previous one. If you read music and love to sing call Lydia or email her on decani@batelco.com.bh

Umm Al Hassam Bahrain Welsh Male Voice Choir

Location → Dilmun Club · Saar | 3964 0916
Hours → 18:30 - 00:00 Sun
Web/email → na | Map Ref → 3-B4

Rehearsals are held for Umm Al Hassam Bahrain Welsh Male Voice Choir at 18:30 every Sunday evening at the Dilmun Club in Saar. Further details can be obtained from Nigel Preece on the above mobile number. Newcomers are always welcome.

Social Groups

Other options → **Support Groups [p.75]**
Clubs & Associations [p.149]

Due to the unique situation in Bahrain with respect to the various clubs and societies here, there is a natural tendency for newcomers to gravitate towards 'their own', whether it be for sport and recreation, socialising or support and advice. The clubs featured in Sports Clubs [p.144], as well as offering sports facilities and various activities, also act as the hub of social life for many in Bahrain. Other options can be found in Clubs & Associations [p.149] but if they don't fill the gap, people in Bahrain are generally so friendly and hospitable that newcomers will have no difficulty in meeting people and finding likeminded people to socialise with.

Summer Camps & Courses

What do you do when the schools close for summer and the heat begins to take its toll on good humour and patience? The answer is the summer camps that spring up around Bahrain to keep kids entertained and happy.

Al Bander Hotel & Resort

Location → Nr Bahrain Yacht Club · Sitra | 1770 1201
Hours → See below
Web/email → www.albander.com   Map Ref → 6-E4

The Resort holds summer camps for children (4 to 14) in July and August. These include swimming, squash, fitness programmes, board games, drawing classes, canoeing, boat rides, arts and crafts, pinball and video games. Monthly tuition is BD60 (three days a week) and BD100 (six days a week) and trained first-aid staff are in attendance.

Gulf Hotel

Location → Nr Gudaibiya Palace · Juffair | 1772 6184
Hours → 08:00 - 13:00 Thu & Fri closed
Web/email → na   Map Ref → 14-C2

The Gulf Hotel offers a summer camp for youngsters (4-13) from the beginning of July to the end of August. Activities include art and craft classes, trampoline games, face painting, dancing, cooking classes (with hotel chefs), field trips and fun sports such as swimming, football, badminton and volleyball. Weekly tuition is around BD25 with discounts available for extra children and additional weeks.

Regency Intercontinental Hotel

Location → King Faisal Highway · Naim | 1722 7777
Hours → 08:00 - 15:00 Wed - Fri closed
Web/email → www.ichotelsgroup.com   Map Ref → 11-E3

The Regency Intercontinental holds summer camps for children (6-13) from July to August. Activities include arts and craft, puzzles, sports and neighbourhood tours around the hotel and also educational trips outside the hotel. Tuition fees are BD60 per month.

Regional Institute of Active Learning (RIA)

Location → Nr Ramada Hotel · Adliya | 1771 6871
Hours → 08:00 - 14:00
Web/email → www.ria-institute.com   Map Ref → 14-C2

The RIA runs summer camps for children for eight weeks through July and August, five mornings a week. Camps offer themed activities including arts and crafts, acting, cooking and dance classes, and sport. The centre also offers classes (all year round) for children with special needs, with a caring and integrated approach to education and personal development. For more details on this year's programmes contact the organisation.

Riffa Golf Club

Location → East of Awali | 1775 0777
Hours → 06:30 - 11:00   Thu & Fri
Web/email → na   Map Ref → 8-A1

Riffa Golf Club offers a children's golf package in the summer with two 45 minute lessons for a special price. Both lessons must be taken on Thursday or Friday morning before September. Contact the club for further details.

Ritz Carlton Hotel & Spa

Location → North Seef | 1758 0000
Hours → 10:00 - 17:00   Wed - Fri closed
Web/email → www.ritzcarlton.com   Map Ref → 3-E1

The Ritz Kids programme for children takes place at its beach and private island. Youngsters are divided into Juniors (6-8) and Seniors (9-11) and activities include tennis, water sports, swimming, boat trips, snorkelling, culinary classes, arts and crafts, camp fires and barbecues. The tuition team is comprised of tennis professionals, fitness experts and internationally certified coaches. Each camp consists of 20 youngsters and costs BD75 per month.

The Diplomat Radisson SAS Hotel

Location → Off Al Fatih Highway · Diplomatic Area | 1753 1666
Hours → Call for timings
Web/email → www.manama.radissonsas.com   Map Ref → 12-C2

Two summer camps for children (7-14) are held at the Mirage Health Club between July and late August. Activities include swimming, tennis, chess, tae kwon do and karate. Monthly tuition is

BD45, snacks and drinks are provided and staff are on hand at all times.

Kids Activities

Bahrain has a great deal to offer children with amusement parks and centres, sports clubs and entertainment venues. Most clubs have their own children's programmes and hotels also often provide programmes particularly during school breaks.

Chaka Zulu

Location → Dana Mall · Sanabis	1755 8500
Hours → 10:00 - 24:00	
Web/email → na	Map Ref → 11-B4

Chaka Zulu has two large floors of indoor entertainment including small boat rides, roller coaster rides, bumper cars, games and food.

Foton World

Location → Bahrain Mall · Seef	1755 6112
Hours → 10:00 - 24:00	
Web/email → na	Map Ref → 11-E1

Foton World is an indoor entertainment area where waterfalls, bridges and tropical flora and fauna provide a magical setting for carousels, rides and games. Games generally cost between 400 and 600 fils, although rates start from 100 fils per game.

Funland Centre

Location → Al Fateh Corniche · Hoora	1729 2313
Hours → 10:00 - 23:00	
Web/email → http://funlandcenter.tripod.com	Map Ref → 12-D3

Funland Centre has 18 top class bowling lanes and the only full size ice skating rink in Bahrain. The centre organises all kinds of competitions; local, international and even friendly or family games. It is great fun for the kids with video games and a cafe.

Magic Island

Location → Seef Mall · Seef	1758 2888
Hours → 10:00 - 24:00 Wed & Thu 10:00 - 01:00	
Web/email → na	Map Ref → 3-E1

Magic Island is the home of the only Rollerblade Rink in Bahrain and many more games and attractions. such as the Roller Coaster Simulator, the Motion Theatre and the Chamber of Horrors.

Entrance is free but you have to pay for each ride. Children cannot enter alone or remain unattended.

Playland

Location → Above Fuddruckers · Adliya	1774 2266
Hours → 10:00 - 22:00	
Web/email → na	Map Ref → 4-C2

Playland is an indoor centre full of games and rides. Each ride costs 100 fils and tokens are available.

Rally Town

Location → Nr Shk Isa Bin Salman Highway	1761 2992
Hours → 15:00 - 23:00	
Web/email → na	Map Ref → 3-C4

Go Kart racing for all ages, for more details see their entry on [p.131].

Soft Play

Location → Dilmun Club · Saar	1769 0926
Hours → 09:30 - 11:30 Sun & Wed	
Web/email → www.softplaybahrain.com	Map Ref → 3-B4

SoftPlay has soft mats, squashy shapes, tents and about 800 colourful balls. There are educational toys, soft toys and just plain fun toys. Nursery songs and rhymes set the atmosphere and at 11:00 it's 'Song Time' where everyone is encouraged to join in. If adults feel a bit shy jumping around, don't worry, Shelly has bags of energy to entice the little ones into singing and dancing to well known nursery songs.

Monkeying Around

MARKS & SPENCER

Shopping
EXPLORER

Shopping

Highlights...

Weekend Shopping Spree

If you fancy a weekend shopping break then why not head to Dubai for the Shopping Festival (middle of January to middle of February). Not only can you stock up on bargains galore but also there is a whole host of exciting entertainment going on from Global Village's fairground rides to educational displays in the shopping malls. There are events all over the city, and everything is on sale. Pick up a copy of the *Dubai Explorer* for more information.

Clothing Sizes

Women's Clothing					
Aust/NZ	8	10	12	14	16	18
Europe	36	38	40	42	44	46
Japan	5	7	9	11	13	15
UK	8	10	12	14	16	18
USA	6	8	10	12	14	16

Women's Shoes					
Aust/NZ	5	6	7	8	9	10
Europe	35	36	37	38	39	40
France only	35	36	38	39	40	42
Japan	22	23	24	25	26	27
UK	3.5	4.5	5.5	6.5	7.5	8.5
USA	5	6	7	8	9	10

Men's Clothing					
Aust/NZ	92	96	100	104	108	112
Europe	46	48	50	52	54	56
Japan	S	-	M	M	-	L
UK	35	36	37	38	39	40
USA	35	36	37	38	39	40

Men's Shoes					
Aust/NZ	7	8	9	10	11	12
Europe	41	42	43	44.5	46	47
Japan	26	27	27.5	28	29	30
UK	7	8	9	10	11	12
USA	7.5	8.5	9.5	10.5	11.5	12.5

Measurements are approximate only; try before you buy

Table of Contents

Shopping

Shopping

As shopping paradises go, Bahrain doesn't quite rank up there with Dubai, but there's plenty here to delight even the most dedicated shopaholic. Shopping is one of the major leisure activities in Bahrain and whatever your shopping preferences are, you'll find them well catered for. From window shopping in the upmarket, designer-label boutiques, rummaging through fabulous bargains in huge discount emporiums, to trawling for treasures in the souk, Bahrain has it all.

Prices vary a lot depending on the quality or quantity of what you're buying, and in the souks and small retail stores your bargaining skills will also affect the price. On an international level, there aren't really any bargains in Bahrain. Computers and electronic goods are generally cheaper in Dubai or in South East Asia. Designer label clothes are as expensive, or more expensive, than in the UK or the US. The joy of shopping in Bahrain is the variety offered and the chance of stumbling upon a really special item or genuine bargain. Recommended buys are gold, pearls, carpets and antique Arabic furniture.

The major malls are located in the Seef district; Al Aali Shopping Complex and Seef Mall are within walking distance of each other, but with a major road bisecting the area, a car is essential if you want to fight your way through the traffic to visit the other big malls. The souks are well worth a visit, not just for the shopping, but for the atmosphere. Generally the retailers are not too pushy and your shopping experience is guaranteed to be an interesting one.

Refunds and Exchanges

The key to getting refunds and making exchanges is the same as everywhere else in the world. Make sure that you keep your original receipts, especially for big-ticket items. The large international stores all have reasonable and clearly defined policies. Marks & Spencer is the best, as they do not put a time limit on refunds or exchanges and you can buy something in one store and return or exchange it in any other Marks & Spencer store worldwide.

Debenhams has a two-week limit and Bhs a 30 day limit on full price items and a seven-day limit on sale items. Geant hypermarket will only exchange or give credit, and goods must be returned within seven days.

For purchases made in other stores, the refund or exchange policy will depend on the shop owner. If it is an electronic or expensive item, find out what the policy is before you buy. Once again, you will need to produce the original receipt for any chance of getting your money back. If you are not satisfied with your attempts to get a refund or exchange see the 'Consumer Rights' section below.

Consumer Rights

There are no legal consumer rights in Bahrain at present. The Ministry of Commerce is apparently trying to get some laws passed through parliament with regards to consumer rights, but they are still 'under discussion' with no anticipated date of completion. If you are unfortunate enough to have an unsolved problem with something you have bought, you should go to the Ministry of Commerce, Consumer Protection department (1753 0200) and complete the necessary forms required for an enquiry. The department will research the problem and take action as they see fit. Nobody seems to know whether or not this process is effective, but as they say in this part of the world, 'What we can do?'.

If you still feel very strongly that you have been treated badly, there is one other course of action; write a letter to the local newspaper, the *Gulf Daily News*, which is known colloquially as the GDN. One of the GDN's main features is the popular 'letters to the editor' section and bad publicity is not something most retailers welcome.

Shipping

The most popular items to be shipped to home countries from Bahrain are furniture and carpets. Both antique and more modern Arabic-style furniture are favourites with western expats. You can find unique designs in Bahrain and particularly at sales time you'll find good stuff worth shipping home. Other items that are popular to ship include carpets, framed Arabic jewellery, picture frames and models of dhows, the traditional local fishing boats.

Most retailers don't offer a shipping service. The major consumer groups here, the American Navy personnel and people contracted to management positions, generally have shipping arrangements as part of their contracts, but shipping out of Bahrain by air or sea is relatively straightforward. Things to take into consideration are how soon you wish to receive the goods in your home country and the most economical way to do it. Airfreight is generally, but not always, the more expensive option. The cost will depend on the actual weight or size of the item. If you are considering shipping things home, it would be a good idea to phone around the major relocators and shipping agents to get quotes or to ask their advice. It's very important to check with the shipping companies whether your country allows the import of particular items, since every country has its own customs rules and regulations for the import of personal effects. GAC International Moving (1781 4500), and Crown Worldwide (1722 7598) are two well-known international shipping companies in Bahrain that you can contact for this information.

How to Pay

Cash, credit and debit cards are all popular means of payment in Bahrain. If you're shopping in the souks and smaller retail shops, it's best to take cash, as many retailers do not accept credit cards. Cash also gives you an advantage when it comes to bargaining power. Retailers incur a 3% charge on credit and debit card sales and you can use this factor to your advantage when it comes to bargaining. For expensive items, the retailer may want to add the 3% to your purchase price to cover the cost of this bank charge. Visa and Mastercard are the most common credit cards and American Express and Diners Card are also readily accepted. The annual charges for having a credit card in the Gulf are high compared with other countries. Generally, the annual fees are around BD 20 – 30 for a Visa or Mastercard, so expats tend to use credit cards from their home countries.

You'll find ATMs everywhere in Bahrain and there are money exchanges in the malls and main shopping areas. Most retailers will readily accept currencies from the other Gulf countries, US dollars or UK pounds, but the exchange rate will probably not be the best in town and it is much less confusing to use the local dinars to ensure you are paying the right price.

Bargaining

Other options → Souks [p.187]

The large department stores, supermarkets and international stores have fixed prices and an attempt to barter in these stores is considered to be bad form. In the smaller retail stores, particularly those selling jewellery, furnishings,

electronic items and souvenirs always ask politely 'Is that your best price?' or 'What is your final price?' and you may be pleasantly surprised with an instant 5 – 25% discount. If you revel in the challenges of bartering for a bargain, head straight for the souk. However, there are a couple of things to keep in mind. Firstly, the shopkeeper you are bartering with probably has a lot more experience at this game than you have. Secondly, do your research before you go shopping, if you are serious about getting bargains. You need to know the value of an item locally and in your home country, to know if it is a true bargain or not. Finally, keep smiling and enjoy yourself.

What & Where to Buy

Listed in the following section are the various shopping product categories and information regarding all you need to know about where and how to buy products in Bahrain. The main shopping area for modern mall-type shopping is in the Seef district, which has Seef Mall, Al Aali Shopping Complex, Dana Mall and Bahrain Mall. The largest souk area is in Manama, south of the Bab Al Bahrain (which means Gateway to Bahrain), but there are also lots of interesting shopping areas, smaller malls, street shopping and souks scattered throughout Bahrain. These are listed in the final sections of this chapter.

Alcohol

Other options → Drinks [p.193]
On the Town [p.227]
Liquor Licence [p.45]

Unlike the other Gulf countries, it is not necessary to have a permit or licence to buy alcohol in Bahrain. There are four companies, with three outlets each, which sell retail alcohol products. The shops are open from 11:00 to 19:00 from Saturday to Thursday, except during Ramadan, when they are closed for the whole month, though you can still get alcohol in the top-class hotels and restaurants. It seems that although there is no actual legal age limit, the shops will not sell alcohol to young people under the age of 18.

Alcohol shops are also not permitted to sell alcohol to Muslims in national dress, but visitors from across the causeway manage to circumvent this rule by using the services of a willing Asian expat, who may be hovering around outside the outlet for this very purpose.

Because they are selling alcohol, there are many restrictions about the location of the shops. For example, they are not allowed to be located on main roads, near schools, or where women might gather, and they are not allowed to advertise. Therefore, the biggest problem is actually finding out exactly where the shops are. However, if you ask any resident expat, they are sure to be able to give you directions.

There is a 125% import tax levied on alcohol coming into Bahrain, so don't expect to find a multitude of great deals. However, because some of the alcohol shops are located quite close to each other, it pays to check each one out, and you may find occasional sales of beer (from BD 12 - 15 a case) and wine special offers (such as buy three and get one free). The best time for exceptional deals is the day before Ramadan starts when you can sometimes buy one and get one free.

Many expats buy their favourite spirits from the airport duty free each time they come into Bahrain from overseas, and buy their beer and wine locally.

Alcohol

African & Eastern	Hoora	1753 4362
	Adliya	1771 3448
	City Centre	1722 4920
B.M.M.I.	Central Market	1727 7261
	Adliya	1771 5616
	Diplomatic Area	1753 4234
Gulf Cellar	Central Market	1727 3020
	Adliya	1771 4205
	Umm Al Hassam	1772 9834
N.H.S.C.	Umm Al Hassam	1772 8636
	Hoora	1731 0782
	City Centre	1722 6295

Art

Other options → **Art Classes [p.146]**
Art Galleries [p.99]
Art Supplies [p.159]

Bahrain has a thriving art culture and the most well-established galleries and shops in the Gulf region. There are two big art societies, the Bahrain Art Society and the Society of Contemporary Art, who organize at least two major art shows (mainly local artists) every year in the National Museum. There are a number of combination galleries and shops, which also have regular art exhibitions and promote both local and international artists.

Arabesque Art Gallery, with branches in Umm Al Hassam and the Al Aali Shopping Complex, has

been established for nearly 30 years and showcases local art and the well-known traditional local scenes of artist Wahab Al Koheji. Small, framed Koheji prints are popular gifts for expats leaving Bahrain. The gallery also specialises in antique art and antique maps of the Middle East and sells a range of antique furniture from the Gulf region.

The Al Riwaq Art Gallery showcases mainly Arab artists from the Arab World. Another well-known gallery is the Dar Albareh Art Gallery. There are also numerous framing shops, which not only frame paintings and prints but sell a wide variety of mass-produced prints and paintings.

Art

Al Areesh Gallery for Child Art	Adliya	1781 3043
Al Riwaq Art Gallery	Adliya	1771 7441
Arabesque Art Gallery	Umm Al Hassam	1772 2916
	Seef	1758 1281
Bahrain Art Society	Budaiya	1759 0551
Dar Albareh Art Gallery	Adliya	1771 7707
Faisal Samra Gallery	Juffair	1782 7393
Globart - Dana Mall	Seef	1755 6777
- Marina Mall	Seef	1723 3320
La Fontaine Center of Contemporary Art	Awadiya	1723 0123

Art Supplies

Other options → **Art Galleries [p.99]**
Art [p.159]
Art Classes [p.146]

Art supplies are not cheap in Bahrain. However, the major suppliers of art and craft are all located in the Budaiya Road area, so you can check them out in your search for art, craft and needlework items. Things-To-Do has a good range of art and craft supplies, and surprisingly also sells equestrian equipment like saddles and bridles. Talent has a noticeboard advertising art and craft classes and will order any materials for you if they don't have what you require. Celebrations of Art, in the same area, is also worth a visit for your art and craft supplies. Bashar Art Gallery sells canvas and will also stretch it for you. Some of the stationery stores also sell a range of art materials.

Art Supplies

Bashar Art Gallery	Umm Al Hassam	1772 7326
Celebrations of Art	Budaiya	1759 5791
Talent	Budaiya	1759 4050
Things-To-Do	Budaiya	1759 0409

What & Where to Buy

Shopping

Beachwear

Other options → **Sporting Goods [p.178]**
Clothes [p.165]

Seef Mall is probably the best place to go if you are looking for beachwear. The large British department stores have all got good ranges of the latest swimwear, available all year round, but the new stock generally arrives in the store around April. Debenhams, Marks & Spencer and Bhs are all under one roof at Seef Mall and between them they have a very good selection of swimwear, sunhats and sarongs. Some of the boutique stores may also stock a small selection of swimwear. End of season swimwear sales usually take place around November. Most of the sports clothing stores have a range of Speedo swimwear and the necessary accessories such as goggles and caps for sports swimming. Geant, the hypermarket in Bahrain Mall, has a limited range of swimwear and all the accessories at budget prices, but the range of women's swimwear is limited and the styles are probably far too modest for most westerners. Suntan lotions are readily available at supermarkets and pharmacies.

Beachwear

BHS	Seef Mall	1758 2258
Debenhams	Seef Mall	1758 1166
Geant	Bahrain Mall	1755 8181
Marks & Spencer P.154	Seef Mall	1758 8188

Bicycles

Generally speaking, there are two types of cyclists in Bahrain: sports cyclists who race and cycle with their clubs, and labourers, who clean cars, do odd jobs and use a bike as a means of transport to move from job to job in an area. There are few recreational cyclists, not only because the roads are very busy, but because the standard of driving in Bahrain is diabolical. Neither Bahraini nor expat parents encourage their children to ride on the roads, but the children of families who live in large compounds often have bicycles for use on the compound.

Bicycles are either fairly expensive sports models or cheapish models imported from Taiwan or China. There is a specialist bike shop, the Skate Shack, with branches on the Budaiya Road, in Juffair and at Seef Mall, which has a good range of imported sports cycles, cycle accessories and safety equipment and also has a workshop for repairs. They are fairly expensive, but if quality or top of the range is what you are after, this is the place to visit.

Geant, Toys R Us and some of the sports stores sell a limited range of bikes. Cheap children's bikes can be bought in the small bike and toy shops in the suburban street shopping areas such as Isa Town and Riffa, and in the large discount stores such as Al Anwaar Discount Centre and Bahrain Pride Trading.

Bicycles

Al Anwaar Discount Store	Tubli	1787 4141
Bahrain Pride Trading	Salmabad	1778 9504
Geant	Seef	1755 8181
Skate Shack	Budaiya	1769 7176
	Juffair	1772 5168
	Seef	1740 4792
Toys R Us	Seef	1758 0860

Books

Other options → **Libraries [p.150]**
Second-Hand Items [p.177]

The range of books in Bahrain is not very comprehensive. You will find a range of fiction bestsellers (although not always hot off the press), the best selling authors, and popular non-fiction books, but the selection is limited, probably due to the small size of the population. There are three main bookshop operators in Bahrain, all offering a fairly similar range of titles.

The largest store in Bahrain is Jashanmals Bookstore in Seef Mall, and they have another branch in the Al Aali Shopping Complex. Both carry a large range of books; fiction and a wide range of non-fiction topics, cards and gifts. The Bookcase, near Alosra Supermarket on the Budaiya Road, is a pleasant place to visit and has a gift section as well as a large stock of books. It specialises in children's books and educational materials. It has a good range of greeting cards and a new-age gift area. A word of warning; the Bookcase outlet in Seef Mall is primarily a gift shop, with a really paltry array of books. The Family Bookshop is a well known name in the Gulf area and is situated between the Sheraton Complex and the American Mission Hospital.

Bookshops are generally willing to order titles for you, but it can sometimes take a while for them to arrive. If the local stores don't have what you're looking for, it might be worth ordering them yourself online (and this option can be quicker and cheaper, although you will have to pay postage on top of the price).

International newspapers and magazines are available in abundance, in bookshops and large supermarkets. Both newspapers and magazines are generally current and they don't seem to suffer from black-pen censorship too much. Charity

FIND YOURSELF IN OUR PAGES

JASHANMAL BOOKSTORES

Bahrain: Seef Mall, Tel: 17581107, Al Aali Shopping Complex, Tel: 17582424
Dubai: Mall of the Emirates, Tel: 04 3406789, The Village Mall, Jumeirah, Tel: 04 3445770
Jashanmal Department Store, Wafi City, Level 2, Tel: 04 3244800, Abu Dhabi: Abu Dhabi Mall,
Level 3, Hamdan Street, Tel: 02 6443869, Sharjah: Sahara Centre, Tel: 06 5317898

shops are probably the best source of second-hand books. Garage sales, car-boot sales and the Isa Town Market are other sources. There are no second-hand bookshops. The libraries in the community clubs (British Club, Dilmun Club, Bapco Club) order most of the best-selling fiction and non-fiction and are popular with avid readers, but are open to club members only.

Books

Book Island	Seef	1758 1224
Family Bookshop	Nr Sheraton Cmplx	1721 1288
Jashanmal Bookstores	Al Aali Complex	1758 2424
P.161	Seef Mall	1758 1107
The Bookcase	Budaiya	1769 0566

Camera Equipment

Other options → **Electronics & Home Appliances [p.167]**

There is a good selection of cameras and camera equipment in Bahrain. It is a booming and competitive market at present, with film cameras being replaced by digital cameras. Generally, prices are about 10% higher for new cameras than you would pay in Dubai. The main stores for some of the major brands are listed in the table. Geant, the hypermarket, is a good place to check out the models and prices available, as they stock most of the major brands and cheaper brands as well. For expert advice, it is best to go to the agent for the brand and model of camera you are thinking of buying. Cameras are often sold in film-processing stores and home-appliance stores in the souks. Be aware that the quality and brands may not be as reliable as those in the agencies' authorised showrooms.

International warranties are available in all the major retail stores. Check that you understand what the warranty offers and that you complete all the necessary paperwork before you leave the store. Falcon Cinefoto in Isa Town has a selection of more than a million negatives of fascinating black and white photos of old Bahrain. Some of these prints are on display and can be purchased. They are also specialists in aerial photography, which requires a special licence in Bahrain. This is probably the place to go if you need any specialised processing with still or movie film. You can also hire their film crew to record your special events, at a price! Camera film and film processing is widely available in the malls and shopping areas. The film-processing business is highly competitive and you can

expect some special offers with your film developing, such as free enlargements, free film and free photo albums.

Camera Equipment

Ashrafs - Nikon agent	1753 4439
Electo - Canon agent	1729 0893
Falcon Cinephoto	1762 4222
Gajira - Casio agent	1721 5353
Geant	1755 8181
Kewelram & Sons	1721 0982
Yaquby Stores	1721 0956

Cards & Stationery

Other options → **Art Supplies [p.159]**
Books [p.160]

Cards and stationery are usually sold in separate shops in Bahrain, with the stationery shops selling mainly stationery and office supplies. The card shops, on the other hand, usually specialise in cards, postcards, wrapping paper, ribbons and bows, and small gifts or souvenirs. There is a reasonable selection of greeting cards available in Bahrain, though those of a slightly more racy nature are not generally available. Having said that, one sometimes comes across cards featuring quite startling innuendo that has obviously bypassed the censor.

Bahrain Greetings has five outlets in all the main malls and they specialise in Hallmark cards. A limited range of cards is also available in the supermarkets and hypermarkets. The Bookcase on the Budaiya Road has a selection of cards that are a bit different, being somewhat artier than the general run-of-the-mill cards. The range won't be as good as in your home country, but if you shop around you should be able to find something suitable in any of the card categories, particularly if sentimental slush is your preference.

Gift packaging is big business in Bahrain and you will find a huge selection of gift wraps and boxes. There are small, specialist gift-wrapping shops such as Papermoon in Al Aali Shopping Complex and Seef Mall, and depending on the arrival of

> ### Explore the GCC
>
> *If you want to drop in on your neighbours, then go prepared. Be it for a shopping spree in Dubai, a luxury holiday in Abu Dhabi, to find tranquility in the wilderness of Oman, or to see the colourful heritage of Kuwait, don't leave Bahrain without an Explorer!*

Copper wall panel (5m high) · Art paint effects

stock, a staggering selection of boxes and ribbons and wraps in the discount emporiums like Ramez Trading in Central Market and Isa Town.

Stationery shops are generally not in the malls, so if you require stationery, check where you will need to go before you step out of your door. Most of the stationery shops stock a good range of personal, school and business stationery and requirements. Almoayyed Stationery also sells computer furniture, geometric instruments and professional measuring equipment. Awal Stationery has engineering instruments too and a good selection of top brand pens. Geant hypermarket also has a basic range of stationery and greeting cards.

Cards & Stationery

Almoayyed Stationery	Bab Al Bahrain	1722 5454
Awal Stationery	Bab Al Bahrain	1722 3337
Bahrain Greetings	Al Jazera Complex	1774 1839
	Alosra Centre	1769 9723
	Bahrain Mall	1755 2142
	Dana Mall	1755 6138
	Seef Mall	1758 1120
Geant	Bahrain Mall	1755 8181
Papermoon	Al Aali Complex	1758 1020
	Cypress Garden	1769 2189
	Seef Mall	1758 1090
Ramez Trading	Nr Salmabad R/A	1725 5519
Salman Int'l Stationery	Bab Al Bahrain	1723 3004
The Bookcase	Budaiya Highway	1769 0566
Union Stationery	Exhibition Rd	1771 4461

Carpets

Other options → **Souvenirs [p.178]**
Bargaining [p.158]

Carpets are a best-selling item in Bahrain. Most of the villas and apartments have tiled, marble or wood-veneer floors, and carpets are needed for both practical and decorative purposes. Oriental carpets originating from Iran, India, Pakistan, China and Asia are available.

The main shopping street in Adliya is lined with carpet stores. The neighbouring personnel from the US Navy base spend a lot of money on carpets and keep the carpet business booming in Adliya and Juffair. Some of the carpets are displayed out on the street and some in the shop windows, but in the shops they are rolled and stacked. The shops all have a relatively similar stock, but each carpet is unique, so you should take your time when selecting one to buy. Once the shopkeeper has determined your requirements he will have the carpets rolled out for you to view. Often you will be served tea or coffee and the shopkeeper will do his best to develop a personal rapport with you.

Bargaining is expected, and after you have bought one or two carpets from a particular dealer over a period of time, and are debating whether or not to buy another, he deals the killer blow, something along the lines of 'Why don't you take it home and live with it for a week or two, and then decide if you want to buy it'. Most of the dealers are also willing to come to an 'arrangement' when you want to buy a really expensive carpet; put some money down upfront and pay the rest over a couple of months.

If you are considering buying an expensive carpet, do some research about the areas where the carpet was made, the family that made it and what to look for to test the quality of the carpet. This will enable you to know whether you are being offered the carpet at a fair or inflated price. Certificates of authenticity are available for the higher priced carpets. Isam at Tehran Handmade Carpets in Adliya is always willing to talk carpets and give genuine advice. Classes are sometimes advertised in the GDN and there are books about carpets available in most book shops.

Carpets are also available in hotel shops, gift shops and home furnishing shops. Isa Town Market has a large number of carpet shops selling a wide selection of machine-made rugs in the lower price range and bargaining for price is expected.

Magic carpets

Carpets

Bardran Persian Store	Bab Al Bahrain	1722 8655
Carpet House	Adliya	1771 0163
City Carpets	Adliya	1771 6158
Handmade Carpet Centre	Hoora	1729 3695
Magic Carpet	Adliya	1771 4618
Oasis Handmade Carpet Centre	Adliya	1771 3197
Peacock Carpet Centre	Adliya	1771 3152
Persian Carpet House	Seef	1758 1239
Red Sea	Adliya	1771 7785
Royal Carpet	Adliya	1771 3600
Tehran Handmade Carpets	Adliya	1771 2153

Cars

Other options → Buying a Vehicle [p.80]

All the major car manufacturers are represented in Bahrain and many of them have their showrooms in the Sitra area. The driving in Bahrain is of a fairly low standard, so 4WDs and SUVs are popular from a safety point of view, although there are basically no off-roading areas to speak of. However, because Bahrain is a small island, has heavily congested traffic, terrible parking, lots of traffic islands and millions of speed bumps, the driving is constantly stop-start and erratic.

A small automatic car is maybe the most practical to own and drive in Bahrain. Cars are definitely affordable although they are probably about 20% cheaper in Dubai. However, the paperwork required to import them to Bahrain means that most people buy locally. Bank loans are readily negotiated and all models and makes are available. Most of the major car dealerships also have their own second-hand car sections to sell their trade-in models.

There are plenty of second-hand car markets and cars are often displayed at major roundabouts with a contact phone number displayed in the windows. If you see one you fancy, act fast,

Off-Road Explorer

If you've just nabbed yourself a 4WD but are disappointed with Bahrain's lack of dunes, why not plan your next mini break around the desert, mountains and wadis of the UAE. The UAE Off-Road Explorer has route maps, satellite images, step-by-step guidance, and safety info to help you find your way and also includes safety tips.

because the police often carry out a blitz and clamp them. The supermarket noticeboards advertise used cars for sale, usually with a photograph, and the local daily paper also has a small classifieds section. Japanese cars have a good resale value, but European cars are generally less popular because spare parts are expensive. Many Bahrainis look down on Korean cars, so they are generally cheaper, but you may find it difficult to sell yours when you decide to move on.

Clothes

Other options → Sporting Goods [p.178]
Shoes [p.178]
Tailoring [p.179]
Lingerie [p.172]
Kids' Items [p.172]
Beachwear [p.160]

All the major fashion designer labels are well represented in Bahrain, especially at the Al Aali Shopping Complex and Seef Mall, and there are some interesting Arabian designer boutiques too. Some of the major international family shopping stores like Debenhams, Marks & Spencer, Bhs and Woolworths are also here, but the prices are usually considerably higher than they would be in their home countries, so sales time is the best time to shop in these stores.

There are some great menswear bargains to be had in Geant, Sana and Discount Home Store. If you have time to sift through the shelves, you will sometimes find designer label items at very reasonable prices, but they may be pirate goods, so check the quality carefully. It is purely a matter of good timing to chance upon these bargains. Fashion-conscious and average-sized ladies are spoilt for choice, but clothing for larger-sized women is restricted to the international family stores listed above. However, don't forget that you can buy your choice of fabric in the souk and have a tailor make an item to your very own design (see Tailoring on p.179).

Clothing sizes vary considerably depending on which country the garment has been made for. An Asian size 14 is very small compared with an Australian size 14 for example, so check the size or try the garment on before you buy it. Refund or exchange policies vary enormously, so it is best to be quite sure an item will fit before you leave the store.

What & Where to Buy

Shopping

Clothes

BHS	Seef Mall	1758 2258
Charles & Keith	Seef Mall	1758 7020
Debenhams	Seef Mall	1758 11 66
Discount Home Store	Nr HSBC Bank	1764 4110
Esprit	Seef Mall	1758 1565
Evans	Seef Mall	1758 1064
Geant	Bahrain Mall	1755 8181
Gerry Webber	Seef Mall	1758 2272
Giordano	Al Aali Complex	1758 2267
Giordano	Bahrain Mall	1755 4201
Lacoste	Seef Mall	1758 1139
Liz Clairborne	Seef Mall	1758 1061
Lui & Elle	Al Aali Complex	1758 1199
Marks & Spencer P.154	Seef Mall	1758 8188
Monsoon	Seef Mall	1758 1804
Next	Seef Mall	1758 1681
River Island	Seef Mall	1758 1129
Sana	Bahrain Mall	1755 6430
Studio Collection	Al Aali Complex	1758 2330
Top Shop	Seef Mall	1758 1126
Truworths	Bahrain Mall	1755 3328
United Colors of Benetton	Seef Mall	1758 1278
Vogue	Al Aali Complex	1758 2555
Woolworths	Al Jazira Complex	1774 0111

Clothes – Nearly New

There are no second-hand clothes shops or factory outlets in Bahrain. The majority of nearly new clothes are found in the charity shops or garage sales. Some stunning outfits and good bargains can sometimes be found, but you need the time to do the rounds of the charity shops on a regular basis. The selection available will depend on the number of expats leaving and the quality of their social life and throw-away clothes! See Second-Hand Items (p.177) for the names and locations of the Charity Shops. They are mostly run by volunteers and the opening hours will vary.

Computers

Other options → **Electronics &
Home Appliances [p.167]**

All the latest computer technology is available in Bahrain in a competitive market. Geant, the hypermarket in Bahrain Mall, has a reasonable range of computers and accessories and is a good place to find out what is available, and how much it costs, but don't expect to find a salesperson who has any technical knowledge of the stock. If it's expert advice you are after, go to one of the larger computer stores and speak to the agent's

representatives. It is a good idea to give the salesperson a very clear idea of what you will be using the computer for, eg. mainly emailing, games, graphics, research, etc. Prices are higher than in the US and slightly higher than in Dubai. However, if you buy in Bahrain from a major supplier, you should have no problems getting the computer serviced. All of the major suppliers have authorised service centres. Check whether your purchase comes with an international warranty and exactly what it includes if you are going to take your computer to another part of the world.

There are usually two computer fairs a year in Bahrain, the Bahrain Computer Shopping Festival and the Future IT Show, which are both held at the Bahrain International Exhibition Centre in Seef. They are probably worth a look if you want to check prices or see what's new in the field of computer technology.

Until quite recently there was a huge amount of pirated computer games and software available in Bahrain, but the authorities have clamped down on this fairly rigidly during the past few years. Be careful of buying computer package deals with unauthorized software already loaded. The dealer should be able to supply the original packaging and manuals for all software they provide.

Computers

Advanced PC	City Centre	1731 0056
Al Majal Advanced Technology	City Centre	1729 6477
Almoayyed Computers	City Centre	1770 0777
Apple Centre	City Centre	1753 3771
Equinox	City Centre	1729 3778
Geant	Bahrain Mall	1755 8100
Hilal Computers- Dell	City Centre	1729 3749
Mars Information Technology	City Centre	1729 2181
Microplus Computers	City Centre	1729 7939
North Star Computers	City Centre	1729 1351
Venus Computers	City Centre	1724 2184
Zayani Computer Systems	City Centre	1745 7007

Costumes

Geant has a great range of Santa Claus costumes and Christmas hats at very cheap prices in December. Manazel also has some Christmas costumes and Halloween items. A variety of children's fancy dress costumes are available in Toys R Us, Mothercare and Geant and sometimes if you scratch around in the charity shops (See the Second-hand Items on p.177) you may find some costumes and hats.

What & Where to Buy

Shopping

If you are looking for a fancy dress costume, one option is to contact the local amateur dramatics Manama Theatre Club (p150), who have a large range of costumes available for hire. The other option is to buy some fabric and take a picture to your favourite local tailor and get him to make it for you.

Costumes

Geant	Bahrain Mall	1755 8181
Manazel	Salmabad	1778 6727
Mothercare	Seef Mall	1758 1010
Toys R Us	Seef Mall	1758 0860

Discount Cards

Discount cards can be expensive in Bahrain, because they are usually part of a credit card scheme. Having the discount card involves paying the large annual fees associated with the credit card, so you need to consider carefully whether the 'discounts' will outweigh the administration costs. Geant La Carte Credit Card is a Visa Card and is based on a points scheme. You get points on all purchases in Bahrain and worldwide and special discounts on some items. Jawad's discount card is a Diners Card with a BD 25 annual fee, and is also based on a points scheme. However, the good news is that Al Jazira Supermarket's Loyalty Card is free with no annual fees. If you spend more than BD 25 in a month in the supermarket, you will receive a voucher for 2% to 5% of the total spent, and you can redeem this voucher at the supermarket or at Woolworths. Manazel, Bahrain's leading DIY store, has a loyalty card which gives you a BD 10 voucher for every BD 100 you spend in their store.

Electronics & Home Appliances

Other options → Camera Equipment [p.162]
Computers [p.166]

If you are considering bringing home appliances or electronic equipment to Bahrain or buying them locally, you will need to check whether they are compatible with your home country requirements. Bahrain's electrical current is 220 volts, 50 cycles, and doesn't suit US goods. Even with a transformer, items with timers run more slowly, causing motors to work less efficiently. Many of the apartments in Bahrain are rented complete with all the appliances, particularly in the Juffair area where competition is fierce for the US Navy personnel. Villas and compound houses, on the other hand, will usually include a washing machine, fridge and a stove, which could be gas or electric.

Geant has an excellent selection of electronic and home appliances, although it is difficult to find anyone to give expert advice. At sales time you can pick up some good buys. Ashraf's has a good reputation and sells the latest models of TVs, VCRs, and sound systems. Al Moayyed Electronics is the agent for Toshiba and sells the Kenwood brand as well. Rouben's Store is the agent for Sharp. Gajira Electronics also has a wide variety of electronic goods. You can buy state-of-the-art products with warranties from the authorised agents, and you can also pick up cheap electronic items in the souks and suburban shopping areas. Don't forget to bargain!

The discount emporiums, like Ramez and Bahrain Pride, have some real bargains if you're not too concerned about the quality or life expectancy of the product. Expats leaving Bahrain often include electronic equipment in their garage sales or advertise on the supermarket noticeboards.

Electronics & Home Appliances

Al Moayyed Electronics	Bab Al Bahrain	1721 2555
Ashraf's Department Store	Hoora	1753 4439
Bahrain Pride Trading	Salmabad	1778 9504
Equinox Electronics	Hoora	1729 2611
Gajira Electronics	Bab Al Bahrain	1722 5356
Geant	Bahrain Mall	1755 8181
Homebase	Seef	1755 6750
Kewelram & Sons	Bab Al Bahrain	1721 0982
Ramez Trading	Central Market	1725 5519
Rouben's Store	Bab Al Bahrain	1722 3330

Eyewear

Other options → Sporting Goods [p.178]
Opticians [p.73]

If you are looking for new glasses or sunglasses you will be spoilt for choice. There are numerous opticians in the shopping malls and shopping areas. All the designer frames are available. There is also a plentiful supply of contact lenses in all the usual shapes and colors. Yateem Optician and Bahrain Optician have many branches all over Bahrain. Keep an eye out for sales at Ehsan Optics. At sales time you can get prescription glasses and sunglasses at real bargain prices. If it is just a fashion accessory you are looking for, cool cheap sunglasses can be found in supermarkets, the hypermarket and discount stores, but the range is limited and quality is obviously poorer.

What & Where to Buy

Shopping

Eyewear

Al Noor Optical	Bab Al Bahrain	1721 2153
Bahrain Optical	Bahrain Mall	1755 2533
	Isa Town Mall	1768 5535
	Seef Mall	1758 0955
Carmel	Seef Mall	1758 1153
Eshan Optics	Dana Mall	1721 3478
Sunglass Hut	Bahrain Mall	1755 1993
	Seef Mall	1758 2875
Yateem Optical	Al Aali Complex	1758 1085
	Manama Complex	1725 3397

Flowers

Other options → Gardens [p.169]

Adliya is the main area for fresh flower shops. Here you will find several specialist florist shops selling fresh flowers, bouquets and houseplants. Most of the large hotels also have an in-house flower shop. There are the usual supermarket posies available in all the major supermarkets, but you won't find any bargain prices. Pop into Singapore Flowers if you feel like transporting yourself to downtown Singapore. They have a huge variety of fresh orchids in every imaginable colour and shape, as well as flower arrangements and small ornamental trees in pots.

The best buy in flowers used to be the bunches of small fresh orchids flown in from Thailand and sold for about 500 fils a bunch at the Rachanee Thai supermarket on a side street in Adliya next to the Wang Thai Restaurant. However, someone has realised that they were selling them too cheaply and now the Rachanee Supermarket has opened a florist shop next to their supermarket, repacking the orchids and selling them at BD 2.500 for a bunch of five orchids (but if truth be told, this is still quite reasonable!).

The range of flowers in Bahrain is not vast, but the standard roses, carnations and orchids are generally available, and whatever other flowers are in season in Holland, where most of the fresh flowers are imported from. Expect to pay about 500 fils for a fresh carnation and between 800 fils and BD 1.500 for a rose. Unfortunately, cut roses seem to droop depressingly quickly in Bahrain, so you have to learn by experience which varieties will last longest.

Check the Yellow Pages for Interflora florists if you want to send flowers overseas or check out the internet for online florists in the destination city. There are also some delightful combination flower, chocolate and small gift shops dotted around

Bahrain. One of these is Verandah Gifts and Flowers in the Verandah Restaurant complex in Adliya, which has a great range of fresh flowers and colourful, interesting knick-knacks and gifts.

Flowers

Alia Flowers	Adliya	1771 4696
Bloom-N-Fantasy	Seef	1758 0393
Lily The Flower Shop	Adliya	1774 9194
Rachanee Flower Shop	Adliya	1771 4412
Riviera Flowers	Seef	1771 3677
RolandaChocolates and Flowers	Adliya	1771 5158
Singapore Flower	Adliya	1774 2456
Verandah Gifts and Flowers	Adliya	1771 7232

Food

Other options → Health Food [p.170]

Because of the cosmopolitan population in Bahrain there is a huge selection of food items available from all over the world. The main supermarkets that the westerners frequent are Alosra, Al Jazira, Jawad, Geant and MegaMart. Geant has a huge food section but the variety of some items can be quite restricted. The bakery (French) and the fish section are popular attractions. For squeamish people, who don't fancy the sights and smells of the fish souk, Geant is the next best option for fresh fish. The checkout operators and packers often look depressed and bored, and are not known as the most efficient in town, but convenience is a major factor, because you can pick up any other household item, clothes, books, tools or toys while you are there.

Alosra in Saar is very popular with the expat community. It probably has the best quality and selection of fruit and vegetables in Bahrain. The bakery, butchery and deli departments have inviting displays and the pork section is very popular. It's best to avoid the pork section on Thursdays and Fridays, when expats based in Saudi come over the causeway to stock up on their bangers, rashers and pork pies. They tend to buy in bulk and everything has to be specially wrapped to avoid the unwelcome attention of the customs officials on the Saudi side of the causeway, so you can end up waiting half an hour to be served. The pork section is also the place expats go at Christmas and Easter to get the special food items for these seasons.

Jawad is a group of large, modern supermarkets that specialise in Tesco and Waitrose products from England. They have an excellent butchery section and friendly, helpful staff. Al Jazira has three branches, in Mahooz, Budaiya Road and Adliya, and sells the usual range of expat favourites. Al Jazira is also very popular with Filipinas and Thai ladies early on a Friday morning, when its stock of fresh fruit and vegetables arrives from Thailand.

If you are after American food items, the MegaMart stores, particularly the one in Juffair, cater for the American Navy personnel as well as the local population. Another large supermarket chain is Al Muntazah, which caters mainly for the Bahraini and Asian markets, and sometimes you will find their prices for basic items, such as rice sold in bulk, are cheaper than in the other large supermarkets.

One of the problems of food shopping in Bahrain is the erratic supply of stock, so if you have a favourite product, stock up on it while you can. The word tends to get round very quickly, so if a friend tells you that Jawad has Twiglets, you'd better go there quickly, before everyone else has snaffled them all. There are many small food stores, known as 'cold stores', which are little corner shops that are open from early until late and sell basic food and household products. Central Market is a great place for fresh fruit and vegetables and in the same location is the fish market, which requires stout footware and is not for the faint hearted. Go early before the heat and smell have built up to stifling levels.

Food

Al Jazira	Adliya	1771 4914
	Budaiya	1759 0845
	Mahooz	1774 0111
Al Muntazah Market	Hoora	1729 5777
Alosra Supermarket	Saar	1769 7558
Geant	Seef	1755 8181
Giant	Sanabis	1755 6226
Jawad Supermarket	Sanad	1769 1010
MegaMart	Muharraq	1734 3266
	Juffair	1782 6884

Gardens

Other options → Flowers [p.168]
Hardware & DIY [p.169]

Gardening is a very popular pastime in Bahrain. Once upon a time Bahrain was known as the Garden of Eden. Unfortunately, the water table has dropped significantly and Bahrain is no longer the lush place it once was. However, it is still a fairly green area for this part of the world and

there is an abundance of trees, grass and flowers, particularly in the winter. Bougainvillea, frangipani, jasmine and hibiscus grow relatively easily and make a wonderful show. Books on plants that grow well in the Gulf are available in the bookshops. There is a very active Bahrain Garden Club (1772 7625) which organises a major garden show each year to promote gardening in the area. Most of the nurseries are along the Budaiya Road and they sell a very similar range of indoor and outdoor plants, and all general gardening requirements. The major supermarkets also sell indoor plants and potting mixes.

There are a few roadside stalls, mostly in the Saar area, that sell outdoor plants. Geant and Manazel are the two major stores for buying garden tools, equipment and furniture. Many expats and locals employ gardeners to look after their lawns and garden areas, but many of the gardeners don't know much about gardening and will basically just water the grass and hack bits off trees and shrubs when they get too big. Word of mouth is the best way to find a good gardener in your area. Be bold! If you see a garden that you like, knock on the door and make enquiries about the gardener.

Gardening Shops

Agro Flora	Jidhafs	1755 5676
Al Khair Agricultural Centre	Budaiya	1769 7881
Al Mazra'ah Garden Centre	Hoora	1773 1300
Gardenia	Zinj	1725 1025
Geant	Seef	1755 8181
Jassim's Garden Centre	Jidhafs	1755 2808
Manazel	Salmabad	1778 6727
My Garden	Tubli	1778 6878
Tree of Life	Hoora	1773 0111

Hardware & DIY

Other options → Outdoor Goods [p.174]

Manazel and Bokhammas seem to be the most popular places to go for home handyman requirements. They have tools and all the other bits and pieces a home handyman needs. They will also mix paints and give good advice. Manazel has a much better layout than Bokhammas, so it's easier to find what you are looking for. Geant also has a good range of handyman items but you are unlikely to find anyone to give you advice.

Isa Town Souk has a large selection of second-hand tools and there are plenty of little hole-in-the-wall shops in the town areas selling plumbing and carpentry supplies. The large discount stores, like

Al Anwaar and Ramez Trading, usually have a huge range of very cheap tools, paintbrushes and much more, if you are not too concerned about the quality. There is a timber yard and carpentry shop called Al Nooh in Qurayyah off the Janabiya Highway if you need to buy timber, and there are plenty of small carpentry shops where you can get things made. If you need a home handyman ask around. Ask at the hardware store, or ask your work colleagues or neighbours if they can recommend anyone and what price you should expect to pay.

Hardware & DIY

Al Anwaar Discount Store	Tubli	1787 4141
Al Nooh Carpentry Shop	Budaiya	1769 4569
Bokhammas	Salmabad	1778 4404
	Adliya	1771 6669
	Hoora	1771 4174
Geant	Seef	1755 8181
Manazel	Salmabad	1778 6727
Ramez Trading	Central Market	1725 5519

Health Food

Other options → **Health Clubs [p.143]**
Food [p.168]

Most of the large supermarkets stock a range of health food and supplements. Alosra has a 'Healthy Selections' range and also imports a limited range of fresh organic fruit and vegetables. Jawad and Al Jazira supermarkets also have health food sections. The Mahooz branch of Al Jazira has a 'Live Well' section in their store, which has a good selection of health food, organic food, diabetic products and associated health products. Vitamin and mineral supplements are available at most pharmacies.

GNC (General Nutrition Centre) has two stores in Bahrain, one in Seef Mall and one on Palace Road, selling vitamin and mineral supplements, weight loss and sports nutrition products, and natural herbs. In Bahrain Mall there is a shop called Organic Nutrition (1755 3151), which also sells health food supplements. Whole Earth Products is situated in West Riffa near Al Muntazah supermarket. The name of the store may be changed to either Health Solutions or Health and Healing in the near future. Karen, the owner, will give natural health advice or consultations for a health plan. She researches and personally selects the products they stock, to ensure that they have no chemical components and are of the best possible quality. She also stocks personal care and aromatherapy products.

Some other health food stores of interest are the World of Herbs in the old souk in Manama near the Adhari Hotel, which sells herbal medicines. Nature Valley has two shops, one in Manama and one in Juffair. They are currently introducing both fresh and frozen organic foods to their stock. Dr Lamia, the owner, is a family physician and specialises in treating obesity problems.

Health Food

Al Jazira Supermarket	Mahooz	1774 0111
Alosra Supermarket	Saar	1769 7558
GNC	Hoora	1753 0343
	Seef	1758 7740
Jawad Supermarket	Sanad	1769 1010
Nature Valley	Juffair	1782 5554
	Seef	1723 2959
Whole Earth Products	West Riffa	1766 6271
World of Herbs	City Centre	1722 8218

Home Furnishings & Accessories

Other options → **Hardware & DIY [p.169]**
Furnishing Accommodation [p.62]

Whatever your budget, shopping for home furnishings and accessories in Bahrain is great fun. The large discount emporiums have an interesting range of home accessories at really cheap prices. There is a rapid turnover of stock, so if you see something you like, you need to buy it there and then. There are plenty of large furniture shops all over Bahrain, many of them on Sheikh Salman Highway,

Home furnishings

selling a wide variety of different types of furniture. They are worth visiting just to check out the range of hugely ornate furniture, commonly known as Louis Farooq, which often has a crazed marble finish and curlicues elaborately picked out in gold. Some of the lamps and ornamental items are splendidly bizarre, featuring giant flowers or palm trees in brass, full-sized falcons or camels. THE One has recently opened a large store in the Al Aali Shopping Complex and has an excellent stock of home furnishings, as does Home Centre in Marina Mall.

There are many upmarket stores like Jashanmal and Artikel, selling exquisite ranges of home accessories, at a price. Second-hand furniture shops are listed in the Second-Hand Items section (p.177), and some also sell a range of new budget furniture from Asia. For some reason they are known as Auction Houses, though the items are not sold by auction. A general rule is that anything with 'Auction' in its name sells second-hand furniture, while anything with 'Exhibition' in its name sells new furniture. If you have time, you can get some good buys at garage sales or from the supermarket noticeboards. Visit some of the carpentry shops such as Al Wasmi or Rosewood Collections for custom-built furniture. Check out the quality of the varnish finish and get a guarantee that the item is free from pest infestation if you are thinking of taking the furniture back to your home country. One other option is Pronto Décor, who offer high quality, custom-made furniture, mostly in wood. Designs are modern, funky and functional, and they are made locally in Bahrain.

Home Furnishings & Accessories

Al Wasmi	Busaiteen	1733 3499
Almoayyed Furnishing	Sehla	1740 0004
Artikel	Budaiya	1779 5038
Bukannan Furnishing	Sehla	1740 0600
Chinese Fine Arts & Crafts	Gudaibayah	1723 2338
Home Centre	Central Market	1725 0034
IDesign	Budaiya	1759 2404
Jashanmal at Al Aali P.161	Seef	1758 2424
Pronto Decor		1722 5456
Rosewood Collections	Bab Al Bahrain	1722 5666
THE One	Seef	1758 7178

Jewellery & Watches

Other options → Souks [p.187]

Bahrain is world-renowned as a centre for gold and pearls. As well as an abundance of jewellery shops everywhere in Bahrain, in the malls, in the shopping centres and even in the small villages, there are two major locations for buying jewellery. One is the Gold Souk (See p.187), which is housed in a three-storey building in the middle of the Manama Souk, and the other is Gold City, another large building opposite the Delmon Hotel in the centre of Manama. The Sheraton Complex also has a large number of enticing, upmarket jewellery stores. If you can't find what you're looking for in any of these locations, it doesn't exist! Most of the gold is 18, 21, 22, or 24 carat, which is a very different colour to the 10 to 14 carat jewellery commonly sold in the west. Gold is sold by the weight, so it pays to check out the current price in the daily newspaper before you go shopping. You will also need to consider the workmanship when pricing an item.

Worth its weight in gold

Jewellery & Watches

A La Mode	Seef Mall	1758 1588
Ahmed Alwazzan		
Jewellery	Sheraton Complex	1753 5231
Al Mudaifa Jewels	Sheraton Complex	1753 2300
Al Zain for Jewellery	Seef Mall	1758 2232
	Sheraton Complex	1753 5331
	Yateem Centre	1722 9191
Asia Jewellers	Al Aali Complex	1758 1444
	Seef Mall	1758 7888
	Sheraton Complex	1753 4444
Bahrain Jewellery Centre	Sheraton Complex	1753 4443
Behbehani Bros	Yateem Centre	1722 5343
Bhasker Devji Jewllers	Al Aali Complex	1758 2588
Bvlgari	Al Aali Complex	1758 2559
Desert Diamonds	Gold City	1721 1963
Gold City	Government Av	1721 0404
MM Sharif Hatam		
& Sons	Seef Mall	1758 1999
Taqi's Jewellery	Sheraton Complex	1753 5544

What & Where to Buy

Shopping

Diamonds and other precious gemstones are also available and can be set to your own design. Bahrain has always been a world-class centre for pearls and it is still one of the major global markets for selling natural pearls from all over the world. If you have a large disposable income you will be able to choose from an incredible selection of all the world's top label watches and designs. There are several specialist watch shops in the malls and shopping complexes, and you can also find a good selection of bargain brands in the souks. Remember to use your bargaining skills and if you are not comfortable with bargaining, at least ask for 'the best price'.

Kids' Items

Other options → Clothes [p.165]

It's unlikely that you'll be stuck for whatever you need in the way of kids' toys, clothes, games and furniture in Bahrain. Geant has all the basics for baby gear and kids' requirements at reasonable prices. The maternity shops (see the Maternity section on p.173) all stock nappy-bag items and basic requirements for babies.

Most of the kids' clothing designer labels and stores have branches in Bahrain. Sana and Discount Home Store both have a huge range of children's clothing at excellent prices. There are always the large department stores like Mothercare, Debenhams, Bhs, Marks & Spencer and Woolworths, but prices here are usually higher than they would be in their home countries.

Toys range from the very expensive to the very cheap and the latest trends in toys and games from overseas are here fairly promptly. You won't be

Watch out - kid drivers!

able to resist the stuffed toys in The Bear Factory in Seef Mall. They can be personalised with birth certificates, voice boxes and clothing, and are totally enchanting. A good place to start with items for kids' parties is probably Geant, but a lot of kids' parties are held in the fast-food restaurants such as McDonald's and Fuddruckers, or Magic Island at Seef Mall and Foton World at Bahrain Mall which provide entertainment and cater for kids' parties.

Kids' Items		
Al Anwaar Discount Store	Nr Train Station	1787 4141
Bahrain Pride Trdg	Nr Salmabad R/A	1778 9504
Bear Factory	Seef Mall	1758 3236
Bhs	Seef Mall	1758 2258
Debenhams	Seef Mall	1758 1166
Discount Home Store	Adliya	1771 6370
	Riffa	1777 9818
	Sanad	1762 2156
Geant	Bahrain Mall	1755 8181
Identity	Bahrain Mall	1755 0959
Jeunesse Parisienne Boutique	Sheraton Complex	1753 5377
Kid Cool	Seef Mall	1758 1505
Marks & Spencer P.154	Seef Mall	1758 8188
Mothercare	Bahrain Mall	1755 4557
Sana	Bahrain Mall	1755 6430
	Salmaniya	1725 9522
Toys R Us	Seef Mall	1758 0860
Woolworths	Al Jazira Complex	1774 0111

Lingerie

Other options → Clothes [p.165]

Lingerie is currently a hot topic in Bahrain because some members of parliament want to ban lingerie displays in shop windows. In the meantime, there is a wide selection of lingerie in all price ranges in Bahrain. If you have a healthy income there are specialist lingerie shops in all the malls and shopping areas selling label brands and some rather interesting and exotic creations.

Mexx in Al Aali Shopping Complex sells a range of Triumph lingerie. Sarah's Secret has two branches, one in Marina Mall and the other in Riffa Mall, and sells underwear in both Asian and western styles for women and children. The department stores like Debenhams, Marks & Spencer, Woolworths and Bhs all have a good range of designer and basic underwear for both men and women. The ladies' underwear in Geant is more suitable for the Bahraini and Asian market, but the men's range is standard, as it is in most of the supermarkets and large discount emporiums.

Lingerie

Bhs	Al Alawi Complex	1770 0123
	Seef Mall	1758 2258
Debenhams	Seef Mall	1758 11 66
Etam	Bahrain Mall	1755 6504
Geant	Bahrain Mall	1755 8181
La Senza	Bahrain Mall	1755 1670
	Seef Mall	1758 2110
Marks & Spencer P.154	Seef Mall	1758 8188
Mexx	Al Aali Complex	1758 1287
Sarah's Secret	Marina Mall	1723 1090
Woolworths	Al Jazira Complex	1774 0111

Luggage & Leather

Other options → Shipping [p.157]

Because of the climate there is little demand for leather clothing in Bahrain. Al Maz in the Sheraton Complex has a small range of men's leather jackets and you might find an item or two of leather clothing in the designer label shops. On the other hand, leather handbags and belts are very much in demand and range in quality and price from expensive to cheap. If you need custom-made leather goods for corporate promotions you could contact Hide N Chic. There is a good selection of luggage available across the price range. Check out the discount emporiums, the souk or the Indian shopping areas for bottom of the range suitcases. For mid-range luggage try Geant, while for quality luggage look in the boutiques in Al Aali Shopping Complex or Seef Mall.

Luggage & Leather

Al Maz	Sheraton Complex	1753 5075
Charriol Boutique	Sheraton Complex	1753 5551
Geant	Bahrain Mall	1755 8181
Hide N Chic	Capital Centre	1723 2110

Maternity Clothes

There is a limited range of maternity clothes available in Bahrain and they can be quite pricey. Nine Months, in Al Alawi Complex, is probably the only specialist maternity shop in Bahrain. They stock selections from North American designers like Belly Basics, Duet Designs and Tummi Designs. They also sell a range of interesting baby shower gifts and other maternity needs, such as an excellent nappy bag with an insulated bottle holder, changing mat and key clip (what do babies need keys for!?). They are also developing a popular and more conservative range of maternity clothes for Arab women. Mothercare has some maternity wear but it is quite pricey, as is Debenhams, which has a limited selection of maternity clothes in their Dorothy Perkins section. Woolworths also has some maternity clothes. Marks & Spencer sells maternity bras.

Maternity Clothes

Debenhams	Seef Mall	1758 11 66
Marks & Spencer P.154	Seef Mall	1758 8188
Mommy 2 Be	Al Aali Complex	1758 1246
Mothercare	Al Jazira Complex	1772 2901
	Marina Mall	1727 2780
	Nr New Bridge	1733 0980
	Riffa Mall	1766 0080
	Seef Mall	1758 1010
Nine Months	Al Alawi Complex	1770 0920
Woolworths	Al Jazira Complex	1774 0111

Medicine

Other options → General Medical Care [p.71]

You will have no problem locating a pharmacy in Bahrain. There are pharmacies in the malls, shopping areas and in the souks. The Ruyan Department Store Centres each have a well-stocked pharmacy and they are open 24 hours a day. Hospitals have their own pharmacies and clinics usually have a pharmacy nearby. A wide range of medicines is available over the counter, including some antibiotics, but there is a list of controlled medicines that require a prescription. Codeine is an illegal substance in Bahrain and is strictly controlled.

As well as medicines, pharmacies stock cosmetics, perfumes, vitamins, baby care products and personal care items. There are ten 24 hour pharmacies scattered throughout Bahrain and these are listed in the GDN and in the following table.

Medicine

Al Hilal Pharmacy	Muharraq	1734 1700
Al Maraya Pharmacy	Tubli	1778 4029
Al Muwasaa Pharmacy	Muharraq	1733 5666
Al Rahma Pharmacy	Isa Town	1768 7117
Awal Pharmacy	East Riffa	1777 2023
Hamad Town Pharmacy	Hamad Town	1741 0114
Jaffar Pharmacy	Hoora	1729 1039
Majeed Jaffar Pharmacy	East Riffa	1777 6500
Nasser Pharmacy	Mahooz	1774 0900
National Pharmacy	Sanad	1779 0121
Ruyan Dept Store Centre	Budaiya	1759 4901
	Sanad	1762 3744
	Muharraq	1733 1164

What & Where to Buy

Shopping

Mobile Telephones

Other options → **Telephone [p.67]**

It seems that everyone in Bahrain has a mobile phone, so the latest, greatest, ever-changing technology is available. It is a competitive market and there are mobile phones and accessories everywhere you go. Prices are reasonable and specials are available from time to time. Shop around if you are looking for a new phone, remember to ask for 'the best price' before you make a decision to buy and check what after-sales service is available. All the large electronic shops sell mobile phones, as does Geant. The GOSI Commercial Complex has many mobile phone shops. Batelco and MTC Vodafone, Bahrain's mobile phone service providers, each have their own shops in various locations. Batelco has five shops located mostly in malls, while MTC Vodafone has ten branches all over Bahrain with one central contact number, see the table below.

Mobile Telephones

Batelco	Alawi Complex	1770 2933
P.IFC P.v P.69	Bahrain Mall	1755 6391
	GOSI Complex	1788 7022
	Muharraq Market	1788 3411
	Seef Mall	1758 2706
Cellucom	GOSI Complex	1729 4026
	Marina Mall	1736 4323
	Nr Yateem Centre	1721 2628
	Seef Mall	1758 1470
Fono Mobile	GOSI Complex	1758 7158
Geant	Bahrain Mall	1755 8181
MTC Vodafone	Various locations	3610 7107
P.31 P.IBC		
Nokia	Alawi Complex	1770 3325
	Exhibition Rd	1729 1700
	GOSI Complex	1729 8080
	Nr Yateem Centre	1721 3377
	Nxt to Basma	1772 7177
Yaquby Stores	Bab Al Bahrain	1721 0956

Music, DVDs & Videos

Like most of the cities in the Gulf, because of the cosmopolitan nature of the residents, the variety of music and movies is vast. When you arrive in Bahrain as a resident, customs will usually take your music, movies and books for a few weeks to check that they are not considered offensive. Since the Israeli boycott was discontinued several years ago few people seem to have had problems with items being confiscated.

In the music shops there will usually be three main sections. One is for Arabic Music, one for English or European music and one for Asian music. All of the main titles and the latest titles will be there, and in the English music section, you can find titles you haven't seen for 30 years or more! The large international music shops, like Virgin, are not yet in Bahrain, but Geant has all the popular titles in music cassettes, CDs and DVDs, and there are numerous music and DVD stores in all the shopping centres and souks. One of the biggest and best is Euphoria in Seef Mall, which also has an excellent website (www.euphorialive.com) with information on all the latest music, movies and games.

Music, DVDs & Videos

Delmon Video and Audio	Al Khalifa Rd	1721 1865
Euphoria	Seef Mall	1758 2040
Geant	Bahrain Mall	1755 8181
Ghadeer Video and Audio	Manama Souk	1727 7729
Music Master	Yateem Centre	1721 2619
Thomsun Cassette Centre	Nr Awal Cinema	1727 5367

Musical Instruments

Other options → **Music, DVDs & Videos [p.174]**
Music Lessons [p.150]

There is not a great deal of choice when it comes to musical instruments in Bahrain. One of the most well-established and popular stores for musical instruments and information is Moon Stores on Bab Al Bahrain Avenue in Manama. Some of the other stores are listed below.

Musical Instruments

Ambassador Stores	Bab Al Bahrain	1722 5513
Beethoven Music Centre	Juffair	1772 7116
Marshall Musical Instruments	Bab Al Bahrain	1722 5664
Moon Stores	Bab Al Bahrain	1721 1005
Music Spot	Hoora	1729 2994

Outdoor Goods

Other options → **Camping [p.125]**
Hardware & DIY [p.169]
Sporting Goods [p.178]

Camping is a major winter event for the local Bahrainis who set up camps and spend their weekends and holidays with their families and friends in large groups in the Sakhir Desert, so there is a plentiful supply of everything required for outdoor living from sophisticated tents to basic

Fruit & vegetable market

barbecues. Attractive camping spots for expats are much more difficult to find, but outdoor home living is very popular as so many of the villas have their own gardens. Geant and Manazel are two of the main shops for outdoor goods and most of the furniture shops have an outdoor furniture section. Many of the smaller hardware stores sell barbecues, folding chairs and camp beds, as well as other camping items. Prices are cheap to reasonable and easily resold when it is time to leave, so there is no real need to bring outdoor goods with you when you come to Bahrain.

Outdoor Goods		
Geant	Bahrain Mall	1755 8181
Manazel	Nr Salmabad R/A	1778 6727

Party Accessories

You'll find all your basic requirements for a child's party at Geant, the supermarkets, stationery and card shops or the speciality gift shops. There's the usual supply of balloons, candles, cards and wrapping paper, table decorations and games. Fancy-dress costumes are a bit harder to find, but there is usually a reasonable supply of masks in the stores and you can always get your favourite tailor to run up a costume from a picture or your own design. For adult parties you can hire glasses, ice buckets and catering needs from Caterworld and Music & Lights can provide a mobile DJ and light and sound systems, or you can very cheaply buy strings and strings of outdoor party lights to drape over your house and garden. Geant and Manazel usually have a good selection of Christmas decorations and some of the specialist gift shops, such as Artikel and Galleria Sophia at Jawad on the Budaiya Road, have expensive but exquisite decorations.

Party Accessories		
Caterworld	Exhibition Rd	1729 6363
Geant	Bahrain Mall	1755 8181
Kumar's Home & Kitchen	Exhibition Rd	1729 6363
Manazel	Nr Salmabad R/A	1778 6727
Music & Lights	Nr Bab Al Bahrain	1723 1012

Perfumes & Cosmetics

Other options → Souks [p.187]

You won't have to go far to find a shop selling perfumes and cosmetics. There is plenty of choice, regardless of whether you require expensive, mid-

range, or budget cosmetics and perfumes. All the usual brand names are here in the department stores, pharmacies and speciality shops, and the prices compare favourably on an international basis. The shop assistants, although very polite, are often not as informative or as ready to demonstrate products as they might be in your home country, so it helps if you know exactly what you want.

The range of perfumes is staggering. It is a fun experience, particularly if you are visiting or have visitors from overseas, to take them perfume shopping in the speciality Arabic perfume shops. First of all you choose a bottle, and there is a large selection of delightful ornate bottles to choose from. Next you need to choose your fragrance and once again the range is vast. The salespeople are charming and very knowledgeable about their products, the finished product makes a great gift or souvenir and it can be as cheap or as expensive as you wish to make it.

Usually these shops will also sell incense and incense burners, and once again the sales people are only too happy to pass on their knowledge. Asghar Ali & Sons have eight shops around Bahrain and specialise in making their own perfumes for men and women.

Perfumes & Cosmetics		
Ajmal Perfumes	Bahrain Mall	1755 4897
	Seef Mall	1758 2244
	Souk Area	1734 1426
Al Ezz Trading Company	Nr GOSI Complex	1729 0055
Al Hawaj	Al Aali Complex	1758 2525
	Bahrain Mall	1755 5339
	Nr Salmaniya Hosp	1723 0088
Al Hawaj	Seef Mall	1758 1228
Asghar Ali & Sons	Al Aali Complex	1758 1013
	Dana Mall	1755 6494
	Nr Gold Souk	1725 3170
Faces	Seef Mall	1758 2226
Jashanmal [P.161]	Al Aali Complex	1758 2424
Lush	Seef Mall	1758 2400
Mac	Seef Mall	1758 2757
Make-Up Forever	Seef Mall	1758 0300
The Body Shop	Sheraton Complex	1753 5354

Pets

Other options → Pets [p.176]

Bahrain has a very active BSPCA (Bahrain Society for the Prevention of Cruelty to Animals), which is well supported by the entire community. This is the place to go if you are looking for a pet. They usually have a great variety of pets available and can give plenty of advice about the type of pet you are considering adopting (www.bspcabahrain.com). Alternatively, there are plenty of pet shops all over Bahrain. Every village market has a pet shop or two, but unfortunately the conditions the pets are kept in are often horrifying and there are no laws for the protection of animals. You can see cats kept in bird cages on display out in the hot sun. Fish and birds are the most popular pets for the local markets.

Animals with pedigrees are available in some of the pet shops but the prices are high. If you are considering purchasing an animal with a pedigree, check with the BSPCA for advice. Supermarket noticeboards also advertise pets for sale or needing homes. Bahrain subscribes to the international Pet Passport Scheme, whereby pets are blood-tested, checked for rabies, micro-chipped, and are able to travel anywhere in the world.

The best place to buy pet accessories is the Pets Shop on Budaiya Road (1755 0564). Cat and dog food is available at Alosra and Al Jazera supermarkets, but the supply can be erratic, so if your pet is addicted to a particular flavour of Doggydins, keep a stockpile.

Portraits

Should you need to have any portraits done there are plenty of talented portrait artists and photographers. A good place to start would be to contact one of the arts societies, either the Bahrain Arts Society (1759 0551) or the Bahrain Contemporary Art Society (1772 8046), or chat to the people in the picture framing shops about who they might recommend for the style of portrait you require.

Moosa Al Demistani (3947 1993) is an artist specialising in portaits, either from a sitting or a photograph. He will do them from a sitting or from a photograph. A pencil head sketch would cost BD 2 - 3, a charcoal sketch would cost BD 7 for A4 and BD 10 for A3, and a pastel sketch would be BD 10 for A4 and BD 15 for A3. A portrait in oils would cost BD 25 for A4 and BD 50 for A3.

Shahran Sohani (3912 0800) is another portrait artist based in the Al Aali Shopping Complex (up on the first floor near the Emirates Airline office). Apart from doing portraits he does cariacatures and is also available to do caricatures for parties. He charges BD 50 for three hours and he can complete 14 to 18 caricatures in an hour.

If you require passport photos, or photos for driving licences or ID cards, pop in to one of the numerous photo developing stores and they will be able to do them for you straight away (try Digimax in Adliya, 1771 6765). For portrait photographs, try Ali Kofi (1759 0551).

Second-Hand Items

Other options → Cars [p.165]
Books [p.160]
Furnishing Accommodation [p.62]

Charity shops in Bahrain are well-established and well-patronised. Like most second-hand shops anywhere in the world, it is a matter of luck what is in stock when you visit, but you can always pick up a bargain or two, especially clothes, books and items for setting up home. The shops are run mostly by volunteers, so opening hours are not standard. It's best to phone or check in the GDN for opening hours before you visit.

There are occasional weekend garage sales, which are most commonly advertised on the major supermarket noticeboards, particularly those in the Budaiya/Saar area and sometimes in the GDN. If you are serious about buying, you will need to get to the garage sales early to pick up the best bargains.

Car boot sales are also held from time to time, usually as fundraisers for sports groups. These are also mainly advertised on local supermarket noticeboards.

The Isa Town Market has a large number of stalls selling second-hand goods of every type imaginable. This is a particularly good place for finding second-hand tools and hardware, but there is an amazing variety of second-hand tat available and it is a great place to wander if you enjoy the ambience of a market place. Take a Bahraini with you and let him or her negotiate on your behalf, preferably while you lurk out of sight. There can be quite a variation in price between what an expat will be expected to pay and what a Bahraini will pay.

Second-Hand Items		
Al Rabea Auctions	Nr Toyota	1727 1447
Arabian Auctions	Nr Pak. Embassy	1727 3736
Bahrain Auctions	Batelco Bld	1727 7568
BSPCA	Budaiya Highway	1759 3479
Gulf Auctions	Beh British Club	1772 7011
Khalid Old Furniture and Antiques	Budaiya Highway	1769 9950
Manama Auctions	Salmaniya Roads	1727 4067
Umm Al Darda Centre Thrift Shop	Umm Al Darda	1771 6300

What & Where to Buy

Shopping

Second-hand furniture shops also sell budget ranges of new furniture, sourced from Asia. Prices in these shops seem to be fixed and bargaining is not encouraged, which is quite an unusual feature for a second-hand shop.

Shoes

Other options → Beachwear [p.160]
Clothes [p.165]
Sporting Goods [p.178]

There is a plethora of shoes in Bahrain, whatever your style, size, or preference. Clarks and Shoe Mart are two of the most popular shoe stores for family shoe shopping, but there are some wonderfully exotic shoes available in some of the women's specialist shoe stores, like Pinks, which are well worth visiting just to marvel at the fanciful shoe creations on offer. Sports shoes are widely available in all price ranges.

Shoes		
Aldo	Seef Mall	1758 2081
Clarks	Seef Mall	1758 1121
Connecxion	Seef Mall	1758 2110
Florsheim	Seef Mall	1758 2110
Milano	Seef Mall	1758 1073
Nine West	Seef Mall	1758 3038
Pinks	Al Aali Complex	1758 7011
Pretty Fit	Bahrain Mall	1755 0005
Shoe City	Seef Mall	1758 2258
Shoe Mart	Marina Mall	1727 2802
	Riffa Mall	1765 1775

Souvenirs

Other options → Carpets [p.164]

Gold and pearls are very popular souvenirs of Bahrain, but there are lots of other items that will also make interesting and unique souvenirs or gifts. For information on where to by gold and pearls, refer to the Jewellery section (p.171). There are many excellent Bahraini artists, so you could browse the art galleries for a painting or print to take home (see the Art section on p.159). Some interesting antique Arabic pieces from Bahrain and the Gulf area can be found in the furniture shops, second-hand shops and gift shops.

Carpets, rugs, perfume and coffee tables made from old Arabian doors are other popular Bahraini mementos and many of these can be found in shops in the Adliya area, which services the US Navy base. There are several local handicraft

shops that make and sell traditional items such as Bahraini chests, model dhows, pottery, woven baskets and fabrics, and silver jewellery, as well as items imported from India.

Souvenirs		
Al Jasrah Handicraft Centre	Al Jasra Village	1761 1900
Craftland	Nr Yateem Centre	1721 1783
Craftland	Shawarma Alley	1771 5348
Kasmir Art Emporium	Manama Souk	1725 3234
Khazana	Nr MegaMart	1782 5909
Oriental Handicraft	Yateem Centre	1722 5469
The Crafts Centre	Nr American Hosp	1725 4688

Gold Centre

Sporting Goods

Other options → Outdoor Goods [p.174]

You should be able to find any sports equipment that you require in Bahrain, but depending on the item, the choice may be limited and the prices higher than in your home country (golf clubs and sports cycles, for example). Geant has a reasonable selection of basic sports equipment and sometimes you can pick up a bargain in one of their frequent sales. However, you do need to know exactly what you are buying as there is little advice available.

The Skate Shack (branches in Budaiya and Juffair) specialises in bikes, skating equipment, roller hockey gear and high tech kites. Olympia Sports has several branches throughout Bahrain, and as well as sports equipment, they stock branded sports accessories, apparel and footwear. One of the key attractions at Baraka Sports in Hoora is that, as well as a comprehensive selection of sports goods, they also have a large selection of soccer jerseys and can custom make jerseys for local sports groups.

Sporting Goods

Athletics Trading	Nr British Club	1772 3395
Baraka Sports	Palace Ave	1753 1553
Geant	Bahrain Mall	1755 8181
Olympia Sports	Nr Ramada Hotel	1771 4334
	Seef Mall	1758 2344
	Yateem Centre	1722 6600
Skate Shack	Mannai Plaza Bld	1772 5168
	Nr Osra Supermarket	1769 7176
Sports Horizon	Seef Mall	1758 1911
Sportsland	Baraka Bld	1753 4718

Tailoring

Other options → Textiles [p.179]
Souvenirs [p.178]
Clothes [p.165]

There are hundreds of tailors in Bahrain. They are usually located in clusters of small shops on the main roads in the areas of Isa Town, Manama, Riffa and the Budaiya end of the Budaiya Road. As a general guideline, you should expect to pay around BD 2.500 for a garment such as a shirt, a pair of trousers, or a skirt, although this price will vary according to the skills of the individual tailor, the amount of sewing required for the item and your bargaining skills. The best way of finding a good tailor is to ask for recommendations from the local Bahraini expats or residents.

The tailors do not sell fabrics so you will need to buy your fabric and take it to the tailor. Be very clear with your instructions. It is best to take a garment for the tailor to copy. If you want it copied exactly, be sure to say so. Don't take anything for granted; just because you don't think the manufacturer's gold lettering down the selvedge of the fabric would be an interesting decorative feature on your blouse, you can't expect your tailor to have the same opinion.

A lot of the tailors are used to making loose-fitting kaftan-type garments for Bahraini women, where the actual fit isn't important. Most of the tailors will include accessories such as zips, buttons and cotton, but if you want a particular type of accessory it is best to buy it yourself and take it to the tailor with your fabric. The tailor's idea of an attractive set of buttons may not match your expectations. Some of the better tailors will also make a garment from a picture. Once again, be

sure to stress the features that are important. If you are not satisfied that the tailor has followed your instructions, he will usually correct the problem. It is extremely important that you make your instructions clear at the start, if you don't want to be disappointed.

The tailors in the tailoring shop in the Awali/Bapco compound (Al Roosha Fashions - 1775 4617) are used to making garments for expats, which is convenient if you live in that area of Bahrain. There are also two tailors in Budaiya who are popular with expats: Al Mubarakiya Tailors (1769 3221) and Al Budaiya Modern Tailoring Centre (1769 2388). Their shops are almost next door to one another in Budaiya Village opposite the small children's park. The Al Rodha tailor shop (1729 0654) is quite close to the group of fabric shops in Gudaibaya, so you can buy your fabric and take it straight to the tailor to be made. This tailor will also make children's clothes. Mrs Pan at the Ladies Best Tailoring (1759 1556) in Budaiya is recommended for being friendly and efficient, and having reasonable prices. In Umm Al Hassam you could check out Farah Tailoring (1782 6032).

Textiles

Other options → Tailoring [p.179]
Souvenirs [p.178]

It's good news if you are looking for fabric! There is an excellent choice of fabrics in Bahrain from quality velvets to cotton and silk, and from imported Liberty Prints (Mohamed Jamal in Al Aali Shopping Complex) to cheap cotton prints from India and men's suiting fabrics. The best place to start is probably the textile section of the Manama souk. Most of the shops there are Aladdin's caves of colour, glitter and shimmer. This is the place to shop for fabric for party costumes and dresses for pantomime dames.

There are also good selections in fabric shops in the Old Palace Road area, the Lulu Centre and in the main out of town shopping areas like Riffa, Isa Town, Hamad Town and Muharraq. Prices are usually considerably cheaper than prices in the UK, the US or Australia. Keep an eye out for sales time and always ask for the 'best price'. The main shopping malls may have one or two fabric shops, but because their overheads are higher, the prices are also higher, but in the heat of summer it may be better to pay a little more for the luxury of shopping in air-conditioned comfort.

Textiles

Mohamed Jamal	Al Aali Complex	1758 1301
Suiting Corner	Bab Al Bahrain	1725 3652

Toys, Games & Gifts

There is a huge variety of toys and games widely available in Bahrain to suit every price range. Toys R Us and Mothercare are large, customer-friendly stores with the usual range of toys and games for every age group, and of course Geant, the hypermarket, also has a good selection. There are many branches of Mothercare and each one has a different selection of toys and games, so don't take it for granted that what you will find in one store will necessarily be in another. There are also many smaller toyshops in the suburban areas selling a good selection of toys and games. You should also check out the large discount stores like Ramez, Bahrain Pride Trading and Al Anwaar Discount Centre, which all have a good selection of very cheap toys from Asia. For something different, The Goodlife Gallery has a range of handmade wooden toys. They are pricey, but quite special. On the ground floor in Bahrain Mall there is a large shop called Lucky Stores, which is bursting with computer games and PlayStation games for all ages (see also Kids' Items on p.172)

Toys, Games & Gifts		
Al Anwaar Discount Store	Nr Train Station	1787 4141
Bahrain Pride Trading	Nr Salmabad R/A	1778 9504
Geant	Bahrain Mall	1755 8181
Lucky Stores	Bahrain Mall	1755 5991
Mothercare	Al Jazira Complex	1772 2901
	Marina Mall	1727 2780
	Nr New Bridge	1733 0980
	Riffa Mall	1766 0080
	Seef Mall	1758 1010
Ramez Trading	Nr Salmabad R/A	1725 5519
The Goodlife Gallery	Nr Osra Supermarket	1769 9002
Toys R Us	Seef Mall	1758 0860

Places to Shop

You are really spoilt for choice when it comes to shopping in Bahrain. There are a number of large, modern malls like Seef Mall, Al Aali Shopping Complex, Bahrain Mall, Dana Mall and Marina Mall. In the heat of the summer, when you need to get out of your house or apartment and it's too hot to do anything outside, the malls are a much needed escape and a pleasant place to shop, browse and socialise in air-conditioned comfort. There are also some exciting new shopping centres being planned and developed at the moment, such as the new City Centre and Sitra

Mall. There is also talk of modernising the Manama Souk, so if you have time, go for a wander and soak up the sights and smells, and admire the old architecture of the bustling traditional souk before it is sanitised beyond all recognition. Banter with the stallholders, barter for a bargain, or just watch the incredible variety of faces and costumes thronging the narrow alleyways. There are also many other shopping areas and experiences to enjoy. The large discount emporiums are full of amazingly garish knick-knacks and there are smaller malls and interesting shopping streets in the outer areas of Bahrain.

Shopping Malls

Bahrain is well catered for with five major shopping malls at present, but there is a gigantic new Bahrain City Centre currently being developed by the UAE-based developer Majid Al Futtaim. It will be similar to the very popular City Centres in Dubai, Abu Dhabi and Doha. This $400 million development will include a huge shopping area with more than 400 stores, including the first Carrefour hypermarket in Bahrain, a 20 screen cinema, a large indoor water park and two hotels that will be directly linked to the mall. It is planned for completion in 2007 and is a very exciting development. The new Financial Harbour and World Trade Centre, currently under construction, will also open up new shopping areas.

Shopping malls in Bahrain are generally open from around 10:00 until late in the evening. On Thursdays and Fridays they open a little later; these are the days when the malls are at their busiest, so if you don't like crowds you should pick another day to do your shopping. Plenty of free parking, adequate air conditioning and a variety of shops to satisfy even the most ardent of shopaholics make 'cruising the mall' a noteworthy pastime in Bahrain. Seef Mall in particular is the place for cool young people to see and be seen. All of the malls have either a foodcourt (mainly fastfood or takeaway options), several cafes and restaurants, or both, so you can fill up and recharge before dragging all your shopping bags around for a few more hours.

Shopping Malls		
Al Aali Complex	Seef	1758 1000
Bahrain Mall	Seef	1755 8100
Dana Mall	Sanabis	1755 8500
Marina Mall	Central Market	1727 7800
Seef Mall	Seef	1758 1111

Shopping Malls - Main

The malls in Bahrain are all relatively new, have excellent air conditioning and plenty of parking. Each mall has its own unique style of shopping outlets from upmarket to everyday, most have foodcourts and, because of the very hot summer climate, hugely popular entertainment areas for children. Some of the malls also include cinema complexes. You will find many familiar shop names and international brands in the shops in the malls and it would be most unusual not to be able to find whatever it is you want to buy.

Al Aali Shopping Complex

Al Aali Shopping Complex

Location → Nxt to Seef Mall · Seef	1758 1000
Hours → 09:30 - 21:30 10:30 - 16:00	
Web/email → na	Map Ref → 11-E1

Al Aali is retail heaven if you need to satisfy your lust for designer labels. The complex is located alongside Seef Mall and with its distinctive Arabic architecture has established itself as a true shoppers' destination and one of the country's tourist attractions. Al Aali embodies the spirit of today along with the heritage of the past, featuring superior designers such as Sergio Rossi, Gucci, Bvulgari and Jimmy Choo. A new addition is THE One, which offers a large area of luxury living ideas and home furnishings. It also has an enormous display of artificial flowers of every type and colour. You will also find Mexx, Giordano and Guess to

tempt the purse strings. Explore some of the finest jewellery stores and department stores such as Jashanmal and Al Hawaj. The foodcourt is located on the upper level of the mall and the new outdoor restaurant walk offers diverse eating options while you enjoy the ambience of the outdoor gardens.

Bahrain Mall

Location → Opp Seef Mall · Seef	1755 8100
Hours → 10:00 - 22:00	
Web/email → na	Map Ref → 11-E1

Bahrain Mall has a distinctive, pink-brick, fortress style of architecture. It is currently the only mall to have a hypermarket; the large and hugely popular French based Geant, where an amazing range of goods is available at very reasonable prices. The mall has 120 retailers and targets middle-of-the-road family shoppers. There is a great play area for kids called Foton World and a large foodcourt selling all the western and Arabic favourites. It has a number of very convenient features. Firstly, nearly all of the parking is undercover and secondly, it has a post office on the ground floor. It also has the usual banking services and a currency exchange. It is a true 'one-stop' shopping experience.

Main outlets include: Claire's Accessories, Geant, Guess Accessories, Foton World, Giordano, Cinnabon Seattle Coffee, KFC, Shoe Mart.

Bahrain Mall

Places to Shop

Shopping

Marina Mall

Dana Mall

Location → Sanabis
Hours → 10:00 - 22:00
Web/email → na

1755 8500

Map Ref → 11-B4

The anchor store in Dana Mall is called Giant, which is not related in any way to Geant, the hypermarket in Bahrain Mall, just up the road. Confused? It is confusing for visitors and newcomers to Bahrain. However, Giant in Dana Mall is a much smaller store. It is a Saudi-based supermarket and also sells a selection of assorted goods like clothes, electrical products and household furnishings. The main attractions at Dana Mall are the undercover parking, the cinema complex, the mini amusement park for children, the excellent restaurants and the Arabian-style foodcourt.

Main outlets include: Chakazoolu, Giant, Alfa Mart, Teatro, Haagen Dazs, Hardee's, McDonalds Pizza Hut, CK Jeans, Versace Collection, Dana Cinema.

Dana Mall

Marina Mall

Location → Nxt to Fish Market · Central Market
Hours → 10:00 - 22:00
Web/email → na

1727 7800

Map Ref → 11-C4

Marina Mall is a family shopping complex with a group of medium-sized department stores selling good value items for the family. The major stores are Home Centre, Mothercare, Shoe Mart and Sarah's Secret. There are a couple of good coffee shops and foodcourts. The kids will love the Jungle foodcourt and you will love its bargain prices.

Seef Mall

Location → Nr Al Aali Shopping Complex · Seef
Hours → 10:00 - 22:00
Web/email → na

1758 1111

Map Ref → 3-E1

Seef Mall is currently the biggest and probably the most popular mall in Bahrain. It is very much a standard international shopping mall, complete with over 220 retail shops, four large department stores, two foodcourts, a children's entertainment centre and two cinema complexes. It is modern, air-conditioned, has a huge parking area and all the other services you would expect in a large international shopping mall. Fashion is probably the main focus of the mall.

Main outlets include: Shoe City, Bhs, Debenhams, Marks & Spencer, JC Penny, Toys R Us, Jashanmal Bookstores, The Bookcase, Claire's Accessories, Six Accessories, St Du Pont, Ashraf's, Euphoria, Radio Shack, Massimo Dutti, Oasis.

Seef Mall

Places to Shop

Shopping

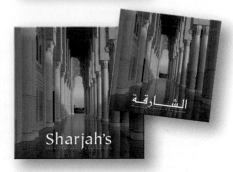

Beautiful Cities, Beautiful Sights

From Dubai's dreamy deserts to Geneva's joie de vivre, our photography books have captured the beauty of the world's most captivating cities. Whether you buy one as a gift or as a souvenir for your own coffee table, these books are packed with images that you'll want to view again and again.

Phone (971 4) 335 3520 • **Fax** (971 4) 335 3529
Info@explorerpublishing.com • www.explorerpublishing.com
Residents' Guides • Mini Visitors' Guides • Activity Guides • Photography Books • Lifestyle Products • Maps

EXPLORER
www.explorerpublishing.com

Shopping Malls - Other

Apart from the large inner-city malls, there are a number of interesting smaller malls dotted around the outer areas of Bahrain. Unlike the larger international malls, the smaller malls are much more individual and usually cater to the needs of the local market.

Al Alawi Complex

Location ➜ Sitra · Sanad | 1770 0123
Hours ➜ 10:00 - 22:00
Web/email ➜ na   Map Ref ➜ 6-C3

The major stores in this complex are the Jawad Supermarket and Bhs department store. There are a number of other speciality stores and several of the major fast-food outlets including McDonald's, Dairy Queen, Hardee's, KFC and Papa John's Pizzas. The complex caters well for everyday shopping for both the local Bahrainis and the expats who live in the area. Jawad Supermarket opens daily at 08:00.

Bahrain Commercial Complex

Location ➜ Nr Sheraton Hotel · Diplomatic Area | 1753 0250
Hours ➜ 10:00 - 13:00 16:00 - 22:00 Fri 16:00 - 22:00
Web/email ➜ na   Map Ref ➜ 12-A2

More commonly known as the Sheraton Complex, this centre is situated alongside the Sheraton Hotel and on the site of the new Bahrain World Trade Centre development. It is the place to go for those special expensive items and gifts. Some of the outlets in the centre are Al Zain Jewellery, Robert Cavallis, Cartier and Escada. The centre is due to undergo extensive renovations starting in 2006. It will increase in size, with over a hundred new shops being added. There is one cafe in the centre, Foody's (1753 3533), which is very popular with people who work in the local offices.

GOSI Commercial Complex

Location ➜ Exhibition Avenue · Hoora | 1729 1551
Hours ➜ 10:00 - 13:00 16:00 - 22:30 Fri 16:00 - 22:30
Web/email ➜ na   Map Ref ➜ 12-C3

The GOSI Complex is a very pleasant place to be, but not if you want a wide range of shopping choices. The building is very interesting with a stunning domed roof and a giant wall-mounted aquarium. The big business in GOSI is Batelco Customer Services and lots of shops selling mobile phones. There are a few interesting shops and restaurants, and it really is a pleasant place to escape from the very busy and noisy Exhibition Road area.

Jawad Dome

Location ➜ Budaiya Highway · Budaiya | 1725 3032
Hours ➜ 08:00 - 23:00
Web/email ➜ na   Map Ref ➜ 3-B2

Jawad Dome is well signposted just off the Budaiya Road. It has a large, modern, spacious Jawad Supermarket and a very pleasant circular foodcourt with a large glass dome overhead and overlooking a garden at the back. It has a few speciality stores and the wonderful Artikel and Galleria Sophia selling an excellent range of home furnishings and accessories.

Jawad Dome

Yateem Centre

Location ➜ Manama Souk · City Centre | 1721 5615
Hours ➜ 09:00 - 13:00 16:00 - 21:00
Web/email ➜ na   Map Ref ➜ 12-A3

The Yateem Centre was the first major shopping mall, built in Bahrain in 1980. It is actually more of a shopping centre than a shopping mall and still has a loyal following of customers. It is situated on the edge of the souk in a busy part of Manama and has reasonably priced clothing, footwear, sportswear (Olympia Sports), and electronics (Gajira Electronics). It has a very popular perfume and cosmetics shop (Faces) and also has coffee and food outlets. The only problem is the parking. The centre has an underground carpark, accessed from the side

Yateem Centre

on display. They are also a good place to pick up Arabic souvenirs, as they usually stock local jewellery boxes, incense burners and the infamous plastic mosque clocks at very reasonable prices.

Al Anwaar Discount Store

Location ➜ Tubli Service Road · Tubli	**1787 4141**
Hours ➜ 09:00 - 23:00	
Web/email ➜ na	Map Ref ➜ 6-A4

Al Anwaar Discount Store is a large two-storey building full of all sorts of amazing items, mostly imported in bulk from Asian countries. This is the place to go if you are setting up home for a brief stay and need to stock up on all the basic home requirements such as cutlery and crockery, pots and pans, linen, cleaning equipment, ridiculously cheap electrical appliances, pictures for your walls, tools, etc. The quietest time to go is early in the morning or mid-afternoon. It gets very busy on Thursdays and Fridays.

Bahrain Pride Trading

Location ➜ Nr Salmabad RA · Salmabad	**1778 9504**
Hours ➜ 09:00 - 23:00	
Web/email ➜ na	Map Ref ➜ 3-D4

Bahrain Pride Trading is another large, well-organised discount emporium or department store stocking a large range of imported goods from Asian countries. Like Al Anwaar Discount Store, this is the place to go if you are setting up home and want to buy cheap and cheerful basic equipment.

Debenhams

Location ➜ Seef Mall · Seef	**1758 11 66**
Hours ➜ 10:00 - 22:00	
Web/email ➜ na	Map Ref ➜ 3-E1

Debenhams markets itself as 'Britains favourite department store.' They have one store in Bahrain, situated in the Seef Mall, and it is one of Bahrain's favourite department stores too! The western expat women in particular, find Debenhams very useful if they are looking for clothing. Debenhams offers a unique combination of their own brands, exclusive designer ranges and leading international brands. so the shopper can be confident that they will be able to find, in their size, whatever item they are looking for. It doesn't have a huge selection, but it has a good selection of ladies', men's and children's clothing. It also has a cosmetics and perfume section and a small selection of home furnishings items.

street immediately before the building, but it is much more expensive than the open-air car park between the Post Office and the Regency Hotel. It has a large area reserved for people who work in the building and the rest of it fills up very early in the morning, so you'll be lucky to find an empty slot. Unfortunately, they haven't installed a system to warn you that the car park is full, so you take your ticket from the machine at the entrance, and then have to trundle around looking for a space before pleading (to no avail) with the poor gentleman at the exit to let you use one of the empty reserved spaces.

Department Stores

There are a mixture of international and local department stores in Bahrain. The international department stores, including Debenhams, Woolworths, Marks & Spencer and Bhs, sell womenswear, menswear, children's clothing and a limited range of home accessories such as sheets, towels and duvet covers. The local ones include Zaina and the magnificent Jashanmals & Sons.

Another unique shopping experience in Bahrain is a visit to the large discount emporiums or department stores (listed below). They are more numerous and bigger in size than elsewhere in the Gulf Region. They stock vast quantities of cheap imported goods, generally from Asia, and if you are a bargain seeker who can't resist hunting out a bargain, this is the place for you. Even if you're not a bargain seeker, they are an interesting place to go just to see the unbelievable and unusual variety of items that are

Places to Shop

Shopping

Geant

Location ➔ Bahrain Mall · Seef
Hours ➔ 08:00 - 24:00
Web/email ➔ na

1755 8181

Map Ref ➔ 11-E1

Geant hypermarket opened in Bahrain four years ago and has proved extremely popular. It is a French-based hypermarket very similar to the Carrefour hypermarkets and it will be interesting to see what happens when the new Bahrain City Centre with its Carrefour hypermarket opens soon. One wonders if there is a big enough population in Bahrain to support two large hypermarkets, but it can only mean good news for the consumers. It has a large supermarket and stocks a huge range of product lines. It has frequent promotions and, particularly with regular specials, its prices are hard to beat. It has its own product range in the supermarket, called Casino, but the price is similar to the other products. It's a great one-stop shopping store.

Giant

Location ➔ Dana Mall · Sanabis
Hours ➔ 10:00 - 22:00
Web/email ➔ na

1755 6226

Map Ref ➔ 11-B4

Giant is a Saudi-based store in Dana Mall, not to be confused with Geant, the hypermarket in Bahrain Mall. It can be difficult for newcomers to Bahrain to sort out which is which. The Malls are quite close to each other and fairly similar in design. Giant is probably suffering due to the competition from Geant. It is difficult to compete with Geant's range of products and prices. Giant has a basic supermarket section and a selection of mid-range household goods and electronics.

Jashanmal at Al Aali

Location ➔ Al Aali Shopping Complex · Seef
Hours ➔ 09:30 - 21:30
Web/email ➔ www.jashanmals.com

1758 2424

Map Ref ➔ 11-E1

Jashanmal at Al Aali is a very well-established, upmarket department store in the Al Aali Shopping Complex. This store sells beautiful home accessories, appliances, Delsey luggage, linen, cosmetics and perfumes, and includes a Jashanmal Bookstore. Jashanmal & Sons is a leading retailer in the Middle East with a variety of stores offering everything from home accessories to books, shoes, cameras, fashion and cosmetics. Departments include Clarks Shoes, House of Tobacco, Casa Mia

and Dior. The staff are professional and the products are very high quality.

Marks & Spencer

Location ➔ Seef Mall · Seef
Hours ➔ 10:00 - 22:00
Web/email ➔ na

1758 8188

Map Ref ➔ 3-E1

Marks & Spencer is a well-known British store that has 400 stores in the UK and over 150 worldwide. The Bahrain Marks & Spencer store is located in Seef Mall. It has a large selection of clothing for men, women and children, and has small selections of home furnishings, own-brand cosmetics and specialist food items. Marks & Spencer is well-known for the quality of its clothing. UK expats may find the prices for items are higher here than at home, but it is still a popular place for clothes shopping, especially at sale times.

A name you can trust

Ramez Trading

Location ➔ Various locations · Central Market
Hours ➔ 09:00 - 24:00
Web/email ➔ na

1725 5519

Map Ref ➔ 6-A1

Ramez Trading is another of the huge discount department stores and it has two outlets in Bahrain. One store is in the Central Market and the other is in the Isa Town Market. The shops are piled full of all sorts of practical necessities and frivolous junk, and like Al Anwaar and Bahrain Pride it is a great place to get everything you need to set up a temporary home or to search out a few gift or souvenir bargains. Be alert at the checkout because nothing is price marked. Ask for the prices as you put things through the checkout and just leave behind anything that is not the price you want to pay. If you're buying a lot, don't be afraid to ask for a discount on the already heavily discounted goods.

Sana & Discount Home Store

Location → Nxt Andalus Hotel · Adliya | **1771 6370**
Hours → 10:00 - 22:00   Fri 16:00 - 22:00
Web/email → na   Map Ref → 6-B2

Discount Home Stores and Sana are Gulf-based department stores. They started in Bahrain in the 80s as clothing stores and have expanded to sell a range of good-value family clothing, shoes, home appliances, home furnishings and luggage. They have excellent specials that change regularly and you can sometimes find designer label clothing in the racks, mixed in with all the other clothing, at budget prices. Most of the women's clothing is in small sizes and Asian styles, but there are some excellent bargains to be had in men's and children's clothing and shoes.

The Sana Stores are in Salmaniya (1725 9522) and Bahrain Mall (1755 6430). The Discount Home Stores are in Adliya (1771 6370), Sanad (1762 2156) and Riffa (1777 9818). Sana and Discount Home Stores both sell the same range of stock.

Woolworths

Location → Nxt American Embassy · Hoora | **1774 0111**
Hours → 10:00 - 22:00
Web/email → na   Map Ref → 13-E4

Woolworths is a South African based department store located in the same shopping complex as the Al Jazira Supermarket in Hoora. Like the other international department stores in Bahrain, it sells mainly clothes and a few home accessories. The clothes are of good quality, but once again, comparatively highly priced. However, sales time is a good time to buy when prices are more reasonable.

Zaina

Location → Seef Mall · Seef | **1758 2110**
Hours → 10:00 - 22:00
Web/email → na   Map Ref → 3-E1

Zaina is a large local department store in Seef Mall. It took over from JC Penneys and now still stocks some JC Penneys items in the home accessories department. On the ground floor it has a large area of women's and children's clothes and items, and on the upper floor it has menswear and home furnishings.

Streets/Areas to Shop

Apart from the large malls and markets in Manama, there are plenty of interesting shopping areas all over Bahrain. Exhibition Road and Adliya are two popular street shopping areas in Manama. Exhibition Road is a noisy, busy, place with a wide variety of well-established small shops serving the businesses in the area. Parking and traffic are a nightmare, especially at night.

The car park area behind the GOSI Commercial Complex is a good place to park if you need to do any business in Exhibition Road. Many of the people who shop and dine out in Adliya are from the US Navy base and the shops and restaurants reflect this in the items they sell and the prices they charge. There are lots of carpet shops, souvenir and gift shops and the majority of Bahrain florists are here. Once again, parking is difficult, particularly around the restaurant section in the evening. A good place to park to keep out of harm's way is in the Gulf Hotel car park. Government Avenue has many of the airline offices and travel agencies.

For budget shopping the Central Market area is the place to go. There are the noisy, busy, colourful produce markets and a large Ramez Trading discount department store, a large Al Muntazah Supermarket and the Marina Mall all in the same area. Budaiya Road has some interesting sections of strip shopping lining the highway. Cypress Gardens is now a very pleasant spot for coffee or a meal in one of the restaurants, set among the garden nursery and supplies. As well as these, each town and village has its own unique shopping area.

Souks

Other options → **Bargaining [p.158]**

The word 'souk' is an Arabic word that means market, and there are many interesting souks, both modern and traditional, in Bahrain. The best-known is the Manama Souk, which has several markets within the market, selling textiles, spices, jewellery, perfumes, electronics and a wide assortment of goods, both practical and

Places to Shop

Shopping

ornamental, within a maze of narrow lanes and alleyways. It also houses the very large and popular Gold Souk with its vast range of glittering 18 or 21 carat gold jewellery. The Central Market is the place to go for fresh fruit, vegetables, meat and fish, and Isa Town Market is known as the flea market of Bahrain and is a great place for bargain hunters to rummage through. Bargaining is expected in all of the souks and it is best to have Bahrain currency.

Central Market

Location → Central Manama | na
Hours → 05:00 - 17:30
Web/email → na   Map Ref → 11-D4

Central Market was established in 1978 as a produce market for fresh fruit and vegetables, fish and meat. It covers a large area in Central Manama by Marina Mall, Ramez Trading and the large MegaMart Supermarket. Nearly all of the fruit and vegetables are imported from all over the world and there is a diverse range catering for all the different nationalities that live in Bahrain. This is your best chance of picking up produce when it is most fresh. The traders will want you to buy in bulk, but will usually be quite happy to sell smaller amounts of their fruit and vegetables. The fruit and vegetable market opens as early as 03:00 and everything is operating by 05:00. It closes at about 17:30.

The fish market is also a popular place to find very fresh local and imported fish and seafood if you have the stomach for it. Wear your wellies and go early before the heat and smell get too oppressive. It also opens really early (before 05:00), but the arrival of the fresh fish depends on the weather. If the weather is bad, the fish will arrive later at the market. The fish market closes at about 14:00.

Gold Souk

Location → Manama Souk · Central Market | na
Hours → 08:00 - 12:30 15:30 - 19:30
Web/email → na   Map Ref → 11-E3

The Gold Souk is amazing! Shop after shop after shop of row after row of gold: gold necklaces, gold earrings, gold rings, gold bracelets, huge, ornately crafted Arabic gold necklaces and head pieces. It is bewildering to decide what to buy. The majority of the items are 18 or 21 carat gold

and they carry a hallmark. You can also get a piece of jewellery custom-made to your own design. Take a picture or photo with you and chat to the goldsmiths. Know the current gold prices and negotiate a price before you make an order or buy anything.

Isa Town Market

Location → Off Quds Avenue | na
Hours → 08:30 - 12:00 16:00 - 20:00 Fri closed
Web/email → na   Map Ref → 6-A1

The Isa Town Market or Souk is known by several names. It is sometimes called the Souk Al Haraj or the flea market, and sometimes referred to as the Iranian Market. It is an interesting local market, used by residents as opposed to tourists, and there are some good bargains to be had in second-hand items, tools, carpets, furnishings, textiles, household items and antiques. There is also a large discount emporium, Ramez Trading, as part of the market. It is well signposted in the Isa Town area with signs indicating Isa Town Local Market off Quds Avenue.

Manama Souk

Location → Nr Bab Al Bahrain · City Centre | na
Hours → 08:30 - 12:30 16:00 - 20:00
Web/email → na   Map Ref → 11-E3

You enter the Manama Souk through the old seaport gate, Bab Al Bahrain. The seafront has been reclaimed and is now quite some distance away, but the bustling traditional souk remains. Don't even think of taking a car anywhere near the souk. The roads are narrow and very busy, and it is very easy to get lost or trapped in a dead-end street with no way to turn or back out. The souk is divided into areas, the most well known of which is the Gold Souk.

There is also a textile souk, a colourful, aromatic spice souk and a tin souk, but everything is sold in the souk, including cheap clothing, electrical goods and some interesting souvenirs. Check out the singing camels and plastic mosque alarm clocks – some of the most popular souvenirs for visitors to Bahrain. You will find stalls selling traditional herbs, leaf tobacco, local craft items and all sorts of fascinating odds and ends. You will be expected to barter and most stallholders will not accept credit cards, so take plenty of dinars with you.

Manama Souk

Spoil Yourself

SIMPLY DECADENT

With décor that recalls the past era, Café Lilou is a magnificent representation of a turn of the century Parisian brasserie - a place where the grandeur and elegance of that time remains. For more information Tel: +973 17714440

Mezzaluna

ELEGANT, SOPHISTICATED, VIBRANT

If you are looking for a unique dining experience, Mezzaluna should come top of your list. An exquisite ambience coupled with food that embodies the Mediterranean makes Mezzaluna the restaurant to be. For reservations and more information Tel: +973 17742999

ZOë

monsoon

SEEING AND BEING SEEN

Inspired by New York's loft style architecture, Zoë restaurant offers a delicious variety of first class cuisine. The atmosphere is cool and stylish, with our resident DJ to entertain on a nightly basis. For reservations and more information
Tel: +973 17716400

PAMPERING, EXOTIC, RELAXING

Experience the exotic flavours and aromas of Asia at Monsoon restaurant. Built to resemble the Royal Palaces of Bangkok and Bali, the restaurant offers richness in the food and hospitality served in a relaxed and casual atmosphere. For reservations and more information Tel: +973 17749222

Going Out
EXPLORER

Highlights...

Sample the Shisha
[p.227]

When in Rome... or Bahrain...you have to sample the shisha. Not just for the sweet taste, but also for the atmospheric experience of a shisha cafe. There are plenty of places where you can try shisha, from specific cafes to various restaurants that will serve shisha with or after a meal. Alternatively you can pick up your own shisha pipe and fruity selection and host a dinner/shisha party. If you have family or friends in town, it is also an excellent cultural experience for them.

Try the Local Cuisine
[p.199]

While Bahrain may be packed with as many cuisine types and menu styles as your stomach could dream of, dining on local dishes is a must. Whether it is fine dining Arabic restaurants or street side shawarma stands it won't take long until your taste for hummus, tabouleh, arabic breads, falafel, kofta and baklava becomes a regularity. There are a plethora of Arabic restaurants to choose from so feeding your habit won't be a problem!

Eat, Drink and Be Merry

Bahrain may have its fair share of fine dining options, budget bites and funky bars but if you're looking for a different scene then why not pop on a short haul flight to Dubai for a big night out. Just pick up a copy of the delectable *Posh Nosh, Cheap Eats and Star Bars* which showcases some of the best locations on Dubai's social scene. Whether you want to romance your loved one or get your dancing shoes on, you will find the perfect place, picture perfect in this perfect book!

Table of Contents — Going Out

Often overlooked, Bahrain is actually buzzing with an incredibly unique vibrant social scene that – better than some GCC countries – mixes local and expat communities. It's one of the few places in the Gulf where hanging out with the locals and getting a real taste of the culture is easily accessible. And despite its size, it manages to cater to a variety of tastes and budgets, whether it be a la-de-da dinner or a cheap and cheerful night out.   Live entertainment is big here, and black-tie events are practically de rigueur.

Much of the hustle and bustle is located in the Adliya area of the capital city, Manama, where the night is always young and the attitude free and easy.   Alcohol is available in Bahrain, so a glass of wine with your dinner or a few jars to loosen you up for the nightclub dance floor is not out of the question.

Eating Out

You would have never guessed it (well, maybe you would), but this place is a gastronomic delight. Have a hankering for it and you are bound to find a restaurant or cafe to cater to your craving. The array of international cuisine is enough to make your belly ache with indecision and as if that were not enough, Bahrain – like everywhere else in the world – has every fast food franchise known to man and a few you'll discover tucked away and only here.

Friday brunch is very common as is the good old fashioned buffet, leaving you spoilt for choice and a little tight round the waist if you don't adopt some self discipline! The chefs here are remarkable and it's easy to get carried away.

Many places have kids menus, and little ones are always welcome during the day, but less so in the evenings.

Delivery

If you're staying for a while expect a lot of invites to people's homes for dinner, and when the weather holds up it's all about the barbeque. Even though dining out is big, dining in is even bigger. It's not unusual for your host to bring in a catering firm, in fact if you're throwing a shindig yourself and with a spirited guest list, consider your options. Practically every restaurant here has a service for private parties and for remarkably reasonable prices. Some places will even throw in extra dining bits and pieces and high-end wait staff to look after your guests. When a quiet night in wouldn't go amiss, then pick up the phone and choose from a fabulous variety of quick home delivery.

In fact, you may never actually have to leave home (besides for work of course), thanks to Gourmet Taxi, a service that will deliver from a choice of 65 restaurants around Bahrain. Operating from 11:30 till 23:30, you can also have your grocery run done and dropped off as well as get them to pick up a DVD for a night's entertainment. For more information visit www.gourmettaxi.com.

Drinks

Other options → **Alcohol [p.158]**

Bahrain enjoys quite a relaxed attitude to alcohol and visitors are guaranteed to find their favourite tipple at a host of hotel bars, restaurants and social clubs all licenced to serve. Special promotional nights are often organised where drinks are ridiculously cheap, so be on the lookout and check local press for details.

The holy month of Ramadan is the only time that the public sale and consumption of alcohol is prohibited.

Picking up a six-pack or a bottle of wine is easily done here through specially licenced shops – slightly off-the-beaten-track but easily found by asking around. By law, the stores cannot sell alcohol to Muslims but buyers and sellers can often be very ingenuous. This law does not apply to restaurants and bars. Rules state that alcohol will not be sold or served to anyone under the age of 18 and beware, there is a zero tolerance attitude to drink driving with absolutely no legal limit and no easy get-offs, so leave the keys at home and take a cab. If caught, you face a hefty fine or a spell in jail.

Staying on the wagon can be just as fun. A local penchant for fresh juices means that these are on offer at nearly every establishment and with a wonderful variety of concoctions to choose from. If you are new to the region the 'Lemon and Mint' juice is a stunning discovery, or be brave and try an Avocado Smoothie.

When it comes to the water, it's best to stick to bottled or filtered; local brands are cheap and readily available.

Hygiene

Technically speaking all hotels, restaurants, bars and clubs in Bahrain are subject to stringent rules and regulations from the Ministry of Health. Quarterly inspections do take place but can be quite casual. The majority of restaurateurs take pride in the cleanliness of their kitchen. If the restaurant looks clean and if the waiting staff are well turned-out, then it probably is clean.

Tax & Service Charges

Eating out comes at a price; a government levy of 5% is added to your bill. Some establishments hide this cost in the prices on the menu but others, in particular large hotels, will add this to your bill at the end. On top of a near mandatory 15% service charge, it can often be a bit of a wallet-worrying moment when you discover that a total of 20% (service and government levy combined) has been added to your bill. The menu will specify the restaurant's policies on this matter so do check before you eat.

Tipping

Most restaurants add a 15% service charge to your bill. Of course this amount should go to the waiter or waitress who has served you, however if you pay by credit card, it often ends up in the till and your server never sees it. Keep some cash on you and leave a cash tip, especially if the service was good.

Restaurant Listing Structure

With an ever-increasing range of venues for eating out in Bahrain, the **Bahrain Explorer** lists only the best selection of restaurants in each category, highlighting those that are recommended as must-dos.

Explorer has compiled reviews for over 150 outlets, and the Going Out section provides a comprehensive listing of the places worth checking out.

Listed alphabetically by cuisine styles, each review contains as much information as possible on the individual outlet.

In order to categorise the restaurants by cuisine we have placed restaurants that serve varying cuisines or styles either under their prominent cuisine or under International if the mix is truly varied.

If you want to know what outlets are in a particular hotel or venue you can flip to the index at the back of the book and look up the hotel, under which there will appear a list of all the outlets with their corresponding page numbers.

> ### Location, location
> *If you have a specific location in mind, such as a hotel where you have guests staying, then just flick to the index at the back of the book and look up the specific hotel for a list of its reviewed outlets.*

To avoid any confusion concerning a particular restaurant's listing, as a rule, any non-English names retain their prefix (ie, Al, Le, La and El) in their alphabetical placement, while English names are listed by actual titles, ignoring prefixes such as 'The'.

Bon appetit!

Icons - Quick Reference

Quick Reference Explorer Icons

	Explorer Recommended!
	Live Band
	Alcohol Available
	Will Deliver
	Kids Welcome
	Reservations Recommended
	Outside Terrace

Vegetarian Food

Vegetarians are well looked after in Bahrain, since the local cuisine offers a rich variety of non-meat mezzes and every restaurant will have a few dishes that are strictly vegetarian on their menus. Indian and Persian cuisine is particularly worth considering, and some Indian restaurants offer nothing but vegetarian fare. Should you find yourself stuck, don't fret, Bahrain chefs are incredibly accommodating and will more often than not recreate a dish sans meat. In fact, making a dish your own is not unusual and if you ask nicely, you'll rarely be refused.

Perfectly Pure

Welcome to Al Bander Hotel & Resort, the best 'Seaside Resort' in Bahrain. Set on a small peninsula with a stretch of sandy beach, this intimate and luxurious Resort is a soothing escape!

Facilities include: Cabanas, Chalets, Restaurants, Conference Centre, Fitness Centre, Pools, PADI Dive Centre, Tennis, Squash, Bowling Centre & Indoor games, Water sports and Marina. It is 10 minutes drive to a Golf Course!

فندق ومنتجع البــنــدر

AL BANDER
HOTEL & RESORT

P.O. Box 28567, Riffa, Kingdom of Bahrain
Tel: +973 17701201, Fax: +973 17701491
E-mail: albander@batelco.com.bh • Website www.albander.com

Restaurants

American

Applebee's

Location ➜ Next to Bahrain Mall · Sanabis
Web/email ➜ www.trafco.com

1755 5834
Map Ref ➜ 3-E1

This international Tex-Mex chain has a refreshingly modern decor, is lively and well-stocked with young couples, singles and families. The menu is also packed with favourites guaranteed to leave you feeling well and truly satisfied and the free soft drink refills are all part of the excellent service. Basically go hungry and leave having eaten far too much!

Tex-Mex

Brenigan's

Location ➜ Country Club · Budaiya
Web/email ➜ na

1759 3593
Map Ref ➜ 3-C1

Known for its grilled meat and seafood, Brenigan's is a little off the beaten track and as such has yet to be discovered by the masses. With consistently good food it is one of the few eateries in the Budaiya area and offers an excellent English-style bar with an impressive selection of beer on tap and pool tables for the energetic. Pub or not, Brenigan's has itself a remarkably picturesque tropical garden and during the cooler months actually manages to turn into one of the most romantic outdoor dining venues on the island.

Chili's

Location ➜ Seef Mall · Seef
Web/email ➜ www.jawad.com

1758 1221
Map Ref ➜ 3-E1

In case you've never been introduced, Chili's is a big Tex Mex chain restaurant but the quality of the food is high and the beef here is excellent. Admittedly, the menu is a tad generic, with the usual fajitas, burgers, steaks and nachos piled high with every sauce known to man and guilt-inducing deep-fried side-orders. The beef spare ribs are fall-off-the-bone tender and a must-try. The sizes are gargantuan and a starter and main course are usually enough for even the biggest appetites, so be sure to save room for desert. Dieters need not worry; one of Chili's strong points is an excellent 'guiltless' menu that gives delicious low-fat and low-carb equivalents to the regular fare. With its location only a stone's throw from the Seef Mall, Chili's is a winner for all the family. Thursday lunchtimes especially are child friendly with entertainers, including a magician who also conjures on Friday.

Dairy Queen

Location ➜ Jawad Dome · Budaiya
Web/email ➜ na

1769 6032
Map Ref ➜ na

Dairy Queen's many outlets around Bahrain offer a slight variation on the traditional burger-cum-fast food joint. Yes, you can order the usual plethora of burger variations, but here's where Dairy Queen differs: chicken strip salads and crispy deep-fried shrimps will brighten up the face of any been-there-done-that fast food addict. Forget the calorie counting here, this place is about greasy self-indulgence. Desserts are equally as fun with delicious chocolate-dipped icecream cones, banana sundaes and blizzard concoctions full of crunchy candies. A real sugar rush for the little ones and great value for money.

Fuddruckers

Location ➜ Adliya
Web/email ➜ www.fuddruckers.com

1774 2266
Map Ref ➜ 14-B3

Another great basic, no-frills, popular American-style diner. Servings are substantial and you can

American

Going Out

A square book but not for squares

Explore Dubai's decadent range of restaurants, bars, cafes and clubs in this beautiful book with stunning images and informative reviews. More than just a guidebook, it's at home on a coffee table while you're out on the town.

pile it on at the well-stocked salad bar. Drink refills are unlimited and free. Choose your own burger toppings for an interesting and unique combination. Their potato wedges are amazing, but most meals on the menu are definitely not low-sodium so, for the health conscious, an extra word in the waiter's ear would not go amiss. There is no pressure to hurry and Fuddruckers is a popular place for families and the hip and trendy crowd to hang out at weekends. Their branch next to the F1 racetrack in Sakhir was long awaited, and is very popular during race meetings.

Hard Rock Café

Location ➜ Exhibition Ave
Web/email ➜ www.hardrock.com

1729 1569
Map Ref ➜ 12-C4

The interior of this American chain is a real treat: walls covered with movie memorabilia, guitars, jackets, signed photos, gold albums and much more. Kids are welcome here and are provided with fun drawing activities, while hungry grown-ups peruse the extensive menu. American favourites and Tex Mex combinations feature highly with huge portions served (staff will provide a doggy-bag at the end of the meal). The kids' menu is reasonable and will keep them satisfied until dessert. A requisite trip to the Hard Rock shop will set you back a dinar or two especially if you succumb to the many collectibles on sale, from the usual T-shirts and baseball caps to quite pricey jackets.

Ric's Kountry Kitchen

Location ➜ Juffair
Web/email ➜ na

1772 5550
Map Ref ➜ 14-D2

This restaurant is as close as you will get to a home-made American meal, without actually eating at an American's home! Everything from grits to blueberry pancakes feature on the menu. This place will cure any home-sickness for those who can't wait to go home to eat their mom's good old-fashioned cookin', and the rest of us who aren't from the States but still appreciate finger-lickingly good comfort food. The Kitchen has a fun lively bar where the friendly staff keep customers smiling. The ambience is very welcoming, with walls adorned with photos of happy nights and wide-eyed grins from previous

good ol' shindigs. Whether it's for breakfast, lunch or dinner, Ric's has a unique, homey feeling – it's almost as good as comfort food from your momma's kitchen!

Spice Buffet and Grill

Location ➜ Nr Al Aali Shopping Complex · Seef
Web/email ➜ www.bflc.com.bh

1758 2550
Map Ref ➜ 11-E1

Neatly tucked between Al Aali Shopping Complex and Seef Mall, Spice Buffet and Grill is an ideal spot for a quick bite after an exhausting shopping trip. The menu offers a great choice of diner-style food. Alternatively, the buffet is fantastic value at BD 3.800 per adult and BD 1.500 per child. Portions are American in size so don't let your greedy eyes get the better of you as you choose from steak, pastas and more. If it's not diet time, finish the meal with a yummy pick of icecream and desserts and distract yourself from the calories by browsing through some fascinating memorabilia displayed around the restaurant. Spice is family-friendly, fun and light-hearted with a very enjoyable atmosphere, and a fantastic place to bring the kids. It is extremely popular at weekends.

The Outpost

Location ➜ Country Club · Budaiya
Web/email ➜ na

1759 3593
Map Ref ➜ 3-C1

Tucked away off the Budaiya Highway, the Country Club's Outpost restaurant is a fantastic little treasure. The atmosphere at The Outpost is as warm as the sunshine and as welcoming as any Country Club eaterie can be. Leather sofas, fake fire and faux animal skins on the wall complete the cowboy country setting. This place is straight out of a western movie, complete with swinging saloon doors and horses rolling around in the sand just outside. Don't come if you want subtlety, this is 'in your face' good solid tucker! Come in hungry and fill up on the sizzling steaks and fajitas, then top it off with something sweet and a cooling beverage. The Outpost features an excellent, good-value menu for kids, with a door leading out to a play area if they get bored, leaving you to some quiet time with your meal.

Arabic/Lebanese

Other options → Persian [p.218]
Moroccan [p.218]

Al Berdaouni

Location → Regency Intercontinental
Web/email → na

| 1722 7777
Map Ref → 11-E3

The night comes alive in a truly Middle-Eastern atmosphere when the entertainment starts at Al Berdaouni. Start by picking your way through the incredible array of hot and cold Lebanese mezzes as the belly dancers come a-shimmying-and-a-shaking on to the stage. The epitome of an Arabian night, the gourmet fun really starts when the entrees arrive. Authentic spices make the succulent meat and fish dishes mouth-wateringly tasty. Have a go with the dancers and shake up some room for dessert, sweet tea and top your night with a classical shisha. The friendly staff and dimly lit dining room attracts a good crowd of both local and expat patrons.

Al Fanar Supper Club

Location → Diplomat Radisson SAS Hotel
Web/email → www.radissonsas.com

| 1753 1666
Map Ref → 12-C2

Located on the top floor of the upmarket Diplomat Hotel, Al Fanar's panoramic views of Manama and the very professional waiters are two of the best features of this Lebanese restaurant. There is a wide choice of the usual Lebanese mezze and grills on offer. Portions are unsparing and the service is adequate to say the least, but the overall quality of Al Fanar's food doesn't go far enough to justify the fancy prices. A relentless rhythm of international music interspersed with the gyrations of an (amateur) East-European belly dancer will distract you from the mediocre cuisine. The supper club is popular with Saudi weekend visitors, seeking a shot of kitsch Arabic culture.

Al Sawani Restaurant

Location → Nr Marina Club
Web/email → na

| 1729 7333
Map Ref → 12-C2

Enter Al Sawani and you step into a world of chic and simple sophistication: this is Bahraini decor at its finest, with less of the frou-frou and a lot more

taste and simplicity. A calm, quiet and unhurried atmosphere pervades until the lights are dimmed and the nightly live entertainment begins, and even then just a few diners are enticed to join in with the singing! A sumptuous array of authentic Lebanese and Bahraini dishes awaits and they are well worth waiting for. Portions are sufficient, beautifully presented, colourful and tasty. The assortment of mezze is mind-boggling and includes some genuine home-made dishes and some unexpected treats. Come with friends, come when you are really hungry and come with the intention of spending the whole night. You can't just 'pop in' for a quick bite, you have to stay for the long haul so as not to miss any of the fun.

Khan al Marjan

Location → Al Safir Hotel
Web/email → na

| 1/82 7999
Map Ref → 4-C2

Khan Al Marjan lives up to the Al Safir Hotel's policy of pure entertainment for its many customers. The focus here is on the live entertainment as opposed to the nightly buffet on offer. The fun begins at 22:00 and continues on well into the wee hours. A rather stern looking Iraqi lady booms out melancholy melodies for the benefit of the expectant male audience, while three nubile young dancers, spilling out of their sequined and bejewelled skin-tight costumes, gyrate around her on the small, well-lit stage. A lot of tress-tossing and body popping goes on for the obvious appreciation of the predominantly male diners. One gets the impression that food is the last thing everyone here is thinking of. A BD 25 pp cover charge keeps the riffraff away.

Layali Zaman

Location → Nxt to Funland
Web/email → na

| 1729 3097
Map Ref → 12-D3

Situated on the corniche, Layali Zaman is a quiet little retreat from the neon noise of Funland next door. Delightfully ramshackle-like and perched precariously right on the waterfront, you can sit down, loosen your belt and tuck into an extremely cheap and cheerful meal or a puff on a shisha while you sip your fruit juice. The sea view and the island of Muharraq make this an idyllic place to unwind, relax and do nothing very much at all. Ample parking in front and easy access to the main road make it a convenient spot to sample the unpretentious fare of sandwiches, salads and grills, all with an Arabic twist. Patroned, encouragingly, by locals, but obviously everyone is most welcome. Choose the family room, inside dining area or the outside terrace fanned by gentle sea breezes. Open from 10:00 to 05:00!

Chinese

Other options ➔ Far Eastern [p.203]

Bam Bu!

Location ➔ Adliya
Web/email ➔ na

| 1771 4424
Map Ref ➔ 14-C2

This restaurant is excellent value for money and especially popular for groups of all sizes. Drink and eat as much as you like for BD 12. The service is very efficient and accommodating. You can order a set menu and as the dishes arrive just ask the waiters to replenish the ones you especially fancy. The food at Bam Bu! is Asian fusion and boasts a tantalising menu of classic favourites as well as a taste of something a little more unique. Sophisticated decor – peppermint green walls and dark wood floors – gives the place an upmarket feel despite its low prices.

Beijing

Location ➔ Adliya
Web/email ➔ na

| 1771 7969
Map Ref ➔ 14-C2

You can't miss Beijing's huge red lanterns hanging at the entrance gates. Red denotes good luck in Chinese and this simple little restaurant is a lucky find. Huang You-Sheng, manager and owner of Beijing, greets all customers at the door as if welcoming you into his own home. The decor is homely in a minimalist way. Shabby chic in an oriental style sums up Beijing to a tee. Huang serves spicy Szechuan delights and Shanghai's light yet sweet cuisine. The prices are ridiculously low with most appetisers starting at around BD 1 and entrees around BD 3. The portions are excellent and all the accompanying sauces are imported straight from Huang's hometown of Shanghai. A good selection of wine and beer includes a 10 year-old, extremely potent Chinese wine. Beijing is a great place to take the family for a cheap and cheerful introduction to fine Chinese cuisine.

China Garden

Location ➔ Gulf Hotel · Adliya
Web/email ➔ www.gulfhotelbahrain.com

| 1771 3000
Map Ref ➔ 14-C2

Situated amid the lush grounds of the Gulf Hotel, visitors delight in the relaxing atmosphere of a babbling brook which overlooks the distinctly Eastern architecture of a nearby Thai restaurant. The food is very traditional yet up-market Chinese. The soups are fresh, the vegetables crunchy and there is a complete absence of gloopy, MSG-laced sauces or greasy pastry. The sizzling main course options are delicately flavoured and all portions are large. The menu's extensive choices will gladden even the fussiest of eaters and sea-food fanatics will fall hook, line and sinker for just about every option. Prices are reasonable, extremely so for the 'quick lunch' menu. There is a whole array of daily set menus to choose from. Private parties, at home or away can be catered by this rather chic Chinese restaurant.

Chinese tea

We mind your business.

The pleasures of home.
The comforts to do business.

Hospitality is our Heritage

فندق السفير
AL SAFIR HOTEL

PO Box 55222, Manama, Kingdom of Bahrain
+973 17827999, Fax: +973 17827888, e-mail: alsafirh@batelco.com.bh, safirsal@batelco.com.bh, Website: www.alsafirhotel.com

Foli

Location ➜ Adliya
Web/email ➜ na

| 1772 2199
Map Ref ➜ 14-C4

A little off the beaten track (opposite the DHL office in Adliya), Foli is especially popular with a loyal group of local ladies and the odd spattering of expat diners. Offering an extensive range of typical Chinese delights, the restaurant's in-house special of vegetable noodles is a must-try. Szechuan, Cantonese and Peking are some of the various flavours on offer, and each more finger-licking than the last. Waiters are friendly and professional and are supported by Joe the manager, whose 20 years of experience shows through his skilled staff. Generous portions can be enjoyed at reasonable prices and in subtly chic surroundings. Foli gets quite busy at the weekends, so booking ahead is highly recommended.

Hong Kong

Location ➜ Budaiya
Web/email ➜ na

| 1772 8700
Map Ref ➜ 14-C4

The restaurant opened in Bahrain back in 1978 and quickly established an enviable reputation for its fine Chinese cuisine and superb service. Since then, they have increased in popularity, winning numerous awards for excellent service, amongst other things. It is absolutely essential to book in advance, this place is always packed and reserving ahead of time will avoid any disappointment. At Hong Kong, real Chinese chefs create delicious authentic meals using a wide and varied selection of fresh produce flown in especially from varying regions of China, making every forkful lip-smackingly good. The crispy duck is a must-try. Meal sizes are ample and served on authentic Eastern crockery for an added touch of class. A visit to Hong Kong is a great experience, both in terms of culture and cuisine.

Jade Garden

Location ➜ Adliya
Web/email ➜ www.jade-garden.biz

| 1782 6100
Map Ref ➜ 14-B3

Jade Garden is a quiet, unassuming little restaurant hidden away down the narrow streets of Adliya. Popular with Indian expats and Bahrainis, who take advantage of the excellently priced business lunch: starter, main course, dessert and a drink and all for the very reasonable BD 3. The menu choice is good, featuring the usual range of Chinese cuisine, with a particularly good choice for vegetarians. And this may very well be the way to go: chicken dishes can be slightly chewy and the chef seems to hail from a province in China that considers garlic a main food group! Set away from the bustle of Adliya's hotspots, Jade Garden is a no-fuss way to get your quick Chinese food fix. Special occasions warrant the wheeling out of a fun but mediocre entertainer, still worth a visit if just for a giggle and some greasy grub.

Magic Wok

Location ➜ Jawad Dome
Web/email ➜ na

| 1769 4105
Map Ref ➜ 3-B2

Magic Wok is a fast-food joint with an impressively large and varied Asian menu. Noodles and all-in-one stir-fries are the Wok's specialities. The usual collection of starters include the time-honoured spring rolls and wantons with a small variety of dips. The chef cooks your stir-fry there and then and right where you can see the action, with no MSG added. The beef teppanyaki seems to be the established favourite. Ask and ye shall get, the staff and chef are incredibly accommodating and can tweak any dish on the menu including adjusting spice level. The Magic Wok is a very popular venue among businessmen on a quick lunch break. It may not be haute cuisine, but the woks are constantly flipping fresh ingredients and the meals are tasty and always filling.

Soie

Location ➜ Sheraton Bahrain Hotel & Towers
Web/email ➜ na

| 1753 3533
Map Ref ➜ 12-A2

Soie staff warmly welcome diners to their cocoon of modest, lush colours. The background music, while recognisably Chinese, is mellowed to a relaxing arrangement. The menu is varied and offers a tempting range of dishes. The attention to detail of the place settings is mirrored by the customer care proffered by the staff. The starters are quite delicious and the rich Beijing shrimp soup is a must. While the pancakes accompanying the crispy duck are perhaps a little too doughy, in general the food is delicious and of a high standard. Classical Chinese fare awaits you and vegetarians will not be disappointed. All in all Soie offers a very relaxing and enjoyable evening and is certainly a place you will want to revisit.

European

Other options ➜ Mediterranean [p.217]
French [p.205]
Italian [p.212]
Pizzerias [p.220]

Braids

Location ➜ Riffa Golf Club
Web/email ➜ na

1775 0777
Map Ref ➜ 7-A1

Braids at the Riffa Golf club is where players and their families can relax and have a bite to eat after a long and arduous round on the greens. To complete the atmosphere the walls are decorated with pictures of golfing greats from days gone by and the constant buzz of sports TV keeps customers up-to-date on the latest scores. The menu offers a fair choice of starters, main courses and snacks, with the emphasis on the latter. What you do order will be well-presented and enough to satisfy the heartiest of appetites. Desserts are few in number and ordinary in taste. The full English breakfast (BD 3.500) is popular, especially at weekends. For a relaxing light meal and an informal place for golfers to gather and reminisce, Braids is perfect to a tee!

Krumz

Location ➜ Adliya
Web/email ➜ www.krumz.com

1771 2767
Map Ref ➜ 14-C2

Everything on the menu here at Krumz is delicious. The dishes are richly flavoured and portions are good. It has an extensive menu full of traditional English pub fare with plenty of variety. They have a reasonably priced early bird menu that includes unlimited quantities of wine and draught beers. Comfort brunch food is served everyday and again unlimited alcohol is included if you wish. The atmosphere is casual and congenial and the service is renowned. You can hire parts of the restaurant for private parties

or even weddings. Enjoy the annual 'Alternative Kristmas Dinner at Krumz' on 25th June where you can experience Christmas over again with turkey and all the trimmings.

La Cave

Location ➜ Adliya
Web/email ➜ na

1771 7705
Map Ref ➜ 14-C3

This place combines a little bit of everything: succulent steak cooked to perfection, the freshest salads, delicious side dishes, to-die-for chocolate brownies and as much vino as you can drink, and all for a fixed price. La Cave's speciality is their set menu. You get three choices of salad, a choice of meat, fish or chicken and three options for dessert. The steaks are cooked exactly to your requirements and come with a delicious house sauce. The salads are proper salads with no damp lettuce or soggy tomatoes in sight and the brownies are worth the two trips to the gym that you'll promise to take but talk yourself out of. La Cave is a great place for a romantic meal during the week and equally good for party gatherings. The staff and service are some of the best in the country. With a beautiful stonewall finish and water garden, the ambience is all French chic. The only thing left to say is bon apetit!

Far Eastern

Other options ➜ Chinese [p.200]
Japanese [p.216]
Thai [p.221]
Polynesian [p.220]

Asia

Location ➜ City Centre Hotel
Web/email ➜ na

1722 9979
Map Ref ➜ 11-E3

Aesthetically stunning, the decor in Asia is wickedly chic and very sophisticated. Walking through the door to your table will feel like a trip to a five-star hotel restaurant, the difference is, the prices are a lot more reasonable. Typically of Japanese food, the portions are on the small side, but tasty. A lovely light Thai lunch comes in at a mere BD 2. The a la carte menu is extensive and caters for all tastes in sushi, sashimi and Thai delights. Asia is quiet during the day and on evenings when there is no scheduled entertainment. However, the place

Chinese • European • Far Eastern

Going Out

becomes a very hip and happening joint when the DJ arrives (Mon, Wed, Thu, Fri) with an incredibly young and trendy crowd, so dress to impress. An extraordinary selection of drinks is available from the well-stocked bar so be adventurous and try a Hong Kong Fuey cocktail or something equally oddly named. Conveniently located across the corridor from the Likwid nightclub and close to other evening hotspots.

Central Café

Location → Various locations | 1726 3271
Web/email → na | Map Ref → na

Central Café is a vegetarian's paradise and an excellent spot for good cheap eats. A full range of Indian delights are on offer here and you can feast until you're full, leave with a doggy bag and still only have spent BD 3 per person at this undiscovered gem. Nothing is on offer for meat-lovers but that should not spoil the experience of eating here. The BD 1 bowl of curry, enough for two people, is a must-try. As you can imagine this little restaurant is nearly always full with families upstairs and couples and singles downstairs. The melamine tables and plastic table-cloths add to the busy kitchen-like atmosphere as do the long wooden benches piled high with metal serving dishes. No alcohol is served but plenty of fresh juices will quench your thirst and cool your mouth after a truly scrumptious meal.

Chaing Saen Restaurant

Location → Budaiya Highway/ Cyprus Gardens | 1759 2105
Web/email → na | Map Ref → 3-B2

You wouldn't choose to come here for the atmosphere or the ambience, but the fact that Chaing Saen is moving to Cyprus Gardens bodes well for its popularity as a diner. The food is delicious, and despite the large selection of dishes, it seems impossible to choose badly. There are three main options: Thai, Chinese and Japanese. Choose the fresh tasting sushi, the piquant Chinese stir-fries or the Thai soups and curries, all of which are cooked to order, full of flavour and as close to authentic as you'll get here. Table settings are attractive with simple decor, the staff are extremely efficient in a discreet kind of way, and any night of the week you come here, you won't be disappointed.

Kontiki Asia

Location → Diplomat Radisson SAS Hotel | 1752 5210
Web/email → na | Map Ref → 12-C2

This restaurant, offering a great range of Far Eastern cuisine, is something of an enigma. Dine here on a busy evening and the vibrant, tropical atmosphere is a celebration of sensations. However, when Kontiki is empty the atmosphere deflates and you may feel dwarfed by the over-sized Asian fixtures, with only the delicious food for comfort. Dine alfresco on balmy evenings and enjoy a cocktail or alternatively savour a cool beverage at the bar in the restaurant. Reminiscent of a tropical Polynesian island, if your timing is right, Kontiki can be an elegant choice for fine diners. You can always bring along a large party of friends and provide your own ambience.

Monsoon

Location → Adliya | 1774 9222
Web/email → www.misfu.com | Map Ref → 14-C2

Monsoon is an impressive establishment, the decor being inspired by a Balinese palace, with a raised central dining area and serene water features. With two distinct menus available to diners, there is a clever blend of Asian food with a comprehensive selection of Japanese fare. Visit the sushi bar and watch the expert chef create your order. All dishes on offer are mouth-watering, with generous portions cooked to perfection. The presentation, quality and taste of everything here is superb. This is a popular establishment so if you're planning to visit on weekends, prior reservations are essential.

Monsoon

French

La Fontaine

Location → City Centre
Web/email → www.lafontaineartcentre.com

1723 0123
Map Ref → 12-B3

A truly romantic step back in time, La Fontaine is a rambling old Bahraini villa whose counterparts have all perished through the years, and has been lovingly restored by dedicated French architect Jean-Marc Sinon. The result is a truly stunning fusion of the old with the modern. Part spa, part zen room, the restaurant portion is situated in the main courtyard with a titanic-sized fountain in the middle. Quiet during the days, the place really comes into its own for specially arranged parties and scheduled events. It is essential to call and book for a meal. This is a place for all things, films are shown monthly in the Moon courtyard, concerts held, art displayed and anything that represents culture has its place. The food in the restaurant is of a high standard and covers a spectrum of cuisines. The whole venue is presided over by its owner, Fatima, and her attention to artistry renders La Fontaine health-giving and soul-restoring.

GCC easy as ABC

If you want to drop in on your neighbours, then go prepared with Explorer. Be it for a shopping spree in Dubai, a luxury holiday in Abu Dhabi, to enjoy the wilderness of Oman, or to get a slice of Kuwait's colourful history. Also look out for Explorer's new guides to Singapore, Hong Kong, London, New York & Sydney.

La Perle

Location → Novotel Al Dana Resort · Bab Al Bahrain
Web/email → www.novotel-bahrain.com.bh

1729 8439
Map Ref → 4-C1

This unique restaurant, tucked away in the coral-coloured streets of a faux Arabian village, is a true pearl. The 'village' itself is located right on a causeway joining the main island of Manama to the smaller one of Muharraq. This ideal situation provides a stunning ocean backdrop from practically every table. Delicious lobster, hammour and other seafood delights are served on huge blue and white designer plates, especially fashioned for the Novotel. This colour scheme, in keeping with the coastal location, is continued throughout the restaurant. A real treat, La Perle specialises in seafood, but also offers many other fabulous culinary treats. La Bellevue Bar, upstairs, entertains guests with a lively Latin American band in a comfortable club atmosphere.

La Perle

Versailles

Location → Regency Intercontinental
Web/email → na

1722 7777
Map Ref → 11-E3

This upmarket restaurant makes the perfect venue for romancing that special someone. Offering a mouth-watering selection of dishes that are exceptionally prepared, the Resident chef (who's French, of course) is joined once a month by a different Michelin Star chef, lending a global touch to the already out-of-this-world experience. The set menu is complemented by an impressive list of daily specials, and the wine list is extensive and of the highest quality. In terms of decor, think tasteful, think 18th century, think French and most importantly, think romantic. Friendly yet unobtrusive waiters round off Les Versailles experience, which on the whole is Tres Magnifique!

French

Going Out

Indian

Clay Oven

Location ➜ Adliya
Web/email ➜ na

| 1771 7008
Map Ref ➜ 14-B3

Clay Oven is a much-overlooked little gem, entirely due to its location slightly off the beaten track. It is hard to find fault with this homely, yet rather elegant, restaurant that serves exquisite Indian food cooked to your requirements while attending to your every whim. The Tandoori items are indeed cooked in a traditional clay oven and you can tell. If you are looking for an intimate meal, you can have a private little room all to yourself, if it's a small private party, book out the Georgian-style dining room or hire out the whole top floor for a large gathering. Children are welcomed and amply catered for. What particularly sets this restaurant apart is their care of their customers. Stuck for a lift? They might even arrange to pick you up. Other items of interest include an old swing seat that keeps bored children amused while the adults savour their meal and a traditional Indian hut in the garden selling old Indian wares.

Lanterns

Location ➜ Budaiya Highway
Web/email ➜ na

| 1759 0591
Map Ref ➜ 3-D2

Suitable for every occasion, this restaurant is an ideal place for family meals, large parties, business outings or a meal *a deux*. Feast yourself on bountiful selections of tasty Indian food and you'll be eating like a king. The setting is charming with its traditional Indian decor and little kiosks and benches, and drinking from tankards is a pleasant added touch. The all-you-can-eat-from-the-menu on Saturdays and the buffet on Mondays are great value, think elasticated waistband! Live Indian music is unobtrusive and enhances the atmosphere. Extremely popular among Indian and European expats as well as the local community, Lanterns is a fail-safe option for good Indian food and is one of the few establishments in the area serving alcohol. Call ahead for reservations to avoid disappointment.

Samarakand

Location ➜ Budaiya
Web/email ➜ na

| 1769 7996
Map Ref ➜ 3-B2

This well-located restaurant has a rather important looking entrance, complete with giant Arabic coffee pot and umpteen garden fixtures ensuring this is a 'couldn't-miss-it-if-you-tried' kind of place. Oddly there's an abundance of tubular steel and red plastic and the decor is a little dusty and unkempt, so consider Samarakand more for take-away then sit-in. This cheap-n-cheerful restaurant offers tasty international, Iranian and Chinese dishes with fantastic portions, all at great value. This is a great place to entertain a large crowd of people on a tight budget who will bring their own atmosphere and easily ignore the drab insides. The management emphasises their expertise in catering private parties and will deliver copious amounts of delicious delights and even stay around to serve you and your guests.

International

Al Abraaj

Location ➜ Sehla
Web/email ➜ na

| 1759 0123
Map Ref ➜ 3-E1

Al Abraaj has many outlets across Bahrain and is popular with locals and visitors alike. Offering a large selection of Iranian, Chinese, Indian and continental fare, it is easy to see why all of its stores are so popular. Good quality food comes to your table in generous portions and at fantastic prices. Traditional entrees, such as mezze, are accompanied by delicious hot Turkish bread, freshly made in the authentic clay ovens. The Chinese dishes are always very popular and the shredded chilli beef and mixed fried rice ridiculously tasty and definitely worth a try. The restaurants outside the malls all have family rooms and are child-friendly. Al Abraaj's main forte is their home delivery service – their fleet of motorbikes can be seen zooming around the city at all hours of the day and night. If ordering takeaway, order early and anticipate a wait, especially at weekends – but it's well worth it.

Other branches: Adliya (1771 4222), Riffa (1762 4666), Busaibeen (1735 3535)

Indian • International

Going Out

Al Wasmeyyah

Location → Golden Tulip · City Centre
Web/email → www.goldentulipbahrain.com

1753 5000
Map Ref → 12-B2

The Golden Tulip's coffee shop is bizarrely located right in between the hotel lobby and the main entrance to the swimming pool. It really is something of a transit area, with lots and lots of comings and goings. If you can tolerate the hustle and bustle then indulge, because the food on offer is quite good with a wide range of Italian, Asian and Arabic dishes. A good-value, weekday lunch buffet is popular with the business and suit-n-tie folk, and a separate tea menu is a novelty feature with specialities from China, Germany and South Africa. Be sure to be quite specific when ordering from both menus, and to avoid any disappointment ask the waiter to read your order back to you.

BAPCO Club Restaurant

Location → BAPCO Club · Awali
Web/email → na

1775 3377
Map Ref → 8-A2

The BAPCO Club Restaurant is located in the expat-populated area of Awali, a 30 minute drive from Manama. It is one of the quietest restaurants in Bahrain, and undeservedly so. Serving up first-rate food and with excellent service it really should be busting at the seams with patrons. BAPCO is big on themes and Saturday is 'Seafood Night', the most popular dish of the evening being the grilled hammour – an absolute must-try. Wednesday is 'Indian Thali Evening' when professional serving staff tempt you with several small portions of Indian goodies – great for those who can't make up their minds! Portions are just perfect and value for money is spot on. Old colonial decor and chic grandeur bestow an atmosphere of a bygone era. The restaurant is mainly visited by Awali residents, which is a real pity as it deserves to be on everyone's list of must-go eateries.

Caesar's

Location → Adliya · Hoora
Web/email → na

1771 6955
Map Ref → 14-B2

Hidden away on the second floor of a rather unimposing building in Hoora, Caesar's embodies elegant dining, a pleasant surprise if ever there was one in Bahrain. The term Fusion permeates through everything here, from the decor – which is proudly faux Louis XIV – to the cuisine, an eclectic mix of Chinese, Indian and European. Tasty, piping hot and extremely filling, almost everything on the menu is worth trying, especially the freshest, crispiest spring rolls on the island. The waiters are extremely helpful and always on hand to advise, without being in-your-face obtrusive. An international clientele frequents Caesar's and reservations are essential at weekends.

Camelot

Location → Nr British School · Adliya
Web/email → na

1771 7745
Map Ref → 14-C3

Architecturally this place is awesome, you can't miss this pseudo-medieval castle rising up from the surrounding Bahraini villas. Taste is a different matter, but this is Camelot after all. The medieval theme extends to the interior and the decor, but forget the roast hog on a spit and the straw on the floor, Instead it's all wooden chairs and tables, sofas in quiet corners and outside dining by the moat. The menu includes lots of vegetarian options as well as steak, fish and pork. The influence of the notorious Irish manager, Jim Lawless, can be seen in the inclusion of traditional Irish dishes, just like 'the mammy' used to cook. A must-try is the Irish soup or full Irish breakfast including black pudding. Large pots of traditional Irish tea are served after the meal, or you can continue quaffing and revelling with Jim and his friends until the wee hours of dawn.

Cantina Spanish Court

Location → Budaiya
Web/email → na

1769 7552
Map Ref → 3-B2

Without doubt the finest restaurant in Bahrain. Benoit Ducray, owner of the award-winning 'The Tipsy Lobster' in Mauritius, has brought his love of fine cuisine and wines, along with an entire kitchen crew, to Bahrain. The interior is all low-walled dining areas at different levels, hacienda-style seating in rich upholstery and a dance-floor for the afterwards, calorie burning dance off. It's perfect, right down to the individual hand towels in the elegant bathrooms. Benoit endows his menu with the freshest of ingredients, including tuna from Japan, salmon from Norway and lobster from Oman. The espresso-sized lobster bisque is an absolute must. Breads and desserts are baked on demand and the menu is updated every four or five months. Every offering on the menu is worth trying and easily complemented by a glass (or bottle) from the very classy wine list.

Charcoal Grill

Location → Bab al Bahrain
Web/email → na

1721 3410
Map Ref → 11-E3

Situated in the heart of Manama, beside the Bab Al Bahrain gate, Charcoal Grill is a convenient place for a quick meal for tourists exploring the souk area and also for businessmen working in the locality. It makes for a great takeaway joint, but if you are hanging around then it's all formica in the little restaurant upstairs. Don't get your best threads on, this place is simple, cheap-n-cheerful, with Filipino covers of Chris Rea as background music. The food is surprisingly good and regulars tout the chicken curry as the best in Bahrain. Choose from a wide selection of Chinese, Indian and Tandoori dishes or go for a standard sandwich. Tacky, kitsch, call it what you will, leave the pretension at the door and get ready for a fabulous feast.

Dilmun Club

Location → Off Avenue 77 · Saar
Web/email → na

1769 2986
Map Ref → 3-B3

Technically, the Dilmun club restaurants are open only to members, however sometimes it seems the entire expat population eats at Candles, Amigos or the Bistro at least once a week. With an emphasis on family friendly, it's hard to beat these outlets for the mind-boggling range and budget price of the food. Amigos next to the pool, serves quick, light lunches and snacks, while Candles, as its name suggests, is best enjoyed in the evening. On Tuesday nights, 'Four Corners of the World' is simply a brilliant concept for the hungry diner and the Friday buffet is unsurpassable good value at a few dinars per head. Portions at all outlets are generous and well-presented by a happy and busy staff. Murthy, the manager, will organise catering for your private parties. With regular bingo nights,

kids' discos, quizzes, concerts, comedy nights and sporting events, it is challenging to find a more friendly club with superior entertainment and dining options.

Bohemia

Location → Adliya
Web/email → na

1771 6715
Map Ref → 14-C2

Bohemia (formally known as Fou) is worth a visit for its decor alone. Downstairs is a cafe in deep tones with a tribute to Marilyn Monroe, and private, cosy niches for small parties. There is also a fantastically funky lounge bar done up Salvador Dali style – all purples and greens, huge pictures, mirrored ceilings and zany lip-shaped settees. Upstairs is for more formal dining: the textured walls, gilt mirrors, ambient lighting and still but subtle Dali-esque touches give the main dining hall a funky flavour. The cafe serves standard light snacks – sandwiches, salads, pastas and curries – while the upstairs restaurant goes for wide-ranging Mediterranean dishes with fish aplenty. The hammour with capers does great justice to Bahrain's favourite fish.

Jim's

Location → Adliya
Web/email → na

1771 0654
Map Ref → 14-C2

Knock on the heavy wooden door of Jim's international restaurant and the staff will usher you into a conservatory-style environment. Wicker chairs with over-stuffed cushions, terracotta-shaded soft furnishings, seascapes set in alcoves and orchid-decorated round tables create a cosy, homely atmosphere in this very popular eatery. Jim's offers all the traditional English comfort food you would expect and more. Portions are fantastic, and you will be hard pushed to clean your plate. The daily farmhouse breakfast is true to a traditional English in every way. On Fridays enjoy a celebratory Buck's Fizz breakfast for a mere BD 5. Jim's cannot be rivalled for its BD 5.500 three-course Roast-of-the-Day meal, where you can choose from two roasts (the delicately flavoured pork is a must). Jim's is quiet and romantic on weekdays, and lively and fun-filled at weekends.

La Mosaique

Location → Crowne Plaza Bahrain | 1753 1122
Web/email → NA | Map Ref →12-C1

La Mosaique offers a delightful introduction to Arabic food. While the starters are more international in flavour, it's the entrees that you're here for and each has an amazingly unique and delicious distinct Arabic flavour. The buffet is generous and readily replenished presenting excellent choice for dedicated carnivores. A lavish array of fresh fish and traditional Arabic dishes such as machbous and ozzi fills the trays on the buffet line. In addition, kebabs and lamb chops can be cooked in front of you and brought to your table sizzling. The ambience is comfortable, so eat slow and just relax. In cooler months the outdoor terrace is great for alfresco dining with the added advantage of a sea view.

Le Bistro

Location → Regency Intercontinental | 1722 7777
Web/email → www.intercontinental.com | Map Ref →11-E3

Overlooking the busy lobby of this city-centre hotel, Le Bistro is the perfect place to watch the world go by. The ambient lighting and French bistro-style decor make the ideal setting for a business meeting or personal down time, and for even more privacy you can squirrel yourself away in one of the private booths. Graceful waiters provide super-smooth service, but speak your order clearly to avoid any surprises caused by the language barrier. The diverse menu offers outstanding quality – particularly recommended is the shrimp and avocado in chili dressing. Every night a different buffet theme lets you sample a world of culinary delights, or if you choose something a la carte you'll find the portions generous and elegantly presented.

Mano's Restaurant at the Rugby Club

Location → Bahrain Rugby Football Club · Saar | 3661 1960
Web/email → www.bahrainrfc.com | Map Ref → 3-B3

Well-known for its good, wholesome, no-frills-no-fuss grub, you can expect man-size portions with only a slight veer towards healthy eating. The food here is all it should be, its job being to fill the bellies of hungry rugby players, and it meets the challenge successfully. Friday brunch is popular with expat families who enjoy a variety of predictable dishes at excellent prices. Kids are welcome and have loads of outdoor space to play. The service can be somewhat slow at times but patrons are fiercely loyal and extremely forgiving. The social side of the club is important: visiting rugby teams, locally produced plays and even an occasional touch of light opera bring in the crowds. The bar is decorated with a selection of proudly exhibited trophies while rugby shirts, once worn by prominent players, adorn the walls. Call ahead to avoid disappointment.

Mezzaluna

Location → Adliya | 1774 2999
Web/email → na | Map Ref → 14-C2

Beautifully romantic, with food equally as exquisite, this restaurant is an authentic old Bahraini house with a covered courtyard. Lighting is low, the waiters attentive and the general atmosphere is conducive to good times. Little surprises arrive on your plate every so often to make you feel really looked after and it is this kind of attention to detail that makes this restaurant a cut above the rest. The food is artistically presented and delicious. Expect to find timeless classics such as excellent steak as well as more adventurous dishes like veal with melted foie gras. One of the most extensive wine lists on the island complements the menu and the manager is only too happy to advise. A grand piano and jazz quartet entertain diners on Fridays and the restaurant is open for hire and can accommodate parties of all sizes. Perfect for a really special, fancy evening out.

Mezzaluna

Neyran

Location → Mercure Grand Hotel · Seef
Web/email → na

| 1758 4400
Map Ref → 3-E1

Newly opened, and as yet undiscovered by the masses, Neyran Restaurant is a real treat of an eaterie. The lunch buffet is quite extraordinary with servings of such sophisticated dishes as lobster thermidor and beef in veal liver gravy. It's not just fancy cuisine though; good ol' Indian, Arabic and Italian dishes are all here for you to enjoy. The service is smart and attentive, while the atmosphere is quiet and relaxing and the setting is light and open but with a distinct Arabic twist. The cocktail and wine lists are extensive with wine from all over the world on offer. While the drinks are quite pricey, lunch at BD 9 is an absolute steal considering the choice and quality of the food. An ideal place for a business lunch with important clients or a rather fancy dinner just for the sake of it. Go on, you deserve it!

Olivo's Brasserie

Location → Diplomat Radisson SAS Hotel
Web/email → na

| 1753 1666
Map Ref →12-C2

Expect to be spoilt for choice at a buffet at Olivo's. Everything is beautifully displayed and fabulously tempting, so dig in and try everything. A wide selection of food is on offer from French to Indian and, all in all, features delicious and unusual flavours. Every dish looks appetising and choosing just one is difficult. Time is spent on presentation at this establishment and it shows. Everything is finished off just perfectly with the correct accompanying garnish. The buffet is immaculately laid out with starters easily identifiable from the main courses. The staff are professional, efficient and on hand to look after you. The decor is tasteful and Olivo's offers a very peaceful and enjoyable lunch away from the rush of the city. Very family friendly with high chairs on hand for the little ones.

Overlook Café

Location → Ritz Carlton Bahrain Hotel & Spa · Seef
Web/email → na

| 1758 0000
Map Ref → 3-E1

Overlooking the white sands of the Ritz Carlton lagoon and the turquoise sea of the Arabian Gulf,

this venue has one of the best views in Bahrain. Cool breezes calm you as you eat alfresco in this informal beach setting and watch the colourful sails of the wind-surfers go by or the fleet of old fishing boats head out to sea. Children are most welcome and amply catered for and can trot off to the neighbouring play-park while the adults enjoy their meal. The menu rarely changes and you won't be disappointed. If the mere idea of making it from the beach to the cafe causes fatigue, you can order from your sun-lounger and your food will arrive in takeaway dishes. The restaurant is only open to hotel guests and members, or guests of the Royal Sporting Club. Overlook Cafe opens at 09:00 for coffee only, and lunch is served between 12:00 and 17:45.

Plums

Location → Ritz Carlton Bahrain Hotel & Spa · Seef
Web/email → na

| 1758 0000
Map Ref → 3-E1

With its deep plum walls, velvet plum seating and sensual plum lighting, this is the perfect setting for a romantic dinner or a small party for a special occasion. Its deep ambience gives it a unique sense of class, and coupled with the awesome menu, Plums is a five-star restaurant in a five-star hotel. The appetisers are mouth-wateringly phenomenal, but it's the sumptuous steaks that are the speciality of this restaurant and they are arguably among the best in Bahrain. The food is beautifully presented and the service attentive, but make sure you bring something warm as the air conditioning reaches Arctic proportions.

Savoy

Location → Al Safir Hotel
Web/email → na

| 1782 7999
Map Ref →4-C2

The Savoy coffee shop at the back of Al Safir's lobby will remind you of a Greek taverna, with its cascading potted plants and terracotta colours. Quite where the feathered curtains fit in is anyone's guess and the same goes for the cordoned-off, yet very audible, Thai massage parlour. Hoots of hidden laughter and gales of giggles will entertain you while you order what very well could be the freshest Caesar salad in Bahrain. While US navy hunks and mysterious Thai masseurs banter away behind flimsy screens, enjoy a somewhat less gripping all-day-long buffet at BD 5.500 per person. If the entertaining banter that emanates from the massage parlour isn't amusing enough for you, then you can always log on to the broadband computers available in the coffee shop. An interesting little place that has to be seen to be believed and perhaps appreciated!

Silk's

Location → Mövenpick Hotel Bahrain
Web/email → www.movenpick-bahrain.com.bh

1746 0000
Map Ref → 2-C4

Renowned for its Monday night seafood buffet and because of its location right next to the airport, expect to find this place full to capacity – all the time. A favourite among airline crew, transit passengers and seafood lovers alike, the food here will not disappoint. Perhaps serving the freshest sushi in town, Silk's also offers you a choice of hammour, clams, squid, prawns and more, cooked to preference with your choice of vegetables and spices. Difficult decisions lie ahead when so many tempting offers are right in front of you, but be sure to leave space for the tastiest desserts on the island. Enjoy the international ambience in a well-lit, open and airy environment with a beautiful garden view. Friday brunch is a treat for families with live entertainment on hand.

Silk's

Upstairs Downstairs

Location → Nr British School
Web/email → na

1771 3093
Map Ref → 14-C3

Upstairs Downstairs is on everyone's list of absolute favourites and George, the maître d', will welcome you and make you feel like a regular on your first visit. A smart dining area upstairs is complemented by a relaxed, informal lounge area downstairs. Ingeniously and tastefully done up, the restaurant partly resembles a cosy jazz club and partly a 1920s London street, complete with bakery and Georgian windows. Try Bahrain's national dish, Machboos, a spicy combination of prawns, rice and vegetables. A regular jazz musician keeps the atmosphere buzzing and international artists fly in regularly to perform at a monthly 'Friday Night Live'. For that extra special occasion, hire out the Royal Suite upstairs where you have a bird's-eye view of the restaurant, your own 'sitting room' with fireplace, silver service courtesy of real butlers, and a delicious seven-course meal. This taste of luxury will set you back around BD 25 per person, but it's worth every dinar.

Wholesale

Location → Budaiya Road
Web/email → na

1759 5950
Map Ref → 3-C2

The extensive menu offers the unique concept of ordering food by weight, alongside the more traditional food-by-portion. This idea comes into its own when catering at home for large parties. There are over 200 choices offered on the menu ranging from Chinese to Indian with a small selection of continental dishes such as pastas and pizzas. Every noodle and curry dish you can think of is listed here with a fantastic choice of dishes for vegetarians. The portions served are substantial and if you order for a party at home you'll have very satisfied guests. On Tuesday nights, starting at 19:00, you can enjoy an all-you-can-eat dinner buffet for BD 2.750 per person, with children under six eating for free. With a kids' play area on site, Wholesale is a winner for families. The restaurant specialises in takeaway, home delivery and outdoor catering with Chinese delights, curry specials and party menus for groups of all sizes.

International

Going Out

Yum Yum Tree

Location ➜ Off Exhibition Ave
Web/email ➜ na

| 1729 6296
Map Ref ➜ 12-C3

The Yum Yum Tree is really six restaurants rolled into one – almost like a food court. It's ideal for large groups as everyone can choose their preferred cuisine and still eat together. Order chicken teriyaki at the Japanese outlet, an Italian pasta, nachos from the Mexican counter, umpteen salads and fantastically fresh juices. Guaranteed there will be something here for everyone. The Yum Yum Tree has plenty of space with a kids' play area that will keep them happy while you finish your meal. This is definitely a cheap and cheerful place to take the kids at the weekend, though it gets both loud and busy.

Zoë

Location ➜ Adliya
Web/email ➜ na

| 1771 6400
Map Ref ➜ 14-C2

Zoë is a safe bet for everyone. Easy to find, with a prominent location in the major row of restaurants in Adliya, this place is both chic and unique. Sophisticated in style with large (mercifully north-facing) windows that give it a bright and airy feel. The menu offers a wide range of food with pastas and pizzas, seafood and steaks, mezze to share, and the fresh-baked breads are to die for. For lunch it is quiet and pleasant, while in the evenings it is more convivial. Its formal yet relaxed undertones make it an ideal place to entertain your friends or business colleagues. Later in the evening it becomes even funkier as the DJ cranks up the volume and folk flock up to try out the cocktails and generally 'hang out'.

Zoë

Italian

Other options ➜ Pizzerias [p.220]
Mediterranean [p.217]

Cico's

Location ➜ Adliya
Web/email ➜ na

| 1771 3710
Map Ref ➜ 14-B3

An excellent choice for those hankering for tasty, simple Italian food, you ask and Cico's will deliver. The quality and quantity is excellent though a little predictable, which works in its favour with good solid appetiser options like the avocado, tomato and mozzarella, and a healthy variety of pasta entrees. The choice of desserts is limited but again safe, and the tiramisu never fails to fulfil. There's always a hustle and bustle here, the tables are closer together, cafe style, to allow more folk to eat and add to the buzz. The maitre d' consistently welcomes regulars, giving the restaurant a homey and friendly feeling. The low ceilings are festooned with bunches of grapes and wine flagons; the decor doing what it can to instigate a Mediterranean ambience. All things considered, Cico's is a solid choice for good, tasty, basic Italian dining.

Ciro's Pizza Pomodoro

Location ➜ Opp Gulf Hotel · Adliya
Web/email ➜ www.pomodoro.co.uk

| 1771 4001
Map Ref ➜ 14-C2

If you absolutely adore Italian food then Ciro's Pizza Pomodoro is perfect for you. The selection of tempting pastas, salads tossed to perfection and pizzas galore makes this a good venue for large groups with varied tastes. Special lunchtime menus pull in the business guys and gals looking for a little fun during their desk-bound day. The tastiest lasagne in town is served here along with an extensive collection of interesting cocktails. Pizzas are named after movie stars or celebrities so you can savour a Sylvester Stallone or munch on a Madonna. Live entertainment every evening draws party people, and the noise level can sometimes be quite staggering. Diners can feel free to boogie, and the party goes on until 02:00 on most nights. The large windows provide a bright and spacious atmosphere during the day, but once the sun sets, anything goes!

or Banquets and Seminars with Style.

s seminars and banquets in a Hi-Tech environment
nidst the most modern audio-visual amenities.
th the new state-of-the-art Grand Ballroom and
smaller meeting rooms, there is something

to match every taste and size. The entire hotel is
a Wi-Fi zone and our Meet and Dine team ensures
that your event has an unmistakable class of its
own.

venpick Hotel Bahrain
Box 24009, Muharraq Town, Kingdom of Bahrain
ne +973 17 460000, Fax +973 17 460001
l.bahrain@moevenpick.com

www.moevenpick-hotels.com
True Excellence in Swiss Hospitality.

MÖVENPICK
Hotel Bahrain

Italian

Going Out

La Pergola

Location → Gulf Hotel · Adliya
Web/email → www.gulfhotelbahrain.com

1771 3000
Map Ref → 14-C2

Less of a traditional trattoria and more like a five star fine dining establishment, La Pergola pleases Italian food lovers as well as sophisticated diners. The clean modern interior and intimate space lends itself not only to business dinners but also a romantic liason. The menu is packed with all the usual suspects, as well as a few surprises! Of particular note are the desserts. One thing everything has in common is quality. Quality of flavours, quality of presentation and quality of delivery. All in all, this is one of Bahrain's most distinguished Italians.

La Pergola

Luigi's

Location → Budaiya Highway · Budaiya
Web/email → na

1769 3533
Map Ref → 3-B3

Luigi's is a family-run pizzeria, and the proprietor and his charming wife, Marie take their pizzas very seriously indeed. All the ingredients are fabulously fresh and hand-picked by Luigi himself, so it's little wonder this place is generally considered to serve the best pizza on the island. Its tantalisingly thin crust and interesting toppings taste authentic, and the salads are generous in size and include delicious grilled cheese and rocket. The decor is rustic and homey and the walls are adorned with cityscapes of Italian metropolises.

Mamma Mia

Location → Al Muaskar Highway Crossing · Riffa
Web/email → na

1777 2321
Map Ref → 6-B4

Mamma Mia is reckoned to be among one of the best Italian restaurants on the island and a firm favourite with those living in the area. This is not a fine-dining restaurant but is wonderfully cosy with a real Italian feel with its intimate seating, red-checked table cloths, low-lighting and warm welcome. Traditional Italian cooking pervades with garlicky starters and superb home-made pastas and pizzas at excellent prices. The service is friendly and accommodating, and before long (a couple of visits actually) you'll feel right at home and quite the regular.

Mondo

Location → Diplomat Radisson SAS Hotel
Web/email → www.radissonsas.com

1753 1666
Map Ref → 12-C2

Mondo is chic Italian at its best. The decor is strikingly modern and you will feel you have arrived at a rather upmarket Milanese restaurant. A powerful use of colours in the restaurant's design is mirrored in the very impressive menu. Expect to spend some time just reading, deciding, changing your mind and then deciding something else all over. There's a good variety and everything sounds delicious. An excellent array of meat, pasta, fish and vegetarian entrees and mains fills the menu, and when you do finally get your food, fills your belly. Service here is friendly, relaxed and very unpretentious which is a pleasant surprise. Despite its chic and expensive appearance, there is nothing nouveau about Mondo's food and you might find yourself trying to justify the fairly high prices.

Oliveto

Location → Adliya
Web/email → na

1771 6747
Map Ref → 14-C3

It's all about ambience here since it is above and beyond the usual and just plain excellent; warm and welcoming with a touch of chic. The comfortable bar area often becomes smoky so arrive early if you prefer to enjoy a relaxed aperitif on the sofa without the fog. The wine list is more than substantial, with expensive as well as

The cutting edge Italian dining experience

MONDO
Bar - Lounge - Restaurant

)% off food & beverage on presentation of this advert

sensibly priced wines available by the glass or bottle. Traditional Italian dishes such as the brilliant Saltimboca alla Romana are hard to beat, and the equally authentic desserts including tiramisu and casatta are superbly presented and flavoursome. The larger-than-life Paolo is very much in charge and will invariably bend your ear with chat and an Italian liqueur on the house – an excellent end to what you should find a memorable and stimulating experience in a place worth discovering.

Pizza Rio

Location ➔ Seef   **1758 2550**
Web/email ➔ na   Map Ref ➔ 3-E1

Only recently opened, this restaurant is connected to its sister shop Spice in the popular shopping district of Seef. The theme here is art deco with faux leather booths, some tall bar tables and a plasma screen pumping out music videos from diners' own CDs and DVDs – so make it good. The menu is extremely colourful despite the choice being somewhat limited. Nevertheless, the pizza that you order will look exactly as good as it did on the menu and will taste delicious. A small salad bar is positioned next to the open kitchens where you can watch your pizza being created and baked. The service is good, if a little grumpy at times, but this seems to be of little consequence to the gangs of teenagers who frequent this restaurant in great numbers at the weekends.

Primavera

Location ➔ Ritz Carlton Bahrain Hotel & Spa · Seef   **1758 0000**
Web/email ➔ www.ritzcarlton.com   Map Ref ➔ 3-E1

No matter what you eat, any place that manages a picturesque beach backdrop is worth a visit or two. If it's romancing or just a little privacy you're after, then tuck yourself and your significant other away into a private corner for an intimate dining experience. Expect the extremely attentive staff to politely help you through your visit. The head chef frequently visits each table during the evening, a fabulous personal touch. An extensive wine list accompanies the noveau cuisine menu that lists freshly made pastas and breads. Everything is served in hearty portions. A set menu offers some innovative choices including the baked eggplant

with fresh tomato coulis, an absolute must-try. This restaurant prides itself on having the best seafood in town. Meals are well presented by a clearly happy and dedicated staff.

Japanese

Other options ➔ **Far Eastern [p.203]**

Kei

Location ➔ Golden Tulip · City Centre   **1753 5000**
Web/email ➔ n/a   Map Ref ➔ 12-B2

Kei, at the Golden Tulip Hotel, offers an exceptionally warm and friendly welcome amid a cool, serene, mirrored interior. Taking centre stage is a sleek stainless steel surface upon which your chef will tease, tempt and entertain by preparing, in full view, your chosen meal. The choice is almost bewildering with a strong bias towards seafood, including the exotic cuttlefish. Quality, not quantity, is top priority at Kei. Meals are immaculately presented on miniature wooden tables and are accompanied by heart-warming sake for those in need of a little mellowing.

Mirai

Location ➔ Adliya   **1771 3113**
Web/email ➔ na   Map Ref ➔ 14-C2

Mirai is, without a doubt, one of Bahrain's most sophisticated restaurants, boasting excellent service and superb food. The sushi chef is also the restaurant's manager, lending a hands-on professionalism seldom found elsewhere. He is full of passion, enthusiasm and true loyalty to the art of Japanese cuisine. The restaurant itself has a wonderful ambience created in part by the sleek, modern, minimalist decor. You almost feel honoured to be eating here. The menu offers plenty of choice, along with the opportunity to witness the renowned chef create, concoct and entertain at the sushi bar. Portions can sometimes leave the famished a little less than full, but the quality of all the dishes is superb. Some of Bahrain's most accomplished DJs add to this hip experience with the latest mixes from the Middle East. Mirai gets pretty busy with the elite crowd at the weekends, so booking ahead is absolutely essential.

Italian • Japanese

Going Out

Sushi Ko

Location → Adliya
Web/email → na

1771 6619
Map Ref → 14-C2

Sushi Ko is a decent place for a quick bite to eat, or for a meal at the beginning of a night out in search of entertainment. The overall effect of the restaurant is spacious, with minimalist interior design, clinical white walls, minimum amount of artwork and pale, pine floors interspersed with grey slate. Tables match the wooden floor and the grey, upholstered chairs tie in with the two-tone effect. The food is satisfactory and prices are reasonable. Portions vary, although you may have to go fishing for your seafood if you order a seafood dish. Sushi Ko offers the usual assortment of Japanese specialities, assorted tempura being the most popular, but watch out for the heavy handed battering. This restaurant does not serve any alcoholic drinks, but the fresh juices are very tasty.

Mediterranean

Other options → Italian [p.212]

Zytoun

Location → Novotel Al Dana Resort · Bab Al Bahrain
Web/email → www.novotel-bahrain.com

1729 8008
Map Ref → 4-C1

Zytoun, on the corniche, is extremely accessible and provides excellent parking facilities. An attractive plant-filled poolside dining area is available as an alfresco option, leading down to the beach. The sunny Mediterranean decor displays tasteful mosaic touches in warm yellow and blue palettes. A large seating capacity offers a welcoming and airy feeling while most tables are reasonably distant for comfort. The Mediterranean-style food is very reasonably priced, delicious and creatively presented. An interesting feature of Zytoun is daily buffets at every meal and a la carte is also available as an alternative. Theme nights offer Italian, Arabic, seafood and grill, and there is a plethora of sauces and dressings to accompany the many innovative side dishes and salads. A thoughtful policy of the restaurant is to keep a children's table set up with simple activities and toys on site to keep little ones happy.

Zytoun

Mexican

Casa Mexicana

Location → Adliya
Web/email → na

1771 5521
Map Ref → 14-B3

This authentic Mexican restaurant guarantees its customers a fantastically friendly atmosphere and an authentic Mexican funfest. Magnificent margaritas flow all night and at some stage you may want to consider tucking in to the fabulously huge portions of hot and spicy (you can ask for the milder version) meals. Good Mexican with a lot of options on the menu you'll recognise and some interesting that you ought to try. If you're still up to it (or just still up), finish off with traditional tequilas. Casa Mexicana is perfect for large parties, with live entertainment throughout the evening. The dancefloor can get quite hot and spicy too as the night draws to an end. This light-hearted restaurant, with Mexican memorabilia on its walls, will keep you and your guests smiling all night!

Senor Paco's

Location → Adliya
Web/email → na

1772 5873
Map Ref → 14-C3

Seductive lighting and authentic Mexican decor is a good guarantee that Senor Paco's will be packed to the oak rafters most nights. Fajitas, steaks and all the Mexican trimmings are served up in a pleasant atmosphere. The menu offers a fine selection for vegetarians but don't expect to stick to a low calorie or carb diet if you dine here. Instead, consider this a good place to cheat on your diet, it's worth the guilt! Margarita night on Fridays always pulls in a big crowd, creating a really fun atmosphere with plenty of partying. George and his team are fast and efficient in an informal way, making sure each diner leaves Senor Paco's looking forward to their next trip to this little Mexican haven in the Middle East. Senor Paco's is a true party-lover's location.

Moroccan

Other options → Arabic/Lebanese [p.199]

Marrakesh

Location → Delmon International Hotel
Web/email → na

1722 4000
Map Ref → 12-E3

Marrakesh serves up one of Bahrain's most interesting Moroccan experiences. Moroccan dishes tend to include a variety of stewed and baked vegetables along with plenty of roast meats. However, food from this part of the world is also famed for its wide and interesting range of vegetarian delights. As in most Arabic restaurants, it is probably best to go with a group of friends so the ridiculously large selection of mezze can be shared and the fun cultural experience can be enjoyed in good company. Desserts are interesting and very tempting and must be accompanied by the traditional Arabic coffee. Marrakesh is authentically decorated and the atmosphere cosy. The serving staff are helpful and friendly but not overly attentive or overbearing. Live entertainment, thanks to a traditional oud player and singer, serves as pleasant background to dinner conversation. Weekends here are wild so book well in advance to avoid disappointment.

Persian

Other options → Arabic/Lebanese [p.199]

Isfahani

Location → Exhibition Ave
Web/email → na

1729 0027
Map Ref → 12-C2

This is a nice find for a cheap meal with a difference. The food is nearly all Iranian and though much of it looks like food you would find on any Middle Eastern menu, the flavours are all subtly different. The starters are so cheap that you can order as many as you like to create your own mezze and of course this comes served with enormous rounds of freshly baked soft bread. The main courses naturally consist of grilled meats, fish and some rice dishes, again all deliciously flavoured. The decor is fairly basic but it has some charming touches, with beautiful Persian enamel tiles on the walls and numerous little booths with curtains for extra privacy. Popular with Iranians who will attest this to be true Iranian cooking. The restaurant attracts locals and interested tourists alike, and does a roaring trade in outside catering.

Takht Jamsheed

Location → Gulf Hotel · Adliya
Web/email → www.gulfhotelbahrain.com

1771 3000
Map Ref → 14-C2

In keeping with its location at the Gulf Hotel, the Takt Jamsheed has a grandiose air and extravagant ambience. The chef, the food and the decor are all authentically Iranian. Traditional Persian ornaments decorate the dining room and live Iranian music rounds off the evenings. When it comes to eating, the best policy is to select your own mezze starters from the extensive first course list. This invariably means that you'll have to restrain yourself for the main course, but restrain yourself a little as the grilled lamb and hammour are absolutely delicious. Squeeze in some traditional desserts if you can or opt for fruit and icecream. This restaurant is particularly popular with Middle Eastern visitors as well as locals and expats. A popular choice for business meetings and conference dinners, Takt Jamsheed's outside catering can handle large numbers.

Going Out

Mexican • Moroccan • Persian

Where Service Counts

Gulf Hotel, a landmark in the heart of Manama offers 366 rooms and suites, Gulf International Convention and Exhibition Centre extends over 4,780 sq. meters of ballroom and exhibition area. Gulf Hotel houses 11 well-known restaurants, bars and lounges.

Pizzerias

Other options → Italian [p.212]

Bahrain boasts a long list of internationally known pizzerias: Pizza Hut, Papa John's, Dominos and Ciro's Pomodoro with its innovative toppings, to name but a few. These establishments offer a standard menu familiar to pizza lovers the world over. In recent years the humble pizza has taken over from the boring burger as the world's most popular fast food.

According to the local grapevine, Luigi's pizza on Budaiya Highway creates absolutely the most delicious, thin-crust, authentic Italian pizza on the island. All the ingredients are hand-picked by Luigi himself and the healthy pizza base is an effective option for the calorie conscious.

Pizzerias	
Caesar's	1769 5592
Domino's Pizza	1782 6222
Luigi's	1769 3533
Pizza Hut	1722 3223
Pizza Papa John's	1727 1701
Pizzabella	1761 1751

Polynesian

Other options → Far Eastern [p.203]

Trader Vic's

Location → Ritz Carlton Bahrain Hotel & Spa · Seef | **1758 6555**
Web/email → na | Map Ref → 3-E1

An international chain, Trader Vic's is as much a restaurant as it is a bar. It sports trendy Polynesian decor and views over the beach. The good news is that you have various options to earn your Trader Vic's badge: you can linger over a delicious, Asian-inspired meal, or munch your way through some very moreish snacks (crispy wontons, prawns and other oriental finger foods), or even just savour a few of their famously exotic cocktails. The wide selection of inventive and artistic cocktails add to the exotic feel provided by the sultry Cuban band. Well worth a visit.

Seafood

Seafood Hut

Location → Yacht Club · Sitra | **1770 0677**
Web/email → www.bahrainyachtclub.com.bh | Map Ref → 6-E4

The Seafood Hut at the BYC is tucked away and hard to find, but it's well worth nosing about until you do. The restaurant and adjacent bar are decked out with nautical paraphernalia, enough to keep the most curious of diners amused for hours. Seafood is the order of the day with a menu ranging from an impressive four choices of lobster dishes to the tried-and-trusted fish and chips (the best British-style chips on the island). Side salads, conjured up into fishy figures, are served alongside hearty portions of vegetables. The service is friendly, knowledgeable and always at hand, and advice from the chef can be sought if you just can't decide on which scrumptious meal to choose. Adjourn to the bar to shoot the breeze with a regular crowd of die-hard sailors or alternatively stroll on the small, moonlit beach and ponder the idea of getting your own sailboat.

Fishmarket

Location → Al Bander Hotel & Resort | **1770 1201**
Web/email → na | Map Ref → 6-E4

The Fishmarket Restaurant at the Al Bander Hotel & Resort is popular with visitors and locals, who keep coming back for more thanks to the excellent

Fishmarket

quality seafood. You can select your choice of fresh fish, crabs and shrimp or lobster and request the style of cooking, whether continental, oriental, Chinese, Thai or one of the Chef's specials, which means no palate will go unsatisfied. The setting of the restaurant is relaxed, although elegant enough for a special occasion with views of the tranquil Arabian waters. Even if you're not a big fish lover, the amiable and knowledgeable staff and pleasant ambiance of the Fishmarket will make you fall in love nonetheless.

Steakhouses

Other options → **American [p.196]**

Ponderosa Steakhouse

Location → King Faisal Corniche
Web/email → na

| 1722 9778
Map Ref → 11-F3

It's hard to find a better deal than the Ponderosa Steakhouse, an all inclusive, all-you-can-eat buffet for BD 3.200 for adults and just BD 1.900 for little ones up to the age of 10. The choice of dishes on display is amazing and includes an extensive salad bar plus all the time tested international favourites such as spaghetti bolognese and lasagne. You can fill up your plate as often as you wish but make sure to leave space for dessert, which includes blue jello and freshly whipped icecream cones. The a la carte menu includes all the well-known steak cuts at reasonable prices. Kids love Ponderosa and the fact that it is situated right next door to an outdoor amusement park doesn't do it any harm at all!

Sizzlers

Location → Mansouri Mansions
Web/email → na

| 1771 6999
Map Ref → 14-B3

Sizzlers is known on the island for its absolutely great steaks, cooked to perfection. There is a huge variety of meaty treats available including the Gaelic steak, Danish steak and the must-try sizzling spare ribs. If that isn't enough to get your mouth watering, then it's well worth keeping in mind that Sizzlers has the island's only 24 hour liquor licence. Extremely popular at weekends, the fajitas are among the best in town and enough

cannot be said about their full-blooded Bloody Mary. Standards have remained excellent and consistent over the 20 years Sizzlers has been feeding the hungry, and it's easy to see why it is on the list of many diners' weekly hangouts. The atmosphere is buzzing at weekends and reservations are highly recommended.

Thai

Other options → Far Eastern [p.203]

Baan Saeng Thai

Location → Adliya
Web/email → na

| 1771 5775
Map Ref → 14-B2

Baan Saeng Thai is a good, solid choice for standard Thai food. Choices include green curry, tom yum soup and the like, and while the menu may not be vast the quality and value are a pleasant surprise. The BD 4 per person buffet is a bargain for all you can eat, with no restrictions on the amount of visits. Lots of diners fill their plates up pyramid style and so get great value for their money. Although the decor is as far from traditional Thai as possible, it is clean, fresh and homely and the 80s pop music playing in the background is pleasant enough. If you are ordering from the a la carte menu, it's best not to be in too much of a rush as 'slow' and 'easy' are the operative words here.

Hash House

Location → Adliya
Web/email → na

| 1771 5094
Map Ref → 14-C2

'Swadee Ka' (meaning welcome) is definitely what you feel when you step into this little taste of Thailand that boasts both authenticity and charm. From the moment you sit down until the moment you have to leave, you will feel looked after, spoilt and fully satisfied during a dinner that easily turns into a wonderful experience. Thailand's famous Papaya salad is a definite must-try, along with the yummy starters, but be careful to save room for the huge choice of Thai main courses available on the menu. This place has great warmth to it so if you are looking for a cultural Thai experience, you're in the right place.

Going Out Seafood • Steakhouses • Thai

Hot City

Location → Palace Inn Hotel	**1772 5000**
Web/email → na	Map Ref → 14-C3

Hot City is an informal, laid-back sports bar serving surprisingly tasty, fresh and well-flavoured food. A selective Thai menu of the usual favourite dishes is on offer alongside a well-stocked bar. Happy hour (from 18:00 to 22:00) daily is very popular with the party-goers, who begin the nights revelling here and often stay till the wee hours of the morning. The sports bar is a large open area with low lighting, three well-used pool tables, one big-screen TV and several smaller ones dotted around the room. The managers and staff are very friendly, chatty and welcoming. The early evening trade mostly tends to be people on their way home from work, stopping in for a quiet drink and perhaps a quick bite. As the night draws on, the nightclub, immediately adjacent to the bar, opens and attracts a good crowd. Takeaway food can be ordered right up to closing time at 02:00.

Lanna Thai

Location → Budaiya Highway · Janussan	**1759 3940**
Web/email → na	Map Ref → 3-C2

Don't be deceived by Lanna Thai's outside appearance. Upstairs is fairly unremarkable but the downstairs dining area transports you to an elegant and cosy Thai-style haven with wood panels, sunken seating and comfy cushions. This is a lovely place for a romantic dinner or a small gathering. The menu offers a wide selection of appetisers, staples and fail-safe green and red Thai curries cooked to your required spiciness. In keeping with the casual atmosphere, serving dishes are simple but the portions are generous. The service is full of smiles and very efficient. This restaurant is popular with those living in the vicinity for its informal nature, good prices, friendly service and the opportunity to enjoy a glass of wine with your meal. If you don't feel like straying out, the takeaway is arguably the best value for money in Bahrain.

Turkish

Other options → **Arabic/Lebanese [p.199]**

Anatolia

Location → Budaiya Highway · Cypress Gardens	**1769 0601**
Web/email → na	Map Ref → 3-B2

Situated in Budaiya at Cyprus Gardens, Anatolia's location in the heart of a busy residential area is one of its selling points. Its others are cheap prices and convenient parking. The pleasant and charming villa atmosphere renders a Turkish feel throughout, bringing the Ottoman right to your table. Choose from a large number of starters and follow up with something from the extensive choice of grilled meats. For an authentically Turkish experience, taste a 'pide', basically a thin-crust pizza with traditional Turkish toppings. Anatolia's will happily and economically cater for your parties too.

Dinner Cruises

Other options → **Boat & Yacht Charters [p.127]**
Dhow Charters [p.126]

Island Tours will whisk you away from the hustle and bustle of the city to the deserted island of Jarada. While away a few languishly lazy hours on the beach while the crew prepare a tasty barbecue complete with endless supplies of your chosen poison. Alternatively, charter Jean-Pierre Cohen's traditional dhow 'Scaramouch' for a real desert island adventure. Shark-feeding for the brave-hearted and pearl diving for the strong are among the choice of escapades he offers. There's food and drink aplenty along with good company and the benefit of the captain's decades of experience on the high seas. Departing from the Novotel Dana Resort prices vary according to the personal needs of passengers.

Island Tours

Location → See below	**1771 0088**
Web/email → www.islandtours.com.bh	Map Ref → 14-B2

The 52 ft custom-built tour yacht 'Island Mermaid' operates lunch and dinner cruises from the Marina Club on the main corniche. Depart at 12:00, cruise through the waves for about an hour and eventually dock on Jarada Island, a tidal sand bar in the middle of the ocean. The crew will prepare a buffet-style lunch while you explore the shallow waters of Jarada from the yacht's swim platform or venture out into deeper water on a jet ski. After a two hour sojourn, the trip back to shore often includes a little dolphin watching. The lunch cruise arrives back at 16:00 and costs BD 25 for adults and BD 12 for kids. The crew is more than happy to organise private parties and weddings for a maximum of 35 passengers. Dig deep though, as prices are steep at BD 300 for a half-day cruise and BD 550 for the whole day.

Jean-Pierre Cohen

Location → Novotel Al Dana Resort · Bab Al Bahrain **3909 4382**
Web/email → na   Map Ref → 4-C1

Jean-Pierre Cohen operates traditional dhow cruises to many of the nearby islands. Departing from the Novotel Dana Resort at 09:15 you can sit back and relax while Captain Cohen cuts through the foam to the pure white sands of Jarada island. Enjoy a Turkish brunch of barbeque meats, fresh salads and plenty of refreshments to cool you down and keep you merry. Prices start at BD 20 per person and decrease as passenger numbers rise. Evening cruises depart at 18:00, touring the coastline and stopping at some of the smaller islands. Shark-feeding, oyster pearl fishing and scuba diving adventures are organised as well as week-long trips to the Mussandam peninsula.

Cafes & Coffee Shops

Other options → Afternoon Tea [p.227]

Coffee drinking is something of a national pastime in Bahrain and one that is eagerly embraced by the multi-cultural expat community. By 08:00 most mornings, the tennis brigade are sipping their frothy cappuccinos and trading weekend gossip and putting off the daily grind. Starbucks and Costa Coffee are among the better known coffee houses in Bahrain. Upmarket, splendidly Moroccan shisha cafes are also to be found where the setting is beautiful, the atmosphere congenial, the shisha pipes fragrant and the opening hours extraordinarily long. Alternatively there are literally hundreds of road-side Arabic coffee shops that offer a blend of local culture and a puff on a shisha.

Expats tend to shy away from these male-frequented Arabic cafes but are usually made to feel extremely welcome. All cafes and coffee shops offer fresh juices, light food, sandwiches, cakes and snacks. The fresh juice culture is thriving in Bahrain, be brave with your choice and you will get a thrilling vitamin boost. Internet cafes are few and far between, most expats have ADSL at home. Costa and Starbucks offer 'Wi-Fi' hotspots where you can access the internet from your wireless laptop or PDA while perking up with the caffeine of your choice.

A Piece of Cake

Location → Off Riffa Avenue · Saar   **1759 6055**
Web/email → na   Map Ref → 3-C2

This delightful little coffee shop is accessed though the very popular art supply shop 'Celebrations' and the arty theme continues on into the dining area. A modern Arabic approach to the decor is created by hanging a rug from the celling – may not sound like much but adds an excellent unique touch. The rest is all watercolours of local scenes and a trickling water feature, all of which creates a serene ambience. Although the menu can be browsed through in seconds, A Piece of Cake offers healthy light snacks, scrumptious gateaux and cute cookies. Fresh and home-made sums up the fare: croissants baked to order and eggs scrambled to creamy perfection. Novelty cakes and catering for parties are this coffee shop's forte with huge orders being taken at Christmas and other seasonal times.

Al Bareh

Location → Off Shaikh Isa Avenue · Adliya   **1771 3535**
Web/email → na   Map Ref → 14-B2

An absolute haven of tranquility and culture tucked away in a picturesque old house in the narrow streets of Adliya, once found it will never be forgotten. Al Bareh serves a selection of superb Arabic fusion cuisine encompassing many healthy and low-carb delights and perhaps the best foul beans in town. The other wonderful thing is the fact that upstairs is a modern art gallery featuring big names in Middle Eastern art. Carefully nurtured by curator Luciana Farah, this magical little cafe and gallery holds monthly art exhibitions featuring

Cafés & Coffee Shops

Going Out

works from artists as far away as Brazil. She also runs classes for the young and young-at-heart who want to dabble in oils and watercolours. If that's not for you, try immersing yourself in thought during one of Luciana's many poetry evenings. Menu prices are reasonable and the charming outdoor terrace is an ideal spot for a light lunch in winter.

Al Noor Lounge

Location → Regency Intercontinental
Web/email → www.intercontinental.com

1722 7777
Map Ref → 11-C3

The Al Noor Lounge is open, spacious and a perfect place for people watching. It is a pleasant place to relax, with plenty of plush armchairs, although the presence of large screen TVs and the constant comings and goings in the busy lobby means it's full of distractions. The performing jazz pianist adds to the commotion and somehow the waiters seem more interested in the lobby activities than in attending to the needs of diners. If you have time on your hands, the Al Noor Lounge is a great place to hide away from mundane routines, at least for a few hours. High tea, more of a full meal with many little snacks and nibbles, is served from 17:00 until 23:00 and is well worth the BD 3.900 price tag.

Al Osra

Location → - Budaiya
Web/email → na

1769 7558
Map Ref → na

If you are new to the island then this is probably one of the best spots to park yourself and meet the expat gang. Buzzing from 08:00 till the sun goes down, this little coffee shop is smack bang in the centre of one of the handiest shopping centres in the expat-dominated Saar area. Before long you'll become part of the crowd, recognised by all and sundry and swapping gossip and local news with the school-run mums. Known as 'the goldfish bowl', you can't beat it for a quick snack and a lengthy chat. The menu is limited and the fare standard (club sandwiches, beef bacon, eggs and the like), all of which are prepared by the friendly staff. Al Najibi Centre offers banking, an optician, a barbershop, supermarket, video store and gift shops, so it's near impossible to live in Bahrain for long without stopping by for a latte and a chat.

Aroma Café

Location → Seef Mall · Seef
Web/email → na

1725 2343
Map Ref → 3-E1

Hidden in the heart of Seef Mall, the cafe tries to be all things to all people and surprisingly achieves this very successfully. The beach bar kiosk, complete with clay pizza kiln in the middle of the dining area, is surrounded by elegantly dressed tables and the walls are bedecked with Mexican throws and Moroccan carpets. The true spirit of this coffee shop is Arabic though, with unobtrusive Arabic music and mainly local, but very laid-back, clientele. An Italian focus to the menu adds to the sweet confusion and keeps Aroma full most evenings. Mondays are seafood nights with the most popular item being the mixed seafood grill. Prices are decent, portions are substantial and the presentation is impeccable. This interesting, if somewhat hard to find, little spot is a unique retreat for shell-shocked husbands while shopaholic wives strut their stuff in the mall.

Brovar

Location → Shaik Isa Bin Salman Highway
Web/email → na

1787 7343
Map Ref → 13-D4

Brovar is a little oasis on an extremely busy highway. It seems to be the only cafe for miles around and as such can often be quite busy, especially with the young and hip local lads and lassies. Offering light snacks and salads, with an emphasis on pizza, American-style food and American-style big portions and all for great value. Brovar also supplies fabulous fresh juices all served up in front of a large screen TV showing the latest MTV gyrators and on occasion, some sporting events. This place really accommodates the trendy and wannabes and considering there's not much else around, it works and is often pleasantly packed. Its airy, minimalist decor is complemented by the wide-windowed restaurant front that makes it unmissable on the highway.

Cafés & Coffee Shops

Going Out

Café Lilou

Location → Adliya **1771 4440**
Web/email → na Map Ref → 14-C2

Minimalist it most certainly is not. Café Lilou is all decadence and old Paris romance with a plush interior and languid atmosphere. It is primarily known for its delectable cakes, baked in-house, but that's not where the goodness ends. Why not enjoy afternoon tea or come in for a delicious breakfast? You'll find no traditional fry-up though (this place is much too chic for grease); instead, think creamy eggs with luscious smoked salmon, or steaming fragrant mushrooms on toast, each beautifully presented and washed down by fresh fruit juices galore. Whether you're dropping by for lunch or dinner, the menu shifts for bigger, more exotic choices, still healthy and still very posh sounding. There is some room for self-indulgence here, try the big hearty bowls of pastas or a succulent steak.

Café Najjar

Location → Salmaniya Roundabout · Salmaniya **1725 5044**
Web/email → na Map Ref → 13-D2

A calm oasis just beside the busy Salmaniya Roundabout, this is a central spot for a quiet coffee, surprising considering the hustle and bustle outside. Floor to ceiling windows and bright colours give an airy feel to this spacious mixture of modern and traditional meshed and merged into this delightful coffee shop. Café Najjar has a wide variety of Lebanese coffees served in the traditional style along with a selection of nicely presented sandwiches and salads. Comfortable chairs, complementary newspapers and attentive service, coupled with easy parking in the rear, make this a friendly alternative to the usual franchise chains.

Cappuccino Cafe

Location → Nr Jawad Supermarket · Saar **1779 0404**
Web/email → na Map Ref → 3 B3,1

Cappuccino Cafe is a little haven in Saar, away from the rush of the many other coffee shops in the area. With a focus on light breakfasts, quick bites and elegantly presented snacks, this coffee shop is

a step above the rest. With the best fresh juices in Bahrain, the 'Lemon and Mint' is a must-try as is the 'soup-in-a-bun'. Portions are acceptable and prices reasonable. This cafe has an indoor garden feel, with cascading creepers practically obscuring the ceiling and walls. A small outdoor courtyard beckons sun-lovers, but keep in mind that if you're sitting outside, the traffic can be noisy. You won't be overwhelmed with the range of options on the menu nor by the speed of the waiting staff, but for a leisurely rendezvous with friends or a lengthy browse through the daily paper, then the Cappuccino Cafe is ideal.

Cinnabon & Seattle's Best Coffee

Location → Juffair **1753 0010**
Web/email → na Map Ref → na

In Bahrain, Cinnabon operates side by side with Seattle's Best Coffee, a perfect partnership that allows you to indulge your senses to the fullest. A Cinnabon, for the unfortunates who may have yet to have come across the term, is basically what in Europe is referred to as a cinnamon roll. Cinnabons are baked on the premises and are sold piping hot, fresh and sensuously soft. They come warm and indulgently sticky with the sauce of your choice. Eat them on site with a coffee from Seattle's Best's tempting array of macchiatos, mochas and iced drinks or ask for a box of Cinnabons (or the more bite-sized Minibons) to take away, which make excellent gifts for breakfast or luncheon get-togethers – think of how popular you'd be!

Coco's

Location → Adliya **1771 6512**
Web/email → na Map Ref → 14-C2

Rustic-style flooring and cutlery, soft lighting, and a converted Venetian monastery look is not exactly what you'd expect of an eaterie (this is a franchise, right?) big on continental cuisine in super huge portions. If the weather permits, than grab a table outside in the courtyard: it's pretty and you'll appreciate the cool breeze. The food here is reliably good, though the menu won't confuse you with choice. It's pretty straightforward, but in its favour the prices are fair and the shisha is excellent. During the day this is a great place for a late breakfast or a light lunch. In the evenings the charmingly lit courtyard is perfect for meeting with friends, discussing business or for a romantic meal. This is not the place to be in a hurry, the waiting service will remind you of that, so sit back and enjoy the shisha and the quiet.

Delifrance

Location ➜ Jawad Dome · Budaiya   **1769 6031**
Web/email ➜ na   Map Ref ➜ 3-B2

Crammed in the popular Budaiya-based mini-mall called Jawad Dome, Delifrance bakes some of the island's most exquisite cakes and breads on site and the waft of fresh baking alone is enough to make your mouth water. The place is good for the lazy, serving all day breakfast and special menu choices that you can eat in or take away with you. Light snacks, healthy soups, subs and sandwiches are also on the menu, as is delicious espresso and cappuccino to wash your meal down. The atmosphere is a little hectic due to its location (you'll find it in a food court) and the service can be somewhat slow at times. Delifrance's range of dishes is limited but it's just fine for a quick post-shopping snack. A healthy option next to all the fast-food joints which this shopping centre houses.

La Maison du Cafe

Location ➜ Seef Mall and Dana Mall · Seef   **1759 3376**
Web/email ➜ na   Map Ref ➜ 3-E1

La Maison du Cafe in Seef caters for two very distinct clientele: those keen on the Arabic style of dining with mixed cuisines, lounge-style seating and shisha pipes galore and then everyone else. Downstairs, although a quiet place for lunch, features lively Arabic music in the evenings drawing a young crowd. Alcohol is not served, but the young party on regardless till the early hours. Entrance is BD 3 for men and BD 1.500 for women, though a ladies night on Tuesdays is well worth coming down for since entrance and shisha are free. Upstairs is much quieter and nicely arranged in semi-private sections, more suited to families and couples looking for something more relaxing. The decor is lavishly Egyptian while the wait staff are immaculately kitted out in Moroccan traditional

dress. The food is sumptuously presented and consists of an eclectic if fairly pricey collection of elaborate dishes from Arabic and Indian to Moroccan, Tex-Mex and Italian. An enormous selection of juices and shisha is also on offer.

La Ventana

Location ➜ Adliya   **1771 6771**
Web/email ➜ na   Map Ref ➜ 14-C2

La Ventana's home-made and freshly prepared food is its main attraction and it is famed for its fantastic salads. The emphasis is on simple, clean presentation and the enormous selection of interesting sandwiches available. The large salads offer a good selection of unique ingredients and are interestingly topped off with nuts and raisins. Over-stuffed baguettes, out of the ordinary baked potatoes and hearty soups are the makings of La Ventana. The pies are freshly made with that loving homey touch, well filled and full of flavour. While you eat, sit and admire the works of prominent local artists displayed and the colourful, but not loud, decor and furniture that conjures up a cosy, yet bohemian feel. The owners change the colour of the walls and the chair coverings on a monthly basis. Choose from an extensive list of teas and coffees and sit back and relax in this European-style cafe.

Le Chocolat

Location ➜ Seef   **1758 2259**
Web/email ➜ na   Map Ref ➜ 3-E1

Le Chocolat is light, airy and with lots of windows that offer a panoramic view of the Seef area. The wide-open patio at the front is pleasant during the cooler winter months. This qaint coffee shop is well known for its delicious Belgian, Italian and French chocolates all elegantly gift-wrapped if that's the way you want your treats. A French patisserie feeling fills the conservatory-style dining area, which is popular with ladies who lunch and well-heeled shoppers from the home decor store next door. The menu offers a fine selection of cakes and pastas, sandwiches, soups and light main courses, all very well presented with an aesthetic appeal. Portions are good, as are the prices.

Med Cafe

Location → Nr Adliya Post Office · Adliya | **1771 3088**
Web/email → na | Map Ref → 14-B2

The Med Cafe offers a refreshing change to the usual franchise 'been there done that' restaurant. Its cool blue and white decor, quirky underground aquarium and oversized comfy chairs, present a funky different one-of-a-kind look. This is a delightful place to enjoy a light lunch or dinner. The extensive menu presents a budget-priced choice of many Lebanese and Italian dishes including everyone's favourite – Lebanese mezze. Salads and light snacks are well represented on the menu and the waiting staff are always on hand to recommend specials of the day. Themed evenings for students and ladies make this restaurant practically unbeatable for value. The atmosphere is laid back and relaxed making it perfect for quick business lunches or light meals on your way around town. Med Cafe is no run-of-the-mill restaurant and deserves a look-in if you find yourself peckish in Adliya.

THE One

Location → Al Aali Shopping Complex · Seef | **1758 7178**
Web/email → www.theone.me.com | Map Ref → 3-E1

The perfect place for ladies who lunch (or breakfast), but also a quiet and alternative venue for an early evening meal, considering it's set inside the fashionable homeware store with the same name. The decor is to-die-for and is taken from the showrooms. It's not just the furnishings that work, the food is absolutely superb, with an extensive and mouth-watering menu to choose from. There are some classic salads, sandwiches created with a variety of breads, dreamy, creamy fondues and more adventurous items such as chicken with spiced chocolate sauce. The drinks are as delightful as the food. Try the banoffee and rosemary latte. A classy kids' menu with healthy pizzas, sandwiches and a 'kids deli' round off this rather excellent eaterie. The staff are efficient, most obliging and are more than happy to adapt the menu to suit your personal tastes.

Shisha Cafes

Other options → Arabic/Lebanese [p.199]

Shisha cafes are common throughout the Middle East, offering relaxing surroundings and the chance to smoke a shisha pipe (aka 'hookah', 'hubbly bubbly' or 'narghile') with a variety of aromatic flavours. Traditionally the preserve of local men to play backgammon and gossip with friends, these venues are now popular with locals and visitors alike, especially in the cooler winter evenings. Most cafes offer a basic menu of Arabic cuisine and a few international options, plus coffees, teas and fruit juices. So, choose your flavour of shisha, sit back and puff away – this is what life is all about!

Shisha Cafes

Shisha Cafes	
Aroma Café	1725 2343
Casa Blu	1771 0424
Chez la Cafe	na
Coco's	1771 6512
La Ancien Cafe	1700 0000
La Maison du Cafe	1759 3376
Veranda Cafe	na

Afternoon Tea

Other options → Cafes & Coffee Shops [p.223]

The Lobby Lounge

Location → Ritz Carlton Bahrain Hotel & Spa · Seef | **1758 0000**
Web/email → na | Map Ref → 3-E1

Nestled beneath the vast impressive atrium that is the foyer of The Ritz Carlton Hotel lies The Lobby Lounge – an oasis of calm and tranquillity where guests can sip afternoon tea while being serenaded by the dulcet tones of a string quartet. Spoil yourself, this is the loveliest way to spend an afternoon. Alternatively come for a working breakfast and help yourself from the elegant central buffet, or try a fresh wholesome sandwich or a crisp seafood salad for lunch. Feeling a little more indulgent? Then order one of the flavoured frappucinos and a cake freshly baked by the resident pastry chef and displayed in the patisserie across the lobby – that is, if you can decide which delectable delicacy to choose! But of course this is The Ritz, could you imagine it being anything less than fabulous?!

Cafés & Coffee Shops

Going Out

Internet Cafés

Other options → Internet [p.68]

Internet cafes are few and far between, most expats have ADSL at home. Starbucks and Costa offer 'Wi-Fi hotspots' where you can access the internet from your laptop or PDA while perking up with the caffeine of your choice. Funnily enough, there seem to be no restrictions or censorship when it comes to the internet here in Bahrain so proceed with caution. Among the most popular internet cafes on the western side of the island are 7 in 1 upstairs at Spinneys, Al Osra in Budaiya who charge BD 1 per hour, and Cyberzone at Jawad Dome on Budaiya Highway, also BD 1 per hour. Both offer special rates to regular customers.

Food on the Go

Bakeries

In addition to bread, bakeries offer a wonderful range of pastries, biscuits and Lebanese sweets. Arabic foods include 'borek', flat pastries, baked or fried with spinach or cheese, and 'manakish', hot bread, sometimes doubled over and served plain or filled with meat, cheese or 'zatar' (thyme seeds). Biscuits are often filled with ground dates. All are delicious, and should be tried at least once.

Fruit Juices

Other options → Cafes & Coffee Shops [p.223]

All cafes and coffee shops offer fresh juices, light food, sandwiches, cakes and snacks. The fresh juice culture is thriving in Bahrain, be brave with your choice and you will get thrilling vitamin boost. Once you've tried it, you're bound to get hooked and make it a regular staple. They are delicious, healthy and cheap, and made on the spot from fresh fruits such as mango, kiwi, strawberry and pineapple (have the fruit cocktail if you can't decide). Yoghurt is also a popular drink, often served with nuts, and the local milk is called 'laban' (a salty buttermilk that doesn't go well in tea or coffee).

Food in Colour

The delectable *Posh Nosh, Cheap Eats and Star Bars* (by Explorer) has some of the best locations on Dubai's social scene. Packed with independent reviews and stunning images this beautiful book is at home on your coffee table while you're out on the town!

Shawarma

Other options → Arabic/Lebanese [p.199]

Shawarma is a popular local snack consisting of rolled pita bread filled with lamb or chicken carved from a rotating spit, and a bit of salad to boot. You'll see countless roadside restaurants and stands offering shawarma for as little as 250 fils each, and they make a great alternative to the usual fast food of burgers and fries. In residential areas, the small cluster of shops at a mosque is often a good place to start looking for your local shawarma outlet. These restaurants and stands usually sell other dishes, such as 'foul' (a paste made from fava beans) and 'falafel' (or ta'amiya), which are small savoury balls of deep-fried beans. Many also offer freshly squeezed fruit juices for around 300 fils. The Saar/Budaiya area is home to a well-known Lebanese restaurant, Fakhruddin, whose shawarma are extremely popular with expats and locals. On the Budaiya Highway, it is hard to beat Golden Dough take-away for authentic taste. Don't forget to mention your personal preferences to the vendor at the shawarma stand, or you may find yourself dealing with a chip-filled blow-your-brains-out spicy concoction.

Friday Brunch	
Al Noor Lounge	1722 7777
Bapco Club	1775 3377
Beverage Brunch	1771 3093
Blue Elephant	1758 3555
Bustan Hotel	1771 3911
Champagne Brunch	1759 3593
Diplomat Brunch	1752 5201
Fakhruddin	1779 0090
Far East Seafood Ramee	1772 7230
Friday Roast	1771 6999
Jawad Dome	na
Krumz	1771 2767
La Mediterranee	1758 0000
La Mosaique	1753 1122
La Perle	1729 8439
Lunch by the Beach	1729 8008
Nirvana	1758 0000
Seafood Brunch	1753 1122
Sparkling Brunch	1729 8008
Sparkling Brunch	1746 0000
Surf&Turf Buffet	1752 5210
The Exchange Brunch	1774 2000
The Harvesters	1753 1122
Versailles	1722 7777
Warblers	1790 6600
Zytoun	1729 8008

Food on the Go

Going Out

Friday Brunch

Most hotels in Bahrain offer at least one choice of Friday Brunch. The family is a very important unit in Arab culture and it is virtually unthinkable that parents would dine alone on Fridays, the weekly day off. So, should you choose to take advantage of the fantastic offers available for Friday Brunch, expect to see and hear lots of happy noisy families.

Prices vary, some are unbelievably cheap, and most offer excellent value for money. As these listings are subject to change, it is advisable to call and make enquiries in advance.

On the Town

The night life in Bahrain really kicks into action on Wednesday night and goes full throttle till late Friday night. This is not Dubai, but rest assured you will find plenty of opportunity to don your glad rags and let your hair down. If your focus is on quenching your thirst, pubs and bars abound. Dancers can keep their toes twinkling till the small hours of dawn to a variety of live bands and funky and not-so-funky DJs. Music ranges from mainstream pop to Arabic or House. If you want it, it's there. Alternatively, if the cafe culture is what you are after, there are plenty of modern or delightfully atmospheric coffee houses in which to while away the evenings, many of these staying open as late as the clubs.

During the week you may find some places a little on the empty and dreary side but a little detective work will get you to the hot spots – so make sure you know what's on where. Monday night at Likwid, for example, is extremely popular and kicks off with salsa lessons followed by the arrival of the hot and mind-bogglingly superb salsa band. Free buffets at some of the pubs and clubs have a hungry following, though ladies nights being two-a-penny are not necessarily crowd-pullers.

Most pubs do not fill up until around 21:30 or 22:00 and most clubs not until 23:00 or so. Closing times for these establishments are 02:00 but the ingenious can always find spots to keep the parties going. Clientele in the various establishments varies and you will find there are places frequented mostly by muscle-bound men and 'international' girls, looking to take a step up in the world!

For a wilder night, seek out the 'jungle bars' at the one and two-star hotels where anything goes and drinks are cheaper than cheap (although elsewhere drinks are not necessarily that expensive).

Being drunk and disorderly on the street will lead to unequivocal arrest as will drinking in public and driving under the influence. So ditch your bottle when you leave a hostelry and do your best to look respectable. Ladies in groups have relatively little to fear from a safety point of view when out and about on their own, but be prepared to be approached by every passing monstrous white Saudi-registered vehicle. It pays to be fairly sober, well-covered and resolute of face.

Bars

Other options → **Nightclubs [p.223]**
Pubs [p.231]

Bahrain has a fair number of bars, ranging from sports and pub-style to the more glamorous. Mainly hotel-based, most bars open from 23:00 through to 02:00, seven days a week and entrance age is generally 21 plus. There is something to suit all tastes and budgets. (If partying round the clock is your style check out Sizzlers in Mansouri Mansions, Adliya, the only 24-hour licenced restaurant-cum-bar on the island).

At most bars on the expat circuit, such as pubs like JJ Murphy's, expect to find the diversity of culture and race that Bahrain is famous for. You may find yourself holding up the bar with a crowd of interesting Irish, raucous Russians, animated Americans, outrageous Orientals, spirited Arabs and many more nationalities. Elsewhere the multi-cultural crowd usually turns up for special events only, such as football matches. Outside of these times, you will find many establishments populated by a rather 'interesting' crowd among whom you may feel slightly out of place. (See On the Town)

> **Big Night Out**
>
> A safe bet for the new-to-town partier is to start in JJ's pub and from there you can easily progress along the corridor to BJ's nightclub without much mishap. Fall out of the doors later into the welcoming arms of a traditional fish and chip shop, Maggie's Café, before accepting a ride in one of the waiting taxis to regale the driver with the joys of the old newspaper-wrapped chips you once enjoyed on Brighton Pier.

If you grow weary of the many bars offered in hotels, seek those in the expatriate sports and social clubs such as The British Club, Dilmun Club and Rugby Club. Some of these clubs are for members and their guests only, so be sure to call in advance. Alternatively wind down and change the scene with a leisurely drink and snack in one of the island's many stand-alone restaurant & bars.

Door Policy

Entrance to bars and clubs is largely at the management's discretion. Some clubs encourage membership and offer discounts on entrance fees and special nights. This also excuses the big guys on the door when they point to a sign and turn away anyone they consider undesirable. As with clubs the world over, large groups of men will find it harder to get in than those with a few ladies in their midst. A few clubs have stipulations regarding dress code.

Dress Code

Most establishments are likely to turn away men wearing shorts and flip-flops, however young chicks in the same attire will be actively encouraged! Other than that, almost anything goes. The wearing of traditional Arabic dress, thobe and guthra, is frowned upon in the majority of American and European-style clubs and bars. There's a time and a place for everything, just think of where you're going and be logical.

General Bars

Burlington Club

Location → Ritz Carlton Bahrain Hotel & Spa · Seef | 1758 0000
Web/email → na | Map Ref → 3-E1

The Burlington Club at The Ritz-Carlton Bahrain Hotel & Spa is intimate, comfortable and stylish. With leather sofas and winged chairs, it recreates a typical 'gentleman's club' although one where ladies are naturally, very much welcomed. The Cigar Room boasts some fabulous smart drinks and of course a cigar menu that will satisfy the tastes of the pickiest of aficionados who will find the humidor stocked with some of the finest Havana cigars. The early evening crowd of both Arabic and western businessmen can often be tempted to stay by the lively band that kicks in from 20:30.

Casa Bar

Location → Mercure Grand Hotel · Seef | 1758 7400
Web/email → na | Map Ref → 3-E1

This as yet undiscovered plush nightspot is discreetly tucked away on the first floor of the Mercure. A sumptuous spot decorated in modern Arabic style where you can enjoy a happy hour with a 30% discount on all drinks from 18:00 to 20:00 every day. Afterwards an Eastern European jazz duo takes over from 21:00 until 01:00. Upmarket pub grub is available at all times except on Fridays, when for BD 8.500 you can enjoy a sumptuous buffet from 12:00 to 16:00, inclusive of all the sparking wine you can consume. Drinks start from BD 2

Clipper Bar

Location → Regency Intercontinental | 1722 7777
Web/email → www.intercontinental.com/manama Map Ref → 11-E3

For a place that hasn't changed much in 10 years, the Clipper Room is well known to locals and the international clientele who regularly stay at the Regency. The choice of food is as varied as the beer in this pub and the Thursday lunch buffet is a good opportunity to try the much loved traditional roast and trimmings for a mere BD 3.900. On regular nights, enjoy a few pints during happy hour and watch the talented band play your favourite tunes. The atmosphere is always lively and the Clipper Room has established itself somewhat as a leader in showcasing interesting and talented live bands.

Dariush Bar

Location → Al Safir Hotel | 1782 7999
Web/email → www.alsafirhotel.com | Map Ref → 14-E2

The Dariush Bar at the Al Safir hotel is past its heyday. Don't look too close or you'll start counting the cigarette burns on the carpet and curls of paint peeling off the walls. Still, a regular following of local lads and US navy personnel continue to use it as their regular watering hole. A quiet sports bar, the pool table is in high demand by serious players, and the free nightly buffet helps to buff up the numbers. Ladies are few and far between, however those on a night out will not be harassed or feel intimidated by the number ratios. Sports TV plays non-stop, as does an American radio station, however this is not a noisy bar and is a grand place for quiet serious drinkers.

Flamingo Bar

Location → Mövenpick Hotel Bahrain | **1746 0000**
Web/email → www.movenpick-bahrain.com.bh | Map Ref → 2-C4

The Flamingo bar is an excellent classy lounge in which to enjoy a few drinks with that special someone or to pass the evening with a couple of jars and a group of fun friends. Every night is a drinks specials, like the 'two for the price of one' and 'buy one vodka chaser get one free,' so you can imagine what it is that makes the Flamingo bar so popular. Bar snacks are available for the peckish, and of course Silk's restaurant is available next door for some stomach lining. The soft couches in small groupings or standing bar area are both well served by the professional bar staff. An interesting feature is the walk-in wine cellar located between the restaurant and the bar. A Filipino band plays top 20 hits of days gone by to entertain the international clientele, sometimes cheesy, always fun.

On the town

Tracks

Location → Crowne Plaza Bahrain | **1753 2122**
Web/email → www.crowneplaza-bahrain.com | Map Ref → 12-C1

An interesting little place, where its drink and be merry attitude is perfectly harmonised with ambience, atmosphere and good time regulars. Food is not the main priority of the youthful patrons, whose good-natured bantering over beer brings a buzz to this pavilion behind the Crowne Plaza. Good quality but pricey snack food and full on dinner steaks are available from the ever-smiling waitresses. Pool tables, dart boards, big screen TVs and lots of sporting motifs adorn this unashamed boys bar. Alternatively the panoramic windows offer a fine vista across to Muharaq while waiting for the pool table to be free. A central location to take advantage of the '2 meals for BD 3' lunch special, or for a few beers with your mates while watching the big game.

Pubs

Other options → **Bars [p.229]**

Manama boasts a rather small number of lively pubs, all of which are attached to hotels. Clustered around the Adilyia area, these mainly Irish and British pubs host regular theme nights, live music and comedians, while managing to squeeze in a little space for dancing. Ladies are very welcome and can often drink for little or nothing. Although Bahrain's pubs fail to recreate the cosy feeling of a local village pub, they do appeal to an extraordinary mix of clientele and on weekends are usually jam-packed. Major sporting events are often shown on large screen TVs and the atmosphere is always welcoming and friendly toward both sides. Manama's few pubs offer a lively, if rather noisy, place to sup a pint or two.

Fiddler's Green

Location → Diplomat Radisson SAS Hotel | **1753 1666**
Web/email → www.radissonsas.com | Map Ref →12-C2

Fiddler's Green is a very popular watering hole. It seamlessly caters to a wide variety of customers mixing westerners and locals in a relaxed, down-low atmosphere. Come on in and enjoy a wide range of beverages and good Irish-style pub food. Fiddler's has a great casual atmosphere. Come with a group, or enjoy a quiet drink and in spite of the large, sometimes raucous crowds, you can still hear your partner talk. Enjoy their home-cooked Irish stew or delicious shepherd's pie. Don't miss the carvery roast, choice of beef or lamb, every night (except Friday) 19:00 to 22:00, all for BD 4 and that includes a free half-pint of lager. Fiddler's is one of the only pubs in the country not to have given way to the DJ disco scene. The place is the quintessential London city pub, rowdy Irish country pub and up market hotel bar all rolled into one. Not an easy combination but one achieved very successfully by Fiddler's friendly management and staff.

Harvesters

Location → Crowne Plaza Bahrain   **1753 1122**
Web/email → www.crowneplaza-bahrain.com   Map Ref → 12-C1

Early on in the evening, Harvesters is a typical hotel bar with small groups of Western and Arab businessmen unwinding in hushed surroundings. Later a raucous Filipino rock band transforms the sleepy bar into a quasi-concert venue with their scantily clad dancers and toe-tapping numbers. There is an extensive cocktail list and every night of the week (except Thursdays) there's a different drinks promotion, from free drinks for ladies (Mondays) to extra cheap pitchers of beer (Wednesdays). The food is served in ample portions and is of a standard that you would expect from a top class joint.

JJ's Irish Pub

Location → Adliya   **1774 2323**
Web/email → na   Map Ref → 14-B1

Known generally as JJ's this is undoubtedly one of the best bars on the island. Popular and busy and boasting a genuinely mixed crowd of all nationalities and age groups, JJ's is a large Irish pub with the still amusing 'Limerick this way' signs. Downstairs has a lengthy bar, plenty of standing and sitting room and modest dancing space. Upstairs there's a balcony with its own smaller bar and a few pool tables. The food is decent and comes in fine healthy-sized portions – the stuff any Irish pub in the emerald isle would be

proud of. The music is mainstream and at a perfect volume to dance to or, if conversing, to be just heard but not deafened. Theme nights as follows:

Every night except Thursday – Ladies Night: pay a small entry fee and then drink all night long for free.

Sunday – Quiz Night with Paul Magill as quizmaster.

Monday – Karaoke Night.

Tuesday – DJ Krazy Kev, with prizes and funny money to be won from 21:00 onwards.

Wednesday – 60s, 70s, 80s and 90s Night: dress to impress.

Saturday – Cocktail Night: special offers on jugs of cocktails with KJ Koorosh (DJ Knight).

Maguires Irish Pub

Location → Mansouri Mansions   **1771 6999**
Web/email → na   Map Ref → 14-B3

Maguires very much resembles a real Irish pub. It is all very plain and simple, with Irish fiddles, Guinness posters and other knick-knacks from the good old days on the walls. Unlike the more modern pseudo-Irish pubs, which are far too shiny and full of flat-screen TVs to be anywhere near authentic, Maguire's has that slightly tired and musty feel of the real thing. Weekdays are quiet and ideal if you want to stay far from the madding crowd. It also makes for a perfect hideaway for a late night jar on the way home. Weekends and lunchtimes, however, are more convivial. Live entertainment consists of watching the barmaid, suffering from cross-cultural confusion, furiously scoop the froth off your soon-to-be-not creamy pint of Guinness, so watch carefully and instruct accordingly! Typical pub food such as steak and kidney pie as well interesting renditions of Gaelic cuisine are served along with a mish-mash of familiar international dishes cooked to the decent standards of its parent hotel.

Warbler

Location → Baisan International Hotel   **1729 0128**
Web/email → www.warblerbar.com   Map Ref → 12-C3

The Warbler is situated slightly off the beaten track in the Baisan International Hotel, off Exhibition

Avenue. It is a sprawling affair all in pub style. A more private lounge-room contains two dart boards and the back room is home to two pool tables. A popular venue that draws in large crowds of guys in the partying mood and gals interested in entertaining them, the Warbler prides itself on its dedication to sport and contains two huge screens and numerous other smaller TVs so you can watch all sorts of different games at once. Major events draw large crowds and tend to bring in a more respectable clientele. Bands and DJs play boisterously throughout the week and Monday's free buffet draws a large crowd. The food is a mixture of International, Asian and traditional pub grub all served at reasonable prices. Friday Brunch is also on offer. Special nights as follows:

Saturday and Sunday – live sporting events.

Monday – free buffet between 19:00 - 22:00. Menu changes weekly and includes live cooking.

Tuesday – Karaoke from 21:00 - 02:00, sing for your free Tequila!

Tuesday - Friday – Happy Hour, BD 1 per drink between 17:00 and 19:00.

Friday – brunch: BD 9 with unlimited bubbly, BD 5 without.

Wrangler

Location → Elite Hotel
Web/email → www.wranglerbar.com

1782 7600
Map Ref → 14-E2

One of the few night spots in Juffair, Wrangler (D' Wild West Saloon) is a busy hangout, particularly at weekends. This quirky ranch-style pub is full of old Wild West paraphernalia and seeped in heavy duty Americana. A pool table and the availability of cocktails and shooters sets off the theme. There is a reasonable sized dance floor and a DJ is in full force every night of the week. The music is fairly mainstream but definitely loud so hardly the place for a quiet night or a relaxed drink. Be sure to wear white to show off your tan under the UV lights. A Tex Mex menu is available all day, every day at reasonable prices. Theme nights as follows:

Saturday – Spin the Wheel night: every hour, on the hour, all beverages BD 1.

Sunday and Tuesday – Ladies Night: free beverages for ladies all night long.

Monday – BD 1 night.

Wednesday – free dinner buffet and all regular beverages BD 0.500 from 20:00 – 22:00.

Thursday – BD 9 night, unlimited beverages 8.00pm till close

Friday Brunch – Wild West Brunch from 12:00 noon onwards

Nightclubs

Other options → Dinner Cruises [p.222]
Belly Dancing [p.148]

Talk to even the wildest party-goer and they will acknowledge that there are only really three or four nightclubs that are worth their salt or that meet European or American expectations. JJ's (which is actually a pub), BJ's just next door and Likwid, which is hit and miss, as is Al Layali at the Diplomat Hotel. Other clubs tend to be a bit tawdry depending on the clientele but can often liven up for special events or sporting fixtures. If you are looking for something a bit more classy altogether, some of the restaurants have live entertainment late into the night where the atmosphere hots up as the night goes on. Try Asia in City Centre Hotel for a hip DJ and young crowd or Zoe for more sophistication. Trader Vics at the Ritz-Carlton offers the five-star cocktail treatment where you are guaranteed a sophisticated evening swaying to the cool Cuban band. If it's an 'alternative' night out you want, amble round to the one and two-star hotels for all manner of strange goings on from Filipino karaoke to beautifully attired Eastern European ladies trying their hand at singing but doing a better job at smiling coyly to the appreciative male onlookers. Arabic and Indian shows are everywhere, ideal if puffing on shisha in a dark basement appeals to you. All in all, a good bet for stag parties. Be friendly and polite and the doormen will be charming.

Al Layali

Location → Sheraton Bahrain Hotel & Towers
Web/email → na

1753 3533
Map Ref → 12-A2

A spot for the night owls, this unashamedly western nightclub could be in Paris, New York or Milan. A DJ plays a steady stream of house and rock music to a mixed audience of hip trendy Bahrainis and Westerners. The combination of lounge service and comfortable armchairs provides a welcoming respite from the busy yet spacious dance floor. The

Nightclubs

Going Out

polite but firm door staff have clear views about the smart/casual dress code so no ripped jeans! Best enjoyed at the weekends, get there before midnight to make the absolute most of a 50% discount on the BD 4 entrance.

BJ's

Location ➜ Nr Al Bustan Hotel · Adliya   **1771 6062**
Web/email ➜ na   Map Ref ➜ 14-B1

BJ's is the closest you will find to a Western-style nightclub, from the music and clientele to the decor. There is normally a good crowd, who largely roll up the stairs from JJ's, and consist of a mixture of older expats and younger folk. Leaning on the cheesy side, the dance floor is a good size with a small stage area, mirrors all over the place and an overwhelming sense of sultry red thanks to both the decor and lighting. Upstairs is another bar, purple velvet sofas to take a load off and a gallery that overlooks the dance-floor. Music is generally mainstream pop to suit most tastes and the volume is just right. A VIP area can be hired out for private gatherings. Theme nights as follows:

Monday, Wednesday, Friday and Sunday – Ladies Night.

Wednesday – Crew Night.

Saturday and Tuesday – Dinar Night.

Music policy: Friday – House; Saturday and Sunday – R&B.

Diggers

Location ➜ Delmon International Hotel   **1722 4000**
Web/email ➜ na   Map Ref ➜ 12-E3

One of older bars on the island, Diggers is an undemanding pub, with few concessions to modern fashions. If you want a wholesome steak and a few beers with the lads then Diggers is just the place. Situated downtown, just 50 metres from Gold City, Diggers – with its massive TV screen – is very popular for big games and of course for F1 races. The food is very reasonably priced and ample portions will help soak up the wide variety of beer available. With the longest happy hour in the Kingdom (from noon to 21:00) and regular dinner specials, Diggers is a real hit with Western males.

F1

Location ➜ Metropolitan Hotel   **1729 6464**
Web/email ➜ www.club1_bahrain.net   Map Ref ➜ 12-C3

Perched on the edge of the Arabic entertainment strip that is Exhibition Avenue, F1, like the nearby Warbler, is a Westerner's nightspot and busy most nights of the week. At weekends the thirsty crowd can make it hard to reach either of the two well-stocked bars. A regular winner of the Battle of the Bands competition, the New Zealand cover band draws a loyal following with the young, while big-game nights draw all age-groups. International food is available for reasonable prices in a partially soundproofed area overlooking the dance floor.

Likwid

Location ➜ City Centre Hotel   **1722 9979**
Web/email ➜ na   Map Ref ➜ 11-E3

Likwid has the advantage of being a small and intimate club. The decor is modern and clean and above all 'cool'. Regular and popular DJs play on Wednesdays, Thursdays and Fridays and guest DJs are brought in twice a month, though the club can often be fairly empty. The place really comes into its own on Monday nights when the hotter than hot salsa band, La Movida, takes the floor. From 20:00 you can learn the salsa steps and then when the band kick off at 21:30, you can practise your moves. The atmosphere has a real buzz as some of the more professional (or brave) dancers take to the floor and others come just for the music and to relish those South American beats as the party goes on.

The best quality alcohol is served behind the bar and a funky cocktail list is on offer at reasonable prices so go for an Italian Stallion, Likwid Lover or some more risqué option. Likwid also has a private room behind the main club that is open on Wednesdays for wine-tasting. For BD 2.500 you can try six different wines (repeatedly) and sample from trays of nibbles. A popular start to a night out.

> ### Food in Colour
>
> The delectable **Posh Nosh, Cheap Eats and Star Bars** (by Explorer) has some of the best locations on Dubai's social scene. Packed with independent reviews and stunning images this beautiful book is at home on your coffee table while you're out on the town!

Pulse Discotheque

Location → Al Safir Hotel
Web/email → www.alsafirhotel.com

1782 7999
Map Ref →4-C2

A pulsating rave beat thunders out from Pulse at the side of the Al Safir Hotel in the rapidly developing Juffair area. This is one of the most popular western-style nightclubs for Arabs in Manama and at weekends is packed to the gills with a heaving mass of Gulf male nationals. The timber bar and floors are more reminiscent of a traditional pub, but the music is uncompromisingly cutting edge. Thursday nights it's BD 6 to enter, and BD 3 every other night.

Sharwarma

Rock Bottom Café

Location → Ramee International Hotel
Web/email → na

1772 7230
Map Ref → 14-E3

Rock Bottom is a lively venue offering a good selection of beverages and food with a good standard of Western-style entertainment. A heavy American theme carries this nightclub, but pleasantly there's plenty of space, pool tables, big eats on the menu, and gleaming Harley Davidsons for extra ambience. There is a dress code so no shorts for the boys and be prepared to have your bags checked on your way in. The live band keeps the party going every night except Mondays and

the bar stays open till 02:00. Theme nights as follows:

Monday – BD 1.500 all night on selected drinks only.

Wednesday – From Russia with Love: vodka with a mixer free for ladies.

Thursday – 18:00 - 22:00, pay BD 9.500 and drink all night.

Female cabin crew – flash your ID and drink a vodka and mixer whenever you please.

Tabasco Charlie's

Location → Adhari Hotel
Web/email → na

1722 4242
Map Ref → 11-E4

Always a popular haunt, the catchy named nightclub is lovingly known as TC's and is one of the largest nightclubs in Manama, with two bars, pool table, dining area and an active dance floor. The clientele is a mixture of lonely men and welcoming Asian ladies. Service is swift and the food is surprisingly good and very reasonably priced. A resident Filipino band drives the crowd to a frenzy with a pulsating stream of heavy rock classics. Wednesday and Thursday nights are best to see TC's at its most frenetic.

Entertainment

Cinemas

Manama knows how to do cinema. Modern movie theatres are well decked out with extremely comfortable seating and good quality sound and visuals. Opening hours are from 11:00 until around 02:00 and you will often find you have the cinema practically to yourself, since it's not particularly popular with the locals here. Many cinemas tend to be attached to a ultra-modern shopping mall where you can continue your retail therapy after watching the latest movie.

Movies tend to be shown in Bahrain only a few weeks after the European and American release dates. Expect any scenes with sexual content to fall foul of the censor's scissors. However, numerous violent images somehow avoid the chop. Be forewarned that the previews shown before a family rated movie may be unsuitable for young children.

Although films carry the international gradings PG, G, 13+, 15+ and 18+, tickets vendors seem to ignore these ratings when selling to minors.

Tickets are priced at BD 2.500 pp. Popcorn and soft drinks are always available on-site and delicious – but at the movies popcorn always tastes good!

The vast majority of movies are in English, often with Arabic subtitles. A small selection of Arabic and Hindi movies are shown, but hardly any avante garde or independent films make it over. Movie listings change every Wednesday so check local press for new releases and timings.

Cinemas

Al Jazeera Cineplex	1786 4666
Awal Cinema	1786 4666
Dana Mall Cinema	1755 8558
Saar Cineplex	1779 3444
Seef Cineplex 1(West)	1758 2220
Seef Cineplex 2(East)	1758 2220

Comedy

Skylight Lounge

Location → Diplomat Radisson SAS Hotel | 1753 1666
Web/email → www.diplomatrdsas.com.bh | Map Ref → 12-C2

The only regular and exclusive comedy nights in Bahrain are held monthly in the Skylight Bar in the Diplomat Hotel by the Guinness Comedy Club. Comedians, mostly from the UK doing the Middle East 'circuit,' drop in to entertain a usually very British audience with their biting British banter. The Skylight Bar is set atop the hotel and commands a wonderful view of the city. The venue is just the right size to give that squished-in convivial atmosphere in which to sip a pint, split your sides laughing or, if the guy is a dud, to admire the view. See local press for times and dates.

Concerts

There is no special concert venue in Bahrain at the moment although all that might be about to change with the arrival of an 800-seater auditorium as part of the National Museum. Most concerts take place in the big hotels. Some of these hotels also have talented Eastern Europeans performing what can only be described as background music, although some of the music is recital-worthy (especially at the Ritz where a trio usually plays in the foyer).

Classical Music is a small but growing art-form on the island. The Manama Singers are bastions of this genre and put on regular concerts throughout the year in a variety of venues. For more high-profile performances, like Mozart's Requiem for example, they fly in professional soloists and instrumentalists for the occasion and achieve an excellent standard.

The Young Musician of the Gulf is also held annually in Bahrain during the spring. Young hopefuls from Bahrain and all over the Gulf compete for a place in the final in this musical talent show case.

The Bahrain Music Festival is held in the autumn and features the resident Bahraini orchestra. Most of the music is Arabic but the organizers are now opening the doors to a wider variety of European music.

If it's more rock and pop you are after, the Ritz-Carlton Hotel hosts sporadic appearances of internationally famous pop stars in a special make-shift outdoor venue. Last year saw Brian Ferry entertain the nostalgic children of the 80s, while Westlife came to woo the teenage crowd. Tickets for such events sell for around BD 22 pp.

Then there is the vastly popular 'Battle of the Bands' held annually in August. This competition can be entered by any band which wishes to register and includes Filipino, Arabic, British, Russian bands and more. The finals are held in a large hotel venue and are attended by crowds of about 3,000.

Other expat clubs and societies also fly in well-known wannabes such as 'Surely Bassey' and a plethora of Beatles copy bands. Bands of every variety (especially Filipino) play nightly at the bars and night-clubs. For the scintillating sounds of salsa check out La Movida who play at Likwid on a Mondays.

Jazz and all things pertaining to it can be found in the form of dinner concerts at the restaurant Upstairs Downstairs with live entertainment nightly. They have an excellent regular jazz pianist and some visiting bands and are further promoting this genre by flying in internationally renowned artists on a monthly basis for their Friday Night Live. It's not quite Ronnie Scott's, but good for Bahrain.

Fashion Shows

Fashion shows in Bahrain are rare occurrences and seem to be arranged on a sporadic basis with no rhyme or reason, and certainly no commitment to timings.

Judy Dodwell of the Visual Image Modelling Agency holds a quarterly fashion show for aspiring super-models at the Dilmun Club. This low-key event features ethnic and Arab fashions. Members of the public are welcome, tickets will set you back BD 3.500, but include a buffet dinner. Call 3963 2446 for more details.

Designer's boutiques located at the Sheraton Complex occasionally organize fashion shows displaying leading style brands to potential customers. The GDN newspaper is the best source for information on this.

The Regency Intercontinental Hotel periodically hosts hair, make-up and fashion shows often featuring a leading foreign designer on a visit to the island. Again, check local press for details.

Theatre

Other options → Drama Groups [p.150]

There is not an awful lot by way of theatre in Bahrain. The Bahrain Golden Tulip hosts about three productions a year by a professional theatre group flown in from the UK. These take the form of dinner theatre and are great social events, standards usually being quite high and prices around BD 25 per ticket and BD 29 on the opening gala night. Other enthusiastic amateur theatre groups put on regular performances usually at expat clubs notably the British Club, Rugby Club, Dilmun Club and the Awali Hall. The Indian Club has its own blossoming and innovative group who perform plays written by their members and often written in a number of different languages. There are several Arabic language theatre groups who perform on special state occasions and at the university. From comedy to thriller to panto, theatre productions in Bahrain are eagerly anticipated and well attended.

Eating out is the spice of life!

Maps

Maps

User's Guide

To further assist you in locating your destination, we have superimposed additional information, such as main roads, roundabouts and landmarks, on the maps. Many places listed throughout the guidebook also have a map reference alongside, so you know precisely where you need to go (or what you need to tell the taxi driver).

The overview map on this page is at a scale of approximately 1:400,000 (1 cm = 4km), maps 2-10 are at a scale 1:50,000 (1 cm = 500m) and maps 11-14 are at 1:15,000 (1cm = 150m).

Technical Info - Satellite Images

The maps in this section are based on rectified QuickBird satellite imagery taken in 2005.

The QuickBird satellite was launched in October 2001 and is operated by DigitalGlobe(tm), a private company based in Colorado (USA). Today, DigitalGlobe's QuickBird satellite provides the highest resolution (61 cm), largest swath width and largest onboard storage of any currently available or planned commercial satellite.

MAPS geosystems are the Digital Globe master resellers for the Middle East, West, Central and East Africa. They also provide a wide range of mapping services and systems. For more information, visit www.digitalglobe.com (QuickBird) and www.maps-geosystems.com (mapping services) or contact MAPS geosystems on (+971 0) 6 572 5411.

Online Maps

If you want to surf for maps online, www.bh.map24.com and www.maporama.com are worth a look. Hardcore map fans though are recommended to try Google Earth (http://earth.google.com). This amazing program (you download it from the site) combines satellite imagery, detailed maps, and a powerful search capability, allowing you to fly between various points on the globe and zoom in for incredibly detailed views.

Community & Street Index

The following is a list of the main cities, towns, roads and communities in Bahrain, which are referenced on the map pages. Many roads are longer than one grid reference, in which case the main grid reference has been given.

Town/City	Map Ref	Town/City	Map Ref
Hamad Town	5-C3, 7D2	Manama	4-C1
Isa Town	3-E4, 5E1	Dumistan	5-B4
Sitra	6-D2	Muharraq	2-B4
Riffa	6-A3	Awali	8-A1
West Riffa	5-D3	Jidhafs	3-E2
East Riffa	6-B3	Hawar Islands	1-C4

Bahrain Areas	Map Ref	Bahrain Areas	Map Ref
A'ali	5-E1	Mina Salman	4-D3
Abu Ashirah	14-A3	Naim	11-D4
Abu Ghazal	14-A4	Nuwaidrat	6-C3
Adliya	4-B2	Quraifa	4-C3
Arad	2-C4	Ras Abu Jarsor	8-D2
Awadiya	12-A3	Ras Hayan	8-E4
Bab Al Bahrain	11-E3	Ras Romman	12-B3
Barbar	3-B2	Salmabad	3-D4
Bilad Al Qadim	13-B3	Salmaniya	13-E1
Budaiya	3-A2	Sanabis	11-A4
Dhuwawdah	12-B3	Seef	3-E1
Galali	2-D3	Suqaya	14-A3
Ghufool	13-D1	Suwayfiyah	11-C4
Hoora	12-C3	Tubli	4-A4
Juffair	14-D3	Zararie	11-E4
Kanu	12-A3	Zinj	13-C3
Mahooz	14-B4		

Introduction

Maps

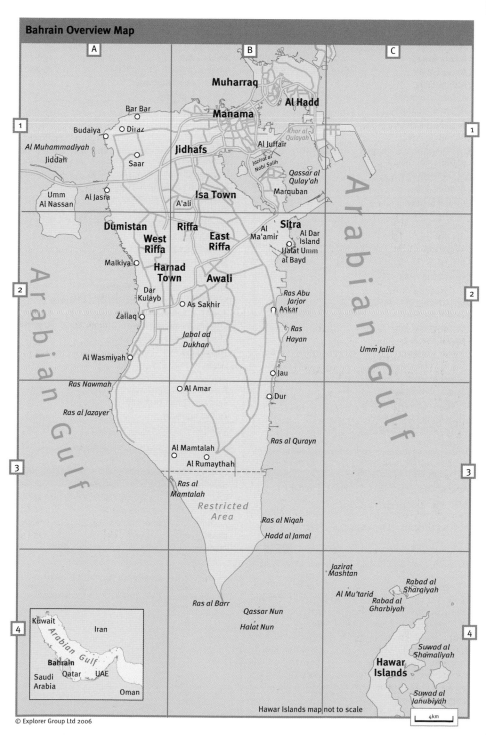

Bahrain Overview Map

Muharraq

Al Hadd

Manama

Bar Bar

Budaiya   Diraz

Al Muhammadiyah

Jiddah   Saar

Jidhafs

Al Juffair

Khor al
Qulayah

Jazirat al
Nabi Salih

Qassar al
Qulay'ah

Marquban

Isa Town

A'ali

Umm
Al Nassan   Al Jasra

Dumistan   Riffa

West
Riffa   East
Riffa

Al
Ma'amir

Sitra

Al Dar
Island

Halat Umm
al Bayd

Malkiya

Hamad
Town

Awali

Dar
Kulayb

Zallaq

As Sakhir

Jabal ad
Dukhan

Ras Abu
Jarjor

Askar

Ras
Hayan

Umm Jalid

Al Wasmiyah

Ras Nawmah

Jau

Al Amar

Dur

Ras al Jazayer

Ras al Qurayn

Al Mamtalah

Al Rumaythah

Ras al
Mamtalah

Restricted
Area

Ras al Niqah

Hadd al Jamal

Jazirat
Mashtan

Rabad al
Sharqiyah

Al Mu'tarid

Rabad al
Gharbiyah

Ras al Barr

Qassar Nun

Halat Nun

Arabian Gulf

Arabian Gulf

Kuwait   Iran

Arabian Gulf

Bahrain

Saudi
Arabia   Qatar   UAE

Oman

Hawar
Islands

Suwad al
Shamaliyah

Suwad al
Janubiyah

Hawar Islands map not to scale

4km

© Explorer Group Ltd 2006

1

Maps

Street Name	Map Ref
Abdulla Ave	12-A3
Adliya Ave	4-C3
Airport Ave	2-B4
Al Fadel Ave	4-D1
Al Fatih Highway	4-C2, 12-C2
Al Ghous Highway	2-B4
Al Hidd Highway	2-D4
Al Khalifa Ave	2-C4
Al Fadel Ave	2-C4
Al Mutanibi Ave	14-A1
Al Qadisiya Ave	13-E2
Amman Ave	4-A4
Arad Highway	2-C4
Aradous Highway	2-D3
Avenue 10	4-D1
Avenue 20	2-B3
Avenue 23	4-A4
Awal Ave	14-D2
Bani Otbah Ave	14-B1
Budaiya Highway	3-B2, 12-B1
Central Market Ave	11-D4
Exhibition Ave	4-C1, 12-C2
Government Ave	11-E3
Gudaibiya Ave	12-C4
Hawar Highway	6-C4
Isa Al Kabeer Ave	4B1, 12-A2
Jamal Al Deen Al Afgani Ave	2-B4
Janabiyah Highway	3-A3
Khalifa Al Kabir Highway	4-D1
King Fahad Causeway	5-A1
King Faisal Highway	4-B1
Kuwait Ave	14-A2

Street Name	Map Ref
Lulu Ave	11-D4
Mahooz Ave	14-C4
Mahzoora Ave	6-B2
Majlis Tawon Highway	4-C4
Mazara Highway	6-B3
Muscat Ave	4-A4
Oman Ave	13-E3
Palace Ave	12-B4
Riffa Ave	5-E3
Salmania Ave	4-B2
Sehla Highway	3-E3
Sheikh Bin Salman Highway	4-A3
Sheikh Hamad Causeway	12-D1
Sheikh Isa Bin Salman Causeway	2-A4
Sheikh Khalifa Bin Salman Highway	3-D3
Sheikh Daij Ave	14-C1
Sheikh Hamad Ave	2-B4
Sheikh Hamad Causeway	5-C3
Sheikh Isa Ave	4-C2
Sheikh Isa Bin Salman Highway	3-D3
Sheikh Jaber Bin Ahmed Alsubah Highway	6-C3
Sheikh Khalifa Bin Salman Causeway	3-D3
Sheikh Mohammed Ave	13-E1
Sheikh Salman Highway	3-E4
Suwailiyah Ave	11-C4
Um Al Nassan Ave	6-A2
Umm Al Hassam Ave	6-A2
Wali Al Ahed Highway	5-B1
Zaid Bin Oman Highway	5-B3
Zallaq Highway	7-C3
Zubara Ave	12-B4

Map Legend

E Embassy/Consulate	**S** Souk/Shopping Centre	**ARAD** Town Name
H Hotel	**O** Hospital	Motorway
M Museum	**SITRA** Area Name	Main Road

Map page 1 is at a scale of 1:400,000 (1cm = 4km)
Map pages 2-10 are at a scale of 1:50,000 (1cm = 500m)
Map pages 11-14 are at a scale of 1:15,000 (1cm = 150m)

Community & Street Index

Maps

2006 | BAHRAIN EXPLORER

Bahrain Map Sheet Index

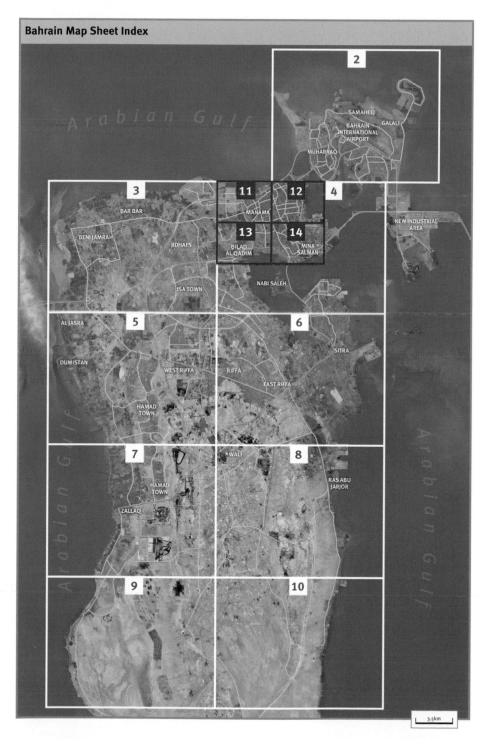

Maps

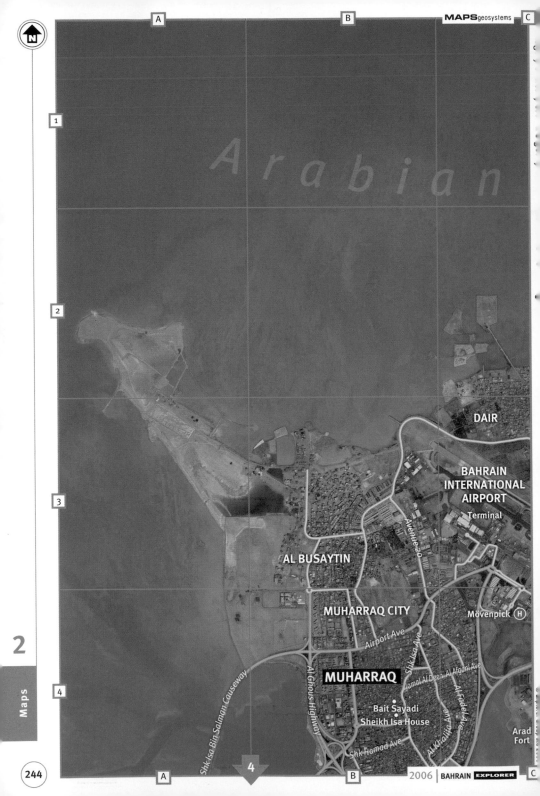

1

A r a b i a n

2

DAIR

BAHRAIN
INTERNATIONAL
AIRPORT

3

Terminal

AL BUSAYTIN

Avenue 20

MUHARRAQ CITY

Mövenpick (H)

Airport Ave

Shk Isa Ave

2

Maps

4

MUHARRAQ

Shk Isa Bin Salman Causeway

Al Ghous Highway

Jamal Al Deen

Al Afgani Ave

Al Fadel Ave

Al Khalifa Ave

Bait Sayadi
Sheikh Isa House

Shk Hamad Ave

Arad
Fort

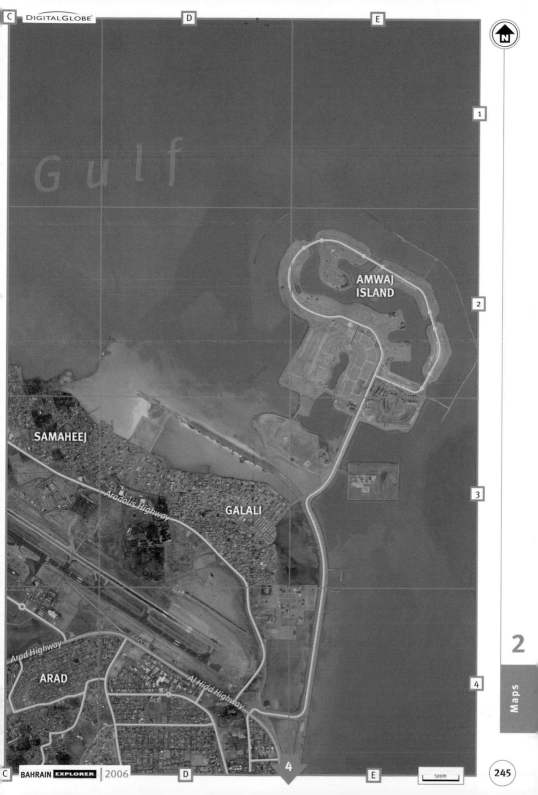

Gulf

AMWAJ
ISLAND

SAMAHEEJ

Aradous Highway

GALALI

Arad Highway

ARAD

Al Hidd Highway

DIGITALGLOBE

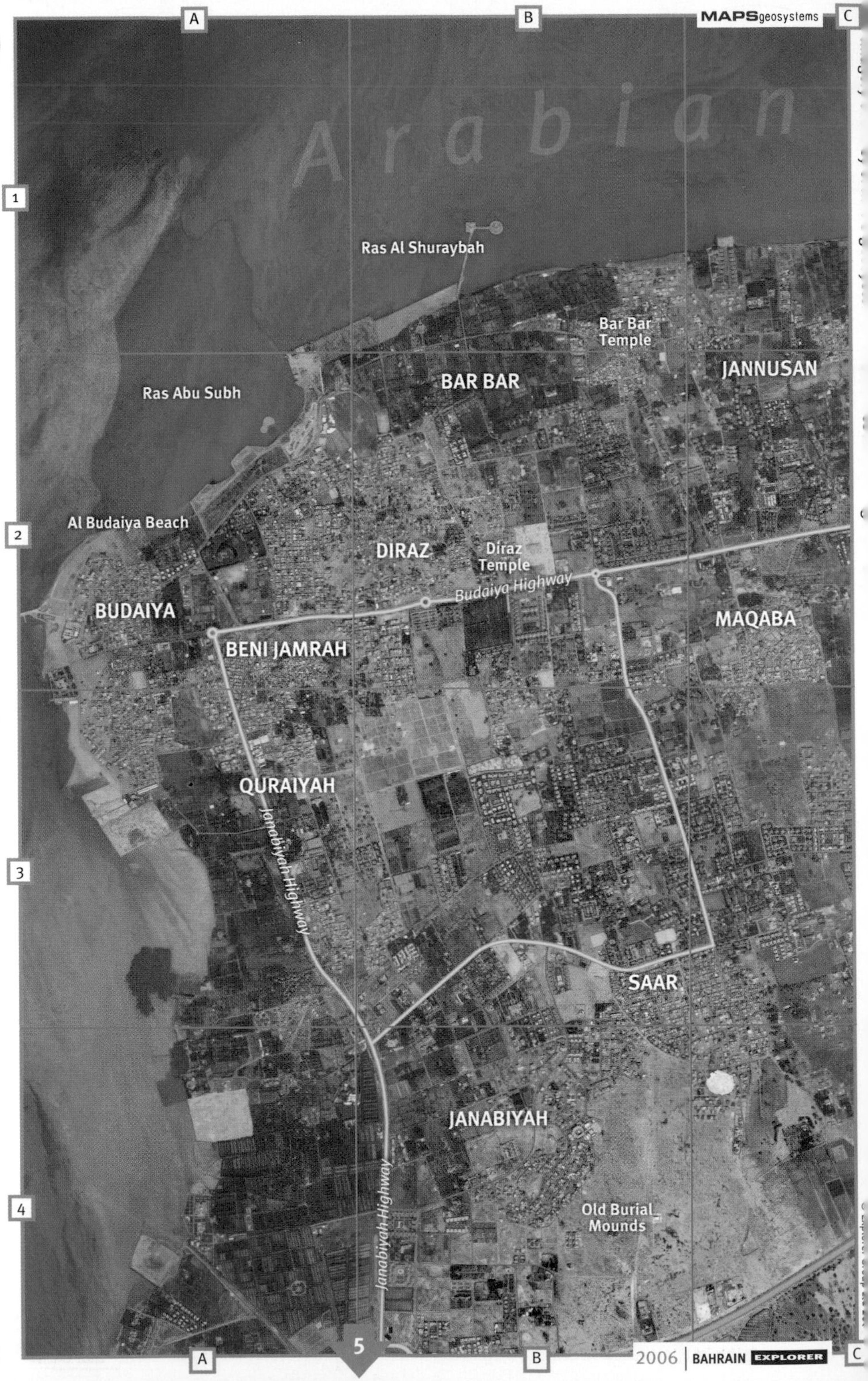

Arabian

Ras Al Shuraybah

Bar Bar
Temple

BAR BAR

JANNUSAN

Ras Abu Subh

Al Budaiya Beach

DIRAZ

Diraz
Temple

Budaiya Highway

MAQABA

BUDAIYA

BENI JAMRAH

QURAIYAH

Janabiyah Highway

SAAR

JANABIYAH

Janabiyah Highway

Old Burial
Mounds

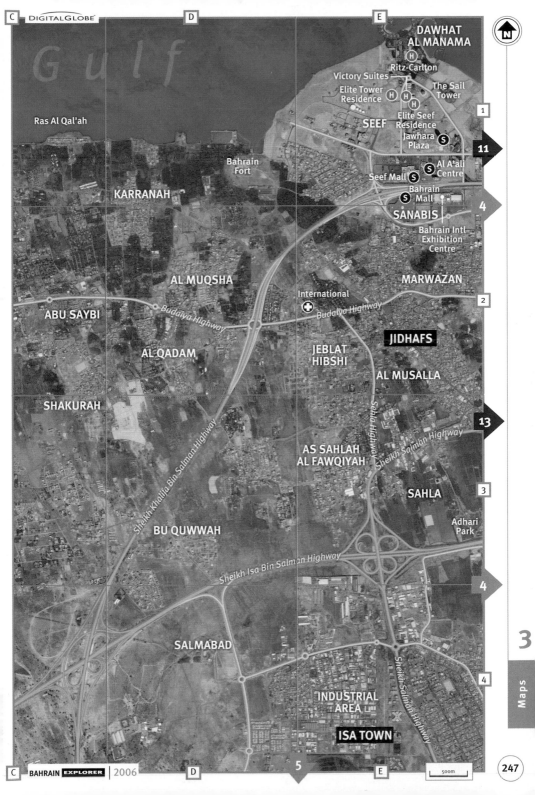

Gulf

DAWHAT
AL MANAMA

Ritz-Carlton
Victory Suites
Elite Tower
Residence
The Sail
Tower

Ras Al Qal'ah

Elite Seef
Residence

SEEF

Jawhara
Plaza

11

Bahrain
Fort

Al A'ali
Centre

KARRANAH

Seef Mall

Bahrain
Mall

4

SANABIS

Bahrain Intl
Exhibition
Centre

AL MUQSHA

MARWAZAN

International

2

ABU SAYBI

Budaiya Highway

Budaiya Highway

JIDHAFS

AL QADAM

JEBLAT
HIBSHI

AL MUSALLA

SHAKURAH

Sheikh Khalifa Bin Salman Highway

Sebla Highway

Sheikh Salman Highway

13

AS SAHLAH
AL FAWQIYAH

SAHLA

3

Adhari
Park

BU QUWWAH

Sheikh Isa Bin Salman Highway

4

SALMABAD

Sheikh Salman Highway

3

Maps

4

INDUSTRIAL
AREA

ISA TOWN

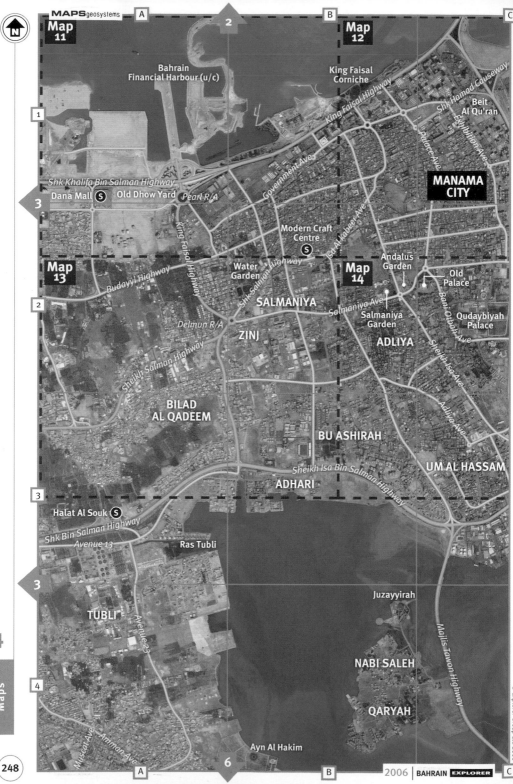

Bahrain
Financial Harbour (u/c)

King Faisal
Corniche

King Faisal Highway

Shk Hamad Causeway

Beit
Al Qu'ran

MANAMA
CITY

Shk Khalifa Bin Salman Highway

Dana Mall (S)   Old Dhow Yard   Pearl R/A

Government Ave

Modern Craft
Centre (S)

Map 13

King Faisal Highway

Budayyi Highway

Water
Garden

Shk Salman Highway

Andalus
Garden

Old
Palace

Map 14

Bani Otbah Ave

Qudaybiyah
Palace

SALMANIYA

Salmaniya Ave

Salmaniya
Garden

Delmun R/A

ZINJ

ADLIYA

Sheikh Isa Ave

Sheikh Salman Highway

BILAD
AL QADEEM

BU ASHIRAH

Adliya Ave

UM AL HASSAM

Sheikh Isa Bin Salman Highway

ADHARI

Halat Al Souk (S)

Shk Bin Salman Highway
Avenue 13   Ras Tubli

Juzayyirah

Majlis Tawon Highway

TUBLI

Avenue 23

NABI SALEH

QARYAH

Ayn Al Hakim

© Explorer Group Ltd 2006

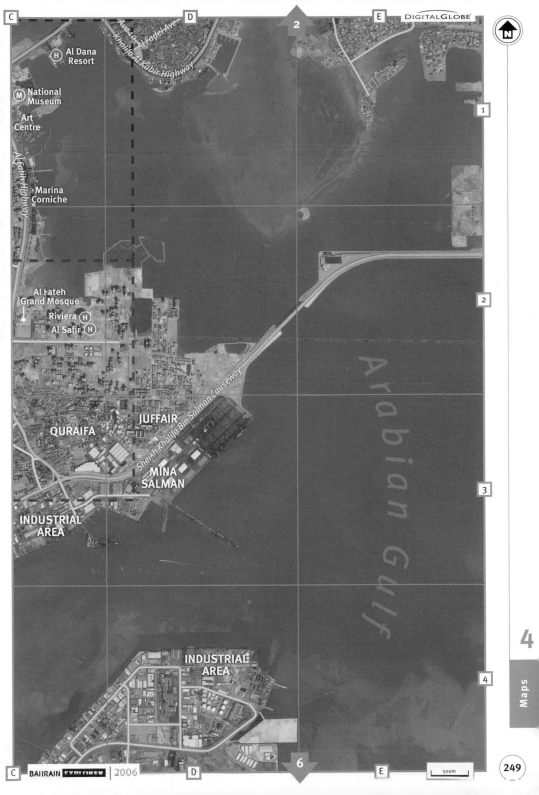

Al Dana Resort

National Museum

Art Centre

Al Faidi Highway

Marina Corniche

Al Fateh Grand Mosque

Riviera

Al Safir

Ave-2o · Al Fadel Ave
Khalifa Al Kabir Highway

JUFFAIR

QURAIFA

MINA SALMAN

Sheikh Khalifa Bin Salman Causeway

INDUSTRIAL AREA

INDUSTRIAL AREA

Arabian Gulf

1

2

3

4

4

Maps

King Fahad Causeway

AL JASRA

Al Jasrah
Handicraft Centre

Al Jasrah
House

Wadi-Al-Ahed Highway

HAMALA

Wadi-Al-Ahed Highway

Al Lazwi
Lake

Zaid-Bin-Oman Highway

Old Burial
Mounds

DUMISTAN

Arabian Gulf

Jazirat
Ya'suf

5

Maps

© Explorer Group Ltd 2006

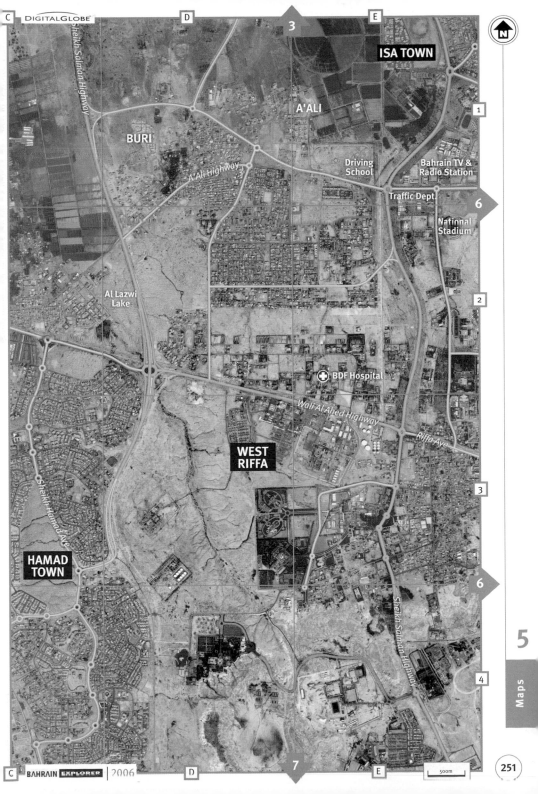

DIGITALGLOBE

Sheikh Salman Highway

A'ALI

BURI

Driving
School

Bahrain TV &
Radio Station

Traffic Dept.

Nationnal
Stadium

A'Ali Highway

Al Lazwi
Lake

BDF Hospital

Wali Al Ahed Highway

Riffa Ave

WEST
RIFFA

Sheikh Hamad Ave

HAMAD
TOWN

Sheikh Salman Highway

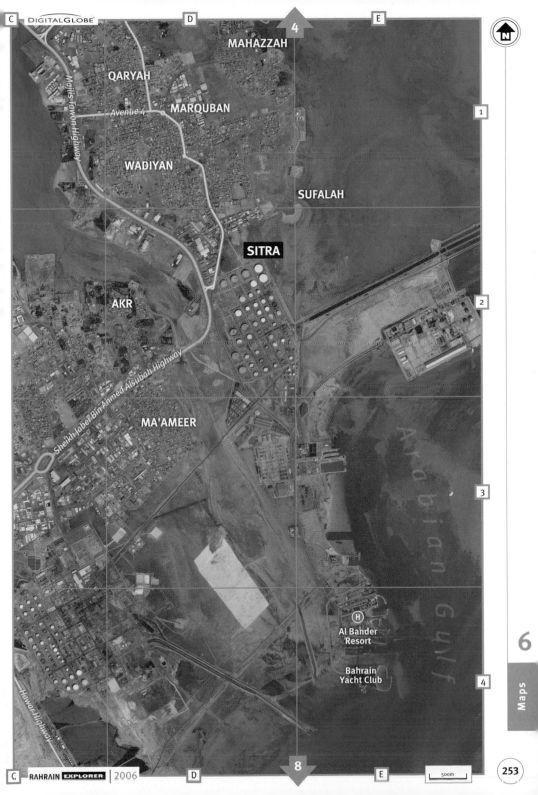

MAHAZZAH

QARYAH

1

Avenue 4

MARQUBAN

Majlis Tawon Highway

WADIYAN

SUFALAH

SITRA

2

AKR

Sheikh Jaber Bin Ahmed Alsubah Highway

Arabian

MA'AMEER

3

Al Bander
Resort

(H)

Bahrain
Yacht Club

4

Gulf

Hawar Highway

6

Maps

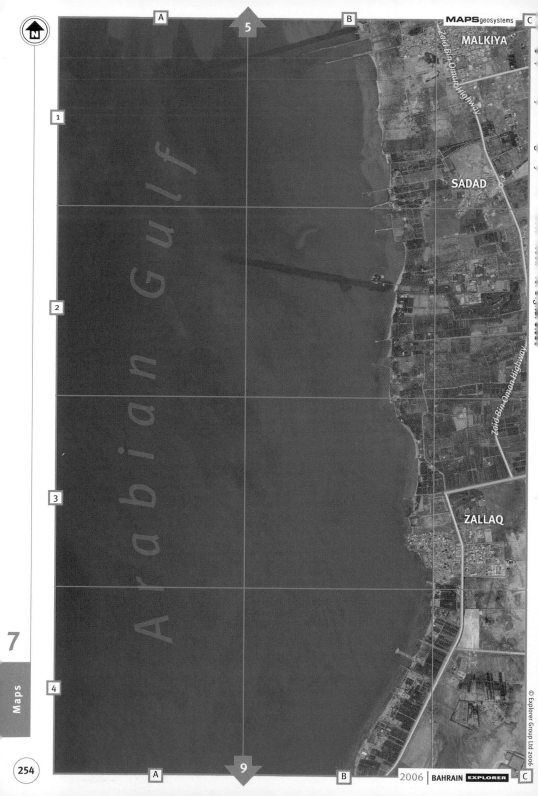

MALKIYA

Zaid Bin Omar Highway

SADAD

Arabian Gulf

Zaid Bin Omar Highway

ZALLAQ

© Explorer Group Ltd 2006

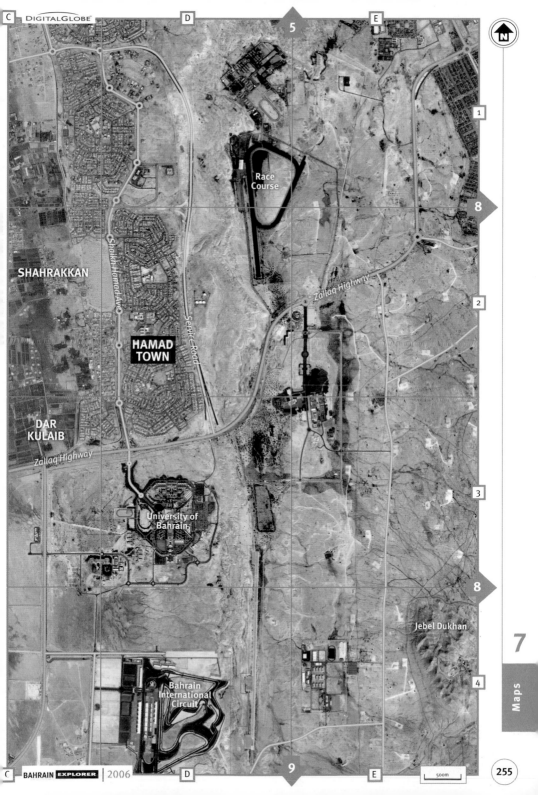

Race
Course

SHAHRAKKAN

Sheikh Hamad Ave

HAMAD
TOWN

Service Road

Zallaq Highwny

DAR
KULAIB

Zallaq Highway

University of
Bahrain

Jebel Dukhan

Bahrain
International
Circuit

1

8

2

3

8

7

Maps

4

Riffa
Golf Club

1

AWALI

7

2

3

7

4

SAKHIR

Oil
Museum

DIGITALGLOBE

Alba
Aluminum

Hawar Highway

RAS ABU JARJOR

ASKAR

Jazirat ash Shaykh

Hawar Highway

RA'S HAYAN

Arabian Gulf

8

Maps

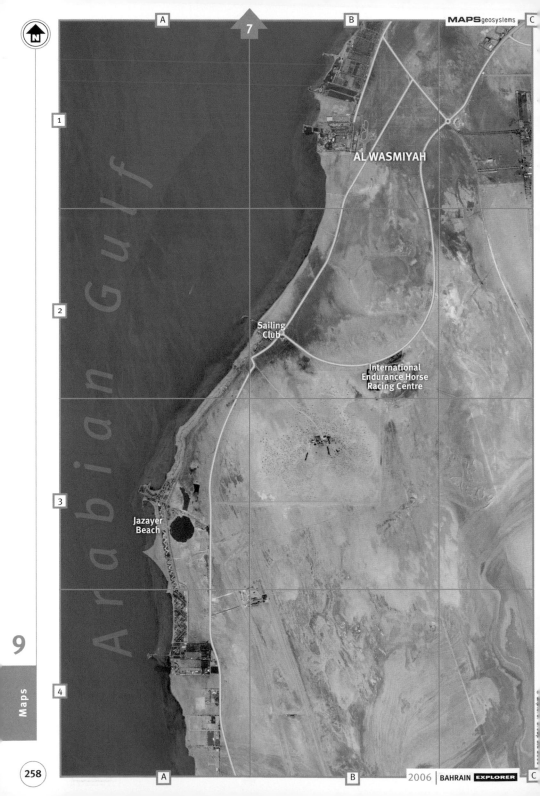

1

2

3

9

Maps

4

Arabian Gulf

AL WASMIYAH

Sailing
Club

International
Endurance Horse
Racing Centre

Jazayer
Beach

Al Areen
Wildlife Park

UMM JIDR

Banyan Tree
Desert Spa and
Resort

2
3

9

Maps

4

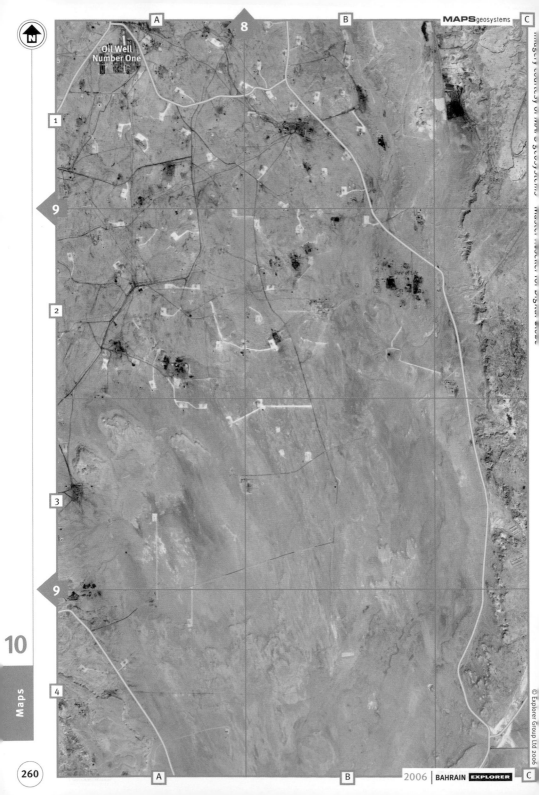

Oil Well
Number One

Tree of Life

10

Maps

Jau Prison

Arabian Gulf

DUR

Jetty to
Hawar Resort

10

Maps

261

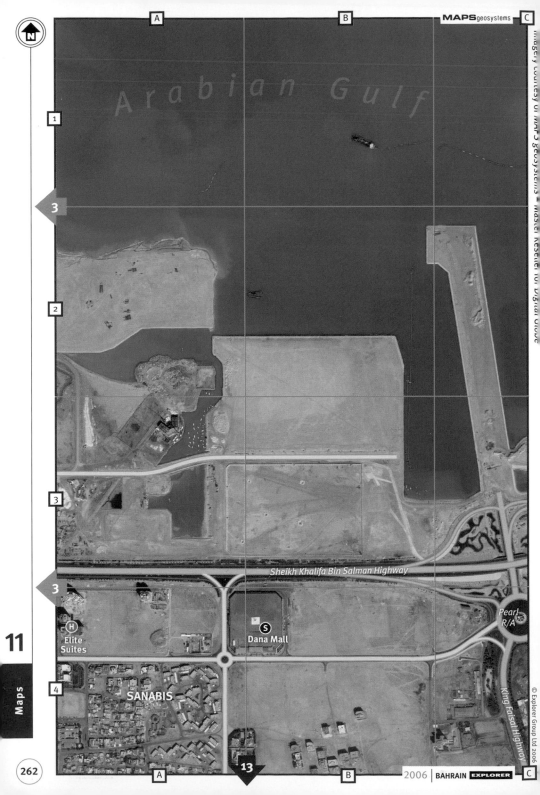

Arabian Gulf

Sheikh Khalifa Bin Salman Highway

Pearl R/A

Elite Suites

Dana Mall

SANABIS

11

Maps

262

13

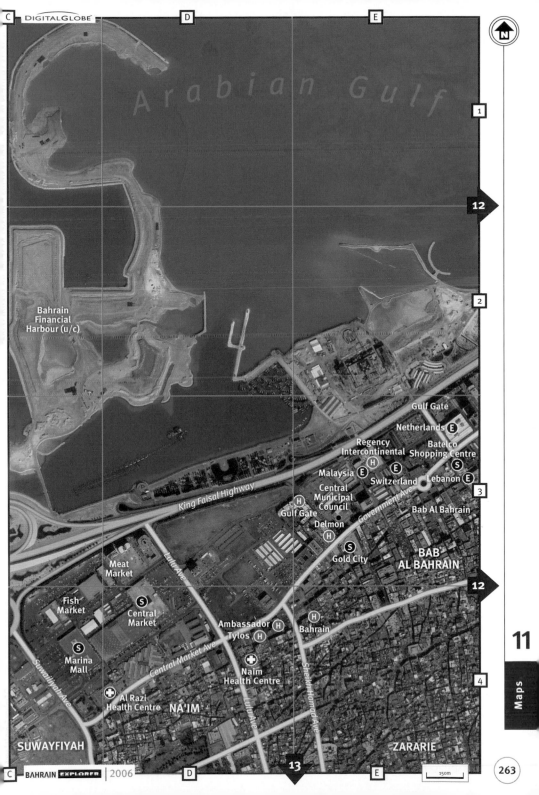

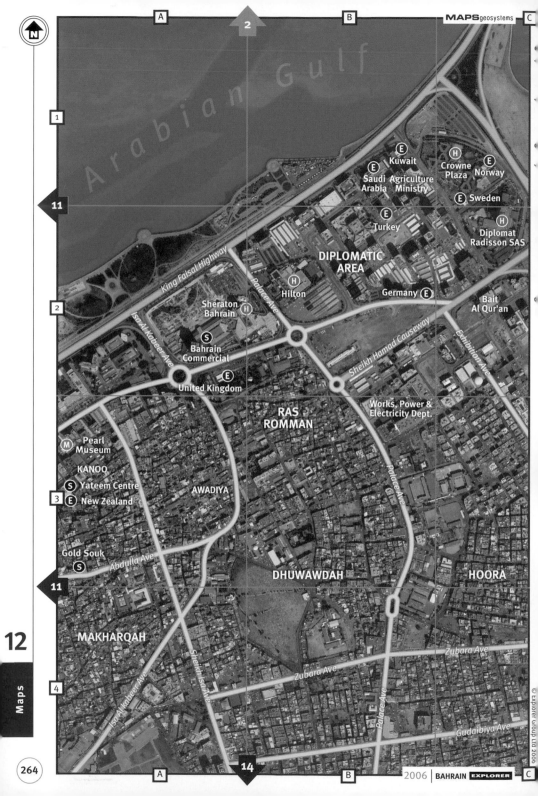

N

Arabian Gulf

1

11

Kuwait **E**

Saudi Arabia **E**   Agriculture Ministry **E**

Crowne Plaza **H**   Norway **E**

Sweden **E**

Turkey **E**

Diplomat Radisson SAS **H**

DIPLOMATIC AREA

Hilton **H**

Germany **E**

Bait Al Qur'an

King Faisal Highway

Palace Ave

Sheikh Hamad Causeway

Exhibition Ave

Isa Al Kabeer Ave

Sheraton Bahrain **H**

2

Bahrain Commercial **S**

United Kingdom **E**

Works, Power & Electricity Dept.

RAS ROMMAN

Pearl Museum **M**

KANOO

Yateem Centre **S**

New Zealand **E**

3

AWADIYA

Palace Ave

Gold Souk **S**

Abdulla Ave

11

DHUWAWDAH

HOORA

MAKHARQAH

Sheikh Isa Ave

Isa Al Kabeer Ave

Zubara Ave

Zubara Ave

Palace Ave

Gudaibiya Ave

4

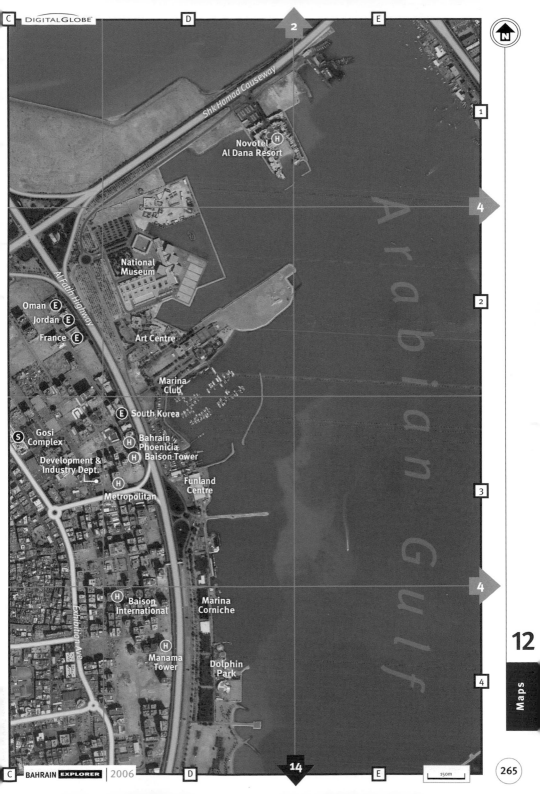

DIGITALGLOBE
2
N

1

Shk Hamad Causeway

Novotel
Al Dana Resort Ⓗ

4

National
Museum

Oman Ⓔ
Jordan Ⓔ
France Ⓔ

Al Fatih Highway

Art Centre

2

Marina
Club

Ⓔ South Korea

Ⓢ Gosi
Complex

Bahrain
Phoenicia Ⓗ
Ⓗ Baison Tower

Development &
Industry Dept.

Ⓗ
Metropolitan

Funland
Centre

3

Exhibition Ave

Arabian Gulf

4

Ⓗ Baison
International

Marina
Corniche

12

Ⓗ
Manama
Tower

Dolphin
Park

4

Maps

1

3

2

3

3

Budaiya Highway

Sheikh Salman Highway

**BILAD
AL QADEEM**

13

Maps

4

© LapidE/ Group llo 2006

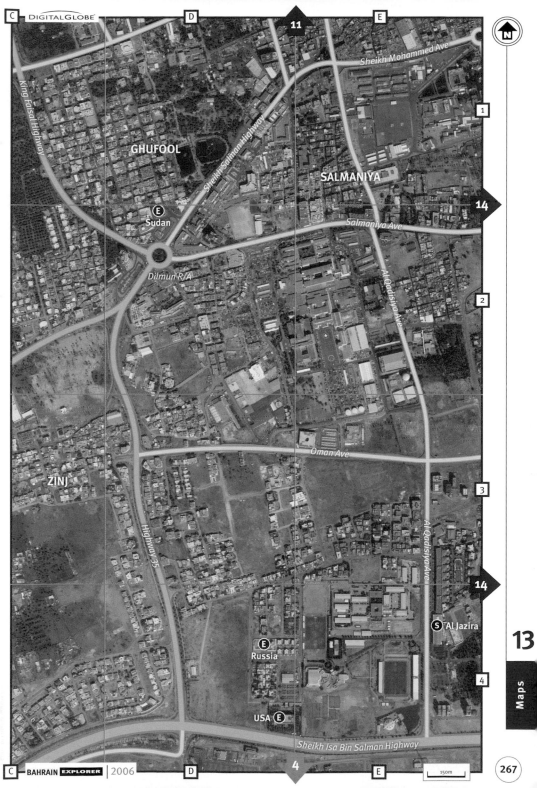

GHUFOOL

SALMANIYA

Sheikh Mohammed Ave

King Faisal Highway

Sheikh Salman Highway

(E) Sudan

Salmaniya Ave

Al Qadisiya Ave

Dilmun R/A

ZINJ

Oman Ave

Highway 35

Al Qadisiya Ave

(S) Al Jazira

(E) Russia

USA **(E)**

Sheikh Isa Bin Salman Highway

13

Maps

150m

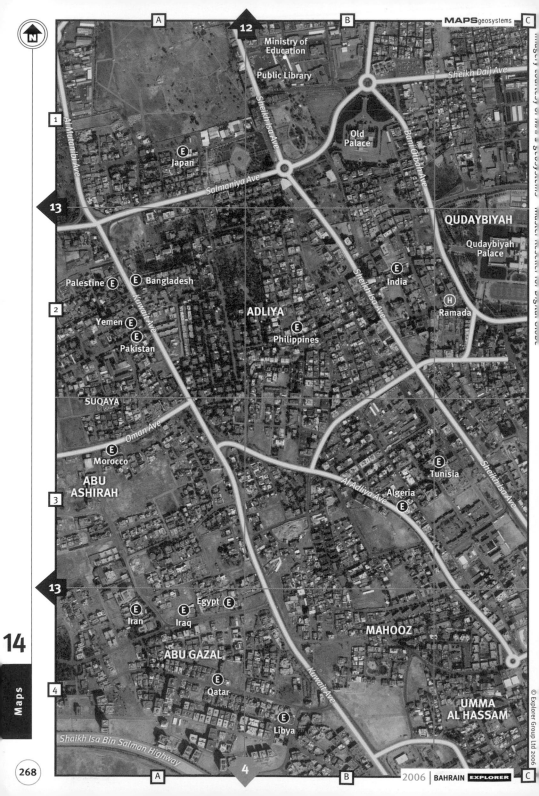

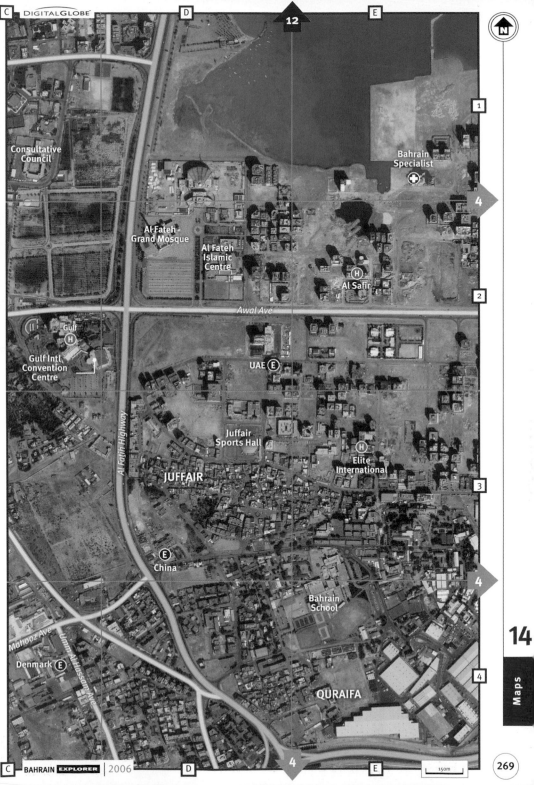

N

C   D   12   E

1

Consultative
Council

Bahrain
Specialist ⊕

4

Al Fateh
Grand Mosque

Al Fateh
Islamic
Centre

Al Safir Ⓗ

2

Awal Ave

Gulf Ⓗ

Gulf Intl.
Convention
Centre

UAE Ⓔ

Al Fatih Highway

Juffair
Sports Hall

Elite Ⓗ
International

JUFFAIR

3

China Ⓔ

4

Bahrain
School

Mahooz Ave

Denmark Ⓔ

Umm Al Hassam Ave

QURAIFA

4

14

Maps

4

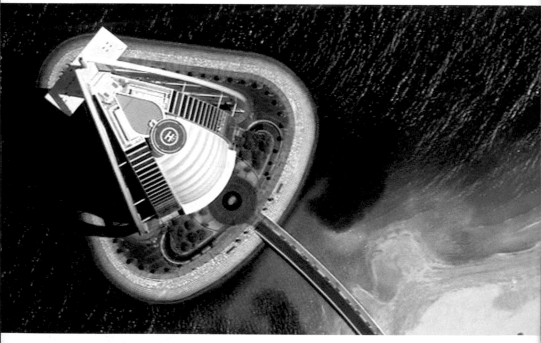

Index

EXPLORER

Index

Index

NOTES

BNH
البحرين الوطنية القابضة
Bahrain National Holding

البحرين الوطنية للتأمين
Bahrain National Insurance

البحرين الوطنية للحياة
Bahrain National Life

Exceeding your expectations

◄ **Home Insurance**

Personal Accident Insurance ►

◄ **Domestic Servants Insurance**

Contractors All Risk Insurance ►

◄ **Motor Insurance**

Future Education Plan ►

◄ **Marine & Pleasure Crafts Insurance**

Future Income Plan ►

Comprehensive cover against all types of risks with exceptional levels of service.

BRANCHES

Seef District
Tel.: (+973) 17 587300
Fax.: (+973) 17 583099

Manama Branch
Tel.: (+973) 17 227800
Fax.: (+973) 17 216464

Budaiya Branch
Tel.: (+973) 17 797888
Fax.: (+973) 17 797878

Sanad Branch
Tel.: (+973) 17 622272
Fax.: (+973) 17 622192

Muharraq Branch
Tel.: (+973) 17 336631
Fax.: (+973) 17 336681

University of Bahrain
Tel.: (+973) 17 449000
Fax.: (+973) 17 448919

P.O. Box: 843, Manama, Kingdom of Bahrain

www.bnhgroup.c